MECHANICS·
MERCANTILE
LIBRARY.

Hello, Everybody!

Hello, Everybody!

THE DAWN
OF AMERICAN RADIO

▲▲

Anthony Rudel

Harcourt, Inc.
Orlando   Austin   New York   San Diego   London

www.HarcourtBooks.com

Library of Congress Cataloging-in-Publication Data
Rudel, Anthony J.
Hello, everybody!: the dawn of American radio/
Anthony Rudel.—1st ed.
p.   cm.
Includes bibliographical references.
1. Radio broadcasting—United States—History—20th century.
I. Title.
PN1991.3.U6R83   2008
384.540973'0904—dc22   2008005629
ISBN 978-0-15-101275-6

Text set in Bembo
Designed by Lydia D'moch

Printed in the United States of America

First edition
A C E G I K J H F D B

For all the dedicated broadcasters
who make American media so incredibly vibrant,
AND
to my wonderful family—with love
and thanks for your patience.

Hello, Everybody!

Chapter 1

▲▲▲▲▲▲▲▲▲▲▲▲

MILFORD, KANSAS. Population 200—not counting animals.

At the beginning of the twentieth century, Milford, Kansas, was a one-horse town on the western plains; there were no paved roads, no sewers, no water system, no high schools, and no sidewalks. Situated across the river and one mile down a dirt road from the nearest train depot, Milford happened to be located about ten miles from the geographical center of the United States. Its other claim to fame was that amid the town's rows of dilapidated structures there was one lone architectural curiosity: a building that had been transported from the 1904 St. Louis World's Fair after the fair had closed. Located on the Republican River, which flows to Junction City, the county seat of Geary County, Milford was near the godforsaken spot of land from where Horace Greeley had been inspired to report that the buffalo hurried through the region, "as I should urgently advise them to do."

But Milford's rise to national fame—or infamy—would really begin in October 1917, when late one evening, the town's new and only doctor welcomed a patient to his neat, simple office. Perhaps the man, a local rancher, was put at ease by the official-looking framed diploma from the Eclectic Medical University of Kansas that hung on the wall; or maybe the fact that the doctor and his wife owned the adjoining apothecary and soda fountain, with its neatly appointed shelves of vials and bottles, filled the rancher with confidence; or maybe the doctor's affable manner and his distinguished red Vandyke assured the new patient that he'd found someone in whom he could confide. Whatever the reason, the man eventually worked his way around to telling the doctor about his real problem.

"Doctor," he said, "I'm forty-six. I've got a flat tire. I'm all in. No pep."

Today an entire pharmaceutical industry has grown around the problem we so loosely call erectile dysfunction, but in the early twentieth century the condition, so vividly described as a "flat tire," was known in polite circles as "lassitude."

The doctor, whose medical experience came primarily from earlier, nomadic years staying one step ahead of the law while working with other quacks, medicine shows, and anatomical museums, was unable to offer much encouragement. Depressed, the rancher talked enviously about his well-endowed goats and their prodigious sexual athleticism.

"Yep," the doctor chuckled. "You wouldn't have any trouble if you had a pair of those buck glands in you."

Intrigued by the idea, and perhaps willing to do anything to ante up the randy factor, the rancher eagerly pressed his case.

The rancher stared intently into the doctor's eyes and enthused, "Well, why don't you put 'em in me?"

And with the breezy air of a man who had nothing to lose, Dr. John Romulus Brinkley, emboldened by the purchased medical degree tacked to his office wall, assented. In one of the more unlikely transplants of the era, by one of the more unlikely medical professionals, Dr. Brinkley, using one of the rancher's own goats as the donor, implanted tissues from the poor animal.

Within two months the rancher was boasting all over town about his resurrected prowess, and other local men who found themselves in the same predicament made their way to Dr. Brinkley's. Among the earliest patients was one William Stittsworth, whose wife gave birth one year later to a healthy son whom they named Billy in honor of the generous donor goat.

Although the procedure was filmed and real medical specialists were later invited to observe the magical rejuvenation surgery that Brinkley called his "Compound Operation," the exact surgical methods and procedures were never completely memorialized. However, Brinkley, who proudly proclaimed he was the first man to take a goat's testicle and implant it in a man, described his operation this way:

> The glands of a three weeks' old male goat are laid upon the nonfunctioning glands of a man, within twenty minutes of the time they are removed from the goat. In some cases I open the human gland and lay the tissue of the goat within the human gland. The scrotum of the man is opened by incision on both sides . . . I find that after being properly connected these goat glands do actually feed, grow into, and become absorbed by the human glands, and the man is renewed in his physical and mental vigor.

In actuality, Brinkley probably did not operate on the patient's testes, but somewhere higher up in the anatomy. The rejuvenation his patients discovered was likely due to psychological factors; just the idea that they had newfound vigor probably allowed them to relax and again become sexually active.

It was sensational. Dr. Brinkley was the talk of Milford, and soon enough, word of the surgery spread and men of all ages from the small towns and villages of the surrounding Kansas countryside were streaming into town, seeking the special surgery by the great man who could reinflate their flat tire: Dr. John Romulus Brinkley. The cost per operation was between $500 and $750, and that included the necessary goat tissue, which was purchased from local ranchers.

DUE TO HIS OWN vague and conflicting rewrites of his personal history, John Romulus Brinkley's years of learning, traveling, and avoiding arrest that brought him to Milford are imprecise. What is certain is that he was born on July 8, 1885, in the Great Smoky Mountains, and that even though his father was the local doctor, his family was poor.

After completing whatever formal education was available in his rural community, Brinkley got a job—with no pay—at the railroad office in Sylva, North Carolina. There the manager taught his young charge how to operate the telegraph, and Brinkley became intrigued by the machine's ability to exchange information with people somewhere on the other side of the mountains. Communicating with an invisible audience was addictive. Brinkley wanted more from life than what was available in this rural world, so he set his sights on becoming a doctor and getting out of the kind of backwoods world into which he'd been born. In 1907 he married and began a career as a "Quaker doctor," which was a cross between a somewhat respected medical authority and a vaudeville showman. This position yielded a platform from which a quick talker who had gained the audience's confidence might convince the crowd of the special curative powers of the liquids and herbs he sold. He may have been called a Quaker doctor, but in truth Brinkley was nothing more than a classic snake-oil pitchman, and his talent for fast talk would play a significant role in his later success as a radio pioneer and broadcaster.

In 1908 Brinkley moved to Chicago, where he worked at the telegraph office. But his dream of becoming a real doctor never left him, so he enrolled in the Bennett Medical College, taking classes during the day and working at night. Before his last year, Brinkley dropped out of school and began his years of wandering from town to town and job to job, including a stint as an assistant to a Dr. Burke in Knoxville. Dr. Burke was a "men's health" specialist who sold guilt-ridden patients worthless cures for the venereal diseases they had contracted. By 1913 the Brinkley family had moved to Chattanooga, where John worked at a satellite office of Dr. Burke's medical practice. By now the Brinkleys had three daughters, but theirs wasn't a happy marriage and they divorced.

In 1914 John Brinkley landed in Memphis, where he met and married Minnie Telitha Jones, the daughter of a local physician. For the next two years Brinkley practiced medicine in small towns throughout Arkansas. One day he saw an advertisement for the Eclectic Medical University of Kansas, which promised to give credit for past experience and would grant a full medical license if the candidate studied in Kansas City for one year. Brinkley managed to "earn" his diploma in a matter of weeks simply by mailing a few payments to the school. In February 1916, the state of Kansas issued medical license no. 5845 to Dr. John Romulus Brinkley. He was on his way to the medical practice he craved. During World War I he served as a medical officer, but the job in El Paso, Texas, was so stressful that after five weeks of service, most of which he'd spent resting in the infirmary, he claimed to have had a nervous breakdown and was discharged during the summer of 1917 by the surgeon general of the army.

In need of work, he ran an ad in the *Kansas City Star* looking for a town that could use his medical services. Milford, Kansas, responded—their only physician had moved away—and after a visit to see the unimpressive place, Dr. Brinkley decided this would be the ideal home for his new medical office. When he told Minnie that they would be settling in Milford, she burst into tears. But when fate, in the form of a flat-tired rancher, walked through his office door a few months later, Minnie's outlook, as well as their fortunes, changed.

Word of mouth built the foundation of John R. Brinkley's practice. The sexual-resurrection business was so lucrative that within months the doctor, using his earnings and money his wife had inherited, bought a large section of the dilapidated town. Overnight, sleepy, dusty Milford was abuzz with construction as Dr. Brinkley's new sixteen-bed hospital was being built.

But local success was not enough; in Brinkley's view, he was a superior man of medicine. "He had begun to realize that he was gifted beyond the run of doctors, and that he could not be bound by the rigid artificial ethics of the American Medical Association." The need to expand his business, to reach more people, to spread the word of his miracle cure, drove Brinkley; he was committed to doing whatever it took to let the world know that he was a top-notch doctor. Informing the world of his talents meant endless days bouncing along the dusty country roads of the vast American middle. He drove from town to town and told people of the sexual fountain of youth he'd found. It was an arduous marketing method, but there was little choice; there was no mass marketing, and doubting consumers would never believe the silent, lifeless words of a print ad. The pitch required the spoken words and confident manner of Dr. Brinkley, who, by his own account, had been "born with the magnetism of a super-powered salesman." Hoping to vastly increase business and gain credibility, he sent booklets describing the operation to members of the medical community, but no one responded. Brinkley, in need of professional marketing help, placed an ad in the *Kansas City Star* seeking assistance from an experienced ad man who could spread the word of the miracles occurring at the Brinkley Clinic in Milford. One interested applicant from Kansas City, a married man with two children who had a low-paying job and needed money, made the trek to Milford. Brinkley told him of the special surgery he could perform and the man instantly recognized its potential, saying, "Dr. Brinkley, you've got a million dollars within your hands, and you don't even realize it."

A new brochure filled with glowing testimonials from Brinkley's satisfied patients was mailed to one hundred newspapers; only two wrote articles. Yet even this modest response led to an increase in the transplant business. But of greater import, Chancellor J. J. Tobias of the University of Chicago Law School saw the article and was intrigued. Despairing of his languishing love life, the chancellor traveled to Milford for the surgery. So pleased was he that in June 1920 he invited Brinkley to Chicago to present him with an honorary Doctor of Science degree, a trophy Brinkley would hang on his office wall. But of greater import was an official statement the chancellor gave to the newspapers—a testimonial about Brinkley's wonderful surgery.

Brinkley's endless shilling was working. His fame—or notoriety— was growing, and a steady flow of hapless men streamed into Milford, driven by dreams of vigor and stamina. Capitalizing on his success, Brinkley again took to the road to further spread the word of his miracle cure. By 1921 the business specializing in sexual rejuvenation, a surgery in step with the comparatively sexually liberal Roaring Twenties, was booming. Telling interested writers that the procedure would turn any man into "the-ram-that-am-with-any-lamb," Brinkley's business became a virtual assembly-line process. The patients paid in advance and could choose the exact Toggenberg goat—a breed that left no unpleasant odors on the recipient—directly from a pen located behind Brinkley's house; it was like picking a particular lobster for dinner out of a tank.

By 1922, thanks to the generosity of the newly wealthy Dr. Brinkley, Milford was a rebuilt town. With medical associates performing most of the procedures at the Brinkley Clinic, or the Brinkley Hospital, or the Kansas General Research Hospital, or whatever he chose to call his place of business, John Brinkley was basically a traveling salesman, the Willy Loman of sexual rejuvenation. In February of that year Brinkley received a letter from Harry Chandler, the owner of the *Los Angeles Times,* inviting him to Los Angeles to perform his miraculous transplant on one of the newspaper's elderly editors. Wanting more business and fame, Brinkley accepted. After examining the patient, Brinkley assured Chandler that the surgery would improve the old man's condition and, as an added benefit, even the man's palsy. Chandler reportedly told Brinkley that if the procedure were successful, he would trumpet the accomplishment in the newspaper, but if the surgery failed he would expose him as a quack.

Harry Chandler was himself a colorful figure: a maverick millionaire, real-estate magnate, and publisher of the *Los Angeles Times.* Chandler had risen to a position of tremendous power in the rapidly growing Los Angeles area and was himself somewhat of a huckster. Indicted by a federal grand jury in 1915 for his involvement in the Mexican Revolution, Chandler was a participant in many questionable, albeit hugely profitable land deals in Southern California. Because of his wealth and position as the head of a major newspaper, Chandler became the leader of the California Republican Party. Politically outspoken, in 1920 he led a failed effort to nominate Herbert Hoover for president. When that attempt collapsed, Chandler backed the Republican ticket of Harding and Coolidge and through the *Los Angeles Times* attacked the Democratic ticket, writing in an editorial that the Democratic vice-presidential candidate "adds no merit to the ticket. He is a radical of unsafe tendencies." That radical was Franklin Delano Roosevelt.

Brinkley accepted Chandler's challenge, and the surgery proceeded successfully. Chandler lived up to his promise to promote the surgeon, and soon Brinkley was the most in-demand doctor in Southern California; his patients, including the famous and infamous of Los Angeles society, flocked to see this miracle man. The *Los Angeles Times* reported that Dr. Brinkley, supported by a group of prominent Los Angeles businessmen, was planning to build a hospital in Ensenada that would be dedicated to performing his amazing surgery. "Goats to supply the glands to be used in the rejuvenation of mankind are being grown under contract by a rancher at El Monte." The story went on to report that "if the undertaking proves successful a group of Los Angeles business men stand ready to erect [their word, not mine] there an institution to cost from $500,000 to $1,000,000."

Owing to Chandler, Brinkley's success in Southern California was assured, and the doctor was kept busy operating on politicians and celebrities, including several of the era's leading silent film stars, all of whom insisted on anonymity. By the end of his visit Brinkley had earned an estimated $40,000.

Los Angeles, April 13, 1922: KHJ, the first radio station west of the Rocky Mountains, goes on the air. The station's one-hour debut program, which ran from 6:45 to 7:45 P.M., began with "The Star Spangled Banner," some opening remarks by station owner Harry Chandler, three arias by members of the Chicago Grand Opera Company, a ten-minute bit by vaudeville headliner Hal Skelly, and bedtime stories and poems read by James W. Foley. "Thousands will sit in their homes, in public places, where magnavox are installed and hear the voices of some of the world's premier artists. Current world events gathered by the *Times* wire and cable news services will be transformed into ethereal waves, a departure in modern journalism."

Owned and operated by the *Los Angeles Times*, KHJ was Harry Chandler's newest toy. Rumor had it that the call letters stood for Kindness, Happiness, and Joy, but actually KHJ just happened to be the next call sign given out by the United States Department of

Commerce, which had control over the brand-new radio broadcasting business. By the fall of 1922, KHJ boasted a program schedule that included a daily, except Sundays, midday forty-five-minute show of "news and concert program of particular value to radio dealers," an evening half hour for children "consisting of songs for children and bedtime story by Uncle John," and a ninety-minute nightly "deluxe program of instrumental and vocal music, news and educational matter." Finally, every Sunday morning from ten to eleven, KHJ aired a "Sacred service—Scripture reading, sermon prayer, and musical program."

One can only imagine John Brinkley, the great marketer and former Quaker doctor and pitchman, when he first encountered radio and realized the power of this new medium. Here was a way to entertain, to educate, and to deliver messages to widely scattered audiences. Here was a way to make your pitch directly to potential patients without having to travel to their towns. Far greater than his rather significant financial windfall, being exposed to KHJ and seeing its cavelike broadcast rooms that were padded with felt to reduce any reverberating noises that might go out over the air would become the most valuable aspect of Brinkley's Los Angeles visit. He returned to Milford and immediately started construction on his own radio facility. A license to broadcast, which had to be applied for and then granted by Secretary of Commerce Herbert Hoover, was easy to secure, and by the end of September 1923, KFKB went on the air. With its 1,000 watts, the station could be heard virtually across the entire middle of the country. Dr. Brinkley, the marketer, had found the ultimate marketing vehicle: radio. Here was the not-yet-understood power of the invisible signal carrying sound across and over all terrains and through walls directly into people's homes. Here was the way to really reach people, to talk personally to the consumer. Brinkley understood that this new medium was far more powerful than his traveling sales pitch, and even more direct than the silent film he had made and showed, called *Goat Gland*

Baby. Radio was a way for him to speak to people, to be that Quaker doctor again, but instead of being on a stump, he used the microphone. His smooth voice, a subtle blend of midwestern intonation and Smoky Mountain drawl, soothed concerned listeners. His knowledge, his comfort with difficult medical subjects such as "being below par," made him easy to listen to, and listeners all over the Midwest agreed with the comment of one fan who said, "There's something about Dr. Brinkley that gets close to your heart."

Dr. John R. Brinkley was a central player in the greatest communications revolution ever seen, or heard: the radio revolution that radically changed the American landscape. And it all started so simply, with his sign-on: *You are listening to Dr. Brinkley speaking to you from Milford, Kansas, over station KFKB. Radio station KFKB operates on a frequency of 1050 kilocycles.*

Chapter 2

▲▲▲▲▲▲▲▲▲▲▲▲▲

UNDERSTANDING RADIO TECHNOLOGY requires a leap of faith, or, more precisely, blind acceptance that the invisible waves that flow through the air do really exist, that they can carry electrically excited energy in the form of sound, that those pieces of information can be received by an antenna, decoded, and then made listenable by a receiving device at some distant point. In simplest terms, radio works by sending an electric impulse through the antenna of a transmitter. Imagine the iconic image shown at the beginning of old RKO Radio Picture movies of a tall radio tower—the kind that still dots the landscape—sending signals out into the air, only in reality the beams can't be seen.

Once the existence of these magical invisible waves had been proved and their nature demonstrated in a series of experiments between 1886 and 1889 by Heinrich Hertz—which is why radio waves were called

Hertzian waves and radio signals were measured in kilohertz—engineers became increasingly intrigued with the possibilities of wireless transmission. But their interest lay primarily in point-to-point communication without having to rely on connected wires; they sought to mimic the way telegraph lines connected two stations. Out of their efforts came the technology known as radiotelegraphy, in which radio waves carried telegraph messages from one station to another to compete with the telegraph lines that crisscrossed the country. While the American Telephone and Telegraph Company, AT&T, was the leader in America's telegraph industry, the new business of sending coded messages through the air was dominated by the Marconi Wireless Telegraph Company of America and its brilliant founder, Guglielmo Marconi.

Born in 1874 to a wealthy Italian family, Guglielmo Marconi became fascinated by the ability to send signals. As early as 1895, using homemade transmitting equipment, he managed to send a signal over a distance of one-and-a-half miles. One year later he went to England, where he was granted the first patents for wireless telegraphy; by 1897 investors had capitalized the Wireless Telegraph and Signal Company to the tune of 100,000 pounds sterling. Marconi worked to extend the distance of his transmissions, and with each new distance record came increased investor interest, and the eventual establishment of an American branch of his company.

By the middle of the first decade of the twentieth century, the idea of transmitting messages to and from ships had become accepted and common, and in 1905 the first distress message was sent via wireless telegraph from an American vessel to a receiving station on shore. But inventors quickly realized that if the telegraph could be supplanted by radiotelegraphy, it was only logical that the telephone, another relatively new communication device, could soon be supplanted by some form of audio radio transmission. As sound could travel through wires from one telephone to another, it was intuitive that voices could be sent via the airwaves, although the idea had its doubters, including the venerable Lord William Thomson Kelvin, who believed that people conversing to one another through the airwaves would create nothing but cacophony in the air. But before that potential roadblock could be dealt with, the main challenge lay in amplifying the sound properly so it could be carried by the invisible waves and decoded at the receiving end. The inventors toying with radio technology originally sought to supplant the wired telephone systems with what would in essence be a walkie-talkie system.

Though there had been trials using phonograph records to provide audio content for radio tests, the experiment that caught people's attention occurred on January 20, 1910, live from the stage of the Metropolitan Opera House, when the great tenor Enrico Caruso sang into a microphone connected to a 500-watt transmitter that sent the sound to receivers placed at the experimenter's Park Avenue laboratory, the Metropolitan Life Building, and a hotel in Times Square. Not only did the fifty or so invited listeners, including some journalists, hear the great tenor's rendition of the role of Turridu in *Cavalleria Rusticana,* but the transmission was also overheard by ship operators and radio enthusiasts in the area who just happened to have their wireless sets tuned to that specific frequency. Despite the poor sound quality that was often interrupted by other random signals being sent through the air, the experiment was deemed a success. Though the test did increase excitement about wireless radiotelephony's possibilities, radiotelegraphy remained the business that seemed to have the most immediate promise, and early in the new decade the Marconi Company began regular American-European telegraph service, cleverly naming the transmissions Marconigrams.

In addition to making a deal with Western Union that extended the reach of Marconigrams, during 1912 the American Marconi Company acquired United Wireless and its seventeen land radio stations and more than 400 onboard ship installations. The East Coast of the United States was dotted with radio transmission and receiving stations, and young radio enthusiasts were hired to man them. It was during an April night in 1912 when news of the *Titanic* disaster was flashed from the *Carpathia* to a Marconi Wireless station manned by a serious radio enthusiast named David Sarnoff, who, legend has it, remained at his post for seventy-two consecutive hours sending coded updates to newspapers and authorities around the United States. In the hours following news of the *Titanic* disaster, President Taft unilaterally ordered all transmission stations not directly involved in the rescue effort to be shut down to eliminate interference with the reception of wireless messages from sea.

Taft's order was timely. These were heady days for radiotelegraphy, but even within the protean, amorphous pathways of business, commerce, and science, the deepening need for some sort of regulation and oversight of the radio waves crisscrossing invisibly through the air was becoming apparent. The airwaves were overcrowded with amateurs and companies alike sending messages through the ether. There were no schedules, no regular transmissions that one could tune in to; it was all free-form and random. Corporations investing heavily in the development of point-to-point communication systems found the signals of hobbyists chatting from their home transmitters—Rube Goldberg–like contraptions of wires, tubes, and dials—frequently interfered with their signals and were disrupting the commerce they were transacting via radiotelegraphy.

As radiotelegraphy and radiotelephony became increasingly prominent, thousands of amateurs from coast to coast became involved in this new hobby. The barriers to entry were low; all one needed was a relatively inexpensive and easy-to-build radio set, and equipment manufacturers were eager to sell the components to this avid audience. Radio amateurs had been active in the United States since before 1910, and they were a devoted, ever-growing group of private citizens who had built their own equipment and who spent countless hours sending and receiving signals. There were radio clubs in high schools and colleges, and associations sprang up to support these hobbyists. It was a terrific activity for young boys, many of whom would later in the decade use their skills to help the military during World War I.

The earliest devotees communicated with one another using the dot-and-dash code. Their "discussions" could be about any subject: the equipment they were using, the nuances of transmission, the distances from which they heard other signals, even just idle gossip, or, in at least one case, an exchange of love notes. Unfortunately for one young woman in Pittsburgh who transmitted personal messages to that special someone, since radio transmission could be received by anyone tuned to that particular frequency, her heartfelt words of love ended up being overheard by amateur operators who were "listening in."

But as quickly as the radio technology emerged, so did the fight to control it. Spurred by the *Titanic* disaster and the fact that many of the first Marconigrams sent from the *Carpathia* could not get through due to all the interference, and in an effort to stem the tide of chaos in the airwaves, on August 13, 1912, Congress approved the Act to Regulate Radio Communication. Rather than banning ham operator transmissions though, which corporations like Marconi's wanted, Congress decided to limit amateur broadcasts to a wavelength of 200 meters, or 1,500 kilohertz.

The Act to Regulate Radio Communication limited how amateurs could transmit and placed control over the licensing of transmitting stations with the Department of Commerce. The law required anyone who sought to transmit to apply for a license from the Department of Commerce, which reviewed the applications, granted the license, and assigned a call sign, usually a combination of letters and numbers. Though an earlier piece of legislation had required seagoing vessels to install transmission and receiving equipment, the Radio Act of 1912 was the first acknowledgment by the United States government that this new technology needed to be more fully organized, and the government's control would only increase as the decade unfolded. It was a battle in what would become the war over who actually owned the radio spectrum: individuals or the government. Nonetheless, the Radio Act of 1912 gave the government the power to decide who would be granted a license to transmit, whether those transmissions were of a telegraphic nature, or whether they used sound. The government had ostensibly stepped in to organize what was becoming a crowded field, but the net result was that corporations with large investments in the business and technology of radio had found a protector in the government, with its ability to control individuals who wanted to fill the air with their own messages.

By 1913 the American Marconi Company was the unquestioned leader in radiotelegraphy, and it quickly expanded into the field of radiotelephony with the goal of bridging the vast communication gap that existed between the United States and Europe. Yet its aggressive domination of the market woke a sleeping giant and its greatest future competitor. Sensing a grave challenge to its domain, the American Telephone and Telegraph Company struck with a preemptive move. Throughout 1913, AT&T negotiated for and bought the patent rights to new transmission equipment developed by a young radio prodigy named Lee De Forest.

Lee De Forest was one of history's unfortunates, an incredibly talented inventor who somehow always seemed to end up on the losing side of every battle. It was De Forest who had organized and run the 1910 test transmission of Caruso's arias sent from the stage of the Metropolitan Opera. Yet despite his talent and his successes, he found himself embroiled in a series of legal battles over patents and was virtually penniless when during the summer of 1913 a lawyer representing AT&T came to his lab and made him an offer he couldn't refuse. De

Forest's work was so advanced that AT&T's $250,000 investment in his company made them the instant leader in the new field of radio.

Ironically, even with companies investing relatively large amounts of capital, during these early days no one was certain of what the actual business model of radio would become. It seemed the real money to be made depended on selling not the medium but the equipment. But the government, and in particular the military, saw the value of being able to communicate without being constrained by connected wires. Radio's commercial potential, though sensed by some, was as yet ill-defined. Individual operators sitting night after night in their garages using homemade transmitters existed side by side with the corporate powerhouses casting about for a way to put radio to work for them. World War I changed all that.

THE OUTBREAK IN 1914 of World War I dramatically increased the importance of radio transmission. The need to communicate from point to point was vital for military success, and telegraph lines were vulnerable to attack; it took only one soldier to cut a line to interrupt crucial communications. Yet despite the problems with telegraphy, the military's continued dependence on telegraph and phone lines is reflected by the fact that by the end of the war the army had set up more 96,000 miles of wire across the battlefields of Europe. The importance of wireless telegraphy in the war zone was unimaginable to an America still trying to grasp what this technology could be used for. Europe was actually far ahead of the United States in terms of radio development; a September 1914 assessment calculated that the warring parties—Austria-Hungary, Russia, Great Britain, France, and Germany—controlled a total of 135 transmitting stations.

During the early years of the war, engineers desperately tried to improve the technology of sending the human voice across distances so it could be picked up and decoded by a receiver at a specific point.

Through improvements of the amplification equipment at both the transmitting and receiving ends, engineers managed to reduce the static and improve the quality of the sound, making radio transmissions clearer and easier to understand.

While the United States declared its neutrality, it did loan leading radio technology pioneers, including Lee De Forest, to Allied governments to assist with wireless technology. Meanwhile the German and British navies were increasingly dependent on wireless communications, but while the British navy sailed under wireless silence, except in emergencies, the Germans communicated frequently from boat to boat or ship to shore, always expecting the British to interfere with or block their signals. But that interference rarely came because the British were far more interested in monitoring the Germans' signals and using the overheard information to anticipate their enemy's military moves.

Despite being officially neutral, the United States was slowly but ineffably being drawn into the war. At the outset of the war the United States government staunchly enforced a rule that forbade the sending or receiving of any radio messages that might be anything other than absolutely neutral, and the price for failing to observe the neutrality rules was steep. In September 1914 Secretary of the Navy Josephus Daniels, as instructed by the president, informed the Marconi Wireless station in Siasconsett, Massachusetts, that it would be shut down for violating the neutrality rule. "The Siasconsett station is closed to the transmission of radiograms of whatever character. You will further keep a close watch on that station and immediately report to the Secretary of the Navy any attempt on the part of any employee of the Marconi Co. to send or receive any message to or from ships at sea or to or from another radio station." The station's criminal violation was that it had transmitted a message to a merchant in New York directing him to provide provisions for the British cruiser *Suffolk,* which was operating off the East Coast. Furthermore, the message had been sent while the naval officer assigned to monitor the station was not on site.

Marconi Wireless challenged the order, claiming they were being censored, but when Attorney General Thomas Watt Gregory ruled that the government's action was indeed legal, the station was closed. At the heart of the issue was whether President Woodrow Wilson had the power to control communications through executive order. In his landmark opinion, the attorney general wrote, "If the President is of the opinion that the relations of this country with foreign nations are or are likely to be endangered by actions deemed by him inconsistent with a due neutrality, it is his right and duty to protect such relations."

As the likelihood of American involvement in the war increased, so, too, did concomitant fears about the threat of wireless technology being used against the United States. There were more than 300,000 amateur radio enthusiasts in the country, and by April 1916, Navy Department wireless experts and agents from the Department of Justice were keeping most American transmitting stations—amateur and corporate-owned—under constant surveillance.

With war rapidly moving from possibility to probability, it became clear that the individual radiophoners, the ham operators, were facing a shutdown in the name of national security. Wireless advocates tried to stave off the government takeover, but it was not to be. Radio was still in its infancy, and the government was taking no chances with a technology with potentially limitless powers. Furthermore, it was clear that the government did not fully understand radio, for while it was being used effectively for naval communications, homing pigeons, not wireless messages, remained an important way for the United States to send military dispatches during the First World War.

Despite pleas from amateurs and radio groups alike from all over the country, and even though these radio enthusiasts attempted to demonstrate how they could be of assistance as a nationally mobilized early-warning system for the United States in wartime, all hope for the independent broadcasters ended in April 1917 when, on the day following America's declaration of war, President Wilson ordered the navy to take charge of all wireless stations in the United States that were not already under the military's control. As for the amateur operators, the president's order forced them not only to silence their transmissions, but to dismantle and store their equipment for the duration of the ban. For the next year, radio as anything more than a government-controlled endeavor fell silent. And though the government ordered scientists from different corporate entities to work cooperatively for the national good to advance the technology, it would be more than two years before radio as a means of communicating for nonmilitary purposes would emerge from the mothballs.

Though their equipment was stowed away by government order, America's amateur radio operators were in demand. With a need for "thousands of men trained in the operation of this modern method of communication," the army recruited the young men whose innocent hobby had suddenly become an important component of warfare. They were wooed with the promise that the professional experience they would receive would guarantee them employment after the war. More important perhaps was that these young men would be given an invaluable chance to be of service to their country during "its hour of need."

While the war stymied the efforts of the amateurs, the government was rapidly learning the value of wireless communication; during the summer of 1917, the United States established radio schools to train more wireless telegraphers. Then in January 1918 President Wilson sent out a wireless telegraph message to a war-weary world; the message contained his critical Fourteen Points, and months later, when Germany finally agreed to the armistice, reference was made to the terms the president had outlined in that message. Furthermore, after the war, the Wilson administration revealed that between October 20, 1918, and the armistice, President Wilson had secretly transmitted messages from a station in New Brunswick, New Jersey, to a receiving station in Nauen, Germany. Those messages urged the German people to accept peace on the terms dictated by the Allies. It was the story of how the president broke diplomatic precedent "by direct parley with the German people," but in reality it was inspired use of the radio technology as a tool of propaganda, one the German government would brilliantly and horrifically manipulate fifteen years later.

Even after the war's end in November 1918, radio transmitters in the United States remained under the control of the Navy Department, and what was to be done with these facilities became a matter of national debate. Secretary of the Navy Daniels's position was absolutely clear: He wanted the navy to have full control over all transmitting stations and all wireless communication within the United States. One argument he made was that if the government did not take control there would be chaos in the sky. But that worry was dismissed when Congress decided that well-crafted legislation could solve and control any invisible-wave traffic problems.

Nonetheless, Daniels's supporters did force a debate on the matter, and in October 1919 Congress considered legislation that would have set his request for government control into law, but such a law never came to fruition. The American Radio Relay League, an organization of devoted radio amateurs, urged Congress to not allow a government monopoly of radio. Individual and competitive freedom was too ingrained in the American psyche to permit the government to control something as far-reaching as wireless communication. In essence, the failure to grant full control over the airwaves to the government, though the power to grant or deny licenses remained in the hands of the secretary of commerce, powerfully affirmed that the airwaves did indeed belong to the people.

Six months after World War I, transmitting and receiving stations were released from government control, and the seals—literally, locked wires—that had closed many facilities began to come off the transmitting stations. Then in July 1919 Congress passed a resolution ordering the government to return all telephones, cables, and telegraphs to private ownership, thus launching the race toward commercialization of radiotelephony.

There was one highly significant aspect of the balance of power among the companies involved in the growing business of radiotelephony that was directly caused by World War I. Despite its name, American Marconi was actually a British-owned company, and by the end of the war the Navy Department had come to believe that foreign ownership, even by an ally, of the American airwaves, or even the right for a foreign entity to communicate to the American people through the U.S. airwaves, was unwise. As a result, the government actively encouraged the General Electric Company to buy American Marconi and its domestic assets. On November 20, 1919, the stockholders of the Marconi Company of America authorized the absorption of their company by the Radio Corporation of America, a new entity created and financed with a $3 million line of credit from General Electric for the sole purpose of acquiring Marconi. The business relationship between the Radio Corporation of America, RCA, and General Electric, GE, would serve as the basis for other acquisitions that would later allow RCA to become one of America's preeminent entertainment and communications companies.

By acquiring American Marconi, RCA instantly became America's leader in the fledgling radio business, whatever that business might actually become. Sending messages from one specific point to another had been the organizational idea behind the radiotelephony industry. Even in war, its greatest value was radio's ability to allow one person to speak directly with another person some distance away. But with the war over, radiotelephony would be developed along more commercial lines, and its potential impact on the telephone was causing concern among the leaders of that industry.

With the war over and a new decade about to begin, there were three important competing forces vying for control of radio communication: a government that believed it owned the radio spectrum; emerging corporate giants that saw the potential profit of selling the hardware and dominating the airwaves; and the enthusiasts who enjoyed communicating via wireless and who valued the freedom that implied. Yet even with all that, it was difficult to foresee how the radiotelephone could ever be divorced from the telephone, especially when the intent of radio's developers was to send signals from one point to another. Central to the problem was the technological fact that radio signals had a propensity to scatter about the atmosphere—to be broadly cast about—and therefore received by many people, even those for whom the communication was not intended. It was a conundrum, but eventually the benefit of the scattering signals would be central to radio's growth.

To fully appreciate how confused and confusing radiotelephony's possibilities were, one has only to read the reaction of one anonymous executive of the newly formed RCA who, when told of the idea of building boxes that could receive music in the home, said: "The wireless music box has no imaginable commercial value. Who would pay for a message sent to nobody in particular?"

Chapter 3

▲▲▲▲▲▲▲▲▲▲▲▲

POSTWAR AMERICA WAS AWASH in new and exciting businesses ripe for development, and conveniently there was a market ready for new technologies. By 1920, 6.7 million cars bounced along America's mostly unpaved roads, airplanes were becoming less of a novelty, and for every 1,000 people in the United States there were 123 telephones. But what about that other new electronic gadget known as the radio-telephone? What was it going to be used for, and by whom? Was it merely a plaything for amateurs who liked to build intricate machines that they spent long nights tinkering with in their garages, sending signals to other enthusiasts? Could it be used to enhance telephone communication, eliminating the telephone poles and wires that stretched across the American landscape? Should it be used solely to improve ship-to-shore or transoceanic communication, bringing the United States closer to the Continent, on which it had just fought a bloody war? Was it a technology the government needed to control for national security issues? Would Americans actually pay to bring information and various forms of entertainment directly into their homes so they could gather around a wooden box adorned with dials, meters, and wires and listen?

America's burgeoning radiotelephony companies were wrestling with these questions, and no company was more involved in that debate than RCA. When General Electric purchased the American Marconi Company and formed RCA, one longtime employee of Marconi may have been the greatest asset in the acquisition: David Sarnoff, the young wireless operator who had devotedly stayed at his post to transmit news of the *Titanic* disaster.

Sarnoff, more than any other pioneer, saw ways to exploit the potential in wireless's greatest flaw: the propensity of radio waves to disseminate over a wide field, to bounce around and spread out over great distances. It was this irony that forced the radio industry to develop, for as these early radio pioneers tried to improve the way radio waves could be used to send messages from point to point, they had to fight the scattering nature of the radio signal. Paradoxically, for this very reason early wireless was far from ideal for point-to-point communication, and it was this annoying habit of radio waves to cast about broadly, or broadcast, that led America to the wild possibilities of mass communication.

Born in 1891, in a wooden hut in the southern Russian town of Uzlian, Sarnoff immigrated with his family to the United States in 1900, settling in the tenements of New York City. Like many poor Jewish immigrants, Sarnoff was immediately enrolled in an English language class, and by the end of the year had acquired a passable ability to communicate. He then took a variety of odd jobs, earning enough money to survive by delivering meat for the local butcher and adding a paper route to maximize his income. His determination led neighbors to invest in him: They bought him a newsstand on Tenth Avenue, where he hired other young boys to help out. Intrigued by journalism, he looked for more important work and at age fifteen landed a messenger job at the *New York Herald*. There, in the ground-floor offices of the Commercial Cable Company, he first saw a telegraph transmitter. Fascinated by the device and its communication potential, he spent as much time as he could practicing Morse code until he felt ready to apply for a job at the American Marconi Company. Though turned down for the telegrapher's job, Sarnoff was hired to be an office boy, and he began his employment there on September 30, 1906. He was a determined young man and his diligence and hard work were noticed. When the Wanamaker department stores in New York and Philadelphia contracted to install Marconi wireless equipment in their stores to improve intracompany communication—and as a publicity stunt aimed at giving the stores a leg up on their competition—Sarnoff sought and was given the New York telegrapher's assignment.

His skills as a wireless operator—the ability to transcribe and send important messages rapidly and accurately—and his passion for the technology put him on the fast track. Soon the energetic young man's résumé read like the job list for the entire company: telegraph operator, training instructor, equipment inspector, chief inspector, assistant traffic manager, assistant chief engineer, and commercial manager. Boosted by his amazing handling of the *Titanic* disaster news, he became famous within wireless circles and was the Marconi Company's go-to guy, the man they turned to when new equipment needed to be evaluated and when ideas needed to be considered.

Sarnoff's intense love of the wireless business and his ideas about communication led him to write an incredibly prescient corporate memorandum in November 1916. Aware of Lee De Forest's initial attempts at broadcasting music in New York, Sarnoff used De Forest's hesitant first steps as a launching point, developing that germ of an idea into a full-blown corporate strategy. He wrote:

> I have in mind a plan of development which would make radio a "household utility" in the same sense as the piano or phono-graph . . . The receiver can be designed in the form of a simple "Radio Music Box" and arranged for several different wave lengths, which would be changeable with the throwing of a single switch or pressing of a single button . . . The box can be placed in the parlor or living room, the switch set accordingly and the transmitted music received.

Sarnoff estimated that sound could be sent within a radius of twenty-five to fifty miles, where it would be simultaneously received by "hundreds of thousands of families." He went on to suggest that the same idea could be extended to the at-home reception of lectures and other information. Then, astutely thinking of the potential of different audiences, he imagined how the new technology would interest farmers and others living in outlying districts removed from cities. By simply purchasing a "Radio Music Box," these distant listeners could enjoy broadcasts of concerts, lectures, music, recitals, and other events that might have been taking place in the nearest city within their receiving radius.

Sarnoff presented the memo to his boss, American Marconi vice president Edward J. Nally, who at the time was preparing the company for a possible role assisting the navy in the event the United States should enter World War I. Sarnoff's memo was politely dismissed as being far too visionary and fanciful.

Three years later, on January 19, 1920, Edward Nally became president of RCA, and Sarnoff, who was one of the company's most valued employees, again rose to prominence. Despite being centrally involved in the company's war efforts and seeing the vital role radio could play as a part of national military efforts, Sarnoff returned to his concept of the at-home radio box. During the intervening years he had added marketing strategies to his plan, even going into such detail as suggesting that everyone who bought one of RCA's Music Boxes be given a free subscription to *The Wireless Age,* the radio enthusiasts' magazine that RCA now owned. Sarnoff's plan forecast the number of radios that could be built and sold, and the profits that could be earned by selling each set for just $75. He presented the revised plan to Nally's boss, Owen D. Young, chairman of the board of General Electric and its affiliate, RCA. Young was somewhat interested in the commercial possibilities outlined by Sarnoff, especially his estimate that 100,000 units could be sold in the first year alone; the RCA board granted him $2,500 to further develop his idea.

RCA, though perhaps ahead of the industry in terms of ideas, talent, and resources, was not alone in the desire to build and sell more radio equipment. In Pittsburgh, Pennsylvania, the Westinghouse Electric Company was branching out from its original business of providing electric power and electrically powered machinery. Though he had lost control of the Westinghouse Electric Company, George Westinghouse had anticipated the growing market for electric appliances, and his manufacturing companies forged a strong business during the 1910s building and selling gadgets for America's newly electrified homes, including the electric percolator and the Copeman Stove. Another invention they had been experimenting with was the radio, but Westinghouse—more so than RCA, and before that Marconi, which had developed a solid business in the sending and receiving of signals—was faced with one of the great chicken-and-egg situations to confront a business: Why would anyone buy a radio if there was nothing of value to listen to, and why would anyone create programming to send to a radio if so few people owned the device?

Fortunately for Westinghouse they had in their employ an engineer named Dr. Frank Conrad who had been involved in the company's research in radio technology during the First World War. To test transmissions, Conrad had placed one transmitting and receiving set at the Westinghouse plant and another on the upper floor of his home garage, about four miles away. When the war ended and the government removed the restrictions on amateur radiotelephony, Conrad went back to using the device installed at his home. Working late into the night to improve the sound and signal, he conversed with other amateurs within range. In April 1920 Conrad applied for and received a license for his station from the Department of Commerce. Given the call sign 8XK, Conrad quickly discovered there was an ever-growing group of enthusiasts who wanted to discuss radio technology. But talking to other radio hobbyists over the air bored him, so he decided to try to entertain his listeners. Placing his crank-operated phonograph near a microphone, he played records and transmitted the music. Despite the scratchy sound, his "programming" became so popular that by midsummer Conrad was receiving letters from listeners requesting he play certain pieces at specific times. Conrad had accidentally created radio's first request show, but since he didn't have all the records necessary to fulfill the requests he made a deal with a local phonograph dealer. He borrowed the requested discs and gave the dealer credit on the air, and thus Conrad also stumbled into doing the first bartered advertising.

Obliging his listeners became time-consuming, so Conrad enlisted his sons Francis and Crawford to help out with the on-air duties. The sons in turn expanded the programming, inviting local talent to appear and perform live. Then they added periodic news updates, and while there was no precise program schedule, they found that as word spread of the entertainment they were providing, so did the number of listeners who went out and purchased radio equipment of their own.

The Conrads had become local celebrities, and by the end of September 1920, the local newspaper noted that

Victrola music, played into the wireless telephone, was "picked up" by listeners on the wireless receiving station which was recently installed here for patrons interested in wireless experiments. The concert was heard Thursday night around 10 o'clock and continued for 20 minutes. The music was from a Victrola pulled up close to the transmitter of a wireless telephone in the home of Frank Conrad, Penn and Peebles Avenue, Wilkinsburg. Mr. Conrad is a wireless enthusiast and "puts on" the wireless concerts for the entertainment of the many people in the district who have wireless sets.

The quasi-news item was part of an ad for Horne's, a local department store that had a stock of receiving equipment for sale.

Westinghouse saw Conrad's experiments as something important and potentially profitable, and so early in October 1920 Westinghouse acquired the International Radio Telegraph Company, which owned and operated five transmitting stations along the Atlantic coast. Westinghouse vice president Harry P. Davis, who was one of Conrad's greatest proponents, stated, "The programs sent out by Dr. Conrad caused the thought to come to me that the efforts that were then being made to develop radio telephony as a confidential means of communication were wrong, and that instead its field was really one of wide publicity, in fact the only means of instantaneous collective communication ever devised."

Davis was certain that radiotelephony's "ability to annihilate distance, would attract, interest, and open many avenues to bring happiness into human lives." And so the company, with a team led by Dr. Conrad, erected a new transmitting facility atop the Westinghouse plant in East

Pittsburgh, the construction of which was not completed until the autumn of 1920, just as that year's presidential election headed into its final weeks.

THE ELECTION OF 1920 presented both major political parties with a clean slate; gone were the giants of the previous decade, Woodrow Wilson and Theodore Roosevelt. Meeting in Chicago, the Republicans, despite *Los Angeles Times* publisher Harry Chandler's efforts to nominate his fellow Californian and businessman extraordinaire, Herbert Hoover, settled on Ohio newspaper editor and United States senator Warren G. Harding as their nominee, and Massachusetts governor Calvin Coolidge was selected as his running mate. The Democrats, who met in San Francisco, nominated another Ohio newspaperman and the state's governor, James M. Cox, to top their ticket and Franklin Delano Roosevelt, the former undersecretary of the navy and a fifth cousin to Teddy Roosevelt, to be the vice-presidential candidate.

For the better part of the summer and into the fall the candidates crisscrossed the United States by train, delivering their messages to a national voting public that, since the adoption of the Nineteenth Amendment, for the first time included women. The campaign itself, with the vast distances needed to be covered, was a grueling test of the candidates' stamina. They traveled from town to town, shaking hands, waving, smiling, and tipping their hats in response to the cheers from the assembled crowds. The *New York Times* noted that

> the Presidential party is generally a wreck when it gets back and has to go on vacation. But the candidate, who has worked harder than any one of them, can have no vacation. He has to do the same thing over again. Finally comes the speech, an exhausting labor in itself. Maybe there are two speeches, one at the mills or stockyards and one at the auditorium; every Western city that

thinks anything of itself has an auditorium and the rest have col-
iseums and convention halls. The moment the candidate has finished his last speech he comes out on the run, propelled by Secret
Service men and local committees, shot into another automobile
and put on board a train for which he is already fifteen minutes
late.

In addition to the many public appearances of the 1920 campaign,
the *Nation's Forum* invited the candidates to record speeches onto
phonograph records, which were then distributed for people to listen
to, thus increasing the number of voters who actually heard the candidates speak. But the heart of the campaign remained the whistle-stop.
Trailing their Republican opponents, Democrats Cox and Roosevelt
decided they needed to do something radical, and at the end of August
launched a nonstop speaking tour during which they planned to stay
on the road speaking to crowds across the country right up until election day. It was exhausting, but it was the only way for the candidates
to get their message directly to the voters.

As the presidential campaign drew to a close, Frank Conrad and his
team were putting the finishing touches on their new transmitting facility on the roof of the tallest building on the Westinghouse campus
in East Pittsburgh. Their goal was to have the facility ready for election night so that the fledgling broadcasters could report election results
to radio listeners. On October 27, 1920, Westinghouse's completed
radio facility was granted its license by the Department of Commerce
and was given the now historic call letters KDKA.

The station was little more than a hastily constructed shack that en-
closed not only all the necessary mechanical apparatus—a mass of wires,
tubes, valves, switches, and other electronic gadgetry—but also the
desk from which the announcer would report the results. The facility
was tested on November 1, but the results were so unsatisfactory that

on the next night, election night, Frank Conrad remained at home listening on his old 8XK equipment, prepared to take over and send out his own signal to listeners, if there were any, should the KDKA experiment fail.

PITTSBURGH, PENNSYLVANIA. Tuesday, November 2, 1920. Election night.

In the metal shack atop the Westinghouse plant, four men dressed in dark suits and ties pored over early election returns, numbers reported via telephone from the newsroom of the *Pittsburgh Post*. Once compiled, the results were handed to another man, Leo H. Rosenberg, who, seated at the small wooden desk right next to the engineer, was positioned directly in front of the mass of wires and dials that made up the transmitting equipment. Leaning forward, Rosenberg annunciated the returns into the rudimentary microphone that looked much like an old-fashioned telephone connected to a clunky, metal box apparatus behind the mouthpiece. His voice passed through the tangle of wires and the glowing tubes, up a single wire to the transmitter, and out into the night. On invisible waves, the election results winged their way through the chilly autumn air, landing wherever a receiver happened to be tuned to that frequency. Despite the problems of the previous night, the experiment went according to plan. The team situated in the "penthouse" studio aired regular updates to the invisible audience, keeping them apprised of how the returns from across the country were coming in. It was estimated that between five hundred and a thousand listeners, equipped with earphones or gathered in stores, heard those historic election returns. Those lucky listeners did not have to wait for the newspapers' special editions to hit the streets; they knew instantaneously that Warren G. Harding had won the presidency of the United States; it was as if they had received the news straight from the sky. Since people had to gather around radio receiving equipment to try to make out the far-from-clear sound, it was less than an optimal listening experience, but that night, that moment, marked the debut of broadcasting.

The excitement triggered by KDKA's coverage of the 1920 election set off a national mania. On the morning of November 3, Westinghouse's switchboard was flooded with calls from people wanting to find out how they could get a radio. Within weeks, Frank Conrad and Westinghouse had replaced the makeshift transmitter with a more permanent installation and had increased the station's power to 500 watts, enabling KDKA to be heard by radio enthusiasts as far away as Washington, D.C. Spurred by his success, Conrad gradually added more entertainment programs to his "schedule," completing the transformation of radio from a medium meant to send messages from point to point, into a communications vehicle that could beam entertainment to the world. Conrad had proven Sarnoff's theory that radio's flaw—its propensity to scatter—was indeed its greatest asset.

DESPITE BEING THE FIRST president to have his election called by the electronic media, Harding's relationship with radio got off to a rocky start. In the five months between the election and the inauguration, the inaugural committee's chairman, in conjunction with radio experts from the army and the navy, developed a plan to have the president's inaugural address recorded onto phonograph records and sent out via radiotelephone the night of his inauguration. It was a bold initiative that included sending the president's voice across the United States and to U.S. battleships within range. The committee further anticipated that the airing of the address would encourage citizens who owned the right listening equipment to hold inauguration parties, at which supporters could congregate, enjoy the president's words, and celebrate, thus turning politics into a truly social event. Despite the well-thought-out plan, and a successful test of the transmitting equipment, the broadcast never

happened. Ironically, it was not scrapped because of technological issues, but because of the failure of Harding's speechwriters: The committee was informed "that Mr. Harding's speech would not be finished
in time to have it recorded on phonograph records." On inauguration
day, Warren G. Harding, like every president before him, was heard
only by those within earshot. It was an inauspicious beginning for
Harding and for radio, but as the new administration assembled in
Washington, D.C., one man in the president's cabinet—a cabinet that
also included Secretary of State Charles Evans Hughes and Secretary of
the Treasury Andrew Mellon—would take the reins of the radio industry and shepherd its growth: Secretary of Commerce Herbert
Hoover.

Born in 1874, Herbert Clark Hoover spent his first years in West
Branch, Iowa. There in the American heartland he developed the work
ethic that would guide him throughout his life. Those formative days
were "days of chores and labor. I am no supporter of factory labor for
children but I have never joined with those who clamor against proper
chores for children outside of school hours. And I speak from the common experience of most Iowa children of my day in planting corn,
hoeing gardens, learning to milk, sawing wood, and in the other normal occupations for boys."

Orphaned before age ten, Hoover left Iowa and moved to Oregon
to live with an uncle and attend Friends Pacific Academy. An average
student, Hoover never graduated from high school but did manage to
matriculate as the youngest student into the first class at the newly
formed Stanford University. Having discovered an aptitude for engineering, he majored in geology, but he also had a head for business and
entrepreneurship, and so while still a student he worked as a newsboy,
as a clerk in the registrar's office, and started a student laundry service.
He graduated in May 1895 with a BA in geology, but he could find no
work as a surveyor, so he accepted a job pushing ore carts at a gold

mine near Nevada City, California. Working deep under the earth, seven days a week, in twelve-hour shifts, Hoover earned about two dollars a day.

Hoover stood nearly six feet tall; he was a stocky man with straight brown hair that he parted to the left of center. His face was rounded and fleshy with a ruddy complexion. He was hardworking and seemingly incorruptible, a model of efficiency who had little patience for those who could not or would not work up to his high level. Often unable to grasp the broad significance of issues, Hoover was a stickler for details and concentrated on organization.

Though he was not happy spending his life digging in mines where his coworkers lacked the education he had, he was upset when the mining work slowed and he was fired. He "then learned what the bottom levels of real human despair are paved with." After months of seeking employment, his luck changed at the end of 1895 when he introduced himself to Louis Janin, the leading mining engineer on the West Coast. At first Hoover was hired as no more than a secretarial assistant, but soon enough Janin saw that the young man knew about engineering and sent him to Australia, where he was responsible for inspecting possible mine sites. From Australia he went to China, where he was stationed, performing heroically during the 1900 Boxer Rebellion. Eventually he ended up in Burma, where he made his personal fortune at the Bawdin silver mine. In 1908, now independently wealthy, Hoover formed an engineering company that specialized in unearthing resources all over the world. By 1914 his estimated personal wealth had reached $4 million.

Now a financial success, Hoover had a desire to do public service, to be part of the national life, a desire he claimed he first recognized when he witnessed a torch-lit parade that was part of the Garfield campaign in 1880. Hoover was a superb organizer whose fame grew exponentially during the First World War as he headed the American

Relief Committee, which helped more than 120,000 Americans trapped in Europe. The war and its aftermath provided opportunities for a man with Hoover's organizational skills, and he accepted the challenges with fervor; between 1914 and 1919 he headed the Commission for the Relief of Belgium, and then while serving as the head of the U.S. food administration from 1917 to 1918, he urged Americans to conserve supplies by observing meatless and wheatless days. His nearly evangelical passion for conservation coined a new term meaning the voluntary rationing of one's goods: to *hooverize*.

Following the war, from 1919 to 1920, Hoover, appointed by President Wilson, who called him "a great international figure," directed the American Relief Administration, where he organized the collection and distribution of billions of dollars' worth of food and supplies to the damaged, demoralized countries and people of Europe. At a banquet honoring Hoover for his amazingly successful efforts in behalf of the people of England, David Lloyd George said, "It seems to me, Mr. Hoover, that you represent not only the United States but also Merciful Providence."

Hoover's organizational skills were truly remarkable and his renown spread throughout the United States and beyond. Maxim Gorky wrote to Hoover expressing his deep thanks: "Your help will be inscribed in history as a unique, gigantic accomplishment worthy of the greatest glory." As the campaign for the 1920 presidential nomination got under way, California maverick businessman Harry Chandler pushed Hoover's name forward, getting the returned hero of Europe mentioned as a possible candidate. Hoover was a good man, the "savior of society," seemingly liked by both Republicans and Democrats. But when the Republican nomination went to Warren G. Harding, Hoover dutifully threw his full support behind the candidate. "I took part in the Republican campaign, making two poorish speeches. Will Hays, the Republican Chairman, complained that they were 'too objective.'"

But Hoover had made his mark, and soon after the election of 1920 Harding sent word that Hoover would be welcome in the new administration's cabinet, either as secretary of the interior or as secretary of commerce. "I replied that, as in my mind our major problems were reconstruction and national development, I preferred Commerce although it was considered less important than the Interior." It was assumed that this great man, this humanitarian, this self-made millionaire, was himself too big for the job of commerce secretary.

Three months went by before Harding officially tendered an offer, but when it finally was made, Hoover hesitated. "I told him there were some ideas in my mind that he should consider before the matter was finally settled. I stated . . . that for the Department to be of real service I must have a voice on all important economic policies of the administration. I stated that this would involve business, agriculture, labor, finance, and foreign affairs so far as they related to these problems." Within the wide-ranging plans Hoover told Harding about was the idea that the proper development of communication was inseparable from commerce, and to that end the nominee pledged to "pay especial attention to the extension of commercial radio facilities."

On February 24, 1921, Herbert Hoover was officially nominated to be secretary of commerce. But as Hoover had warned Harding, his idea of a successful secretary of commerce required the building of a department that would have far-reaching and extensive power and influence throughout the United States. What neither man may have realized when Hoover said that he would "build up, not tear down" was exactly how Hoover's organizational genius would eventually influence nearly every aspect of American life and culture.

Unlike his predecessors, one of whom told him the job "would not require more than two hours of work a day," Hoover became the most active and influential person to hold the post of secretary of commerce. As he developed his plans, he divided the tasks of the department and its subordinate bureaus between two undersecretaries, but he kept the bureaus of Foreign and Domestic Commerce and Standards under his direct control. It was the work done by Hoover's newly energized and far-ranging Bureau of Standards that literally reorganized American life. Hoover understood that many of the prewar ways of manufacturing and organizing were no longer viable, however as a probusiness Republican he was also a believer in letting businesses run on their own. He believed the Department of Commerce should be in the widest sense a department of service to the commerce and industry of the country, and not a department for the regulation of trade and industry. To do such service to the greatest advantage, he sought to establish a wider and better organized cooperation with trade and commercial associations.

During his seven years as secretary of commerce, Hoover grew the department by 2,800 employees and increased the appropriation from Congress by nearly 50 percent. His increasingly large team worked to make government help business; by imposing standardization to more and more elements of American life, the work his team did at the beginning of the decade helped America pull out of its postwar economic funk, which allowed it to explode into the decade that would become known as the Roaring Twenties.

The list of goods standardized by the Department of Commerce's Bureau of Standards goes on for pages and includes thousands of items, including many whose consistent nature are taken completely for granted today, such as beds, springs, and mattresses; milk bottles and caps; bank checks; and tissue paper. But the department also dealt with areas that were crucial to the economy, such as construction in which building equipment and materials had been manufactured in a rather haphazard manner. "Through the good offices of Herbert Hoover and the simplified practice division of the Department of Commerce, the brick industry has been enabled to sweep away the infinite variety of odd sizes of brick and establish one standard size for the 7,000,000 bricks produced every year in the United States."

While Hoover and his organizational talents helped the construction industry simplify itself, there were other areas of a rapidly changing country that needed some form of control to establish order. More and more automobiles were being built and sold. As they began to clog America's newly built byways, they created dangerous traffic conditions in a country still accustomed to horse-and-buggy travel. Early in 1924 another of Hoover's committees unveiled its plan for a uniform system of color signals to ease traffic problems, and so was born the red, yellow, and green signal system still in use today.

One other crucial, growing business that needed traffic control if it were to thrive was radio. With its signals that carried messages invisibly through the air interfering with one another while on their way to listeners, who found the constant static made listening difficult, radio in 1921 was an ideal candidate for government intervention and Hoover's brand of organization.

Chapter 4

▲▲▲▲▲▲▲▲▲▲▲▲

THE 1920S WAS A DECADE of fads. Prohibition, which banned the manufacture, sale, and transportation of intoxicating liquors, seemed to be out of step with a country giddy with postwar euphoria. It was, at least in the big cities, the age of the flapper. Women were "hiking up their skirts, wearing makeup, bobbing their hair, and partaking of heretofore forbidden delights." Celebrities like F. Scott and Zelda Fitzgerald personified the freedom that was reflected in the hot sounds of jazz.

As radio began its ascent in popularity and importance, there was a sense that this wire- and tube-laden contraption might be just another craze, a fad that, if nothing else, was reducing unemployment among America's engineers simply because companies had to build so much equipment for the thousands of at-home enthusiasts. It was believed that hobbyists using the complex rigs they built in their homes might, for a while at least, be excited about speaking with one another over great distances, but that eventually—just as sixty years later the CB radio fad would come and go—radio would lose its appeal as a hobby and be relegated to government use, such as ship-to-shore and other military communication.

Though the image of the radio enthusiast alone at night in his garage manipulating antennas and wires in an effort to receive a crackly voice from many miles away remains a popular image, the truth is that the radio hobbyist was a social animal who enjoyed the company of those who shared his excitement. Tens of thousands of Americans, many of them high school boys, began building makeshift home receivers and exchanging sounds with other enthusiasts; the *Washington Post* encouraged boys to "get on the Radio band wagon. Everybody's listening in the world round, and you must keep up with the procession. Radio is a hobby that is worth while. The government is right behind the boy who takes up radio seriously."

As the number of hobbyists grew exponentially, radiophoning became a force that brought faraway places and different kinds of people closer together. Late-night listeners boasted of how their apparatus had pulled in static-filled signals from hundreds of miles away. Hearing sound from great distances became an honor acknowledged and lauded by other enthusiasts. Men involved with this hobby gathered for banquets at which they praised their members and listened to music played at a distant location and sent via radio directly to the banquet hall, where proper listening equipment had been set up. Across the nation, radio clubs at colleges sprang up, and some of these early college stations became petri dishes of programming and technological innovation. Union College in Schenectady, New York, was referred to as the "pioneer college broadcaster" when they inaugurated the sending out of Sunday evening religious sermons. But radio was not for men only, and at women's colleges such as Radcliffe, radio clubs were becoming an important part of the campus social and extracurricular scene. Even high schools and junior high schools were involved in radio, and by March 1922 every one of Washington, D.C.'s high schools boasted its own radio club. "The popular radiophoning craze has seized the students of all the Washington high schools and those active young citizens of the Nation's Capital have forsaken 'flapping' fraternities, sororities and their 'tweedles' for scientific pursuits of the radio wave."

The radio craze was ubiquitous; at one New York City public elementary school commencement ceremony, nine of the students' speeches were about radio, and learning to send and receive radio signals became part of basic training for Boy Scouts. Invitations to high-society parties often included the mysterious marking B.Y.O.H. Given that Prohibition was in full swing, some invitees may have assumed the cryptic message meant "Bring Your Own Hootch," but the initials actually stood for "Bring Your Own Headpiece," as group listening to the wireless radio became a popular party game. Reasons for group listening were as varied as the participants. One group of firemen in a Michigan town, in an effort to "get cultured," purchased a radio receiving set for the purpose of improving the downtime they had between fire calls. New uses for radio were newsworthy as the print media reported on every aspect of the craze. WOMEN HEAR RADIO MUSIC one story headlined. It was a report of the momentous news that the members of the Anthony League attending their monthly meeting had been entertained by an afternoon radio concert.

Radio, with its power to send sounds invisibly through walls, across rivers, and to anywhere there was a receiver, was magic, and gradually it was recognized that radio was more than a fad: The radio telephone had progressed from a hobby to a staple luxury. Radio also became a unifier, not only within communities but between them, as it brought the sounds of urban life to rural areas. Farmers became a particularly desirable audience segment, and the government, eager to help these isolated agrarians, used the navy's radio transmitters to send out daily agricultural reports throughout the United States, an innovation referred to by the Department of Agriculture as "the most important step of its kind in the radio world." A story circulated about one farmer's shrewd mother who was able to negotiate better prices for their fresh eggs because she had heard a report on the radio about the price of eggs in the New York markets. When a local buyer offered her less because the market was weak, she quickly corrected him, quoting what she had heard that morning on the radio.

Understandably some difficulties with the idea of radio itself lingered. The still hard-to-fathom invisible transmissions were blamed for any unusual occurrence, including dizzy spells, bad weather, and all kinds of mysterious sounds. A farmer near Louisville became concerned about radio's evil power when a flock of blackbirds flew over his farm and one of the birds suddenly dropped from the sky, dead. It must have been a radio wave from station WHAS that struck and killed the bird, he reasoned. Another group of farmers in Lewiston, Ohio, grew concerned when while working in their fields they heard voices seemingly coming out of the sky. After some investigation it turned out that the sound was nothing more than the result of the installation of a powerful receiving set and audio speaker on the top of a local school building.

Secretary of Commerce Herbert Hoover, the man who'd made his name organizing relief efforts for the public good and who called for limited government control and regulation of business, was faced with the challenge of shaping the future of radio, the industry he described as a "universal art profoundly modifying every aspect of human life." Appreciative of the potential power of the new medium, even in its still undeveloped state, Hoover knew he had to find a way to help this new business grow in an organized, sensible, and safe manner, all without wiping out the investment made by many individuals who had built their own transmitters, and without trampling on the right of free speech that was clearly going to be affected by any imposition of government control of the airwaves.

Almost immediately after taking office, Secretary Hoover quashed the ongoing attempts by the Department of the Navy to place all radio frequencies under its control. He needed a sensible way to manage this new form of communication no one yet fully understood. "The law authorizing the Secretary of Commerce to regulate radio had been enacted prior to voice broadcasting. It was a very weak rudder to steer so powerful a development," Herbert Hoover wrote years later. In fact, the last time Congress had dealt with regulating radio had been in 1912, when voice broadcasting was still in an embryonic state, and long before anyone in their wildest imagination could even think of a business developing out of the invisible signals that bounced around wildly. It was clear that the Department of Commerce would have to move carefully into uncharted waters, and Hoover was keenly aware of the conflicting interests at play. "I was early impressed with three things: first, the immense importance of the spoken radio; second, the urgency of placing the new channels of communication under public control; and, third, the difficulty of devising such control in a new art."

When Hoover was confirmed as commerce secretary in March 1921, three main companies were involved in the radio business: Westinghouse, RCA, and AT&T. But every day new transmitting stations were being granted licenses to send signals into the air, and the resulting congestion of the airwaves was making receiving and hearing radio signals increasingly difficult, especially since all of these broadcasters, by government order, were sharing the frequency at 833 kHz, the only part of the spectrum then approved for broadcasting. Only limits on a transmitter's power, reducing the distance the signal could travel, kept stations from overlapping and constantly interfering with one another, although most still did create listening chaos. Fortunately interference was also kept at bay by the fact that stations broadcast only intermittently—when they had something they wanted to send out. There was no such thing as a program schedule, and the idea of 24/7 broadcasting was beyond anyone's wildest imagination. The idea of sending messages all the time was idiotic, so radiocasters chose times when they turned on their transmitters, hoping to be heard by an indeterminate number of listeners who might be tuned in.

Radiocasting was a booming hobby-business, and the rate of growth in terms of numbers of stations was staggering. By 1922 there were more than 200 licensed stations with federally assigned call signals transmitting throughout the country, and yet there were naysayers who continued to see radio as nothing more than another craze that would, like a weak signal, eventually fade. Though he appeared on the cover of the March 26, 1922, edition of *Radio Broadcast,* one of the first industry publications, humorist Will Rogers said during an interview on Detroit's WWJ that radio was "bunk." Doubting the power of the new medium, Rogers challenged the invisible audience: "I don't think you can hear. If it isn't bunk, let me know you can hear me." Rogers received hundreds of postcards from all over the Midwest and later went on to host one of the country's most popular radio programs. One now-forgotten congressman likened radio to mah-jongg: just another way for his constituents to while away some of their leisure time.

This skepticism is easy to understand. In 1922 listening to the radio was still a difficult, confusing, and often frustrating undertaking. One need only refer to the experience of one young radio fan who tried to listen to his radio on July 4, 1922. Tuning in to a frequency he usually received, he heard only loud static and made the logical assumption that the station was airing a program of fireworks to celebrate the nation's birthday. Problems and skepticism aside, radio in America was a hot commodity requiring guidance and extensive scientific help from the government.

The Bureau of Standards, part of the Commerce Department, was busily establishing regulations and measurements to help American business. Hoover was the popular front man for the bureau and he often spoke on topics ranging from the standardization of weights and measures used in the baking of bread, to making hotel blankets a uniform size. Alongside all the day-to-day items the bureau worked to standardize and organize, the department's scientists engaged in an intense effort to organize radio technology. To help keep track of the rapid increase in the number of transmitting facilities, the Department of Commerce issued a monthly *Radio Service Bulletin* that reported on advances and new stations. Every issue of the bulletin listed the number of new stations granted licenses by the department, and the list makes clear why organization was needed.

AUGUST 1, 1921:	Two new stations
SEPTEMBER 1, 1921:	Nine new stations
OCTOBER 1, 1921:	Twelve new stations
NOVEMBER 1, 1921:	Six new stations
DECEMBER 1, 1921:	Three new stations
JANUARY 1, 1922:	Twenty new stations
FEBRUARY 1, 1922:	Fourteen new stations
MARCH 1, 1922:	Twenty-seven new stations
APRIL 1, 1922:	Eighty-eight new stations
MAY 1, 1922:	Ninety-nine new stations

Concurrent with this rapid increase in the number of licensed radio stations, a steady stream of technological improvements in the sending and receiving of signals led to further increases in the number of people who wanted to own the wonderful receiving sets on which they could, at least sporadically, hear all kinds of different things. In 1922 alone the American public invested more than $60 million in the purchase of home receiving sets. By midyear the number of receiving sets in the country had reached the million mark, and since there were at that time about 350 stations in the country, it was estimated that the average station serviced approximately 3,000 sets, although clearly there was a higher concentration of signals and audience in more densely populated areas. Selling radios was a hot business, and the work by the scientists in the Department of Commerce gave the buying public confidence. The bureau was instrumental in aiding radio's development and the information they published was extremely helpful to the radio manufacturer and the merchant. Radio's effect on commerce was becoming more and more evident. One newspaperman noted, "It is pretty hard to determine what is a 'radio store' nowadays. In the larger cities, besides any number of shops that specialize in this equipment, nearly all electrical and hardware shops have added wireless sets and parts to their stock. Now drug stores have gone in for it carrying all sorts of sets, from $10 up."

Everywhere people were turning on and tuning their mostly battery-operated contraptions just to pick up signals from distant places. It wasn't about what you were hearing, just that you were hearing something sent by someone faraway. Station program schedules were nonexistent, programming was a hodgepodge of anything and everything that could be fed into a microphone, and so the content itself, whatever form it might assume, was newsworthy. "Mrs. David H. Kincheloe, wife of Representative Kincheloe of Kentucky, will appear at the Hecht Co. radio concert tonight at 7:30 o'clock. Mrs. Kincheloe is a versatile entertainer and will render a varied program of novelty whistling, songs and recitations," reported the *Washington Post* on July 7, 1922.

Perhaps even harder for twenty-first-century consumers of media to fathom was the idea that radio transmission was totally haphazard, occurring mostly in fits and starts. No station operated for more than a few hours per week. It was news when WGY, the GE-owned station in Schenectady, New York, announced that beginning on September 11, 1922, it would offer regular musical programs every Monday evening in addition to the programs of Tuesday, Thursday, and Friday nights that were already on the air. Strikingly, that announcement appeared in the *Washington Post,* whose readership was more than 500 miles away from WGY's transmitter. But because of the way signals bounced, especially at night, WGY's signal, and those of other stations some distance away, could be heard in Washington. The mere fact that WGY was adding programming and had something of substance to air made it a station worth writing about.

Conflicting interests, a lack of real understanding of what this miraculous device was for, and technical issues that made listening difficult could have relegated radio to the category of fads. Hobbyists interested in using the airwaves to converse with one another and listen to signals from distant places were in direct conflict with the companies that were heavily invested in the technology and that saw the new medium as a way to reach as many people as possible. As to the confusion about what the technology was good for, there were those who wanted radio to provide information, those who wanted it to provide entertainment, and there were some for whom it remained the ideal form of person-to-person communication. Some people in tune with the looser morals of the 1920s even thought the radiophone would be an excellent device for couples separated by distance to use to make love over the airwaves, even though their "private" session might be overheard by hundreds of other people listening in.

In his effort to minimize the government's control over radio, Secretary Hoover had hoped licensed stations would negotiate private agreements to avoid interfering with one another. Nearing the end of his first year in office, he realized this would not work and that conflicts were worsening. On February 27, 1922, he called the first Conference on Radio Telephony to order. Hoover invited men from the major corporate interests, representatives from government agencies, and a few engineers and inventors, including Hiram Percy Maxim. Born in Brooklyn, New York, in 1869, Maxim was an inventor who in 1914 cofounded the American Radio Relay League, an association of radio amateurs. Maxim had been the champion of amateurs' rights and had led the fight before World War I to halt the government's takeover of radio equipment. It was only logical that he should represent the country's enthusiasts at the first national radio conference. Hoover opened the meeting by saying:

It is the purpose of this conference to inquire into the critical situation that has now arisen through the astonishing development of the wireless telephone; to advise the Department of Commerce as to the application of its present powers of regulation, and further to formulate such recommendations to Congress as to the legislation necessary.

We are indeed today upon the threshold of a new means of widespread communication of intelligence that has the most profound importance from the point of view of public education and public welfare.

Hoover stressed that

the use of the radio telephone for communication between single individuals as in the case of the ordinary telephone is a perfectly hopeless notion. The wireless spoken word has one definite field, and that is for the broadcast of certain predetermined material of public interest from central stations. This material must be limited to news, to education, and to entertainment, and the communication of such commercial matters as are of importance to large groups of the community at the same time.

During the conference one main point became abundantly clear to Hoover: something needed to be done to straighten out the mess that radiophoning had gotten itself into. But only one resolution resulted from the conference: a nonbinding request that the secretary of commerce should be given "adequate legal authority" for effective control. Those intimately involved with the embryonic business understood they needed stringent government regulation, a desire no doubt endorsed and pushed by the large companies that saw Hoover as probusiness.

America's organizer went to work: Using his department's power, Hoover assigned certain parts of the radio band for use by the army and the navy, and for public service. He even set aside one definitive wavelength for use by boy amateurs. The department then allotted broadcasting stations specific wavelengths to reduce interference. The plan worked somewhat, until the sheer number of stations grew so great that there was even more interference on the dial. Though the Commerce Department regulated frequency distribution, it did not tell stations which days or hours they could broadcast. Hoover again urged stations to reach local agreements about hours of operation, and in some cases this worked. But these unenforceable agreements led to other conflicts. WDAF, the station owned by the *Kansas City Star*, usually signed off at 7 P.M. to allow station WHB to broadcast from 7 to 8 P.M. "One day it was learned that a local politician was going to appear on WHB and 'rake the *Kansas City Star* over the coals.'" During the time scheduled for the politician, WDAF's engineer kept his station on the air without broadcasting any programming, but just by playing with the equipment and changing the frequency, he created some very odd sounds that interfered with the reception and thus the ability of the listeners to hear the politician's remarks.

Legal battles over the freedom of the airwaves erupted. A court case in Joliet, Illinois, pitted the president of the State Bank of Dwight against an eighteen-year-old amateur radio enthusiast, G. Wylie Bergman. The case, the first of its kind, began in November 1922 when the banker Edward McWilliams won a temporary restraining order against Bergman preventing him from using his transmitter because his signals had interfered with the "receiving of radio telephone service at the McWilliams home on election night."

Bergman and his attorney sought to have the order overturned so he could return to the airwaves, but the case was put over to the April term. Prominent radiomen, including Secretary of Commerce Herbert Hoover, New York machine-gun manufacturer Mitchell Lewis, and Hiram Percy Maxim, president of the American Radio Relay League, planned to attend the hearing.

Before that case would be heard, and with no new legislation from Congress to provide guidance, Secretary Hoover called to order the second national radio conference in March 1923. One highlight of the conference was the awarding of the first Hoover Radio Cup. The prize recognized the best amateur station in the nation as selected by a three-judge panel put together by the American Radio Relay League led by Hiram Maxim himself. The criteria for the prize included how much of the equipment was homemade; the ingenuity of the design; consistency of the technical aspects of transmission; obedience to United States law; and accuracy, completeness, and neatness of the station's log of operations. The 1923 winner was Frederick Ostman of Ridgewood, New Jersey. Though they were recognized as an important group, the amateurs were a major culprit in the creation of the bedlam that Hoover sought to ease. Earlier in the year Congress had failed to pass a bill that would have provided the Department of Commerce with the power to supervise all radio communication, "assigning wave length, approving apparatus, licensing operators and otherwise supervising wireless communication to bring order out of the present chaos of jazz bands, sermons, crop reports, sporting services, concerts and whatnot running simultaneously on the same wave lengths."

With no new mandate to regulate radio transmission, Hoover asked the conference attendees to craft some principles to guide amateurs and corporations alike. The conferees agreed, but in the end they merely affirmed their belief that the secretary already had the power to "regulate hours and wave lengths of operation of stations when such action is necessary to prevent interference detrimental to the public good."

Control of the radio spectrum was a balancing act between the need to organize for the good of broadcasting in general, and the desire to allow the airwaves to symbolize American freedom. Fully expecting legal challenges, Hoover reorganized the broadcast spectrum by creating different classes of stations. In April 1923 he announced a plan that divided the broadcasting stations into three distinct categories, which would go into effect on May 15:

1. High-power stations serving many people would receive dial positions close to the center of the dial—between 300 and 545 meters—and would only have to share time when absolutely necessary. There was one interesting caveat: These stations could never play phonograph records; all music had to be performed by live musicians. Since records could be enjoyed by any person with his or her own phonograph at home, it was thought that the magic of radio should be reserved for bringing live music performances into the home; it reinforced Hoover's theory that radio was a public service.

2. Lower-power stations of not more than 500 watts serving smaller areas would broadcast free of interference within those regions and would be located between 222 and 300 meters, although these facilities might face some time-sharing.

3. Finally, all other low-power stations would be located at 360 meters and would serve limited geographic areas, would have to share time, and would most often be restricted to daytime hours so they would never interfere with the larger stations.

The reorganization was hailed as a fabulous achievement: "With the reassignment of wave lengths, a big step has been taken in forwarding the interests of radio broadcasting," opined *Radio Broadcast*'s editor. But his optimism was short-lived, for people who had been using their transmitting equipment without fear of violating laws that didn't exist were unhappy with Hoover's unilateral reorganization, and they abrogated his rules. It turned out to be regulation without the power and benefit of legislation.

However, the reorganization did make it easier for stations to promote themselves, and newspapers began including daily listings of available radio programs that cited call letters, city of origin, and the dial position in meters. For example, on May 15, 1923, the first day of the new frequency assignments, the *New York Times* listed stations WEAF, New York, 492 meters; KDKA, Pittsburgh, 326; WWJ, Detroit, 517; and KHJ, Los Angeles, 400. In general, the reallocation was well received by the public, especially in urban areas where stations from all over the country could now be heard clearly and at a defined dial position. Of course, many, if not most of these preferred, high-power stations were owned and operated by the corporate entities that had been investing heavily in radio. The stations relegated to the frequency at 360 meters, "a place of howls and squeals and eternal misery," were hard to hear and had limited audience appeal.

The more innovative and costly programming offered by large city stations would prove to be just as popular with rural and distant listeners who found the connection to the sophisticated streets of cities like New York and Chicago appealing. Letters from around the country poured into the big radio stations.

KDKA was received with such good volume that the music and other entertainment could be heard about 100 yards outside of the hall. There are about 600 people in the Molokai [Hawaii] leper settlement. The leper colony is located on a long narrow point of land surrounded on three sides by the ocean and backed up by steep cliffs, 1,300 feet high which are practically unclimbable.

Farmers proved to be an open-minded and receptive audience for information and entertainment emanating from urban areas. Sensing an opportunity, the Agriculture Department sent daily market reports to about 150 radio stations that then informed their listeners about everything from crop rotation to how to cure sore eyes in chickens. Though that quaint information may have been useful, farmers had an ear for big-city entertainment and were not shy about letting stations know what they liked.

A fourteen-year-old boy living on a farm in North Carolina, 575 miles from New York, wrote to express his pleasure at hearing the Schola Cantorum concert from Carnegie Hall; when New York's WEAF aired musical comedies direct from the stages of New York theaters, the station received mail containing dollar bills from grateful farmers hundreds of miles away who offered the money as a way to help pay for this wonderful entertainment. And one Ohioan, thrilled to be part of the New York scene, wrote: "We have heard silver clink on the banquet tables in the Hotel Astor; Louise Homer sing from the stage of the Metropolitan Opera House; Lord Robert Cecil's plea for the League of Nations from the ballroom of the Biltmore; a talk by Mr. Schwab from the Plaza and humor by a fellow named Rogers from the Waldorf-Astoria. Radio brings us lots of notable visitors these days."

Signals were clearer; the ever-growing audience understood more about the technology and was investing millions of dollars to acquire the latest available receiving equipment; people were finding new careers as radio engineers, studio designers, announcers, talent scouts, on-air talent, and station managers. Radio was a business, but with its enormous success came the need to confront a significant new question: How do you pay for it?

During his opening remarks to the first national radio conference in 1922, Secretary Hoover warned, "It is inconceivable that we should allow so great a possibility for service to be drowned in advertising chatter." His sentiments were echoed in the November 1922 issue of *Radio Broadcast:* "Driblets of advertising, most of it indirect so far, to be sure, but still unmistakable, are floating through the ether every day.

Concerts are seasoned here and there with a dash of advertising paprika. You can't miss it."

One economic solution was for the manufacturers of radio receiving devices to pay a tax on the sale of their equipment, with the revenue going to fund licensed stations. It seemed like a logical plan except for the fact that since there was such a huge demand for equipment, much of it was made by fly-by-night companies, and it was therefore unlikely the taxes would ever be collected. The editor of *Radio Broadcast* suggested that stations should be endowed by community-spirited citizens who saw the greater good of radio, much in the way some libraries had been funded. Other radio enthusiasts believed that cities and towns should pay for radio stations out of tax revenues, much in the way they might build a park or sponsor public lectures.

Though advertising seemed to be a logical source of revenue, Hoover was absolutely against its use because it sullied the notion that radio was meant for the public good. But on August 28, 1922, the anti-advertising levee was breached when the AT&T station in New York, WEAF, aired a ten-minute message from a real-estate developer who was opening a new housing complex in Queens. The commercial, for which the firm paid $100, was the softest of soft sells: A WEAF staff announcer told the audience that Mr. Blackwell of the Queensboro Corporation would "say a few words concerning Nathaniel Hawthorne and the desirability of fostering the helpful community spirit and the healthful, unconfined home life that were Hawthorne ideals." Mr. Blackwell then read a meandering ten-minute speech that eventually got to the point: *The fact is, however, that apartment homes on the tenant-ownership plan can be secured.*

Eight months later, WEAF boasted a client roster of twenty-five advertisers. Nonetheless, advertising was still not the accepted way to finance the operation of radio stations. Seeking "a workable plan which shall take into account the problems in present radio broadcasting and propose a practical solution," the May 1924 issue of *Radio Broadcast* announced the creation of a special contest in which entries were to address the central question of funding. The panel of judges included Professor J. H. Morecroft, president of the Institute of Radio Engineers; Powel Crosley Jr., president of the Crosley Manufacturing Company; Frank Reichmann, of the Reichmann Company; Senator Royal Copeland of New York; and the publisher of the *Los Angeles Times*, owner of KHJ, and Hoover supporter, Harry Chandler.

While radio enthusiasts composed their entry essays, the industry moved at a blistering pace. In 1923 Americans spent an estimated $136 million on radio parts and sets, an amount dwarfed by the following year's spending, which topped $385 million. The entertainment and information radio provided, even if it was somewhat intermittent, was addictive, and Americans were hooked. Programming became increasingly important. Stations aired anything they could dig up, whether it was a singer with a pianist who happened to stop by the station, to a guest performer who whistled hit tunes, to a children's program provided by a local church that asked listeners to guess what animal they were hearing. When there was nothing to air, stations simply went silent. On October 12, 1924, KFO in San Francisco aired an "undenominational and nonsectarian church service" at 3 P.M. and a concert by Rudy Seiger's Fairmont Hotel Orchestra at 11:30 P.M. (all times Eastern Standard). Between these two wildly different shows, listeners to the frequency at 423 meters heard only the sound of silence. But the quantity and quality of programming increased, a fact reflected in the daily newspapers' radio columns, which gradually focused less on radio technology and more on what was being aired.

By the autumn of 1924, the "hobby" Secretary Hoover had been given control over in 1921 had exploded into a business with potentially huge economic as well as social consequences. Control over the flow of information via the airwaves concerned the secretary, and although

Americans in every survey indicated that they tuned to radio primarily to hear music, it was realized that dominance of the airwaves by a limited number of people or corporations might have dangerous consequences. On October 6, 1924, Hoover called to order the Third National Radio Conference, "for the better voluntary regulation of radio."

The conference's agenda included frequency allocation, improving programs, and licensing. Fittingly, Hoover's opening speech to the delegates was aired by fifteen radio stations from as close as Washington, D.C. (WCAP) and as far away as Oakland, California (KGO). In his opening address, Hoover praised the industry's amazing progress and looked forward to the time in the not-too-distant future when shared programming of high quality would stretch from coast to coast in some form of network broadcasting. While he made clear his opposition to any monopolistic control of the airwaves due to the dangerous nature of this kind of nongovernmental control, he reserved his harshest words for those who were sullying the airwaves with advertising:

> The reader of a newspaper has an option whether he will read an ad or not, but if a speech by the President is to be used as the meat in a sandwich of two patent medicine advertisements, there will be no radio left. To what extent it may be employed for what we now call indirect advertising I do not know, and only experience with the reactions of listeners can tell. The listeners will finally decide in any event.

Later that year, Hoover endorsed a 2 percent tax on radio sales as his preferred method of funding, believing that Americans would never tolerate a direct tax on listening.

The importance of the third conference was reflected by the fact that the conferees were invited to the White House, where President Coolidge, who had assumed the presidency following Warren Harding's death, thanked the group for cooperating with the commerce secretary in his effort to properly develop and control radio. Coolidge called wireless one of the "great blessings" and went on to issue a stern warning, emphasizing to the delegates "the great responsibility on the part of those who transmit material over the radio that there should be no malice of slander through these channels."

But by the end of the three-day conference, little had been resolved. The conferees called for the government to experiment with some superpowered stations and to increase the power granted to stations so that reception would be clearer, but little else was agreed on, and the conferees offered no firm opinion on the advertising issue.

Meanwhile, the *Radio Broadcast* competition was being judged, and out of the thousands of entries, one winner was selected: H. D. Kellogg Jr. of Haverford, Pennsylvania, won the $500 prize with his well-articulated argument in favor of taxing listeners by assessing an annual charge of two dollars on each tube, with a fifty-cent charge for each crystal used in receiving equipment. The funds raised by this tax would be controlled by a newly formed Federal Bureau of Broadcasting, which would dole the money out to stations. Despite selecting him as the winner, the magazine roundly criticized Mr. Kellogg's plan in the very edition that featured his winning essay.

> The officials of the American Radio Association do not feel this plan is the final word in the matter of "who is to pay?" and neither do the editors of this magazine. The broadcasting problem cannot be settled as easily as this plan proposes . . . One of the chief stumbling blocks is the setting up of a federal bureau of broadcasting which seems to be contrary to the entire trend of radio development. We believe that anything that smacks of too centralized federal control or censorship would be resisted as much by the public as by all those administering radio today.

While the question of how to fund this rapidly growing industry remained unanswered, by the end of 1924, radio was permeating virtually every element of society. It was a form of entertainment and a source of information central to the booming American economy of the 1920s. New patterns of behavior were developing as people made radio part of their lives. Farmers were urged by the Interior Department to get the guidelines issued by the Bureau of Standards on the construction of radio receiving equipment so they, too, could enjoy the variety of information and entertainment now available through the airwaves. These features included regularly scheduled daily market and weather reports, while in the evenings farmers and their families could enjoy political discussions, concerts, and lectures, and on Sundays a serving of sermons and good church music.

Radio even spawned a new type of American woman: the "Wireless Widow." "Her's [*sic*] is another portrait to be added to the gallery of those unhappy women whose husbands continually neglect them in the all-absorbing pursuit of their hobbies." Yet perhaps because radio had become more about content and less about technology, women were increasingly seen as an important part of the audience. "The main reason why radio has become so popular with women is that it is no longer a complicated maze of wires and controls . . . Furthermore, leading radio manufacturers are making sets which are ornaments to the home." More significantly, women's organizations were using the medium to further causes. The League of Women Voters, in conjunction with Columbia University, created a program for women to go to college by radio in order to take courses in government and politics that would make them better-informed voters. Meanwhile, other women's suffrage organizations set up meetings at which their members could listen to and discuss the radio speeches given by the 1924 presidential candidates. When in 1924 the *Washington Post* ran a contest for the best essay on "Radio, the Wonder," the winner was a thirteen-year-old girl, Ida Bush, who wrote:

"The invention of radio is another step in the ladder of development. It enables both the rich and the poor to have the same enjoyment of 'listening-in' for a price next to nothing."

Just before the end of 1924, Secretary Hoover withdrew his support for legislation pending before Congress that would have given full control of the airwaves to the federal government. His argument raised the issue that, in retrospect, seems so obvious: "With only limited number of wavelengths and 500 stations—rapidly increasing—we are forced today to a certain duplication of waves and to the division of time between stations. Any attempt to give preference among stations in the allotment of wavelengths on the basis of quality of program raises the question of censorship, the implications of which I cannot at present accept."

Despite some unanswered questions about its future, radio had become so dominant that Christmas 1924 was called the "radio Christmas," because a radio receiver was the best gift to give or receive. The first four years of the 1920s were marked by advancement; at the end of 1924 the radio industry, with its ever-growing, devoted audience, was poised to explode into its greatest years. As Dr. J. H. Dellinger, chief of the radio laboratory of the United States Bureau of Standards, said, "One thing about radio sets that now appears certain is that virtually everybody will have one. Broadcasting is here to stay, and it will bring to the people more and more of the thrill of participation in the real, worth-while things that are going on."

His boss, Secretary Hoover, ended the year by telling American radio fans that

the radio industry can't live on an endless diet of jazz. Radio is becoming more important in the life of the country every day. It is already one of the necessary adjuncts. Right now I think the most important thing is the improvement of what is put on the air.

Chapter 5

▲▲▲▲▲▲▲▲▲▲▲▲▲

BY THE END OF 1922 it had become clear that people *would* actually sit at home and listen to the radio if there was something to listen to, and the corporations with the resources to develop and produce content slowly created programming to respond to the growing demand. Meanwhile, new stations were popping up all over the country at an amazing clip. But who owned these facilities, which were technologically far more advanced than the little rigs enthusiasts had built out of mail-order kits?

Of the more than 300 licensed stations on the air in June 1922, the vast majority were owned by companies and not individuals. Many of these transmitting signals and their facilities were operated by companies involved in the business of building and selling radio equipment, such as Cincinnati's Crosley Manufacturing Company, which owned WLW. Some, like KMO in Tacoma, Washington, were owned by companies like Love Electric, which manufactured other home appliances. A sizeable number of stations were owned by other forms of media, such as the *Detroit News*'s WWJ; and KLS in Oakland, California, which was owned by Warner Brothers. Some stations, such as KOB in State College, New Mexico; WAAC in New Orleans; and KOJ in Reno, Nevada, were owned by colleges or universities. WOO, WIP, and WFU, all in Philadelphia, were owned respectively by the retailers John Wanamaker, Gimbel Brothers, and Strawbridge and Clothier. Some, like WBU in Chicago and WNYC in New York, were owned by the cities themselves, while other stations were built and run by religious associations, including San Francisco's KDZX (the Glad Tidings Tabernacle), Los Angeles's KJS (the Bible Institute of Los Angeles), and WDM in Washington, D.C. (the Church of the Covenant).

But in mostly smaller communities across the country, in places like Wilkes-Barre, Pennsylvania; Lindsborg, Kansas; Fargo, North Dakota; and Waterloo, Iowa, stations were owned by individuals, men who'd probably been experimenting as hobbyists and had decided to transform their facility into an official radio station. Even local doctors found time to operate their own radio stations; one of the more unusual such stations was owned by Dr. B. J. Palmer of Davenport, Iowa, whose WOC went on the air in March 1922 and was licensed to the Palmer School of Chiropractic. Palmer, the son of the nominal founder of chiropractic medical treatment in the United States, took over the leadership of his father's school when the elder Palmer was sent to jail for practicing medicine without a license. Located on the top floor of the chiropractic school building, WOC was credited with being the first privately owned and operated radio station west of the Mississippi. When it went on the air, Palmer wasted no time in using the new medium to promote his business. Every evening he'd fire up his transmitter and take to the airwaves to deliver a lengthy discourse on the benefits of chiropractic care. Within his carefully crafted talks was a constant defense of his father's practice and an attack on the government's regulatory forces. The talks and their not-so-covert messages were marketing genius, but Palmer's craftiness went even further: He embedded his core message right into his station's call letters: WOC stood for "Wonders of Chiropractic."

But no doctor or broadcaster understood the power of sending a message into the ether as fully as Milford, Kansas's Dr. John R. Brinkley, whose radio station helped him amass a fortune and become one of the most well-known, though controversial figures in the entire country.

By 1923 Dr. Brinkley's Milford goat-gland implant clinic had grown into a full-fledged hospital built on a small campus that covered an entire block of the once-sleepy, run-down town. Brinkley's wealth ballooned as he performed his questionable surgery on hundreds of men who came from far and wide seeking sexual rejuvenation. His good fortune allowed the doctor the freedom to travel, a pastime for which he and his wife had a deep fondness. During the summer of 1923 the Brinkleys drove through Canada to Connecticut and to New York, where the doctor visited former patients. They then continued to Washington, D.C., where their congressman offered to arrange for his notable and rich constituent to visit the White House and spend some time with President Coolidge. But Brinkley, through some newfound sense of delicacy, declined because he thought the purpose of his visit to the White House might be misinterpreted and he didn't want anyone to think the president might need *his* medical assistance.

While he was traveling, Brinkley's radio station was being built according to blueprints he had left behind. The cost to erect the first transmitter on the grounds of the Brinkley Clinic in Milford was around $20,000. Brinkley saw his new station as a powerful vehicle through which the people of rural Kansas might fight the big-city folks: His station would be the farmer's mouthpiece. With a metal transmitter tower rising behind the fifty-by-sixty-foot brick building that housed the radio station's studios, all Doctor Brinkley needed before he could begin to broadcast was his license and the station's call letters from the Department of Commerce. That license came through in September 1923, and the call letters assigned to him were KFKB. Always the consummate marketer, Brinkley turned those letters into his station's slogan, declaring that KFKB stood for Kansas Farmers Know Best; or Kansas First, Kansas Best. But not long after he went on the air, Brinkley sensed that his new station might be used for a greater purpose, and so he amended the station's on-air slogan, changing it to "KFKB, the Home of the Gland Transplantation."

The station's mission, Brinkley claimed, was to amuse and enlighten the convalescing patients at the clinic. With a built-in, captive, live audience of bedridden patients, Brinkley experimented by trying out different entertainment and information shows. The programming he developed presented a mixed bag: fundamentalist theology; various entertainments that might include the Old Timers, a guitar and banjo ensemble, and Uncle Bob Larkan and his fiddle; occasional talks about new books and Brinkley's own travels; and a steady supply of medical lectures that never failed to remind the male members of the audience that contentment could be had in a bit of sexual rejuvenation, which coincidentally could be found only at the Brinkley Hospital in Milford, Kansas.

Brinkley didn't waste time in establishing his station, with its powerful, clear signal that stretched far beyond Milford's borders, as a home of radio innovation. The station was highly listenable and entertaining, and KFKB quickly became the greatest marketing tool for Brinkley's hospital and his medical accomplishments. There is no doubt that the experience he had gained in his earlier years as a Quaker doctor, his ability to blend charm, showmanship, and questionable medicine, served him well as he took to the airwaves. His on-air style was folksy; he played the part of the "aw-shucks" country doctor who just intuitively knew exactly what would heal the ailing folks lucky enough to be within the sound of his voice. Using a dignified tone that brought together the gravitas of a member of the clergy with the bedside manner of a caring doctor, Dr. Brinkley answered his mail:

> *I have here a letter from a farmer, a tiller of the soil who has given himself without stint, with his simple generosity that the great cities may live . . . This sufferer requires an immediate operation. I suggest to him that he go to the Brinkley Hospital in Milford, Kansas, for an examination.*

The message, delivered to an audience of men who surely didn't want to be left out of a sexual revolution central to the image of the relatively liberal Roaring Twenties, was precisely on target. Dr. Brinkley offered hope to the unfortunate sufferers who heard his soothing words, and though the goal of his carefully delivered broadcasts was to draw more patients to Milford, he never considered this not-so-subtle call to action to be advertising. The good Dr. Brinkley was on the radio merely to help people; if he got rich in the process, well that was just a happy by-product of his hard work. Brinkley's "helpful," commercial-free broadcasts seemed to be perfectly in tune with Secretary Hoover's core belief that radio must be used for public service, assuming that helping men overcome erectile dysfunction could be viewed as a public service.

Brinkley's manipulation of the medium was astounding; he often aired his medical-advice talks at odd hours, as early as 5 A.M. and as late as 11 P.M., no doubt so his message, carried on the wings of his powerful signal that could be heard as far west as the mountain states and as far east as the Mississippi Valley, reached the ears of many men awake at that time of morning or night who might have been worrying about their own sexual abilities. Shrewdly he played on fears and prejudices: *Don't let your doctor two-dollar you to death . . . come to Dr. Brinkley . . .*

*take advantage of our Compound Operation . . . I can cure you the same as I
did Ezra Hoskins of Possum Point, Missouri.*

Never content to rest on his accomplishments, Brinkley was quick
to implement any programming idea that might further his station's
reputation and image, and possibly in turn increase his audience and
the number of potential patients. Not long after KFKB went on the
air, Brinkley met Sam Pickard, a student at the Kansas State Agricultural College, who had the notion to create a "College of the Air."
The idea of distance education is commonplace today, but in 1923 it
was a new, surprisingly simple idea: Professors from the college would
read their lectures into a telephone; the signal would then be carried
via standard land phone line to Milford, where it would be sent out
by KFKB's transmitter. Seeing the public-relations benefits of such an
affiliation, Brinkley agreed to Pickard's plan, and a phone line from
Manhattan, Kansas, to Milford was leased, and the lectures, sometimes
interrupted by unrelated conversations on crossed local phone lines,
were heard over KFKB. Playing the role of a good public servant,
Brinkley did not charge for broadcasting these programs; after all, radio
was merely his hobby, a means of amusing, entertaining, and uplifting
his audiences. The educational programming was so successful that by
1924 the College of the Air had attracted paying enrollees from thirty-
nine states and Canada. The College of the Air remained on KFKB
until, seeing the value of owning the service, the college was given
funding by the state legislature to launch a radio station of its own.
KSAC, Kansas State Agricultural College's radio station, debuted on
December 1, 1924. While Brinkley ostensibly made no money from
the College of the Air broadcasts, the value of his relationship with
Sam Pickard would be realized a few years later when the president of
the college, William Jardine, was chosen to serve as secretary of agriculture in the Coolidge administration. Needing a radio editor for his
department's reports, Jardine brought Sam Pickard with him to Wash-

ington, D.C., to fill the job, giving Brinkley an important friend in the federal government.

With his powerful radio signal attracting hundreds of new patients to Milford, Brinkley's sex-operation business was booming, so much so that new housing facilities were needed to handle the visitors. Proof of his success was provided by a goat rancher from Arkansas who reported shipping an average of forty goats a week to the Brinkley Hospital. If each goat were used just once at the advertised price of $750 per operation, it could be calculated that Brinkley's hospital facility was grossing $30,000 per week just from surgeries. Brinkley was making money from his radio station without having to accept a single dollar for advertising, which kept the doctor in line with Commerce Secretary Hoover's antiadvertising stance. But late in 1924, KFKB encountered its first crisis: The station was badly damaged in a fire and had to be shut down. Sparing no expense, Brinkley immediately set out to rebuild; the new facility cost more than $65,000. The reborn KFKB boasted a more massive transmitter, towering even higher over Milford, with the power to send the doctor's comforting messages even farther. Of course, by the time the new facility opened more Americans had purchased radios, further increasing the size of his potential audience. The new KFKB opened in 1925 with Brinkley once again using his mellifluous voice to tempt men lacking pep to come to his clinic and avoid the pitfalls of mainstream medicine. He was a modern-day Pied Piper of Hamelin, using a microphone to attract unhappy men from far and wide.

Brinkley continuously refined his diverse program schedule; he sought to entertain and enlighten listeners of all ages and interests, from children who wanted to hear a sweet-sounding woman read them a story, to farmers who tuned in for the information they might need to run their businesses, and to listeners who, once they heard some of the medical advice being doled out, might be susceptible to the suggestion that they, too, needed Dr. Brinkley's medical help.

But with fame and fortune, even if you are able to convince your-self that the work you're doing is for the good of mankind, comes no-toriety, and that kind of attention often leads to trouble. By 1925 Brinkley was a well-known broadcaster with a frequently repeated, singular message about the value of good glands, which he blended into other programs designed to comfort, keep company with, and appeal to a wide range of listeners. But the nature of his talks led certain listeners to complain to the Department of Commerce; one letter stated that KFKB broadcast a talk on "glands [in which] the language was distinctly unsuited to radiocasting or to decent conver-sation even among men. The terms used were nauseating." Despite the relative openness of the era, there was an element of the listening audience not ready to hear about testicles while sitting in the comfort of their living rooms. America was still dominated by old-fashioned fundamentalist behavior and beliefs, and that was brilliantly illustrated during the summer of 1925 when the country was gripped, and amused, by a seminal and vitally important debate about monkeys and evolution.

DAYTON, TENNESSEE, JULY 1925: It was exceptionally hot and humid. Day after day the tiny town seemed to be baking, but despite the bru-tal weather, thousands of people flocked to Dayton. Among the throng that swelled the town's population from 1,800 to more than 5,000 were the two main contenders in a highly publicized legal battle: William Jennings Bryan and Clarence Darrow. Awaiting their dra-matic arrival were hundreds of newspaper and magazine reporters, including columnists H. L. Mencken, Joseph Wood Krutch, and West-brook Pegler, pencils and pads in hand, ready to keep their readers in-formed about the trial, from the buildup right through the proceedings and all the way through the momentous decision. In addition, more than sixty-five telegraph operators had set up their clunky equipment to send reports to Europe and Australia. Also present was the reluctantly famous defendant, high school teacher John T. Scopes, who was charged with violating Tennessee's law regarding the teaching of evolution.

Hawkers selling every kind of monkey-related curiosity crammed Dayton's streets as what was being billed as the trial of the century got under way. But when the judge, twelve jurists, and the crowd jammed into the old wooden courthouse on that July Friday, they saw something new: Placed strategically around the courtroom, which was sixty square feet and could seat about three hundred people, were four microphones installed by radio engineer Paul Neal. He, along with announcer Quin Ryan of station WGN in Chicago, had arrived in Dayton along with the rest of the throng just a few days before the trial's opening session. They were there, with the permission and probably the encouragement of Judge John T. Raulston, to broadcast the trial. So significant was their presence that they were invited to stay at the mayor's house. "We're like moon men here," Ryan reported. "We're the radio guys from outer space."

The technical arrangements for the radiocast were complex. At a cost of about $1,000 a day, the one-year-old radio station owned by the *Chicago Tribune*—the call letters WGN stood for World's Greatest Newspaper—rented AT&T phone lines that stretched from Dayton to Chicago so the proceedings could be heard by anyone able to receive WGN's signal. Though the idea of broadcasting a trial was completely new, the relevance of the broadcast outside of Dayton did not receive much attention, although the *New York Times* did note: "The full proceedings of the trial will be put on the air including the speeches of William Jennings Bryan for the prosecution and Clarence Darrow and Bainbridge Colby for the defense. Microphones in the courtroom will pick up every word spoken and forward them over land wires to the transmitter of WGN, atop the Drake Hotel, Chicago."

Broadcasting the trial was a bold programming move for a fairly new station that was usually heard only in the evenings, when they aired two-and-a-half hours of instrumental and vocal music. But now, as the torpor of a hot summer gripped the nation, listeners could tune in every day for the latest installment of the ongoing courtroom drama. For Neal and Ryan, the setup in the courtroom was a huge success, especially when the judge agreed to reseat the litigants so the famous lawyers' voices could be more clearly picked up by the microphones. It was the first time, but certainly not the last time that a courtroom or a celebrated trial would be rearranged to accommodate the media.

Every aspect of the trial—the issue, the case, the lawyers, even the judge—was good theater. On the night before the opening session, William Jennings Bryan "went up onto a mountain top and spoke to the simple people of the hills of his hope that the South was to lead in a great religious revival that would sweep the country." The next day, Friday, July 10, 1925, the trial began. The Tennessee heat was so intense that every man in the courtroom, except for the judge and one juror, took off his jacket and sported shirtsleeves, a rare informality for the era, especially in a court of law. In his opening remarks, heard beyond the courtroom by the radio audience, Judge Raulston, wearing a linen crash suit but shedding any semblance of objectivity, sought God's guidance: "Therefore I am much interested that the unerring hand of Him who is the Author of all truth and justice shall direct every official act of mine." Furthermore, despite Darrow's repeated objections, Judge Raulston insisted that each day's session open with a prayer delivered by a member of the clergy.

Seated at a table near a windowsill from where he had a perfect view of the main arena, announcer Ryan decided that his job was not to interfere in any way with the trial. He wanted listeners to hear the proceedings exactly as they would have had they been in the courtroom, but he also knew he needed to describe the important movements of the participants and provide some explanatory commentary so listeners would have a clearer visual image of what was happening:

Here comes William Jennings Bryan. He enters now. His bald pate like a sunrise over Key West.

When he felt his listeners needed more complete commentary and explanation, Ryan had at his disposal a private chamber just off the courtroom from where he could narrate with more detail without interrupting or disturbing the actual proceedings.

As the courtroom battle progressed, reporters began calling the trial a circus and the many oral thrusts and parries exchanged by the great lawyers, along with the judge's frequent admonishments to Darrow, including one contempt-of-court charge, were thrilling to hear. These lawyers were showmen and they didn't want to disappoint the audience, seen or unseen. In one ironic instance when Darrow and Bryan argued a legal point, the judge excused the jury, but since the lawyers' comments were being broadcast, the jurors simply stepped outside and listened on a radio. Judge Raulston, who had maneuvered schedules so he could preside over the case, was not exempt from looking for and bringing out the drama of what was taking place in his courtroom. "I approach my duties in the trial of the Scopes case with a deep consciousness that the issues are profound," he announced midtrial.

But as the trial played out, the judge's objectivity became increasingly suspect. On day six Raulston ruled that scientists who had been called by the defense to speak about the science of evolution would not be heard, in effect sealing Scopes's fate. With an inevitable verdict about to be delivered, many of the journalists who had flooded Dayton packed up and left for cooler climes. But Quin Ryan and his WGN engineer stayed on. When the trial was reconvened on July 20, outdoors under the trees where it was cooler, WGN's microphones were still there. That vigilance allowed the radio audience to hear Bryan's powerful closing speech in which he vowed to defend the word of God against the greatest agnostic and atheist in the United States.

The trial, which had to have been really exciting radio if not great law, concluded with an anticlimactic guilty verdict and a $100 fine for schoolteacher Scopes. Thanks to WGN and Quin Ryan, listeners throughout the Midwest and some as far away as New York were afforded a front-row seat at the trial of the century and got to hear one of the era's greatest orators, William Jennings Bryan, deliver his final speech. Bryan died while taking a nap five days after the trial ended.

The Scopes trial was a radio programming coup and it enlivened a few weeks during the summer of what was already developing into a critical year in radio's growth. The industry's evolution was being carefully nurtured by Secretary of Commerce Herbert Hoover, whose control over the medium was so total that the July 19, 1925, edition of the *Washington Post,* in an article titled "Hooverizing Radio," headlined: IT WAS NECESSARY TO CREATE A "CZAR" AND HOOVER IS THE MAN.

Ironically, perhaps the biggest problem facing radio and Secretary Hoover was the spectacular growth of the industry itself. A high-ranking Commerce Department official who chose to remain anonymous, commenting on the stations being built all over the country, said: "Ninety percent of these people build their station in the best of faith, but their knowledge of the subject is surprisingly small. They dash in saying 'I've spent $15,000 on this station and I simply have to have a license.'"

In many ways 1925 was the pivotal year for radio and for the energetic secretary of commerce whose influence over American society was expanding. Among the industries Hoover's staff sought to organize and simplify were textiles, newsprint, fisheries, and, perhaps of greatest import, women's dress sizes. "Aid in attacking the problem of standardizing sizes of women's ready-to-wear will be given by the

Simplified Practice Division of the Department of Commerce. The situation has been growing steadily worse, largely because of the straight-line silhouette and the growth in the use of rubber corsets. All divisions of the trade will be asked to help in providing a solution of the problem."

Radio was the most public example of an industry benefiting from the guidance and careful control of Hoover's Commerce Department. Without curtailing any basic American rights, Hoover encouraged an entire industry to develop into one of the central forces in a country racing ahead through an economic boom of unprecedented proportions. As the summer of 1925 drew to a close, the radio industry prepared for two important events: the Fourth National Radio Conference, set to open on September 12, and the Second Radio World's Fair, which opened on September 14. Both shows were held in New York City, and the attention given to the radio industry and the radio itself spurred the *New York Times* to offer its readers something new: a supplement devoted entirely to radio.

The special radio section appeared on Sunday, September 13. Within its pages were articles dealing with the ever-improving technologies and how they would affect the transmission and reception of signals, since the pursuit of better audio quality and ease of operation for the listener was paramount, especially as the novelty of hearing anything, no matter how static-distorted it might be, had worn off. One article went so far as to imagine a time when a "miniature motion picture screen" would be attached to "radio sets in every household." One article told of the exciting plans for broadcasting educational programs from a transmitter in Mexico. Another essay discussed the ongoing debate about how to pay for this radio business, and why advertising was an unlikely and unwelcome source of revenue. For the fashion conscious, there was a preview of some of the new radio styles on display at the shows, and for those listeners looking ahead a few months, the

Times included a comprehensive survey of the local radio stations and the programming they hoped to offer during the upcoming autumn and winter seasons. Perhaps of greatest significance was a series of blurbs written by leading programmers, engineers, and other industry executives, in which they indicated what changes they foresaw for radio. Among the comments by industry leaders was one short article by J. H. Dellinger, the chief of the radio laboratory in the Bureau of Standards at the Department of Commerce.

"It is well known," Dellinger wrote, "that the trend of public interest is toward the reception of the local rather than the distant station programs." His comments may have been spurred by the results of a study that estimated that 43 percent of the nation's population was reached by only twelve radio stations transmitting from twelve cities. Clearly the idea that control of the broadcast content might be vested in the hands of a limited number of broadcasters was perceived by the Department of Commerce as an emerging problem, one that needed to be addressed.

The 1925 radio conference, the larger of the two New York shows, opened with a ten-minute talk by Secretary Hoover, delivered by phone lines from Washington, D.C., and aired over local radio stations. As was expected, the secretary focused on improving service to listeners, which was always the thrust of his talks about the industry. The radio conferences were a magnet for other important orators; New York governor Al Smith spoke at the opening ceremonies, and his speech on how radio could aid good government was carried by many New York stations. In a speech delivered from the convention floor, David Sarnoff, who was the vice president and general manager of RCA, said: "The mission of radio transcends mere entertainment. It has a cultural function which it can perform only through the cooperation of public spirited elements, and I am confident that in the final solution of the broadcasting problem in the United States these elements will rally to the cause of public service." Politically astute, Sarnoff went on to praise Secretary Hoover for fostering the cooperative relationship "between the public and the industry and between the industry and the Government."

At the gala Radio Industries Group banquet, held at the Commodore Hotel, diners as well as listeners to the twelve radio stations that stayed on the air just to broadcast the festivities heard Will Rogers, once a radio skeptic but now one of its preeminent stars, chat in his humorous, homespun style. They also heard General J. G. Harbord, president of RCA, himself once a Kansas farm boy, explain how radio had transformed the lot of the isolated farmer by linking him to news and events from other parts of the country. On the lighter side, the audience enjoyed music by saxophone star Rudy Wiedoeft and Vincent Lopez and His Orchestra, which premiered a new medley titled "Echoes of New York." The new work was dedicated to the New York City Democratic mayoral candidate, Jimmy Walker.

On September 19 the Radio World's Fair officially ended with the presentation of *Radio Digest*'s Gold Cup, a prize awarded to the nation's most popular announcer. In 1925 that man was WEAF's Graham McNamee, whose initial involvement in radio was a complete fluke. As a young boy McNamee had studied singing. He moved from Minnesota to New York, where he earned money as a church singer. Then one day during the summer of 1923 he wandered into the Broadway offices of WEAF, where the office manager was impressed by his resonant baritone voice. He was hired on the spot as a staff announcer, and since the station was only on the air part-time, his work hours were short—from seven to ten weekday evenings.

In general, the news for radio was all good. Sales and orders for radio sets exceeded even the most optimistic projections, causing U. J. Hermann, managing director of the fair, to wax enthusiastically: "A month ago I predicted a $500,000,000 year in radio. Cancel that prediction.

It looks now as if it will be a $750,000,000 to $1,000,000,000 year." Hermann also reported that during the first twenty-one days of September more than 6,000 new shop owners and other retailers had entered the radio business.

The one warning issued during the radio fairs came from Senator C. C. Dill of the state of Washington, who pleaded with the attendees to never allow the government to control radio. "The day you give to any board in Washington the power to regulate radio, that day will the liberty of radio and the radio industry end." The legislative battle to control radio, though on the horizon, would take a backseat to the overriding belief that the right to broadcast through the airwaves was an extension of the freedom Americans enjoyed.

That kind of open-minded thinking certainly helped keep broadcasters like Dr. Brinkley, with his racy sexual rejuvenation broadcasts, out of trouble. But while Brinkley was at least temporarily safe from the Department of Commerce, he was not free from the investigators of the American Medical Association, who began looking into the qualifications of this famous medical miracle man. Working through local chapters, the AMA succeeded in having the reciprocal licenses Brinkley had received from other states revoked. Angered by this challenge to his livelihood and his professional standing, Brinkley charged back. Using his powerful radio signal, he began a two-prong on-air campaign that at once belittled the mainstream medical profession and reinforced the do-gooder, quaint, self-made qualities of his own story. He portrayed himself as a champion of the hardworking, small-town folks who were being cheated by the forces of the big-city doctors. He was the medical profession's David, struggling against the evil Goliath, the AMA, and he used his underdog status as a centerpiece of his on-air talks. His advantage was that radio enabled him to in effect make house calls to every one of his thousands of listeners, and his bedside manner was a well-rehearsed performance of the role he knew best: the folksy, small-town doc who just cares about the guy next door.

Despite the attacks, or possibly because of the additional attention they brought to him, Brinkley's fortune grew even greater. He was Milford's most important citizen and he cleverly involved as many of his neighbors as possible in his radio operation. His regular employees included a twelve-piece orchestra, a cowboy orchestra, three announcers, along with yodelers, crooners, and other singers. Altogether Brinkley employed about twenty-five staff artists, which cost him around $5,000 per month. Ever the good citizen, Brinkley even funded the local baseball team, cleverly naming the squad the Brinkley Goats and paying for them to attend a tournament in Denver, which they won.

By 1927 Brinkley had decided that his message of good sexual health was too important to be constrained by a 1,000-watt signal. So he applied to the Commerce Department for additional power that, if granted, would increase his transmitter to an incredible 5,000 watts. At virtually the same time, WDAF, which was owned by the *Kansas City Star,* asked for a similar power increase. WDAF's request was denied and KFKB's was granted, inflaming Brinkley's simmering conflict with the *Kansas City Star* that would become central to his fate.

There was little doubt that the seemingly do-good local nature of KFKB made it easier for the government's regulators to grant the increase. The evidence Brinkley could provide that his was a station helping its local community and the public in general was overwhelming. All one needed to do was look at Brinkley's contributions to the town of Milford. While his main business of sexual transplant surgery may have been of questionable character, Brinkley did run his radio station by the book, and even posted the strict policies that were his guiding principles.

First, no price quotations whatever. I own the station. I have a hospital here. I will not ask people to come to my hospital, and if I will not ask for patients, my advertisers shall not make pleas to purchase.

Second, no records shall be played. Records are cheap, but full time talent is far more valuable than its great initial outlay.

Third, the station shall never become an advertising or selling medium. No merchandising shall be conducted from it.

Fourth, the station shall never be used for controversies, but all organizations shall be permitted a hearing, regardless of creed or beliefs. The station shall be an open forum.

Fifth, KFKB shall not be a chain station [a station affiliated with outside broadcast sources, such as a network] *unless the listeners demand it. A recent poll showed that they did not.*

Sixth, the station shall be kept clean, so that none shall be offended. No suggestive language or risqué music shall be permitted. The programs shall be of a nature as to be welcomed in every home.

They were policies to be admired and they indicated that KFKB was a public trust, a facility dedicated to helping the community while bringing no outward gain to its owner. They were standards to which, Brinkley believed, the rest of America's broadcasters should be held.

Another important event in the Dr. Brinkley saga occurred in 1927. Ironically, the Brinkleys had been unable to have children and were resigned to remaining childless. But shortly after New Year's, Mrs. Brinkley announced she was expecting, and on September 3, 1927, gave birth to John Richard, who became known as Johnny Boy. The miracle birth engendered some nasty comments from newspapers that the boy had to have been the result of some goat gland hanky-panky, but Brinkley assured everyone that the conception was absolutely natural. But his son's arrival indirectly gave birth to another brilliant Brinkley business. The doctor realized that with ever-increasing costs of running his station and his hospital, he needed to find additional income, so he looked "with more thoughtful eye at his radio station."

Still refusing to follow the business model being used by many other radio broadcasters and accept outside advertising, Brinkley sought a way to raise money without sullying KFKB's programming with other people's wild claims about their products or services. First he changed his station's identifying slogan to "The Sunshine Station in the Heart of the Nation," which was a line suggested by a housebound crippled child who enjoyed KFKB's varied programming. Then Brinkley used his airtime to comment more and more about how to treat various medical conditions. People from all over, dissatisfied with their local medical care, wrote to Dr. Brinkley seeking advice. "He told them in plain unadorned language the best way to care for their babies, to treat them for minor ills, to use the necessary prophylactics in the constant warfare against germs." Discovering that audience involvement combined with a little sentimentality made great radio, Brinkley read and answered listeners' questions on the air, in turn encouraging other listeners to write in hoping to have their problems solved by the caring, small-town doctor. So many letters poured into Milford that a new post office, paid for by Dr. Brinkley, had to be built.

Brinkley named this new feature the *Medical Question Box* and aired three versions of the program each day. The mail, more than a thousand letters a day, inundated the doctor's ever-increasing staff, who sorted through the letters, carefully looking for just the right ones— those that would emotionally affect as many listeners as possible—for the doctor to answer during his half-hour programs. Sitting at his large wooden desk with a single microphone in front of him, Brinkley, speaking in his mellifluous baritone, probably the very tone he had developed as a Quaker doctor, would read a letter, comment on it, and then suggest that a cure for the problem could be had by writing in for one of the special elixirs he made and sold at his clinic in Milford. He was so generous that all he asked for was a small payment to handle the shipping, and the medicine would be on its way to the patient.

Here's one from Tillie. She says she had an operation, had some trouble ten years ago. I think the operation was unnecessary, and it isn't very good sense to have an ovary removed with the expectation of motherhood resulting therefrom. My advice to you is to use Women's Tonic Number 50, 67, and 61. This combination will do for you what you desire if any combination will, after three months' persistent use.

However, an unforeseen problem developed with the distribution of Dr. Brinkley's special tonics. Druggists complained that customers were coming into their stores asking for the special cures they'd heard about on KFKB, but the compounds were unavailable and the patients left empty-handed. Instead of competing with the druggists, Brinkley stumbled onto another new opportunity, and within short order he had contracted with pharmacies to stock and sell his special elixirs, each nameless compound coded by number to simplify the on-air marketing process. Delighted with this newfound profit center, druggists happily kicked back to Dr. Brinkley one dollar out of each sale, an idea that, Brinkley claimed, came from the druggists themselves. His power and popularity was so great that he was able to consolidate the participating drugstores into an organization known as the National Dr. Brinkley Pharmaceutical Association. But of longer-lasting importance, Brinkley had created, without naming it as such, the infomercial—a commercial disguised as an informative program just like the ones on the air today.

Beyond the brilliant use of the medium to promote and profit from his dubious medical practices, what makes Brinkley one of radio's true early innovators is the way he constructed one of the first nearly full-time broadcast schedules. After only a few years of development, a typical day on KFKB looked, or sounded, like this:

5:30–6:00	Health lecture by announcer
6:00–7:00	Bob Larkan and His Music Makers
7:00–7:30	Hints to Good Health by announcer
7:30–8:00	Bob Larkan and His Music Makers
8:00–8:30	Professor Bert
8:30–9:00	Old Time Entertainers
9:00–9:30	Markets, weather, cash grain
9:30–10:00	Medical Question Box
10:00–11:00	Special Feature
11:00–12:30	Steve Love and His Orchestra
12:30–1:00	Health Talk by Dr. Brinkley
1:00–2:00	Special Feature
2:00–2:30	Dutch Hauserman and Cook
2:30–3:00	Medical Question Box
3:00–4:00	Bob Larkan and His Orchestra
4:00–4:30	Uncle Sam and Dutch Hauserman
4:30–5:45	Arthur Pizinger and His Orchestra
5:45–6:00	Tell Me a Story Lady
6:00–6:15	Professor Bert. French Language Instruction
6:15–6:30	Orchestra
6:30–7:00	Dr. Brinkley

KFKB's broadcast day was long and filled with a variety of programs targeted at the specific audience most likely available at that particular time of day. His station was far more advanced than most other small-town facilities, and was certainly competitive, in terms of power and content, with major-market signals, many of which were owned by the leading broadcasting companies. Brinkley's programming savvy, his

snake-oil pitchman and down-home on-air style, his station's transmitting power, his manipulation of the audience, and his claim to be
doing everything for the public good all combined to make him one
of the most innovative and wealthy radiomen of the 1920s. It is estimated that his income from the prescription business and his surgeries
at the Brinkley Hospital exceeded $2 million annually. He was a local
hero and he flaunted his wealth by driving around town in Lincolns
and Cadillacs with gold-plated hubcaps. The governor of Kansas made
him an admiral in the Kansas navy and he proudly wore his uniform as
he sailed on his large private yacht. He and Mrs. Brinkley sported the
gaudy jewelry they bought, including a diamond-encrusted tie clasp
for the doctor that was two inches long and three-quarters of an inch
wide. Somehow the wild display of wealth did not offend his supporters, who failed to see or simply ignored the hypocrisy in his claims of
working solely for the benefit of others. Of course, the Milford locals,
many of whom also grew rich as a result of KFKB and Dr. Brinkley,
were not going to criticize the man who kept the town growing.

One by-product of the Brinkley medical talks, however, was that
some listeners, swayed by the knowledgeable and soothing voice on
the radio, stopped going to their regular doctors, relying instead on the
medical advice Brinkley doled out three times a day. "Brinkley is going
to be a perfectly impossible problem," one doctor declared.

Another side effect of KFKB, one that Brinkley, through his biog-
rapher, boasted about, was that after he began selling his elixirs on the
air, advertising for pharmaceutical goods in the *Kansas City Star* was
drastically reduced. Brinkley and his radio station were cutting into the
newspaper's revenues and he seemed to relish the ongoing battle with
the newspaper and their weak-signaled WDAF. The simmering conflict helped fuel Brinkley's image as the little guy struggling to overcome the forces of the establishment in both the worlds of medicine
and media.

But the true high point for Brinkley the radioman came in November 1929, when *Radio Digest,* the industry's leading magazine, decided to conduct a radio station popularity contest. The magazine sought to determine which of the now hundreds of stations on the air was the most popular. The results were staggering: Of all the stations in the United States and Canada, Dr. Brinkley's KFKB, broadcasting from tiny Milford, Kansas, won the coveted *Radio Digest* Gold Cup, receiving an amazing 256,827 votes to make it national champion. Perhaps most rewarding to Brinkley was the fact that WDAF, his primary competition in the region, the station owned by his nemesis, the *Kansas City Star,* received fewer than 10,000 votes and was not even mentioned as one of the nation's leading stations.

Brinkley was on top; rich and famous, he had resurrected countless listless men and the town of Milford, Kansas, employing more than 100 people full-time. In an interview he gave to an investigative reporter from the *Kansas City Star,* which referred to him as the "nefarious Milford Messiah," the diamond-laden doctor crowed, "I get fat on fights."

Chapter 6

▲▲▲▲▲▲▲▲▲▲▲▲▲

As a broadcaster, Dr. Brinkley followed the rules. But there were other radiomen less willing to bend to the controls being devised and established by the Department of Commerce. One of those men hailed from the tiny town of Muscatine, Iowa. Located on the western bank of the Mississippi River, south of Davenport, Muscatine was a model of small-town America that once had hopes of becoming a major commerce center but was eclipsed by Davenport. The 1920 census estimated that Muscatine had a total of 7,315 dwellings and a population of 29,042, which was a decrease of nearly 500 people since 1910. Among Muscatine's citizens was Norman Baker, undoubtedly one of the town's most unusual, resourceful, and devious people.

Born in Muscatine on November 27, 1882, Norman Baker was the youngest of ten children. At age sixteen he quit school and took a job as an apprentice machinist at Muscatine's freshwater-pearl button factory. Armed with the skills of a master machinist, he left Muscatine, calling it nothing more than a "two-by-four town," and bounced around from state to state earning whatever he could as a die- and tool-maker for hire. When he saw a traveling vaudeville show that featured a magical mental suggestion practitioner named Professor Flint, Baker abandoned the die- and toolmaking profession. Intrigued by the possibilities of the traveling-show format and the unusual acts one could present, Baker formed a troupe of his own that debuted in 1904. The show's leading attraction was Madame Pearl Tangley, the Mental Marvel. Headlined by Madame Tangley and her amazing psychic talents, Baker's show became a hit throughout the midwestern vaudeville circuit, which led to the troupe's signing a contract with Marcus Loew's vaudeville circuit, and to performances in New York's National Theater. There Madame Tangley astounded the crowd by reading the mind of a man who had risen to denounce her as a fraud. The show was tremendously successful and remained popular until Madame Tangley decided to retire. Needing a suitable replacement, Baker found a college girl named Theresa Pinder who somehow learned to become a mentalist and assumed the position as the show's leading attraction. Taking the name of her predecessor, she became the second Madame Tangley, and soon thereafter the first Mrs. Norman Baker.

The show toured on and off until 1914. During a scheduled hiatus in Muscatine, Baker, who was working in his brother's machine shop, developed a new version of the calliope: His invention was a boxy contraption with shiny silver pipes that was played with air rather than steam, emitting a rich, deep sound. Baker's instrument became known as the Tangley Air Calliope or Calliaphone, and the prototype sold for $5,000. Baker shut down his touring magic show, divorced his wife, and turned to manufacturing the Tangley Calliaphone, which became so popular that his company's revenues in the first year exceeded $200,000. But Baker, like other bold showmen of his era, wasn't content with his initial successes. And so in 1920, despite the fact that he openly admitted he had absolutely no artistic ability, Baker opened an art correspondence school—learn to draw through the mail—which he called the Tangley School. It soon became another profitable business and netted its owner a quick $75,000. Intrigued by the power of sales through the mail, Baker started selling everything from food products to clothing, all by direct-mail response marketing.

A few years later, seeing the success of nearby local radio stations in the direct sale of different products, Baker concocted another scheme. He went to the Muscatine Chamber of Commerce and the city fathers, who were still upset about being less important than Davenport, and offered to build the town's first radio station, which he promised to use to promote their fair city—the same one he had castigated some years earlier—and thus popularize it. He would "lift Muscatine from being a little burg lost in the Mississippi corn fields to a city the whole world knows about," he explained. All he asked in return for his generous civic mindedness was free water, free electricity, and to not pay taxes. The town fathers agreed, and Baker set to work constructing a transmitter on the highest hill in Muscatine; from there its signal could travel greater distances than was intended by the class A designation he had received from the Department of Commerce, a classification that limited his station to 500 watts.

Initially Baker probably saw his radio station as merely a way to sell more Calliaphones and some other products. When construction was complete, Baker filed his final application with the Commerce Department and received a license to operate his station in Muscatine, Iowa. Perhaps the person in the Department of Commerce who granted the license to Norman Baker might have been alarmed by this neophyte broadcaster's request to receive a special call sign, KTNT.

On Thanksgiving Day 1925, KTNT debuted. Right from the outset, there was little doubt that Norman Baker was going to use his new electronic mouthpiece to attack anyone he believed was against the values embodied in small-town America; with his radio commentaries protected by free speech, he vehemently criticized any perceived wrongdoers. His targets included the corporations that owned the patents on radio devices, the big-city radio station owners, and Secretary of Commerce Hoover, whom he blamed for the chaos and interference that increasingly plagued the radio waves. Baker called for complete freedom of the airwaves and a more open and accessible broadcasting world, a credo he brought to life within the confines of his station, which he built without bars or doors; he wanted the whole world to see exactly what was going on, and he allowed visitors to be in the same room as the talent even while broadcasting. He invited listeners to come to the station and to his hometown of Muscatine, and on most summer Sundays a crowd of over 5,000 people congregated on the hill leading up to the KTNT building.

Like most broadcasters of the era, Baker ran his station for only a few hours each day and he used most of that limited time to promote two important causes: his Calliaphones and his viewpoints. Marketing his bizarre musical instrument was a fairly subtle endeavor: Baker featured the dulcet tones of the Tangley Calliaphone several times during each broadcast hour, incorporating them into the programming so listeners would be intrigued and might want to buy one. As to the opinions he brought to the fore, these he incorporated into nightly speeches during which he railed against the big-city interests controlling the people's airwaves. He believed the best broadcasters were local broadcasters who had the interests of their neighbors at heart, a theme that had been articulated by Hoover. But Baker didn't want any interference from the government or the big corporate broadcasters in urban centers; to him radio was a public service, and local publics were best served by local radio. In a way, he, too, was acting the role Dr. Brinkley had mastered, the small-town David against the big-city Goliaths.

Though inexperienced with radio, Baker was a talented, confident showman. Three weeks after signing his station on the air, Baker traveled to Washington, D.C., to attend the meeting of the National Association of Broadcasters. Before the convention officially opened he spoke in the hotel lobby to conventioneers, warning his fellow independent broadcasters about the dominance and control of the airwaves by what he called the Big Five: RCA, General Electric, Westinghouse, AT&T, and the United Fruit Company. His central point was that the stations owned by or affiliated with these conglomerates were being linked by shared programming, or what had become known as "chain broadcasting," in which a program was passed from one station to another. The result was that many stations all aired the same shows, further decreasing the already limited available listening options. He suggested that the stations airing what he called synchronized programming be put on one frequency, thus freeing up other frequencies for independent broadcasters. Baker also warned that the power of the Big Five and their corporate greed would eventually force broadcasters to charge listeners directly for programs, thus creating direct profits from the licenses to broadcast over the very airwaves Baker vehemently believed belonged to the people. Spurred by some positive reaction to his populist rants, Baker even threatened to form his own association of independent broadcasters whose mission would be to fight the "gang."

On December 12, 1925, Baker gave a radio talk in which he articulated his argument. Introduced by Billy, his announcer, who told the audience that Mr. Baker was "conducting a fight to 'Keep the Air Free,'" Baker eased into the speech, saying he "had no ax to grind, excepting that I deem it a pleasure to be able to entertain you with our programs here." He claimed he had been warned not to build a station, that someone like him would never be granted a license. The speech was filled with innuendo and vague concerns about those in power and how they, including Secretary Hoover and the Commerce Department, were controlling the airwaves. Anticipating his talk might enrage some listeners, Baker cleverly preempted negative responses by debunking the attacks before they could be launched: *There are those who do not see the light of day, who do not know the inside of this Radio matter, who will say, "That fellow's crazy," "He's an agitator" and many other unkind remarks, I expect that, after I finish my remarks tonight. But to those let me say: "Time will tell the truth of my statements."*

Baker ended his thirty-minute tirade by thanking his listeners for their time and telling them he had tried, without success, to get the text of his talk reprinted in local newspapers. He urged supporters to use their influence in their hometowns to convince a local editor with courage to reprint the text of his talk, and suggested they send a note to him confirming they had. Normally the signal of a 500-watt station, even one transmitting from atop a hill as KTNT did, would have limited reach, but Baker's station sometimes illegally transmitted with up to 10,000 watts, causing the signal to travel far beyond the area of its license.

In January 1926 the issue of the growing dominance of the big-business radio manufacturers and the big-city radio stations had become central to the debate of how radio should evolve. Leading the charge against the big-market stations was a newly formed organization called the American Broadcasters Association (ABA). Comprised of owners of smaller and lower-power stations, the ABA became a vocal proponent of the familiar, homelike atmosphere available on America's small-town stations. The organization was concerned that these highly vital stations had been discriminated against because they had been given frequencies on the overcrowded wave band ranging from 200 to 275 meters, resulting in tremendous interference among their signals, rendering the stations nearly impossible to receive clearly. They argued that big-market stations had been treated preferentially when they were permitted greater transmitting power and assigned frequencies on a far less crowded part of the dial. With a vocal group of independent broadcasters supporting its every move, the ABA became a force to be reckoned with. The ABA's founder and first president was Norman Baker.

As the spokesperson for America's independent broadcasters, Baker appeared in February 1926 before the Senate Interstate Commerce Committee, which was investigating control of radio by the Department of Commerce. Baker reiterated the charges of discrimination against small stations and urged the Senate to pass legislation that would relieve Secretary Hoover of a "large part of his discretion in administration." The Senate committee listened to his requests but took no action, preferring to study the entire radio broadcasting situation in greater detail. But Baker was relentless and he understood the power of an angry, vocal group of broadcasters, all of whom had radio transmitters at their disposal. In March he asked the Senate to investigate the Department of Commerce for discrimination in the ways they administered radio affairs. Then in June, Baker announced the idea of linking one hundred or more independent stations in a kind of unwired network that would allow paying sponsors to have their products promoted across the whole country. Augmenting his plans, Baker floated the idea of developing a company of performing artists that would travel from one station to another, creating a circuit of stations, similar in nature to a circuit of vaudeville theaters.

The vaudeville showman–*cum*–inventor from Muscatine was superb at getting press coverage, and while he still hadn't actually formed either the network or the performers' circuit, he was garnering lots of attention across the country and especially in New York, where the idea of a nationwide network was foremost in the mind of another important radioman, David Sarnoff.

Beginning in January 1926, negotiations among the corporate radio manufacturers were secretly taking place in New York. The legal entanglements and cross-licensing of patents that had been hammered out at the end of World War I among the large manufacturers—GE, AT&T, RCA, and Westinghouse—were becoming problematic, and the Federal Trade Commission was beginning to examine these deals with an eye toward charging the large companies with restraint of trade. Determined to negotiate a mutually agreeable solution and avoid a public airing of the radio giants' businesses, the discussion gradually moved to David Sarnoff's idea of a "central broadcasting organization."

On July 7, 1926, agreements were signed that completed the sale of AT&T's powerful New York station, WEAF, to RCA. As part of the deal, AT&T agreed to get out of the broadcasting business, content to collect revenues from leasing its miles of telephone wires to what would become a newly formed national radio company. The new venture would be owned by the other three corporations: 50 percent by RCA, 30 percent by GE, and 20 percent by Westinghouse, and the new entity would be called the National Broadcasting Company, Inc., or NBC. Full-page ads in the September 14, 1926, editions of the nation's largest newspapers announced the formation of the new company. The carefully worded advertising copy made the case for a national source for high-quality radio programming, claiming the market for better radio receiving equipment would increase if there were more exceptional, interesting programming available. The stated purpose of the new company was to provide the best programs available for broadcasting in the United States.

Anticipating complaints from those who saw the new venture as a move to further limit access to the airwaves and increase what was perceived as the industry's monopolistic tendencies, RCA, the parent company of the newly formed NBC radio network, included in the ad the statement that

> the Radio Corporation of America is not in any sense seeking a monopoly of the air. That would be a liability rather than an asset. It is seeking, however, to provide machinery which will insure a national distribution of national programs, and a wider distribution of programs of the highest quality.

If others engage in this business the Radio Corporation of America will welcome their action, whether it be cooperative or competitive.

David Sarnoff fended off charges of monopolistic behavior by calling "baseless the fears of a 'monopoly of the air,' most often expressed by those who find themselves without an audience to serve because they have no service to render." RCA also announced it would form a "Public Advisory Council" made up of twelve members from "various shades of public opinion" to advise on what the best type of programs might be. The ad assured the public that the members would be announced as soon as their "acceptance shall have been obtained."

Seeking a strong leader from outside the industry, the newly configured RCA named Merlin H. Aylesworth, who had been the managing director of the National Electric Light Association, to be president of the NBC Radio Network. Aylesworth was chosen not because of his knowledge of radio, but because he had been adept at dealing with the mass psychology behind America's perception and acceptance of the electrical industry. In his initial statement as president of NBC, Aylesworth staked out the position that the new company would help an industry suffering from the lack of organization and permanence that seemed to have plagued radio during its initial half decade. "Stations have been free to come into the field and go out again. Because the supply of service has probably exceeded the demand, there has been no particular responsibility for staying on the air or withdrawing from it. So far the experience of the various broadcasting companies has been somewhat disheartening, financially, because expenses have exceeded the income."

The NBC Radio Network was launched on November 15, 1926, with an all-star broadcast originating from New York's Waldorf-Astoria Hotel. An invitation-only, white-tie audience of more than one thou-

sand celebrities and political leaders watched as performances by con-
ductor Walter Damrosch, pianist Harold Bauer, the dance orchestras of
Ben Bernie, George Olsen, Vincent Lopez, and B. A. Rolfe, as well as
a routine by the comedy team of Weber and Fields went via microphone, through AT&T's phone lines and out to listeners of the network's affiliated radio stations. As an added bonus, listeners were treated
to a speech by humorist Will Rogers. It was the kind of glittering all-
star show that only a network based in New York could offer, and it
launched not only the NBC Radio Network, but the concept of listeners everywhere enjoying the same programming at the same time,
or as Norman Baker had called it, synchronous programming.

Roughly six weeks after the launch of its eighteen-station radio network, of which New York's WEAF was the flagship, NBC announced
the formation of a second network led by its other New York outlet,
WJZ. To avoid confusion, they dubbed the original network the NBC
Red Network and the junior circuit, which originally had just five stations, the NBC Blue Network.

Though the Department of Commerce reported that in the last six
months of 1926 one hundred and five new radio stations had received
licenses and signed on the air, Aylesworth's assessment of the instability of broadcasters outside the major markets was probably accurate. In
most places, days and hours of broadcasting were irregular at best, and
the on-air talent, when some could be found, couldn't match the quality available to stations in big cities. Many smaller stations simply played
phonograph records, as opposed to airing performances by live talent,
which was considered to be a public disservice. Radio was there to be
dynamic, and playing records was far from dynamic, especially when
anyone with a Victrola could do the same thing for themselves. But
while Aylesworth may have been right about the benefits the listeners
would gain from network broadcasting, it was the economics of broadcasting that was truly central to NBC's mission.

Americans had spent millions of dollars buying radio receiving sets, and by mid-decade the novelty of hearing static-filled broadcasts of people speaking, or music that sounded like it came out of a tin can— for a few random hours on inconsistent days—had worn off. Listeners wanted something more; they wanted regularly scheduled, dependable, interesting programming. A natural chain of events had triggered a change in how the radio business operated: People wanted to listen to their radios for more hours each day, which meant radio operators needed to broadcast for more hours, which required more content, which increased costs, requiring more money to cover the larger expenses. Where would this money come from? The obvious source of revenue for radio stations that reached significant audiences was advertising. There had been a sense, repeatedly expressed by Secretary Hoover, that sullying the airwaves with commercialism would be a betrayal of the public trust. But the ability to reach an audience with a special message contained in an environment as exciting as the one provided by a radio program was impossible to resist for ad men at the country's new and growing advertising agencies. Furthermore, by selling airtime, or access to their audiences, broadcasters finally had a way to make the money they needed to operate for more hours each day. Despite Secretary Hoover, who had said that "the quickest way to kill broadcasting would be to use it for direct advertising," the tide pulling broadcasters toward seeking advertising's dollars was simply too powerful.

Excepting some spotty efforts at short-form commercials, the bulk of radio's first advertising took the form of program sponsorships. Advertisers attached their name to some performance or performers heard on stations across America. By January 1927 the NBC Radio Network, not yet three months old, had a long list of sponsored programs, including *The Eveready Hour,* sponsored by Eveready batteries; the A&P Gypsies, a string ensemble sponsored by the Atlantic and Pacific Tea

Company; *The Coward Comfort Hour* of familiar music brought to you by Coward Shoes; the Jolly Wonder Bakers quartet sponsored by Wonder Bread; and Betty Crocker food talks, which were underwritten by General Mills. One other clever tie-in that deserves mention was a program featuring the vocal stylings of the Smith Brothers, which were exclusively sponsored by Smith Brothers Cough Drops.

Meanwhile, back in Muscatine, Iowa, where Norman Baker continued to agitate against the steadily increasing dominance of radio by big-city businessmen, KTNT was doing well as an independent station. Though Baker accepted no outside advertising, his marketing skills and the reach of his radio station were making him quite wealthy. While initially the raison d'être for KTNT was to sell more Calliaphones, the popularity of the station led Baker to other profitable businesses, both off the air and on. To accommodate the thousands of curiosity seekers who flocked to Muscatine to see his radio station on the hill, Baker built the KTNT Café to feed his visitors and the KTNT Oil Station to fuel their automobiles. On the air he added to his offerings of direct-response products—items that listeners heard about and could write away to order. He realized how compelling radio messages could be and didn't hesitate to use his understanding of on-air persuasion to curry favor with political candidates, allowing them to deliver campaign messages over his airwaves. Since the law requiring equal time for opposing candidates did not yet exist, the time Baker gave away was especially valuable and put him in good stead with the political leaders whose intercession he might someday need.

In Washington, radio's maturing complexities did not escape the concerned eye of Congress. The rapid increase in the number of stations broadcasting and the commensurate chaos in the airwaves that had almost reached crisis stage by the end of 1926 made it clear that new legislation was needed to codify control over wavelengths and transmitting power that Secretary of Commerce Hoover had virtually unilaterally instituted. Something was needed to replace the Radio Act of 1912. The thorny questions that delayed Congress from enacting legislation in 1926 concerned who should have the right to grant access to the airwaves, and what kind of limitations should be placed on those who received a license to broadcast.

Representative Wallace White of Maine and Senator C. C. Dill of Washington had a fundamental disagreement: White believed control should remain in the hands of the secretary of commerce, while Dill believed what was needed was an independent commission to control radio. In a December 1926 address to Congress, President Coolidge urged legislative action, saying, "This most important function has drifted into such chaos as seems likely, if not remedied, to destroy its great value." Meanwhile, a group of insurgent progressives, including Idaho senator William Borah, argued that the radio issue was absolutely central to the future of democracy and needed to be thoroughly debated. For Borah, the real fear was that Hoover, who was considering a run for the presidency, would use radio as a tool of partisan politics. Secretary Hoover added his point of view to the debate. He believed that though it had begun life as an amateur hobby, radio needed to be developed by professionals so that news, information, entertainment, and messages from the federal government could be brought directly to the American population in an efficient, effective manner. Hoover wanted the federal government to oversee all aspects of broadcasting, but with an advisory board that would determine whom the government should grant the licenses to transmit to. The administrative aspects, such as issuing wavelengths, setting transmission power, and hours of operation, would continue to be handled by the Department of Commerce.

Underlying the political debate was the notion that radio might be used by one party for political gain over opponents, which further fueled the growing concern that the radio waves could be used for the dissemination of harmful propaganda. After months of hearings and arguments, a compromise bill was hammered out and passed by both houses of Congress. The Radio Act of 1927 put the onus on the government to accept responsibility for "managing the airwaves for the public interest," and it gave the government the right to restrict the number of broadcasters and the power to impose tests for broadcasters to determine if they were indeed acting in the public's interest. At its core the act had five guiding goals: (1) to ensure radio's growth; (2) to protect the public; (3) to protect broadcasters' speech; (4) to create better government; and (5) to serve the public interest.

The legislation established the Federal Radio Commission (FRC), a body made up of five independent commissioners to be nominated by the president and confirmed by the Senate, each of whom would represent one of five geographic zones. "Not more than three commissioners shall be members of the same political party," the law stipulated, as a way to guard against partisan control of the airwaves. The commission was charged with periodically classifying stations and, in general, organizing the way radio stations coexisted. But as part of the compromise, most of the commission's legislated powers and authority were only temporary. "From and after one year after the first meeting of the commission created by this Act, all the powers and authority vested in the commission under the terms of this Act, except as to the revocation of licenses, shall be vested in and exercised by the Secretary of Commerce." However after that time, the FRC could be called on to rule on cases referred to them by the secretary of commerce, or in situations where the broadcaster wanted to appeal the secretary's decision. In essence, the FRC was an experiment to test whether a commission, in cooperation with the secretary of commerce, might help reduce the growing disorder of the airwaves.

On February 23, 1927, President Coolidge signed the second Radio Act into law and promised to nominate the FRC commissioners immediately. The first staggering job faced by the new commission would be to relicense all of the transmitting facilities in the nation, as the law required every license be turned in and reissued. It was as if the radio industry were starting all over. "The completion of the radio legislation makes it possible eventually to clear up the chaos of interference and howls in radio reception. The new commission which is to determine who shall have licenses to broadcast, at what times and with what power will no doubt require some months to make rearrangements of broadcasting stations which will be necessary. It will require some patience on the part of listeners while the commission works out the problem," cautioned Secretary Hoover. To stem the confusion, Hoover proposed that all existing call letters and licenses would be recognized until the FRC could rule on all of the more than 700 existing radio stations operating in the country.

The Federal Radio Commission got off to what could best be described as a rocky start. President Coolidge, with a list of nominees provided by Secretary Hoover, sent to Congress the names of the five men he thought would be good for the FRC. Of the five initial nominees, two died, and two never received Senate confirmation but joined anyway as unpaid employees, working with the one confirmed commissioner to deal with the mess they'd been handed. Despite its staggering workload, the commission, with clerical assistance provided by Secretary Hoover's office, managed to reallocate the frequencies of more than 600 radio stations. In the process, complaints about the annoying radio-wave interference ruining the listening experience led the commission to determine that almost 100 radio stations would have to be eliminated for the others to thrive. In November 1927 two new commissioners were nominated and approved: Harold Lafount, a radio manufacturer from Utah, and Sam Pickard, the Agriculture Department editor who'd begun his career in radio working with Milford's Dr. Brinkley. Pickard's nomination and seat on the commission would have significant political consequences a few years later.

Norman Baker's KTNT seemed to be one of the stations that could easily fall victim to the FRC's new radio order. During a partial reorganization enacted at the end of May, KTNT was ordered to reduce its transmitting power from 5,000 watts—the power they had been raised to in the two years since their sign-on—to 3,500 watts, and to change from their current dial position to a less desirable frequency. Then in October the FRC singled out nine stations for more changes; among them was KTNT, which was ordered to further reduce its power to 1,000 watts, although the commission later reversed itself and agreed to increase Baker's power to 2,000 watts. The explanation was that the mandated cut in power was the result of a stream of complaints received by the FRC from three stations in New York that claimed that KTNT, though more than 1,000 miles away, was still interfering with their signals. Baker's problems grew worse when KSCJ, the station owned by the *Sioux City Journal,* filed a petition with the FRC seeking to take over the frequency granted to KTNT. The challenge was serious, but Baker's political connections and his populist messages garnered powerful support. A team of senators from the progressive bloc of the Republican Party went before the FRC to plead Baker's case. "The Baker station broadcasts the progressive thought in politics, whereas the *Sioux City Journal* speaks for the reactionary school. I see no reason why Mr. Baker should be crowded out, as would happen if his present channel were taken from him. His programs are popular in the farming region, and no good reason has been given by Station KSCJ why they should be discontinued," testified Senator Smith W. Brookhart of Iowa. The very concerns Baker had expressed two years earlier were haunting him and threatening the existence of his station.

Because representatives of KSCJ failed to respond when called by the FRC, their petition was denied, and Baker's station remained on the air. Emboldened by his successful defense and angered by the reduction in power and his inferior dial position, Norman Baker, ignoring the raft of complaints against him, petitioned the FRC to allow him to change his dial position and increase his station's power to either 10,000 or 14,000 watts. Baker's belief was that he was owed a favor by the commission because his station had been treated so unfairly. A hearing was scheduled for January 1928. His application included detailed descriptions of the quaint, hometown informational and entertainment programming he provided to rural citizens; he explained that the power increase would allow his specialized programming to reach more of America's farmers. His request was denied.

March 1928 marked the one-year anniversary of the FRC, and it was expected that until the Congress could pass new legislation extending the life of the commission, Secretary Hoover would opt to reduce the commission to a merely advisory role. But on March 15, as the FRC's power was about to expire, Hoover requested that the commission remain in control of radio. Hoover's close friend Eugene Sykes, who by then had become FRC chairman, agreed, and the FRC continued its work reorganizing the radio spectrum.

When Herbert Hoover stepped down as secretary of commerce to mount his campaign for the 1928 Republican nomination for president, the FRC was steeped in deliberations about stations they had marked for removal from the airwaves. Of the 164 transmitting facilities ordered off the air in July 1928, 57 simply accepted their fate and went silent. The other 107 were given the chance to plead their case before the FRC, one of the most conspicuous being station WEVD, the Socialist and Labor station of New York City. Speaking on the station's behalf, Norman Thomas, Socialist candidate for president, appeared before the commission. WEVD—the call letters were a subtle tribute to Eugene V. Debs—was determined that its message would not be silenced by the government, especially during an election year. "If WEVD is taken off the air and, in fact, is not treated on a parity with others who are richer and more influential, the people of this nation can truly recognize that radio, which might be such a splendid force for the honest clash of ideas, is nothing but a tool to be used by the powerful against any form of disagreement or any species of protest," argued candidate Thomas.

In the end, WEVD remained on the air. The FRC found no appropriate way to silence so many stations and in its final decision forced only five stations in the Midwest to discontinue broadcasting. The FRC did, however, refuse to grant a new broadcast license to a group of atheists seeking to operate a station in New York. The FRC claimed the application by the American Association for the Advancement of Atheism had been rejected simply "because of the crowded radio conditions in New York."

Just as Americans prepared to choose their president in the fall of 1928, the FRC completed the frequency and power reallocation process. With the nation divided into its five geographic zones, a massive moving day of radio station frequencies was scheduled for October 1, but because of logistic complications the big shift was delayed until November 11, by which time Herbert Hoover had become president-elect. A rumor circulated around Washington that Hoover would end the FRC when its term ended in March, preferring that the regulatory power be in the hands of the secretary of commerce and his department. Hoover told one anonymous source that with commissioners each representing and championing one specific geographic zone instead of viewing national broadcasting as a whole, the greater good of radio, a cause the president-elect believed in fiercely, was being sacrificed.

On November 11, 1928, radio in America was completely changed. New frequency and power allocations meant that people around the country, though temporarily forced to hunt around the dial to find their favorite stations, would hear programming they had never before been able to receive. While the primary goal was improved reception, one of the other benefits was improved quality for America's remotest listeners. "Millions of rural listeners in the agricultural sections and in remote towns and villages will be the chief beneficiaries of the new arrangement—especially in their future ability to hear clearly distant large stations and the small stations in their own neighborhoods and States," wrote FRC commissioner Orestes H. Caldwell.

The changes of November 11, 1928, had a direct impact on KTNT, which the FRC ordered be shifted from a full-time station to a day-time-only station, meaning Baker had to sign off at sundown. Baker's complaints to the FRC were answered by commissioner Sam Pickard, whose nomination to the commission Baker, in his role as president of the American Broadcasters Association, had protested. Pickard informed Baker that KTNT was designated as a "limited time" station and went on to urge Baker to improve the quality of his programming: "I feel that you should now take advantage of this opportunity by devoting every effort to providing a high class service to your listeners."

The battle over KTNT's power and hours of operation continued well past Hoover's inauguration and into the spring of 1929. In Philadelphia, WCAU, a station that was part of the Columbia Broadcasting System (CBS), a national network created in 1927 to compete with NBC, complained that KTNT's signal from Iowa was interfering with reception in the City of Brotherly Love. Baker's premonition that the big-city chain stations would eventually crowd out the small-town radio operators seemed to be coming true. He renewed his request to the FRC for more power. His petition showed that KTNT had excellent local programming, that it employed twenty-seven people, including eighteen musicians and artists, and that the slight revenue it generated was not covering its costs because of the loss of advertising caused by the requirement that the station not broadcast at night. Again the request was denied, but Baker would not relent and he wrote directly to President Hoover seeking his intercession.

At the same time, Norman Baker renamed a magazine he had developed to complement his radio station, changing the title from *Why* to *TNT Magazine,* the initials of which, Baker proudly announced, stood for "The Naked Truth." The magazine's editorial content paralleled Baker's radio talks, which by now had taken on a new mission: promoting his cure for cancer. Possibly because to censor him would have created more problems than it would have solved, the FRC allowed Baker to use his frequency to promote his magazine, his products, and now the miracle cancer cures he claimed to have developed. But his cancer talks caught the attention of the Illinois State Medical Society and the AMA, which began to investigate Norman Baker's medical qualifications.

By December 1929 Americans found themselves dealing with a larger problem than Norman Baker's wild claims and KTNT: The economy was coming undone. But despite what was believed to be a temporary economic downturn, the twenties had been a most amazing decade: ten years of women voting, ten years of Prohibition, and ten years of radio. What had started out as a hard-to-fathom hobby enjoyed by a few enthusiasts had evolved into an astounding industry that employed thousands of people from coast to coast. The growth of the business was impossible to predict and even harder to comprehend: It was estimated that in January 1922 there were approximately 60,000 radio sets reaching an audience of around 75,000 people. Seven years later it was estimated that 7.5 million American homes had at least one radio, and that the audience had grown to include one-third of the entire United States population. The industry had overcome chaos and had an organizational structure and accepted regulations in place; even the once-offensive concept of advertising had become an important adjunct industry. Yet despite the rosy future radio seemed to offer, the crash of October 1929 reduced RCA's stock from a post-split high of $110 to below $20 a share.

Once the novelty of listening to sounds from remote places had worn off, Americans wanted more entertainment and information from that wooden box in the living room. It was all about content; radio was the American canvas. As NBC Radio Network president Aylesworth put it, "Radio broadcasting provides a great medium for religion, music, debate, drama, and information," and once the initial problems and natural reluctance to understand a new idea had been removed, that's exactly what radio gave its listeners. In less than ten years radio had evolved from oddity to necessity, and its greatest champion and shepherd had gone from being the reluctant secretary of commerce to the president of the United States.

Chapter 7

▲▲▲▲▲▲▲▲▲▲▲▲

THE IMAGE WAS ODDLY FAMILIAR, only this time instead of being on the roof of the Westinghouse facility in Pittsburgh, the makeshift studio was located beneath the steps of the Capitol in Washington. Seated on wooden crates, three engineers worked around the spaghetti-like mass of wires, turning dials and adjusting meters on the transmitting equipment they'd set up on a long table. Facing them, standing before a microphone, an announcer prepared to introduce the presidential inauguration about to take place on the building's portico, just above the temporary radio studio. It was March 4, 1929, and the radio team and the nation were poised to hear the swearing-in of Herbert Hoover. After the solemn oath, Hoover, who thanks to the many radio addresses he gave as commerce secretary was a confident speaker, stepped up to the microphones to address the nation of which he was now president. One can only imagine the thoughts that went through his mind at that moment; after all, it was radio, the child he had nurtured from infancy to maturity, that would magically carry his words into homes from coast to coast.

In his inaugural address Hoover urged maintaining the status quo, including continuing Prohibition. Noting the increase in gang violence on America's streets, he called for improvements in the justice system to stem the crime wave. The speech, which was organized more like a company's annual report than an inspirational message, pointed to the roaring stock market and the economic prosperity that buoyed the country. Then, near his conclusion, Hoover reminded those assembled on the Capitol steps and the millions more listening at home that

> ours is a land rich in resources; stimulating in its glorious beauty; filled with millions of happy homes; blessed with comfort and opportunity. In no nation are the institutions of progress more advanced. In no nation are the fruits of accomplishment more secure. In no nation is the government more worthy of respect. No country is more loved by its people. I have an abiding faith in their capacity, integrity and high purpose. I have no fears for the future of our country. It is bright with hope.

With those optimistic words Herbert Hoover began his presidency; less than seven months later his vision of and belief in an eternally prosperous America would be shattered by harsh economic realities. Radio's seminal role in helping to calm and heal the beleaguered nation following its economic collapse, and how Hoover tried to use the medium, is a later part of the story; but the relationship between the presidency and the medium, which Hoover benefited from at his inauguration on March 4, 1929, was nearly a decade in the making.

———

EIGHT YEARS EARLIER, PRESIDENT Warren G. Harding was sworn into office, replacing the tired and ill Woodrow Wilson. Harding, a handsome six-foot-tall man with a thick head of white hair, avoided confrontation. During thirty years as a newspaper publisher he never fired a single employee. He was an amiable man who believed in minimizing the stress of his new job. Twice a week he golfed, and at least as frequently played poker. Though he'd been married since 1891, Harding always had a mistress, and that practice did not stop when he moved into the White House, where he and one of his paramours, Nan Britton, often made love in a twenty-five-square-foot closet near the president's office. Though Harding did fill some cabinet posts with excellent people, such as Charles Evans Hughes at the State Department, Andrew Mellon at the Treasury, and Hoover at Commerce, Harding doled out other positions to an unsavory group of men. Loyal, perhaps to a fault, he rewarded friends, relatives, and cronies with jobs and preferential treatment, a practice that would lead to the Teapot Dome scandal and the 1924 congressional investigations into, and hearings on, the administration's cozy relationship with business.

True to his conservative leanings, Harding was probusiness. In his inaugural address he called "for administrative efficiency, for lightened tax burdens, for sound commercial practices, for adequate credit facilities, for sympathetic concern for all agricultural problems, for the omission of unnecessary interference of government with business, for an end to government's experiment in business, and for more efficient business in government administration." But the headline that emerged from his address was that "our supreme task is the resumption of our onward, normal way," echoing his campaign call for a return to normalcy.

Harding's forty-minute-long inaugural address, which angered Democrats and thrilled Republicans, did establish some firsts that would signal the changing nature of the coming years: His was the first inauguration at which the president-elect and the outgoing president rode to the ceremony not in a horse-drawn carriage, but in an automobile; his was the first inaugural address to be spoken into a microphone, amplified and played through speakers to the assembled crowd. Moreover, it was the first time an inauguration was described over the radio waves, as Pittsburgh's KDKA had an announcer read an advance copy of Harding's address while the new president was delivering his rendition of it on the Capitol portico, although only a very few listeners with the right receiving equipment heard the announcer's reading.

For nearly the entire first year of his presidency, Harding did not have to deal with the ramifications of the developing national radio hobby and industry; that was left to Secretary of Commerce Hoover. But it was clear that a dilemma for the Harding administration was developing on the not-too-distant horizon: Its belief in minimal government interference would eventually conflict with the need for the government to control and organize the radio spectrum. But until that conflict needed real attention, radio was a feel-good idea, and Harding, an astute politician, was ready to embrace the positive exposure it offered him. On October 21, 1921, the Associated Press reported that David Sarnoff, RCA's general manager, had completed the installation of a transmission line in the White House. From there, on November 5, President Harding read a message carried by land line to RCA's newest radio transmission facility on Long Island, "said to be the most powerful in existence." The new station, powered by 2,000 kilowatts, which was ten times greater than most broadcast facilities of the time, would send the president's message hundreds, if not thousands, of miles around to anyone with a properly tuned radio receiving set.

Ironically, the president did not himself have a radio receiving set until February 1922, when one was installed in the executive offices so he could stay "in touch with the news of the world merely by picking up the receiver and listening." The installation of the set became a major news story and a topic of conversation at a cabinet meeting, during which the president ordered Secretary Hoover to organize a conference with leading military and commercial radio people in the country to get input on how the government should address the regulation of the radio waves.

Installed in a bookcase alongside his desk in the White House, the president's receiving unit had an antenna that ran along the roof and extended to one of the trees on the south side of the executive grounds. "President Harding has a new toy to play with. It is expected that a similar receiving instrument will be installed in the White House press room where the hard working correspondents, if they can snatch time, may listen to strains of music, concerts and gossip flying through the air," reported the Associated Press.

Harding, like most Americans, quickly became hooked on listening to his radio receiving station during any spare time—those moments between golf and poker—he could find. While the White House installation was far more elaborate than those constructed by hobbyists, Harding realized that, like himself, there were enthusiasts who would listen to almost anything, even dull speeches by the president. And so by the spring of 1922 Harding was using radio to tell the American people—at least those with radio receivers—of his administration's achievements.

But all was not ideal. Despite being president, Harding was not shielded from the burgeoning reception interference issues, and one night in January 1923 he was having such difficulty tuning his receiver that even after fiddling with wires and dials he still received two conflicting signals. "Mr. Harding frantically tried to get one of them off, but the more he labored, the louder came the screeching. Finally in disgust, he turned the whole business off and went to reading. 'The thing sounded like the reports of some conferences,' Mr. Harding laughingly told friends."

Reception problems aside, Harding knew that radio's ability to reach voters could be used to political advantage. In part due to the lack of available programming, every speech the president gave had the potential to fill station operators' broadcast time. Harding's voice quickly became a recognizable sound. When Harding spoke at New York's Metropolitan Opera House, his talk was carried by WEAF, and it was noted that given the strength of the station's signal, this speech garnered the largest audience ever addressed by a president. Then a month later, plans were made to have the president's speech in St. Louis carried simultaneously by two stations so the signal might cover a larger swath of the country. "The step is the first in a plan to link up as many as 30 broadcasting stations in the United States by wire. Then the President, sitting in his study in the White House, could speak into a microphone, with no more effort than if he were speaking to someone in the room, and be heard in all parts of the country."

Harding's trailblazing broadcast work had its problems; speaking directly into a microphone was altering the way the president delivered speeches, and the change was not to his advantage. Critiquing the president's radio appearances, the New York Times wrote: "The fact that President Harding's speeches are heard all over the country instantaneously by radio has its drawbacks as well as its advantages. It gives him an immense distant audience, but hampers him before his immediate hearers. It carries his message far, but cripples his oratory near by." Perhaps Harding's problem lay not only in his delivery, but in his content, for as one pundit quipped, "His speeches leave the impression of an army of pompous phrases moving over the landscape in search of an idea."

On June 20, 1923, Harding and his entourage set out from Washington by train for a "Voyage of Understanding," a transcontinental trip that would include the first presidential visit to the Alaska territory. The journey was an old-fashioned whistle-stop that the Harding administration claimed had no political purpose; the stated mission of the lengthy journey was for Harding to meet and greet the American people and to gather firsthand information about the development of that distant territory. At each stop along the route, Harding delivered a speech; most were aired by small local radio stations. However, the need to speak directly into the microphone continued to have a restricting effect on the president. He was impressed by the wonder of the radio amplifier, which enabled his words to be carried to interested people listening at receivers hundreds of miles away, but this acknowledgment did not modify the evidence that the mechanical contrivance worried him and that he was "tempted at times to revert to the old style of direct oratory, more stimulating to both orator and audience." He could not find that balance between grand oratory and intimate expression.

Following what was called his fact-finding trip, but was really more of a sightseeing, pleasure junket to Alaska, Harding traveled to California, arriving in San Francisco on July 29, where a major speech at the Civic Auditorium was to be the highlight of his visit. According to the announced plans, the president's address was to be carried by a group of radio stations wired together by phone lines from San Francisco all the way to Round Hill, Massachusetts. It was anticipated that the total audience for the president's address would be between three million and five million listeners, the largest audience ever to simultaneously hear an event. It was to be another important first for the president, but fate interceded. When the presidential party arrived in San Francisco Harding was not feeling well, and the surgeon general, suspecting a case of food poisoning, ordered the president to bed. For two days he rested in room 8064 of the Palace Hotel, and though an erroneous report that the president had died was leaked over radio stations, causing some panic in major cities, his condition did seem to be improving. Nonetheless, his radio speech was postponed, and on August 2, at 7:30 P.M., just after hearing his wife read a highly complimentary portrait of him that had been published in the *Saturday Evening Post,* President Warren G. Harding died, probably of a massive stroke. On August 5 radio stations across America broadcast memorial services for the late president, and then in an ironic tribute to a man who had become one of radio's most vocal proponents, most radio stations shut down and remained silent for the balance of the week.

At the time of Harding's death, Vice President Calvin Coolidge was on vacation at his father's farmhouse in Vermont. Awakened by the arrival of a messenger, he learned of the tragic news and of his new job. Once the text of the oath of office was wired from Washington to Vermont, Coolidge was sworn into office by the nearest government official available, his father, who happened to be the notary public of Windsor County. The ceremony took place in the parlor of the family home, but since the house had no electricity, the quaint, historic scene was illuminated only by the flickering light of a kerosene lantern. Once the oath was administered, the capital of the country became Plymouth, Vermont, where the sole telephone was in the general store across the street from the Coolidge farm. That phone line had limited technical capability, and within a few hours of Coolidge's swearing-in a representative of New England Telephone was on site installing a special line connecting the farmhouse with the White House. "This completely tied up one of the three telephone circuits running from the neighborhood of Plymouth to New York and Boston, and increased the difficulty of transmitting information to the newspapers and press associations."

It is hard to imagine that a man whose nickname was Silent Cal could be good for an industry that thrived on the transmission of sound, but in fact the Coolidge administration, again with the help of Secretary of Commerce Hoover, would steward an incredible radio boom during the next five years. Initially Coolidge refrained from speaking on the radio as often as his predecessor had; it was not until February

1924, six months after he took office, that Coolidge made his third radio appearance. But by April he had become a radio regular, and his speech to the Associated Press at New York's Waldorf-Astoria Hotel was heard over a network of ten of the country's largest stations.

Politics and radio were destined to coexist, and radio stations still on the hunt for programming realized that nominating conventions had the potential to entertain an audience that had once found listening to distant static mesmerizing. The presidential nominating conventions helped make 1924 "the summer of radio," the moment in time when radio's power and importance were truly realized. The industry's growth was spurred not only by an increase in the number of broadcasting stations, but by the growth of the size of the audience that was due to the increased affordability of manufactured—as opposed to built-at-home—receiving sets, some of which could be purchased for as little as twenty-five dollars.

As the political season got under way, there was no doubt the next president would have to be a radio president. Predictions were made that the coming presidential election battle would be fought on the air. For the first time in the history of politics the great national conventions traditionally reserved for those lucky to be there would now be accessible to the rank and file.

Expecting a difficult general election due to the fallout from the Teapot Dome scandal, in which Interior Secretary Albert Fall illegally sold the nation's oil reserves in Wyoming's Teapot Dome for personal gain, the Republicans gathered in Cleveland, Ohio, for their convention. Radio stations linked together as an ad hoc network could cover a large portion of the country, and were standing by to play their part in bringing the sounds of democracy to the American people. Unfortunately for the roughly 20 million people who composed the radio audience, the three-day Republican National Convention lacked any drama whatsoever; as Will Rogers quipped, "It could have been done by postcard." In tidy fashion, President Coolidge was nominated on the first ballot and the Republicans went off to prepare their national campaign. Meanwhile the radio technicians packed up their equipment and headed to New York's Madison Square Garden for the Democratic National Convention, hoping there might be something more dramatic to air.

Since the agreement in which AT&T was to get out of the radio business had not yet been completed, two competing groups of stations, one led by RCA–General Electric's WJZ, and the other by AT&T's WEAF, set up in Madison Square Garden to report on the convention. WJZ's coverage featured Major J. Andrew White, the editor of the *Wireless Age* magazine, and a radio neophyte named Norman Brokenshire, while WEAF's coverage was handled by Philips Carlin and Graham McNamee.

When the convention opened on June 24, the radio commentators found a deeply divided Democratic party; roughly 50 percent of the delegates, led by William Gibbs McAdoo, defended fundamentalism, Prohibition, and the right of the Ku Klux Klan to exist, and the other half, championed by New York's Catholic governor Al Smith, sought an end to Prohibition and an explicit condemnation of the Klan.

It was a brutal, politically polarizing battle that played out, day after day, on radio receivers across America; democracy with all its warts was on display. Stations added broadcast hours and moved other scheduled programming so as not to miss a moment of the protracted confrontation. The convention dragged on with neither candidate receiving the delegates required to secure the nomination. Looking for something of interest to report to their readers, newspapers began to cover radio's coverage of the convention. By July 8 the tedium of the spectacle was evident in those reports: "'Good morning, ladies and gentlemen of the radio audience.' For the eleventh day we hear this greeting as the airwaves again take up the burden of the Democratic national convention." It was a divisive, damaging meeting for the Democrats, and though they did try to manage what the audience heard by censoring any particularly nasty speeches, it was impossible for listeners not to perceive a party badly divided. Finally, after the ninety-ninth deadlocked ballot, Smith and McAdoo agreed to withdraw from contention, leaving the field wide open. The exhausted, homesick, and cash-poor Democratic delegates took only four more ballots to nominate John Davis, a lawyer, former ambassador to Britain, and political rookie from West Virginia, to run against Coolidge. Davis, who was visiting a friend on East Sixty-eighth Street, found out about his nomination by hearing the report on a local radio station.

It was an unhappy episode for the Democrats, and it was all heard across the country. There was, however, one humorous side effect of the radio coverage: It made a national star out of an insignificant state legislator from Alabama named Oscar Underwood. Since there were 103 ballots, and each one began with the state of Alabama, the audience heard Alabama's governor William Brandon declare, 103 times, that Alabama's votes were being cast for the state's favorite son: *Allllllllllllllll-a-baaaaaaaaaaaaaaaaaaaaaama casts twennnnnty-four votes for Oscarrrrrrrrr W. Un-der-wooooooooood.* Thanks to radio, that singing vote was the most talked-about part of the convention; it even led to a lawsuit when Mrs. Kuni Schlott, a rooming-house owner whose building was located next to a bird hospital, filed a complaint against the hospital and its owner, Mrs. Pope. The problem was that following each of Alabama's 103 votes, a crow being cared for at the hospital reacted with a loud *Haw-haw-haw, caw-caw-caw,* which made it impossible for people in Mrs. Schlott's house to listen to the convention coverage.

While the radio coverage of the convention was not good news for the Democrats, it was sensational for radio itself. The radio transmission was hailed as being nearly perfect; every speech was heard perhaps better by the radio listeners than by those in the convention hall. The music, shouting, singing, and celebration came in so clearly that a person without the least imaginative power was able to enjoy the proceedings just as well as those who actually were there. Industry experts estimated that coverage of the conventions added more than one million new radio fans to an already burgeoning audience.

Given the popularity of the convention among radio listeners, there was no doubt the magical medium would be a factor in the upcoming campaign. However, the central drama of the campaign did not come initially from either of the two major party candidates, but from a third-party candidate. During the hubbub of the Democrats' disappointing, self-annihilating demonstration, Senator Robert La Follette of Wisconsin announced he would run as an independent representing the Progressive Party, which was holding its convention in Cleveland, Ohio. The concurrence of the two conventions was caused by the unanticipated length of the Democrats' debacle. Senator La Follette's name was placed into nomination by his son, who electrified the delegates with a rousing speech in which he stated that his father had declared that the old parties "could not be trusted to carry out their promise."

Radio was ready for the campaign, and newspaper advertisements promoting the sale of home radio receivers heralded the exciting speeches sure to come.

Everyone agrees that this will be the most interesting and spectacular Presidential campaign in American history. The public is fortunate in being able to avail itself of radio to hear every word of the acceptance speeches, campaign addresses, political debates and discussions of the issues.

The ad, created and paid for by the Radio 'Merchants' Association, Inc., concluded: "If you haven't a radio set, now is the time to buy one. If you have a set, check up on your tubes, batteries, etc."

Airtime was a political asset, and the major radio companies, realizing there was an inherent need for them to be fair with the use of their airtime, joined forces to develop a common policy, agreeing they would give airtime primarily to the major parties, but review requests from minor parties and decide each case on its merits. Though it was the first step toward codifying what would eventually become an equal-time rule, this policy was criticized as unfair as it instantly handicapped La Follette by not granting him airtime equal to that of his opponents. Angered, he warned that his campaign would use radio not only to deliver its message, but as a way to monitor the "utterances of his opponents."

The major parties were fairly traditional in the way they began the campaign, using grueling cross-country whistle-stops as the main method of getting the voters' attention, but they soon realized that radio was a far more efficient way to communicate. The campaigns devised a way to intertwine the old in-person appearance with the new idea of making radio broadcasts part of the train tours. Democratic candidate John Davis even had his train car wired with a microphone and the appropriate electronics to make it easier for local radio stations to "plug in" and air his campaign speeches. And though all three parties had to purchase some of the airtime they used, La Follette's talks were so dynamic that his speeches always raised more money from contributors than the airtime cost.

Of the three candidates, Silent Cal and the Republicans used the new medium most brilliantly. When autumn arrived, Coolidge chose to stay in the White House, from where he delivered more radio speeches than either of his opponents. Radio had brought new power to the president's bully pulpit, and Coolidge, whose natural New England twang seemed to disappear when he spoke over the airwaves, had become a masterful radioman. As the election neared, the radio war intensified; more efforts were made to string together larger networks of linked stations. It was, after all, a national campaign, and the more people reached at one time the better. On the eve of the election

John Davis gave his final radio address from the studio of New York's WEAF, promising to punish "men proven guilty of crimes while holding office and those who conspired with them, and a general housecleaning of the Government." The talk was carried by eight stations and on shortwave, giving Davis coast-to-coast exposure. Likewise, Coolidge's final address was aired on a record twenty-six stations that blanketed the country, probably reaching the largest audience ever assembled simultaneously up to that point.

The real excitement of the 1924 election came on Tuesday, November 4. As Americans sat down to dinner, waiting to find out whether the Coolidge administration would survive the three-pronged assault of scandals and the criticisms of Davis and La Follette, radio stations across America were prepared to report election results as quickly as the numbers became available. Even President and Mrs. Coolidge had an early dinner, then retired to the study soon after 7 P.M. to listen to the radio as scattered reports began to come in. Nearly four years to the day after Dr. Conrad and his team at Pittsburgh's KDKA had pioneered the idea of reporting election results via radio, nearly 400 radio stations from one coast of America to the other were reporting on the presidential election. Since it was all new, no one was really sure what to expect either from the broadcasters' or the listeners' perspective, so many stations, like New York's municipally owned WNYC, offered election results interspersed with weather reports, and entertainment provided by the likes of The Virginians orchestra, Cliff Edwards on the ukulele, and the humor of Joseph Spree. *Election returns by Radio! Tonight from station WEAF. With a continuous Eveready program from early evening until long after midnight. Will Rogers, himself, will call the turn on returns,* announced WEAF on election day, adding, *The Eveready Male Quartet will revive memories with the campaign songs of all time.*

With all that entertainment, it was no surprise that listening to election returns turned into a social event. In addition to good food and company, New York's finest hotel restaurants offered election returns via radio, even though it was clearly stated that "the Volstead Act will be enforced everywhere." In other words, you could get food and news, but not food and booze. All across the country radio stations reported not only on the national election but on local contests as well, interspersing results as they became available; millions of voters kept in touch with the hour-to-hour tallying of the votes and went to bed knowing the outcome of both the presidential race and even the local contests in which they were interested. Even at New York's Sing Sing Prison, inmates were allowed to listen to radio reports until 9:30 P.M. They were interested in the contest between Governor Smith and Colonel Theodore Roosevelt Jr. because the governor had the power to pardon prisoners. Al Smith won.

The signal relevance of the 1924 presidential election was not that Calvin Coolidge won the election, but rather the important role radio played in the campaign. In addition to the free airtime the candidates received, the Republicans spent approximately $120,000 on advertising while the losing Democrats spent about $40,000. If there was any doubt about radio's increasing influence, the election of 1924 removed it, and the first radio campaign spurred three important developments: the power of—and economic need for—advertising; the need for nationally connected networks; and the instantaneous impact of radio news. As the *New York Times* opined, "Tuesday evening, nearly enough to 'everybody' was eager to get the same information, and if they did not all seek it at any single station, at least they all did seek it from one another. Just how large the audience was nobody knows." Judge S. B. Davis, acting solicitor of the Commerce Department, predicted that in the future voters would be able to see, as well as hear, their candidates over the airwaves. Noting that speeches went off on time and were shorter than usual, he went on to comment that "the radio program waits for none and radio audiences do not care for long speeches."

The Coolidge presidency boasted a litany of radio firsts. Unlike his inauguration in Vermont nineteen months earlier, his second inaugural was witnessed by a large crowd at the Capitol and a radio audience of "virtually every owner of a radio set" in the entire country. During the buildup to the inauguration it was noted that Warren Harding had spoken into an amplifier that allowed his words to be heard by a live audience of more than 125,000 people. Just four years later, President Coolidge would recite the oath into radio microphones that would carry his words to an audience estimated to be over 22,800,000. While broadcasting the inaugural was in itself historic, the radio producers saw the need to provide some description of the proceedings for their invisible audience. Again they turned to WEAF's Graham McNamee, who at 11:15 on the morning of March 4, 1925, began the broadcast with *Good morning, ladies and gentlemen of the radio audience.* McNamee described the scene then, at 11:57 A.M., and introduced the United States Marine Band, which played the fanfare calling those assembled to order. The excitement of the radio event far overshadowed the president's forty-two-minute, optimistic though uninspired speech; it had to have been boring radio.

As president, Coolidge used radio to communicate directly with the American people; events heard on the radio ranged from his lighting of the White House Christmas tree to his tedious discussion of the proposed U.S. budget, a talk made more palatable by the inclusion of an introductory concert by the United States Marine Band. Coolidge's ubiquitous radio presence did cause one enemy to cry foul. Senator La Follette, the defeated 1924 Progressive candidate, was troubled by the influence America's largest corporations seemed to wield in the Republican administration, and he questioned the relationship between the White House and the leaders of companies such as General Electric. "I intend to inquire into the extraordinary radio facilities placed at the disposal of the present administration by the General Electric Company without compensation," the senator announced.

La Follette's charges did nothing to curtail Coolidge's use of radio. Moreover, every time the president planned to take to the airwaves, the story was covered by the print media. The talks became so expected and commonplace that they often took second billing to other radio events scheduled for the same day: MME. ALDA TO SING FOR RADIO TONIGHT declared a bold headline, clearly overshadowing the subhead: ADDRESS OF PRESIDENT COOLIDGE ALSO WILL BE BROADCAST.

As the number of radio sets owned by the public increased, the coverage of Coolidge's addresses shifted from what he had to say, to how many people he was saying it to. As was true with his inaugural address, Coolidge's achievement was not the content, but the reach of his messages. In February 1927 he gave a speech honoring George Washington: "A hook-up of 42 radio stations, the greatest chain the world has ever known, carried the President's words and the exercises to the farthermost reaches of the country and abroad. Hardly had the President returned to the White House than he received several messages from distant places telling of the reception of his message." Estimates put the radio audience for the George Washington talk at more than 25 million people, the largest audience ever to hear an event simultaneously. Due in great part to Coolidge's excessive use of the medium, radio and the presidency had become intertwined, and observers eagerly awaited the 1928 campaign for the White House, expecting the contestants to be two radio masters: the incumbent, and "best radio speaker in the nation," President Coolidge; and the challenger, Governor Al Smith of New York, who "has made more effective use of radio than any other man in public life." However, it was acknowledged that if Coolidge decided to not seek reelection, the Republican nomination would be open to "another presidential possibility with a great national radio following," Secretary Hoover, who "makes no mistakes in his delivery."

At noon on August 2, 1927, four years to the day after his father had administered the oath of office, President Coolidge ended the speculation over whether he would run. Assembling the White House press corps in his private office, the president asked the reporters to form a single line. Then as each man passed before him, he handed them folded pieces of paper containing the typewritten phrase "I do not choose to run for President in 1928." For a man who had mastered electronic communication, it was an antediluvian way to disseminate information, but that is what he chose to do, thus leaving the field for the Republican nomination wide open. Initially the leading candidate was former governor Frank Lowden of Illinois, but his candidacy encountered strong opposition from a bloc of senators from Western states who were holding secret meetings. During their conclave, the senators considered a suggestion from a radio owner from Iowa who proposed creating a low-frequency, high-powered radio station over which the insurgent senators could air their views directly to the American people. "Senator Brookhart of Iowa, in whose office the secret conference took place, explained that Mr. Baker was the owner of station KTNT at Muscatine, Iowa, and that he was an inventor and manufacturer of the Calliphone [sic]."

With no clear front-runner, Secretary Hoover, who had never run for any office, was positioned as a challenger for the nomination and was entered in all the major primaries. Hoover found Coolidge's August 2 message to be "cryptic," and was concerned that the president might still seek reelection. By the middle of May 1928, Hoover had secured more than 400 delegates and went to see Coolidge, offering to withdraw if the president had changed his mind. Coolidge's only advice to Hoover was "If you have 400 delegates, you better keep them."

The 1928 national conventions were just the kind of entertainment programming the country's radio networks—NBC, and CBS, which had been cobbled together in September 1927—wanted to air. "Our plans will make it possible for radio listeners to hear every phrase of the conventions. From a point where he can watch the entire convention, Graham McNamee will direct each broadcast and give the running story of each event," announced Merlin H. Aylesworth, president of NBC.

As the conventions neared, it appeared this time that the Republicans were in disarray while the Democrats were in lockstep in their support of Governor Smith. But when the Republicans gathered in Kansas City, the delegates gave Secretary Hoover 837 of the 1,084 votes, which secured the nomination. It was clean and efficient, but not great radio, even though it cost NBC an average of $1.07 for every second the convention was on the air. Then at the end of June, the Democrats met in Houston, and though the convention was not as devastating as the one in 1924, their 1928 version was far from dull. "Demonstrations, battles on the floor, policemen breaking up fights, noise, noise, plenty of noise, and a wild tumult of sound when Franklin D. Roosevelt put the name of Governor Smith in nomination, seemed enough to wreck microphones gathering the din of the Democratic performance for the coast to coast networks of the National and Columbia broadcasting companies."

After what must have sounded to radio listeners like organized hysteria, the Democrats heeded Franklin Roosevelt's stirring speech and nominated Al Smith, who was the first Roman Catholic to run for the office. With the two standard-bearers in place, the four-month campaign for the presidency was under way. But the Republicans faced one unexpected hurdle: President Coolidge's unwillingness to speak in behalf of Hoover. Coolidge's reluctance may be better understood when viewed in the context of this comment he made about his possible successor: "That man has offered me unsolicited advice for the past six years, all of it bad." In mid-August, Hoover delivered his official nomination acceptance speech to a huge radio audience, and again Coolidge did his utmost to snub the nominee, proudly letting it be known that he had gone fishing during the radio address and hadn't heard a word of it.

Governor Smith's campaign got off to a much smoother start; on August 22, 1928, Smith was officially notified that he had been nominated. Through a linking of the stations in the NBC network with some in the CBS network, Smith's acceptance speech was carried by the largest group of stations ever assembled, enabling him to be heard in virtually every corner of the country.

The campaigns began in earnest after Labor Day. The Republicans fired first, announcing an agreement to buy airtime from the NBC network at a weekly cost of $20,000. But the time they were buying was not for stand-alone commercial campaign messages, but for entertainment programs the party planned to sponsor. "The programs would consist of short addresses of not more than ten minutes, with twenty minutes of entertainment."

Radio was the ideal vehicle for candidates running for national office, yet for Hoover the medium he had championed seemed to be a handicap. As the campaign progressed, he learned he had to write new speeches for every stop on his tours. Radio had made it impossible for presidential candidates to repeat the same speech with small variations, as had been the practice in those happier speaking times. Then, paragraphs could be polished up, epigrams used again and again, and eloquence invented by repeated tryouts. Now every speech had to be original and new.

Whether through paid entertainment with speechifying included or with speeches and rallies carried by radio, the candidates and their surrogates took to the airwaves as often and as widely as possible, and from all accounts the American audience was enjoying having the thrill of politicking brought into their homes. Nonetheless, President Coolidge remained disinterested. Enjoying his evening leisure hours, the president did not burden himself with the progress of the campaign. He never turned on the radio to hear Secretary Hoover or Governor Smith or anyone else speaking on behalf of the candidates, this despite the excellent receiving and listening equipment installed at the White House.

While Coolidge was no help to Hoover, the candidate did receive support from one unexpected corner: Norman Baker and KTNT became vocal champions of the Republican cause in the Midwest. Though he gladly sold advertising time to the Democratic campaign, Baker was on Hoover's side—he preferred the Republican to Governor Smith—and even traveled to Washington at the end of September for a confidential meeting with the Republican nominee. After advising the campaign on how to use radio most effectively as a propaganda machine, Baker told Hoover that following any of Governor Smith's broadcasts heard over KTNT, he, Baker, would go "on the air with about a one hour's talk each night after their talk is over and will do all I can to break down this campaign, which you will note is a strong one." The Democrats quickly discovered what KTNT was doing, and on October 25 sent a telegram to Baker:

MANY COMPLAINTS RECEIVED DEMOCRATIC NATIONAL COMMITTEE RE INTOLERANT RELIGIOUS PROPAGANDA EMANATING FROM YOUR STATION AGAINST SMITH. REPETITION OF SUCH SUBJECT MATTER GROUND FOR CANCELLATION REMAINING FARM NETWORK SCHEDULES.

Baker, the ultimate huckster, saw the threat as an opportunity and encouraged the Hoover campaign to respond by buying more airtime from him. The KTNT case was just one particularly nasty manifestation of the national radio campaign, which only intensified as the election neared. Both parties increased their radio expenditures, ultimately doling out more than one million dollars for radio time, which the candidates and their surrogates used to speak directly to the American voters. But despite the relative novelty of the radio campaign, American voters had begun to get irritated by the repetitive messages. Political managers reported that the radio public was growing weary of political speeches and was tuning "the spellbinders out."

During the final days of the campaign, the parties took to the radio waves with unprecedented intensity, buying time on networks made up of as many stations as could be assembled. Every day Republicans and Democrats attacked and defended over the airwaves. On the eve of the election, the candidates bought nationwide airtime for the campaigns' closing speeches. Al Smith spoke from the NBC studios in New York, and Hoover from the campus of his alma mater, Stanford University in Palo Alto, California; but both those speeches were eclipsed by one made by the previously tacit Silent Cal. Speaking from the White House over a nationwide network of stations, President Coolidge gave a heartfelt talk urging the American people to exercise the right given them by democracy: to vote. Much to the Republicans' dismay, the speech never endorsed Herbert Hoover and was entirely nonpartisan. Coolidge closed by using the airwaves in a more personal way than was common, especially for the president: "To my father who is listening in my old home in Vermont, and to my other invisible audience I say 'Good night.'"

When the 1928 campaign and election were over, Herbert Hoover, a man who had never held any elected office, had become president-elect. It had been a brutal campaign, carried into America's living rooms by radio, which during this election cycle had become a mature, vital component of the democratic process. Radio was credited with increasing registration and voter turnout. It had eclipsed all other forms of media, causing one newspaper columnist to opine that "money spent on any other kind of publicity is largely wasted." Predictions were made that in the near future, campaigns would be conducted entirely from the candidates' homes.

Even the transition from the Coolidge administration to the Hoover administration was defined by radio. Highly sympathetic to the departing president, commentators noted how he had become a well-liked, recognizable voice on the American scene, and to mark his contribution to radio, Graham McNamee, on behalf of NBC, presented the outgoing president with the microphone through which he had spoken to the nation. Meanwhile, the incoming president would be saddled with the legal challenges to the government's control over the airwaves. Even before his inauguration, Hoover would face a decision about what to do with the Federal Radio Commission, whose charter was scheduled to expire at the end of February 1929. It was oddly remarkable that the situation turned out as it did: Once given control over radio as commerce secretary, then shorn of that responsibility by Congress, Hoover, as president, would once again hold the fate of the FRC and of radio in his hands.

It had all come full circle; the commerce secretary who had guided radio's growth was now the most powerful, though not the most popular, man in the country. Hoover's March 4, 1929, inauguration was covered and aired by both networks, each sending a phalanx of their best announcers, including McNamee, Carlin, and Brokenshire, to detail all of the solemn proceedings and celebratory parades for the American people. In the concluding moments of his inaugural address, Hoover asked Americans across the nation to give him their aid, tolerance, and cooperation. Speaking into the networks' microphones he called on the Higher Power: "I ask the help of Almighty God in this service to my country to which you have called me." Seven months later, he would need it.

Chapter 8

▲▲▲▲▲▲▲▲▲▲▲▲

APRIL 11, 1921—Pittsburgh's Motor Square Garden. The *Pittsburgh Post's* renowned boxing writer Florent Gibson was ringside for the lightweight bout pitting Johnny Ray against Johnny Dundee, whose real name was Giuseppe Carrora. But Gibson wasn't there merely for his newspaper; he was there to describe the action in a device that resembled a telephone, his oral account to be relayed to Westinghouse's nearby KDKA—the same station that aired election results the previous November—which would then send out the description to its minuscule audience. The modest size of the event and the way it was transmitted were insignificant harbingers of the business that sports radio would eventually become. By simply telling the audience what he was seeing, Gibson was the first of many sportswriters to describe the action, translating what would have become written images into audio pictures for the radio audience. Sportscasting was born, and some of the men who became sportscasters would become almost as well known as the athletes they covered.

Sports radio was a laboratory in which ideas were tried and ultimately kept or rejected. During its infancy, radio experimented with broadcasts of golf, tennis, boat racing, auto racing, horse racing, and almost every other sport enjoyed by professionals or amateurs. But during the early 1920s, sports radio exploded because of America's interest in three main competitive endeavors: college football, the World Series, and boxing.

BOXING

JULY 4, 1919—Even the extreme midsummer heat didn't keep crowds from gathering outside the offices of New York City's major newspapers, waiting for the results of the heavyweight bout being fought in Toledo, Ohio, to be posted on bulletin boards. Within an hour after the end of the fight, newsboys on street corners everywhere hawked extra editions filled with detailed, round-by-round descriptions of the bout. But even before the newspapers hit the streets, New York's telegraph offices and phone circuits had been flooded with messages and calls from people in Toledo to acquaintances in New York eager to be the first to find out what had happened. Word spread that heavyweight champion Jess Willard, a six-foot-six, 245-pound mountain of a man, had been knocked out by the smaller challenger, Jack Dempsey. And so Jack Dempsey the legend was born.

Dempsey had seemingly come out of nowhere. Born in Manassa, Colorado, in 1895, he began boxing in Colorado's small mining communities, and by age twenty-four had won more than eighty bouts. The battle with Willard was his big chance, and he made the most of it, blasting the larger man with a series of wicked left hooks that left the giant dazed. The fight launched Dempsey to stardom and he was given the catchy nickname the Manassa Mauler. Twice during 1920 Dempsey defended his title against lesser opponents before agreeing to a bout against the French champion Georges Carpentier, to be held in New Jersey on July 2, 1921. A shrewd promoter, Tex Rickard, billed the battle as a confrontation between good and evil; Carpentier, a graceful, almost gentle, wounded World War I hero, versus the vicious, powerful American who had shirked military service during the Great War.

In a country where boxing "dominated the sports pages, and coverage of a heavyweight title fight rivaled that of a world war," it didn't take much hype for a fight to generate excitement. Seeing opportunity in the transmission of a description of the battle, RCA's imaginative general manager David Sarnoff arranged to divert a powerful transmitter from its delivery to the Navy Department to Jersey City, where RCA's engineers built a makeshift antenna by stringing wires between nearby railroad towers. Then they connected a microphone at ringside by running telephone wires to a shack where the transmitter had been installed. To draw more attention to the radio broadcast and the fight, Sarnoff and Rickard linked the event with a drive to raise charitable donations to help the reconstruction of war-torn France. The idea was for charitable organizations from northern Florida to southern Maine to set up radio receivers and speakers so people who paid an admission charge could gather together to hear the bout. It was an innovative way to raise money, and to secure even more attention Sarnoff asked Anne Morgan, daughter of J. P. Morgan, who was in charge of donations for France, along with the recently defeated vice-presidential candidate, Franklin Delano Roosevelt, to promote these fund-raising get-togethers. Rickard, wanting to spread his boxer's renown to an even wider audience, encouraged local organizations such as the Elks and the Rotarians, schools, and even movie theaters to set up listening equipment for the bout.

Excitement grew to a fevered pitch; interest was so great that more than 700 sportswriters from all over the world flocked to Jersey City to cover the bout. In Paris, the army arranged to inform people there of the results by flying over the city: If the planes flashed red lights then Carpentier had won; if the lights were white, Dempsey had retained his crown. The *New York Times,* anticipating being inundated with inquiries about the fight, asked its readers to refrain from calling the paper's offices for updates. "Liberal provision has been made by the newspapers and the 'ticker' news service for supplying bulletins in the usual places." Most notable among those provisions was the installation of large loudspeakers in Times Square that could send out the wireless transmission direct from ringside to the throng outside the newspaper's offices. "The whole story of the fight will be told by voice. If the words are lost in the tumult and cheering there will be no doubt as to what happened as carefully written descriptions of the rounds will be posted blow by blow."

On Saturday afternoon, July 2, the grandstands erected at Boyle's Thirty Acres in Jersey City were packed with nearly 90,000 fans who'd paid a record $1,626,589 to see this international bout. Seated next to David Sarnoff was RCA's Andrew White, the editor of *Wireless Age* magazine, who was at ringside to call the fight. Caught up in the excitement of the spectacle, White, seated before a microphone, enthusiastically described every blow. His words traveled to the transmission shed, but ironically that's as far as they went, because there sat RCA technician J. O. Smith, who repeated White's words into another microphone connected directly to the transmitter. So instead of hearing White's excited call from near the epicenter of the bout, the radio audience heard Smith's rather flat description of Dempsey's four-round knockout of his French opponent. Nonetheless, the immediacy of the transmission, which reached an estimated 300,000 listeners and provided a great windfall for the charities, cemented a mutually beneficial relationship between radio and boxing. Perhaps of greater import was that radio had discovered its first real sports personality: the Manassa Mauler.

The bout and the attendant publicity also pushed Tex Rickard into the forefront of sportscasting. A colorful figure in his own right who was well suited to the flashy 1920s, Rickard began his career in the Klondike during the 1897 gold rush. While there he met a young engineer named Herbert Hoover and a man named Jack Kearns, who would become Jack Dempsey's manager. In 1920 Rickard, who had already invested in a hotel, saloon, and gambling hall in Nevada, signed a ten-year lease on New York's Madison Square Garden, where he hosted all sorts of events including marathon bicycle races that lasted for several days, wrestling matches, and even some lesser boxing matches. However, for big-draw events like championship bouts, he preferred large outdoor venues.

And so Rickard picked New York's Polo Grounds, home of base-ball's New York Giants, as the site for Dempsey's next major bout, which would be against the Argentine champion Luis Angel Firpo. Billed as the battle between the Wild Bull of the Pampas and the Manassa Mauler, the fight was set for September 14, 1923. When advance ticket sales surpassed $1 million, Rickard predicted that with attendance expected to be around 100,000 people, gross revenues would exceed $1.3 million. Meanwhile it was announced that Andrew White would again call the fight, only this time the radio audience would be treated to his actual ringside call, including crowd noise. WJZ, with studios atop New York's Aeolian Hall, would be the originating station, but other stations around the country would listen in to White's call and then retransmit the words of his descriptions to their listeners, thus widening the audience.

The first round made for magnificent radio as the champ dropped Firpo seven times, but each time the tough challenger struggled back to his feet. Then Firpo slugged Dempsey with a wicked right, sending the champion through the ropes. Listeners to WJZ heard the huge crowd fall silent, holding its collective breath, as Dempsey slowly climbed back into the ring just ahead of the referee's ten count. The fighters returned to their corners then came out for the second round, but it was short-lived: Dempsey knocked Firpo out fifty-seven seconds into the round.

On the morning after the fight, one of New York's great department stores, Gimbel Brothers, ran a telling ad: "Did You 'Listen In' on the Dempsey-Firpo Fight Last Night?" It went on to remind New Yorkers that radio would be broadcasting all kinds of important events, and that Gimbels was "Radio Headquarters." The tagline of the ad was "Every Home Should Have a Radio!" Thanks to the fight, interest in radio surged. Shops dealing in radios and radio supplies sprang up everywhere. But it would be three years before boxing's biggest draw, Jack Dempsey, would again step into the ring to defend his crown. During that hiatus other fighters boxed, and the sport continued to fill pages of newsprint, but none of the new contestants had Dempsey's swagger or popularity. By mid-decade, Dempsey, a man truly in tune with his era and the growing importance of media exposure, had appeared in as many movies as championship bouts.

Radio, as station managers found out, could also be intimidating, even to boxers; the light-heavyweight champion, Mike McTigue, went so far as to declare during a visit to WGY in Schenectady, New York, that he would rather get into the ring and battle the Manassa Mauler than have to speak into a radio microphone.

Though Jack Dempsey the celebrity remained in the headlines amid speculation about when he might return to the ring, his scheming manager, Tex Rickard, who actively promoted other fighters and bouts, announced in November 1924 that he was banning radio broadcasts of any fight his client was involved in. His reason was simple: economics. Rickard claimed radio coverage was so satisfying to the fight fan at home that attendance at bouts had decreased. As he saw it, the fight fan at home was not paying for his entertainment, and that wasn't fair to the fighters and, more important, to the promoter.

Rickard's pronouncement was hotly debated and a resolution of the stalemate was sought, but in the end a promoter did have the absolute right to decide if his events could be exploited for another industry's benefit. Then in January 1926, Rickard surprised the radio and sports worlds by announcing he would radiocast events from Madison Square Garden from a station with studios in the Garden itself. This announcement came just after Commerce Secretary Hoover, hoping to spur Congress to write new legislation that would relieve the congestion in the airwaves, placed a moratorium on new radio licenses. In need of a frequency and without the ability to get the government to allocate one, Rickard bought WWGL from the Radio Engineering Corporation of Richmond Hill, New York. When asked about the apparent conflict with his earlier position of banning radio, and then acquiring a station, his spokesperson said: "It has never been a question of Tex Rickard being opposed to broadcasting on the grounds that people did not go to the fights because they could hear them over the radio. He believes broadcasting of sporting events is all right, if they are properly handled. What he opposed was the propaganda started by some factions in radio that listening-in was just as good as seeing the fight."

Two months later the new facility, which asked for and was given the call letters WMSG—Madison Square Garden—was in the final stages of construction. Rickard claimed he had changed his position about radio because of "the numerous requests which had come to him from shut-ins and disabled war veterans who were unable to attend these events." On April 5, 1926, while the Ringling Brothers and Barnum and Bailey Circus was in the middle of their annual Madison Square Garden engagement, WMSG debuted with a varied program of talks and music. The speakers included James A. Farley of the New York State Athletic Commission, John Ringling of circus fame, and Tex Rickard himself. The only details given out about the station's future was that it would be devoted to broadcasting sporting events.

Rickard now had control over radiocasts of his sporting events, which increased his already considerable leverage as a promoter. He then announced plans to build an outdoor complex that would seat more than 100,000 people, as well as an agreement with New York Yankees owner Colonel Jacob Ruppert to present championship bouts at the big stadium in the Bronx, making Rickard the greatest sports promoter of his time. But all of these announcements paled in comparison to Rickard's greatest 1926 promotion: Jack Dempsey's defense of his heavyweight title.

The bout, scheduled for September 23, 1926, would be part of the nation's sesquicentennial celebration in Philadelphia. Gene Tunney, a former Marine with a handsome face, elegant stature, and a bookish nature, was the challenger. Unlike Dempsey, who was a boxer through and through and loved his tough, average-guy image, boxing to Tunney was a way to better things: fame, fortune, business success, and a socially upward marriage. This fight was to be *the* event of the year, and Rickard made sure everyone who was anyone would be in attendance. But as the date neared, the main subject of debate was whether Rickard would allow a broadcast from ringside. Well into September, the radiocast remained in doubt, and Rickard made it clear that the right to broadcast this spectacle had a real value, and $50,000 was the sum he would accept from any station, individual, or advertiser interested in buying the radio rights. As the fight neared, leaders of the radio industry, at Secretary Hoover's invitation, were meeting at New York's Astor Hotel trying to help craft legislation to organize the airwaves. At the end of one session, George C. Furness of the National Carbon Company made a motion seeking the authority to raise the $50,000 demanded by Tex Rickard. The motion was never seconded.

Meanwhile, negotiations between Rickard and the RCA-owned stations WEAF and WJZ went down to the wire, with the radio stations threatening that if the rights were not made available they would still broadcast a round-by-round description using copy furnished by newswire services. Rickard retaliated, declaring the fight was a "private show" and banning any newspaper or reporter from covering the event. But Rickard was trumped by the Sesquicentennial Committee, which declared that if the newspapers were barred, then Rickard's rights to hold the fight at Sesquicentennial Stadium would be revoked. With just two days to go, the standoff ended when the rights to broadcast the bout on a network of stations covering about two-thirds of the country were purchased by the Royal Typewriter Company of New York. Rickard received only $15,000, but he increased his take by having the bout rebroadcast in Madison Square Garden, where fans without access to a radio had to pay an admission fee just to hear the call of the fight over loudspeakers.

On the day before the bout, as the network of stations was still being wired together, WEAF and WJZ announced that veteran boxing announcer Andrew White would call the fight, assisted by announcer Graham McNamee. Without doubt, the contest was *the* event of the sesquicentennial: Political leaders, including senators and governors; business leaders such as Hearst, Rockefeller, Mellon, Schwab, and Pulitzer; and Hollywood stars like Tom Mix, Charlie Chaplin, Norma Talmadge, and Flo Ziegfeld streamed into Philadelphia to be among the more than 132,000 people in attendance, a number that paled in comparison to a radio audience estimated to be greater than 15 million listeners.

Andrew White's descriptions captured every move the boxers made:

The champion can't stand this. He seems to be contemptuous of Tunney's punches, but he can't take them all night. They go into a clinch. There is no whirlwind stuff at all in Jack Dempsey. He takes two rights on the jaw. Tunney crosses with the right. Dempsey smashes with a left hook, but just a glancing blow with no steam behind it.

On the morning after the fight, the *New York Times* printed a verbatim transcript of White and McNamee's call, and while the blow by blow was thrilling, McNamee's scene setting had added tremendous visual color to the audio event.

Gene is standing in the corner of the ring now. He has got probably the most up-to-date covering in the bathrobe line that has ever been seen in the history of the prize ring. On the back he has a gigantic emblem of the marines. It is not a bathrobe. It is a dressing gown with a red back.

At the end of the ten-round slugfest, Dempsey was listless, and from the descriptions the radio audience could tell a new champion would be crowned. Moments later, Andrew White was at ringside getting the first statement from the new champ, Gene Tunney: *I have realized all my ambition, and I will try to defend the title that I have worked so hard for six years, and I am going to try to defend it as becomes a marine.*

The fight and the radiocast were huge successes, causing one of radio's harshest and most famous critics, Thomas Alva Edison, a prominent voice among those who believed radio's popularity was no more than a fad, to admit that the broadcast, which he must have had trouble hearing since he was nearly deaf, was "quite satisfactory." Tunney was champ, but Rickard was king, especially when less than a year later Dempsey climbed back into the ring to fight Jack Sharkey, this time at Yankee Stadium.

IF YOU CAN'T SEE THE BIG BOUT—*you can hear it on a Radiola*

So proclaimed an RCA newspaper ad. All it took was an RCA Radiola, and any fan could enjoy "one of the most interesting bouts in all heavyweight history." By signaling that the winner of this fight would get a shot at champion Tunney, Rickard again created a frenzy, intensified by the fact that this would be the first bout carried by the stations of the newly formed NBC network. A sudden convert to the promotional value of radio, at least for now, Rickard told the press, "I am for broadcasting. It is a boon to boxing."

On the night of July 21, 1927, more than 80,000 fans filled Yankee Stadium, while a network of fifty stations crisscrossing the entire country were standing by, ready to air the call. Sharkey, the only man to fight both Dempsey and Joe Louis, had earned professional boxing's number-three ranking and thus the chance to fight Dempsey. The bout lasted only seven rounds as Dempsey knocked Sharkey out, setting up the desired rematch between Dempsey and Tunney. Six weeks later, Tex Rickard announced that Chicago would be the site for the rematch and that NBC was seeking the rights to handle the radio coverage. But the newer radio network, CBS, was not going to acquiesce so easily, and its leverage came from the fact that Andrew White, who was the nation's premier fight caller, was their employee. But NBC eventually did secure the rights from Rickard, and the job of announcing the action went to Graham McNamee.

It was the most anticipated event of the year, even trumping Charles Lindbergh's triumphant return from Paris that had so captivated America earlier in June. "The athletic carnivals of the Greeks and the Romans will pale into insignificance when Gene Tunney and Jack Dempsey step into the ring at 10 P.M. to fight for the heavyweight championship of the world," enthused the *New York Times*. On the night of September 22, America tuned their radios to their local NBC affiliate to hear Graham McNamee, assisted by Philips Carlin, call the fight. Even the convicts in the death house at Sing Sing were granted the special privilege of hearing the bout, as were the participants at a double wedding in Bloomingdale, New Jersey, who postponed their ceremony for two days so that the celebrants could listen to the fight. Apparently the only person who wasn't going to listen was the champ's wife, Estelle Dempsey, who vowed to remain in her hotel room with a companion. She planned to spend her energies pulling for her husband and hoping neither boxer would be injured.

Sensing the magnitude of the event, more than 1,200 newspapers contracted to have wire reports of the bout flashed from ringside directly to them, while sixty newspapers that also owned radio stations arranged to have the Associated Press reports wired directly to their stations' studios so written descriptions of the fight could be read and transmitted. But nothing could be as powerful as Graham McNamee's resonant voice calling directly from ringside, which was sent out by a network of at least seventy stations to more than 50 million people.

The captivating bout was highlighted by the famous seventh-round long count, during which a staggered Tunney received more than the allotted ten seconds to recover because Dempsey hadn't returned to his corner:

Tunney is down! Tunney is down from a barrage of lefts and rights to the face. The fight is going on. Tunney is down. Dempsey is on the other side of him; they are counting—six, seven, eight, nine, and Tunney is up and now they are at it again.

The battle continued through the tenth round; Tunney had again outlasted the former champ. As Dempsey left the ring, McNamee tried to get a comment for the radio audience, but the angry fighter just stormed by and left without a word. The next day it was reported that Estelle Dempsey, who had sworn not to listen to the bout, had collapsed in her hotel suite. "Everything seemed well until near the end of the eighth round, when the tide turned to Tunney. Mrs. Dempsey became hysterical, ordered the radio shut off and locked herself in the bathroom. At the pleadings of the nurse Mrs. Dempsey ordered the radio turned on again and remained there until the decision was announced."

Though he called the event a huge success, Tex Rickard again claimed radio had hurt his profits. Nonetheless, he declared that radio must continue its relationship with boxing because the exposure was good for the sport. "Radio is one of the most wonderful things in the world. I would not be at all surprised if radio television would be developed within a comparatively short time, to the point where it could be applied to fights along with the broadcasting of the announcer's voice from ringside."

For the next two years, Tex Rickard's love/hate relationship with radio continued. When Tunney defended his crown against Tom Heeney in July 1928, McNamee and Carlin were ringside at Yankee Stadium to call the fight over the NBC network, but when the contest ended with Tunney retaining his crown, Rickard again banned broadcasts of bouts, claiming radio had ruined the show. His chief complaint stemmed from the fact that boxing had made millions of dollars for the radio manufacturers while returning virtually nothing to fight promoters. He urged the industry to find a way to reimburse promoters equitably. The next morning he received several small checks from radio fight fans hoping to defray his losses and thus keep boxing on the air. Rickard returned the money.

The other dominant theme of 1928 and 1929 was Jack Dempsey's rumored return to the ring. He was a legend, and fight fans, many of whom believed he'd been robbed in 1927, craved his return. Dempsey's every move was news, and when CBS's Ted Husing interviewed him on May 4, 1929, the story of his radio appearance was the lead item in that day's radio column. Despite immense pressure to return, Dempsey's retirement from the ring was permanent, especially after the sudden death of his promoter, Tex Rickard, in June 1929. That summer Dempsey appeared as part of a touring vaudeville show in which he merely went on stage and talked; his larger-than-life persona made any appearance by the former champ an event. After Dempsey arrived in San Francisco, his immense popularity was proven when a crowd of "several hundred admirers surrounded him and neglected nearly fifty movie stars who arrived on the same train." His brief stage career ended at the end of the summer of 1929, and on October 2 Dempsey became a member of the media, premiering his own radio boxing show and taking to the mike to describe the bout between Jackie Fields and Vince Dundee.

In October 1929, station and network program managers, desperately missing the audience draw of major prize-fight radiocasts, were trying to find a way to get the important boxing matches back on the air. At the heart of the problem was economics: Who was going to pay for the rights to air the fights? What had been learned during the previous eight years was that radio and boxing needed Jack Dempsey, or someone with his magnetism and appeal, to generate excitement and build the audience and the radio business. It was a lesson radio and baseball would inadvertently heed. It was fortunate that on January 2, 1920, the Boston Red Sox sold a hefty, left-handed pitcher to the New York Yankees. New York, Yankee Stadium, the World Series, Babe Ruth, and radio would together be an unbeatable combination.

BASEBALL

When the Chicago White Sox won the 1919 World Series, everything seemed to be just fine with the American pastime. The sport was poised to enter the 1920s more popular than ever, and by selling Babe Ruth to the New York Yankees, the Boston Red Sox put the sport's biggest star in the largest market; it was a marketing bonanza. Without a home of their own, the Yankees played their games at the Polo Grounds, which they rented from their crosstown rivals, the New York Giants. But despite improving attendance and a country enjoying the benefits of a booming postwar economy, a black cloud formed over baseball when eight members of the world champion White Sox were charged with throwing the 1919 series. The trial, which failed to convict a single player yet led to the banishment from the game of all those accused, dragged on into 1921. The accusations, the direct link between the players and gamblers, and the negative feeling created by the incident left baseball in need of something to revive the public's flagging trust.

During the autumn of 1921 New York's WJZ, which was partially owned by Westinghouse, debuted. Announcer Tommy Cowan's voice was the first heard: *You are listening to the radio telephone broadcasting station WJZ in Newark, New Jersey.* Cowan repeated the sign-on several times, but doubted anyone was actually hearing his voice. Shortly after its debut, WJZ sent announcer Sandy Hunt to the Polo Grounds to report on the World Series between the New York Giants and the Yankees; it was the first intracity championship battle, and the Yankees' first-ever postseason appearance, all of which was enhanced by the notion that this was a battle between the old guard—the Giants—and the upstarts, with their brawny lineup newspapers had dubbed Murderers' Row.

The series generated excitement throughout New York, so much so that a crowd of over 15,000 jammed Times Square to see game updates posted on a huge apparatus that reproduced every play made in the World Series, while another 10,000 people who'd bought tickets went to Madison Square Garden, only to see a mechanical simulation of the game played out with little pieces moving around a board. But because so few people had radios, WJZ's coverage garnered little attention, although game one did spur this mention:

The new station of the Westinghouse Electric and Manufacturing Company in Newark was also busy broadcasting the results of the game. The bulletins, which were received as part of the wireless service of a Newark paper, were sent out over a radius of 200 miles. This service has been established for the entire series. Each day the play-by-play bulletins will be sent out as the game progresses.

Anyone who happened to be tuned to WJZ that afternoon heard staff announcer Tommy Cowan, who was in the station's studio, simply repeat Sandy Hunt's descriptions of what was happening at the Polo Grounds, which had been relayed to the studio by telephone. Despite the relative immediacy of delivery, the broadcast lacked the thrill of hearing the ambient noise and was probably only slightly more interesting than what could be heard in Roosevelt Hospital, which used a system of ringing bells to tell the games' stories: The sequence, repetition, and length of rings delineated the inning and the score so doctors and patients could know what was going on.

Despite the buildup and the excitement of the contests, in the end Babe Ruth's injuries kept him out of the last games of the series, and the Giants held off the upstart Yankees to win five games to three.

While big-ticket events like the World Series were just what big-city radio broadcasters and radio manufacturers needed to help get the industry going, local stations all across America were experimenting with sports programming of their own. In August 1922, responding to requests from listeners who wanted to hear reports about local sports, WJAM in Iowa sent announcer Bert Puckett to a Cedar Rapids Raiders baseball game, but the owners of the team, afraid radio coverage would reduce attendance, wouldn't allow Puckett into the stadium. Not wanting to disappoint his listeners, Puckett stood on a nearby roof from where he could see the field. Perched high above the action, Puckett gave his play-by-play.

While the idea of covering baseball games on the radio was intriguing, the day-to-day sameness of the games wasn't going to generate the necessary buzz. Radio needed a captivating, special World Series. Other than being shortened to a best-of-seven contest, the 1922 series looked a lot like 1921's, with one exception: The opponents were the same, the venue was the same, but radio had evolved from a virtually unnoticed experiment to a force to be reckoned with. Before the first pitch of the 1922 World Series was thrown, WJZ announced it would broadcast direct from the Polo Grounds with sportswriter Grantland Rice not only announcing every play as it happened, but also giving "his opinions of the game and comment on all interesting occurrences." With WJZ connected by wire to WGY in Schenectady, and WBZ in West Springfield, Massachusetts, the size of the potential radio audience was estimated at more than 5 million people. Moreover, so the broadcasts could be easily received, all the other broadcasting stations in the New York area agreed to shut down during the games, leaving WJZ a clear spectrum. Baseball was made for the instantaneousness of radio; commenting on its incredible immediacy, the *New York Times* remarked, "The tremendous speed of the radio waves, 186,000 miles a second, will carry the world's series of 1922 around the world seven and one-half times a second, so that if Babe Ruth drives out a home run the radio listeners will know as soon as the ball drops in the bleachers, and before Babe crosses the home plate."

The De Forest Radio Company seized this opportunity to sell radios. In a large ad that appeared the day before the 1922 World Series began, De Forest proclaimed:

NEVER MIND THOSE WORLD SERIES TICKETS.
You're Going to All the Games—You're Going to Thrill with Every Big Play that is Made—At Home!

Unfortunately for the Yankees, the series was far from thrilling; they were crushed by the Giants in four games. Even worse for the Yanks, Babe Ruth failed miserably, going just two for seventeen with no home runs, and even though the radiocasts seemed to be popular, only the first two games of the series were aired.

When the next regular season ended, the same teams reigned; the 1923 series again featured the Giants and the Yankees, but this time the series would be played in two venues: the Polo Grounds and the brand-new Yankee Stadium. The series was billed as a rematch between the brilliance of Giants' manager John McGraw and the brawn of Babe Ruth. WJZ would again broadcast the games, but this time WEAF and a string of other stations as far north as Providence, Rhode Island, and as far south as Washington, D.C., would also carry reports of the contests. WJZ again hired Grantland Rice to provide the play-by-play, and staying competitive, WEAF chose sportswriter Bill McGeehan to announce the action, which was a disappointment to Graham McNamee, who wanted the plum assignment.

This was an eagerly anticipated World Series, and in Washington, radio shops were using the broadcasts heard on WCAP to sell more radios.

2 P.M. TODAY WORLD SERIES; *You are invited to listen-in.*
Today and during the series at our store.
The Broadcast Shop.

Or if you preferred listening in the privacy of your home, Lansburgh and Brother would sell you a compact Audiola receiving set for as little as ten dollars.

The series opened on October 10 at Yankee Stadium, by far baseball's largest and most beautiful cathedral. The crowd of 55,307 that filed in that afternoon included many notables, politicians, and motion-picture actresses eager to be part of the event. The game was a dramatic, tense affair. Tied 4–4 in the ninth inning, Casey Stengel stepped to the plate and smacked an inside-the-park home run to give the Giants the win. The game completely consumed the city; trading on Wall Street was the "dullest experienced in a period of weeks. The outcome of the World Series game was a matter of more concern in speculative circles than was the buying or selling of stocks."

Back at the Polo Grounds, game two was another tight struggle that the Yankees won 4–3 with two Babe Ruth home runs leading the offense. The action returned to Yankee Stadium for game three; the first four innings were a pitchers' duel between the Giants' Art Nehf and the Yankees' Sam Jones. But in the fourth inning an odd thing happened in the WEAF broadcast booth that would change radio history. Sportswriter Bill McGeehan had reached his limit; the great writer was unable to go on describing the action, or lack thereof, and quit, leaving Graham McNamee to step in. McNamee later wrote:

I found myself more than ever falling back on general description. And that is where the imagination comes in—not that we invent, but it takes something of the imaginative faculty to make the quieter times vivid and to avoid the old hackneyed, and boresome expressions. You must make each of your listeners, though miles away from the spot, feel that he or she, too, is there with you in that press stand, watching the movements of the game, the color, and flags; the pop-bottles thrown in the air; the straw hats demolished; Gloria Swanson just arriving in her new ermine coat; McGraw in the dugout, apparently motionless but giving signals all the time.

McNamee called the remaining games of the series—won by the Yankees 4–2—and was the natural choice to be the voice of the 1924 World Series, which pitted the Giants against the Washington Senators. For the first time a city other than New York would be the host for a fall classic heard over the radio, and Washington-area retailers benefited; with the games at Griffith Stadium sold out, sales of radios in the Washington area increased by a whopping 50 percent. Advertisements about radios available in time for World Series delivery filled the newspapers. There was a radio for every fan and every budget; at the Doubleday-Hill Electric Company you could buy an RCA Radiola for as little as $35 or for as much as $425, with seven models between those price points. Even President Coolidge, aboard the yacht *Mayflower,* listened to the second game, and when Washington won by scoring a run in the bottom of the ninth inning, the president sent a congratulatory message to the Senators' manager, Bucky Harris. It was a close, well-played series won by Washington in the twelfth inning of game seven. The attention the series brought to radio was expressed by one writer, who called radio's rush into everyday life "one of the miracles of the age."

"GOVERNMENT BUSINESS suffered virtual paralysis after 2 o'clock yesterday afternoon," reported the *Washington Post* on October 8, 1925. The reason? The World Series game between the Senators and the Pittsburgh Pirates was airing on radio. Annoyed by the behavior of federal workers, Secretary of the Interior Hubert Work—there never was a more fitting name—ordered his employees to log the time they'd spent listening to the game so their pay could be adjusted downward. Graham McNamee, who was already being referred to as a "veteran announcer," anchored the series coverage, but since some Washingtonians were still without radios of their own, crowds gathered every afternoon in front of the *Washington Post'*s offices, where a large magnetic board showed a re-creation of the game as loudspeakers aired WCAP's broadcast of McNamee's descriptions and his trademark opening phrase, *Good evening, ladies and gentlemen of the radio audience.*

The 1925 series was another thriller; Pittsburgh beat Washington's legendary pitcher Walter Johnson in game seven, taking the crown four games to three. As a radio event, the series was another triumph, especially for McNamee, whose talent for filling pregnant pauses led more than 50,000 listeners to write in and express their delight at being able to almost see the game through his eyes. The famous critic, columnist, and member of the Algonquin Round Table, Heywood Broun, wrote of McNamee:

He did a swell job. To a great extent it was a piece of acting. Not only did you get the full detail of the actual happenings upon the field, but the emotion of the moment came over. The roar of the crowd carried an informing eloquence.

In the autumn of 1926, the New York Yankees, starring Babe Ruth and a supporting cast that included Earle Combs, Joe Dugan, and Lou Gehrig, returned to the World Series to face the St. Louis Cardinals. WEAF was again the principal radio station, but it was now part of the NBC network, so its coverage of the game was relayed to a network of twenty-five stations that reached an audience estimated at more than 1.5 million people. If there were any doubts as to radio's growing impact, the fact that almost no one bought tickets to Tex Rickard's Madison Square Garden re-creation of the games told the tale. The success of the radiocasts led one New York newspaper columnist to note that the city got its World Series reports with its thrills and its "disappointments just as poignantly as of yore; but in privacy, for these are the days of the radio."

The 1926 series was another seesaw struggle; the Cardinals led two games to one when game four was played in St. Louis. Listening from his sickbed in Essex Falls, New Jersey, was eleven-year-old John Dale Sylvester, a baseball fan stricken with blood poisoning. His case was dire and doctors were not optimistic, but after listening to the game— a Yankee 10–5 blowout—and the encouragement sent by Ruth and other Yankees who had been informed of the boy's plight, Johnny showed improvement. The physicians claimed the boy's recovery began when he learned the news of Ruth's three home runs.

When the series returned to Yankee Stadium for game six, an improved Johnny Sylvester predicted his hero would again homer, but he would be disappointed, as St. Louis won the contest 10–2 behind the superb pitching of Grover Alexander, which set up a deciding game seven.

We are going to have a cold game. It is cold; it is dreary; it is dark; it is dripping; it is damp and thick and all that, but it doesn't make any difference, you can't dampen the ardor of a real baseball fan.

So began Graham McNamee and Philips Carlin's broadcast of game seven. In the third inning the Yankees struck:

Here it is—a long drive into the right field, and a home run! There you are, a long drive into the right field bleachers, making the score 1–0 in favor of the Yankees, amidst a terrific noise. Babe Ruth comes in after a slow jogging trip around the circuit, bows and takes off his hat to the crowd.

In the fourth inning St. Louis scored three runs; the Yankees answered with a single run in the sixth and it remained 3–2 until the bottom of the ninth. With two out there was a classic confrontation between Grover Alexander and Babe Ruth; not wanting to surrender a tying home run, Alexander walked Ruth, bringing up Bob Meusel. However, the Babe was thrown out trying to steal second base, bringing the game and the series to a sudden end.

The world series of 1926—we will never say it again—is over. It has come to a close, and the championship goes west, southwest, down to the sovereign State of Missouri.

As to little John Dale Sylvester, there were some fans who believed the entire incident was invented by an oversentimental press corps looking for a good story. What is certain is that Johnny Sylvester was a real person, that he recovered from his illness, and that he died in 1990 at age seventy-four.

COMING OFF HIS record-setting sixty-home-run season, Babe Ruth and his teammates were devastating, beating the Pirates in four straight to win the 1927 World Series. Both of America's national radio networks, NBC and CBS, sent descriptions of every play of the series through the airwaves to an audience of millions. Sensing the encroaching power of radio, one columnist noted that in theory a hundred million Americans could tune in on the Yankees and Pirates "without waiting for the box score or the detailed account, with the moral. This is one limitation to broadcasting against the printed word. It is evanescent. The radio is a message, but it is not a record. Mr. McNamee's words are writ in a thinner medium even than water; they are written in air." Perhaps he should have consulted with his editors, who every morning following a series game saw the benefits of printing Graham McNamee's calls, word for word, for their readers.

The next year, the Yankees were again American League champs, and the 1928 series was a rematch of the 1926 battle against the St. Louis Cardinals, only this time the Yankees walloped the Cardinals in four games. Since there were no exclusive rights to the series, any radio station could air the games, which resulted in more coverage than ever before. In New York alone, five stations—WEAF, WJZ, WNYC, WABC, and WOR—carried the series. The national networks, linked by more than fifty stations, provided radio coverage from coast to coast and border to border, entertaining millions of people, many of whom found the highlight of the series to be a game-four, three-home-run effort by the Babe. What made it so special was his second homer, which followed an argument that erupted when pitcher Bill Sherdel attempted to sneak an illegal quick pitch past the Babe. The home plate umpire's call enraged the Cardinals' manager, Bill McKechnie, who argued so loudly that his shouts were picked up by the microphones. The incident was made even sweeter for New York fans when Sherdel's next pitch was followed by *Here it comes! My, what a hit! It's over the fence.*

By 1929 BASEBALL was a fixture on radio stations in every corner of the country. So ubiquitous was radio coverage that in Washington listeners complained that games were being aired every day, not by one station but by three. They couldn't understand why this sports programming, which took time away from other programs, was necessary. "Will you please give a reason for these stations all going full blast on this one subject? No other city acts so crazy over its team and have better ones. [signed] A score of disgusted listeners."

At season's end the American League champs were the Philadelphia Athletics, and the National League standard-bearers were the Chicago Cubs. Both networks aired the series, with McNamee at his post for NBC and relative newcomer Ted Husing anchoring for CBS. Played between October 8 and October 14, the series lacked the star power and sparkle of previous years. Nonetheless, radio manufacturers still found a new way to use the series and its players to sell their wares. In what may have been the first athlete endorsement, the Majestic Radio Company announced that eight of the Philadelphia players, including star first baseman Jimmy Foxx, owned Majestic radios: *My Majestic gives me more than you would expect of any radio—and then some. When it comes to radios, I choose Majestic every time. It's a great set.*

Radio's first decade as part of baseball ended on October 14 when, rallying for three runs in the bottom of the ninth, Philadelphia beat Chicago 3–2, to take the series 4–1. When the excited winning team left the field, waiting for them, microphone in hand, was Graham McNamee: *This is Graham McNamee down under the stands again, a little bit out of breath, as we came down pretty fast. I am going to ask some of the boys if they won't say just a word to tell you how they feel in regard to winning the series.* Six of the Athletics spoke with McNamee, sharing their jubilation with listeners who must have felt as though they were there with the celebrants.

But not everyone celebrated. In Bayonne, New Jersey, fifty-eight-year-old Frank Drudy collapsed while listening to the winning Philadelphia rally. Before the game ended, he was dead. Similar reports of sudden death while listening on the radio to the Cubs' loss were reported from Maine and Chicago. However, despite some individual tragedies, the marriage between baseball and radio was consummated and total as the roar of the 1920s began to fade.

COLLEGE FOOTBALL

In the November 9, 1923, edition of the *New York Times,* Gunther's furriers on Fifth Avenue and Thirty-sixth Street advertised men's raccoon coats that "will be worn wherever football is played." The ad also listed that week's big games: Princeton vs. Harvard at Princeton, and Cornell vs. Columbia at the Polo Grounds. College football was big, so big that Gunther's extended "a cordial invitation to our patrons, their friends and college men who cannot attend the games to visit our Men's Department, Third Floor, to hear the returns of the games, play by play, on the radio."

Men wearing raccoon coats watching Ivy League football today is a clichéd image that goes with the flasks, flappers, and fads central to the Roaring Twenties. But college football was more than a fad; it was a frenzy that by mid-decade had insinuated itself into all aspects of the mass media. Newspaper coverage of college football dominated the sports pages throughout the fall season; radio latched onto college football for audience building; and in 1925 Hollywood's comedic genius, Harold Lloyd, brought the two fads—radio and football— together in his film *The Freshman.* In this silent classic, Lloyd plays Harold Lamb, a college freshman with dreams of being a football star; but alas, he is relegated to scrub status. In what must have been an oddly familiar scene at that time, Lamb's father, a rampant radio enthusiast, is seen tinkering with his receiving equipment when he hears strange whooping sounds. He deludes himself in the belief that he has reached some far-distant country, only to discover that what he is actually hearing are the odd yells of his college-football-mad son cheering in his room.

The initial union between radio and college football, like so many other firsts, took place at Pittsburgh's KDKA when, in 1921, Harold Arlin described the game between the University of Pittsburgh Panthers and the University of West Virginia Mountaineers, an intense annual rivalry known as the Backyard Brawl, a battle won that year by Pittsburgh, 21–14. The radiocast seemed to be a onetime experiment, but as radio stations popped up across the country, the regionality of college football became a logical program source for station owners eager to fill on-air hours. College football provided steady, weekly content that was of special interest to local listeners.

One of the greatest challenges of football radiocasts was the actual announcing. For one thing, unlike baseball, college football was played in inclement and cold weather, and since none of the stadiums of the era had broadcast booths, the announcers were literally left out in the cold, often broadcasting from temporary scaffolding erected near the field. Grantland Rice tried announcing a football game once and decided, given the number of players involved in each play and the pace of the game, that it was simply too demanding. During the 1922 season, a highly anticipated contest was the battle at Chicago's Stagg Field between Chicago and Princeton. From a newly constructed, soundproof booth atop the stadium, an announcer relayed descriptions of the game into a telephone circuit linked to the local phone company lines. Those lines traveled more than 1,000 miles to WEAF's studios in New York, where the descriptions were then transmitted over the air. To draw more attention to radio, the station sent a truck equipped with an antenna to Park Row, where it relayed the game over loudspeakers to a crowd of listeners. The show was so successful that the station decided that from then on it would broadcast the most important eastern game every Saturday afternoon.

But college football was more than just a game, it was a spirited event; radio managers learned that merely to describe the game was not enough; radiocasts needed to capture the atmosphere as well so the radio audience would not only hear the plays the moment they were made, but the cheering and the rousing college songs as well.

The 1922 successes set the stage for 1923, and Graham McNamee, who, too, found the action and number of players difficult to keep straight, was ready for the challenge. When he assumed the mike for the 1923 season, he was aided by an associate who sat near him to serve as an extra pair of eyes. This "spotter" then whispered vital information that made it possible for McNamee to announce the game rapidly and eliminate the long pauses he would have needed as he sorted out what had just happened. This need for reporting accuracy also forced changes on the game itself. So that announcers seated above the field could easily determine where the ball was placed or where a player had gone out of bounds, the markings on the field were enlarged and made clearer. And since the game was being announced instantly to an audience that couldn't see what was happening, the referees and officials learned to relay penalty signals quickly and clearly so the radio audience could be kept au courant with the action.

While college football coverage in the New York area was focused on a few schools—primarily the Ivy League, Army, Navy, Notre Dame, and a handful of others—colleges in other sections of the country began to broadcast games. In 1924 the University of Michigan initiated radio coverage over Detroit's WWJ. On October 18 anyone listening to the game between Michigan and the University of Illinois at Champaign had to be stunned by what they heard, as Harold "Red" Grange, the Galloping Ghost, scored four touchdowns in the first twelve minutes, which was as many touchdowns as the vaunted Michigan defense had given up during the previous two seasons. At game's end, Grange had amassed 402 yards and was on his way to being one of college football's and radio's biggest stars. Author Damon Runyon was moved to write: "This man Grange of Illinois is three or four men rolled into one for football purposes. He is Jack Dempsey, Babe Ruth, Al Jolson, Paavo Nurmi and Man o' War. Put together, they spell Grange."

At the outset of the 1925 season, the need to report quickly and accurately, to translate the collegiate intensity of the game on the field to the now significant at-home audience, forced broadcasters to make another major adjustment. Realizing the task of reporting the constant stream of plays was too great for one announcer, WEAF teamed McNamee with Philips Carlin, "employing for the first time in sports announcing a new technique of cooperative announcing." McNamee and Carlin became known as the Twin Announcers as they worked together, filling in, discussing, describing, and helping each other to bring listeners a constant stream of information that kept up with the game's fast pace.

By the end of the 1926 season, college football on the radio had become an American Saturday afternoon ritual, a habit that even extended to the White House, where President Coolidge forsook his usual Saturday afternoon practice of working at his desk so he could listen to the Army-Navy game. Although everything seemed ideal with the arrangement between colleges and radio—especially since many colleges owned the stations over which their games were broadcast—trouble was brewing, especially in the Midwest.

As the 1927 season was set to open, the University of Iowa began questioning the real impact of radio broadcasts. Following Tex Rickard's example and driven by the belief that radio was hurting attendance, the university canceled the WSUI radiocasts of their games. But that action led to so many complaints from radio fans that the edict was reversed and the radiocasts resumed. The debate over radio's effect on revenue continued throughout the season and even into the next, but by year's end radio had found another stellar event to get listeners to tune in: the Rose Bowl. The import of that particular game, unlike today where there is a bowl game for every sponsor with money to spend, was that the Rose Bowl was the only bowl game played at the time, and it was always an East-West battle. In 1928 the opponents were the University of Pittsburgh and Stanford University, and at the NBC microphone for this coast-to-coast hookup was Graham McNamee.

Played on January 2, 1928, the Rose Bowl radiocast featured Mc-Namee's descriptions of Pasadena's Tournament of Roses parade—its flowered floats, the huge crowds, and all the rest of the splendid pageantry—along with special greetings from the broadcast booth to the national audience by such luminaries as Jack Dempsey, Estelle Taylor, and Colleen Moore. Of course, by this time, Graham McNamee was himself a national star.

Despite the ongoing debate over radio's impact on attendance, the last two years of the decade were prosperous, with more games aired and more people listening. To a degree, the beginning of the college football season marked the beginning of the autumn radio season. When the 1920s drew to a close, Harold Lloyd was starring in another comedy, *Welcome Danger,* a Paramount talking picture; Douglas Fairbanks and Loretta Young were teamed in *The Forward Pass,* which was billed as "a college football romance"; Graham McNamee had become a household name; and football fans from coast to coast no longer had to brave the elements to enjoy their favorite college team. They could stay at home and listen to the radio.

Chapter 9

▲▲▲▲▲▲▲▲▲▲▲▲▲

JUNE 1927—The cruiser *Memphis* steamed across the Atlantic. On-board was Captain Charles Lindbergh, returning to the United States after his successful transatlantic flight. This dashing young man in his flying machine was the embodiment of the bold, adventurous spirit that seemed to define the 1920s, and Americans wanted to get to know him. Radio, with its magical ability to bring distant sounds into homes across the country, would be a central component linking the hero with legions of new, adoring fans. Lindbergh's return was a boon for radio. A hero's welcome, speeches, accolades, and parades were just the kind of events that made people tune in to their favorite radio station, and Lindbergh's return had all the elements that made for dramatic programming. What no one anticipated was that Lindbergh's return would also produce radio's first scoop. The scoop, such that it was, occurred as the cruiser made its way toward the eastern seaboard. From their location in Virginia Beach, radio station WSEA initiated coverage of the ship and its escort's progress. From the moment the convoy was visible to the announcer positioned at the station's rooftop studio, listeners heard descriptions of every detail of the ship's progress, right until it passed into the waters of the Chesapeake Bay to continue its voyage up the Potomac to Washington, and to the celebrations awaiting Lucky Lindy.

WSEA station manager George L. Sutherland Jr. described the scoop and the audience's reaction this way: "The angle of the story which we had to give proved more a bit of spot news than something which was definitely arranged. For our work, we have been favored with hundreds of telegrams and undoubtedly will receive within the next two or three days a large amount of mail."

Despite the popularity of the coverage, spot news, as Sutherland described it, was still a rarity in 1927. Even with radio's instantaneous speed of dissemination, the ability to cover news with that same immediacy was not something radio stations were equipped to handle; during the 1920s that kind of on-the-spot coverage was taken care of exclusively by newspapers eager to sell extra editions. Since stations themselves were not really making any profit—the bulk of the money was being made by radio manufacturers—most stations employed little more than a skeleton on-air crew. Stations scrounged for programming to fill whatever hours they were on the air, and spending money on news reporters was unheard of.

Ironically, the radio coverage of Lucky Lindy's return in June 1927 became itself one of the biggest news stories of the year. But from 1920 until 1927, radio news coverage, and radio's relationship to the established and powerful print-news media, would be slow to develop, encumbered as it was by many issues and problems that needed to be resolved.

IN A SENSE, KDKA's reporting of the 1920 presidential election returns *was* the first news broadcast, but that auspicious beginning did not spur fledgling radio stations to hire newsmen to sniff out stories and report on them as they happened. The spontaneous nature of hard news—crimes, accidents, weather events, and the other kinds of stories that cause today's 24-hour news organizations to interrupt regular programming with special bulletins—required manpower, and stations didn't have the resources, the inclination, or the talent available. Furthermore, since stations, especially in the earliest days of radio, were only on the air a few hours each day, there was no guarantee that breaking news could be aired in a timely manner. Radio's inability to handle news efficiently allowed the newspapers and their extra editions to remain the primary source for news. However, during its infancy, radio became an ideal vehicle for the dissemination of other kinds of information helpful to different elements of America's far-flung and diverse population.

The first and most obvious items useful to listeners were weather reports. From the outset, this staple of local newscasting provided stations with content relevant to every listener. More important, in most parts of the country the regularly changing weather meant listeners would tune in multiple times for updates. America's farmers, whose livelihoods depended on being able to react quickly to changes in weather conditions, found radio particularly beneficial.

As an experiment, on April 15, 1921, the Department of Agriculture launched a service that provided market news, broadcast several times each day, to amateur radio operators. The information was then handed over to local farmers to help them with their planning and operations. In May 1922 farmers in Delaware installed a radio receiver so they could stay apprised of market conditions in New York, Philadelphia, and Boston. Their belief was that by being current on a daily basis with market prices they could react more quickly and send the crop to the market that was fetching the highest prices. Radio's role as a new farming tool was becoming clearer, not only because it linked these rather isolated rural Americans to the rest of the country, but because radio could be a guide that provided vital information. Looking to further the connection radio provided, the federal government also used radio as a vehicle through which to teach the typical farmer about important subjects like "how to deal with maladies among his live stock or insects devouring his crops."

To assess radio's importance to the farmer, late in 1922 a survey was sent to the editors of major farming journals. The results were unanimous: Radio had become central to any well-operated farm. The editors even suggested other uses for the new medium, including a service to inform farmers where to find seasonal laborers and, in turn, where laborers might find employment. One editor noted, "The importance of this service is so readily appreciated, however, that it is accepted without discussion."

The September 1924 issue of *Successful Farming* magazine predicted that radio would do a great deal toward taking those long, sour looks off the farmer's face; it would keep the youngsters at home at night; it would give the whole family entertainment and amusement; and it would pay for itself in a few months if the farmer heeded the market reports. No farmer—unless on the verge of bankruptcy—could afford to do without radio. "It's the farmer's friend."

Of course farmers' interest in radio was also good for the radio business and helped fuel its amazingly rapid growth. Aware of this, David Sarnoff said in 1924 that "radio's greatest contribution to civilization lies not so much in what it does for the city dweller but upon the signal influence it can bring upon the life and action of our farm population." By the autumn of 1924 it was estimated that 370,000 radio sets were in use on farms around the country. Eighteen months later the United States Department of Agriculture claimed that approximately one million receivers were in use on farms, and that the agriculture reports that had been started in 1921 as experimental programming fed to just three stations had become programming that "literally hundreds of stations have requested the privilege of handling."

Other radio news reporting was sporadic at best and usually came about because an announcer felt the need to fill airtime by reading stories from that day's newspaper. In 1921 Tommy Cowan, the first voice heard over WJZ, often read bulletins provided by the *Newark Sunday Call*. The sound of his voice, itself a news story in those days, was heard throughout Greater New York City, where one of his listeners was an editorial writer for the *Brooklyn Eagle* named Hans von Kaltenborn. Intrigued by radio and its possibilities, in April 1922 Kaltenborn delivered a speech that was carried by WJZ, but that limited initial exposure gave no hint of the long radio career that lay ahead for the *Brooklyn Eagle's* columnist.

When WEAF debuted—it went on the air for the first time on August 16, 1922—the station, like most others, was desperate for programming, for content, and so they contacted the *Brooklyn Eagle's* associate editor, who was one of the paper's most impressive and authoritative public speakers, and offered him a spot on the air. Given the radio platform, Kaltenborn used the chance to deliver regularly scheduled talks on issues facing the country. Unafraid to use this far-reaching soapbox to make controversial comments, Kaltenborn was an eloquent commentator who appreciated the innovative nature of what he was doing. "The current events talks that I delivered on the air were something entirely new," he wrote. "They were the first spoken editorials ever heard by a radio audience."

Kaltenborn's outspoken radio commentaries caused all kinds of trouble for him and WEAF during the winter of 1923. His opinions, which were popular with radio audiences, were not so highly regarded by the people he criticized, including a judge presiding over a case involving rate setting by AT&T, WEAF's parent company, and a union leader who had called a strike that Kaltenborn disapproved of. Then Kaltenborn criticized Secretary of State Charles Evans Hughes for his curt rejection of the Soviet Union's request for diplomatic recognition. Hughes, listening to Kaltenborn's criticism in his Washington home—at that time, WEAF's programs were carried by telephone wire to WRC in the nation's capital—was in the company of a group of distinguished guests and was not pleased. Secretary Hughes complained to the president of AT&T, which resulted in Kaltenborn being told his talks would be discontinued unless he agreed to "cease all editorial comment."

Kaltenborn refused to be censored, and AT&T notified the *Eagle* that his talks would have to be discontinued, an order the newspaper passed on to WEAF. Unbowed by the threat and seemingly unafraid of the consequences, WEAF informed the *Eagle* that if Kaltenborn's talks were to be terminated, then the paper would have to announce the cancellation of the commentaries and the reason for it within its pages. The cancellation was reconsidered, and Kaltenborn was allowed to finish the regularly scheduled programs. However, when that series of shows ended, his contract with WEAF was not renewed, ostensibly because there was growing audience pressure to air other programs. But Kaltenborn was not so easily silenced; he ended up delivering opinion talks on a number of different stations, so many, in fact, that the impresario and radio producer Roxy Rothafel dubbed him "the wandering voice of radio." Kaltenborn's experience as a radio commentator revealed an important flaw in the relationship between the day's dominant medium—newspapers—and the upstart medium of radio. "News was still the monopoly of the newspapers, but they feared the new competition," Kaltenborn noted. "A few publishers owned stations but no press association would permit its news service to be used regularly on the air." In other words, by controlling the flow of timely information and keeping it from being used by radio stations, newspapers were securing their territory, protecting it from radio and its ability to get the news to the audience more immediately than the newspapers could.

During the period of radio's rapid growth, many of America's leading newspapers devoted pages and pages of newsprint to the progress of the technology. Then, as reader interest in programming gradually surpassed interest in technology, newspapers increased their coverage of what was available on the air. Not surprisingly, radio was extensively covered by the many newspapers that had started and owned their own stations: The *Los Angeles Times* had KHJ; the *Detroit News* had WWJ; the *Kansas City Star* owned WDAF; and the *Chicago Daily News* owned WMAQ, while their crosstown rival, the *Chicago Tribune,* owned WGN. Many newspapers began daily or weekly radio columns, some written by amateur radio enthusiasts, and regularly printed feature articles about the new medium. Despite the print media's hard-line rule of not providing news copy for radio stations to broadcast, there were natural synergies between the two media: On-air mentions of a particular newspaper column could help that paper's circulation, while editorial coverage of a radio station would naturally drive more listeners to that station. However, one questionable practice evolved when radio station managers, desperate for free, live entertainment to fill their broadcast hours, suggested to the newspapers that owned them that it might be in everyone's interest if artists performing at the station received good reviews in the newspaper. The unspoken guarantee of positive notices made it far easier to rebook those performers and to book new acts for future broadcasts.

Coverage of entertainment and technology was good for newspaper sales and good for radio itself, but when radio ultimately began to find ways to incorporate news into their broadcast schedules, newspaper publishers, even those who owned radio stations, became concerned that the new medium might erode their readerships and their bottom lines. At their annual convention held at New York's Waldorf-Astoria Hotel in April 1923, the members of the American Newspaper Publishers Association discussed how newspapers could be mailed less expensively, and after much debate, adopted a resolution that defined newsprint paper as that used strictly in newspapers. Between such stimulating policy decisions, the publishers managed to fit in a discussion about radio and its impact on newspapers. "Several publishers who operate radio plants said they did so as a general service to their readers and got no financial return from it. They said that they regarded it as good publicity, for they had received many appreciative letters." Nonetheless, the publishers association formed a committee to look into whether the pages of newspaper coverage about radio should be considered to be advertising and not editorial content. Among those chosen to be on the committee was Harry Chandler, publisher of the *Los Angeles Times,* owner of KHJ, and champion of America's sexual rejuvenation surgeon, Dr. John R. Brinkley of Kansas.

At the next publishers' meeting one year later, while concerns about increasing postage rates were still the main topic, radio was discussed at greater length. Perhaps most significant was a report that newspaper ownership of stations had declined from a high in 1922 of one hundred to a new low of forty-five. Most of the stations that had been shut down were low-power operations, and the majority of the remaining stations were nothing more than loss leaders for the newspapers, the stations' parent companies. But the most relevant part of the committee's study reported, "There is no positive evidence in the experience of the last year whether or not broadcasting stations can be used commercially for the dissemination of news to the public which would in any way affect the publication of newspapers and the demand for them."

When the publishers convened again in New York in April 1925, radio's competitive power had become the most hotly debated topic.

The medium's incredible growth forced a complete reassessment of the relationship between newspapers and radio. By a vote of 130 to ten, publishers who jointly owned the leading news service, the Associated Press (AP), authorized their board to rewrite the rules about how radio might use news reports provided by the AP. The official resolution recognized that "the tremendous and continuing growth of radio broadcasting is presenting many new problems not contemplated when the existing by-laws and rules of the Associated Press were adopted." The resolution went on to cite the public's interest in important national events such as presidential elections, and authorized the board to write new rules allowing the broadcast of "such news of the association as it shall deem of transcendent national and international importance and which cannot by its very nature be exclusive." In other words, newspaper publishers believed radio stations had an unalienable right to air any news they collected on their own, but anything gleaned from the wire services that were owned by the newspapers was to be doled out and controlled by the publishers.

Adding to the growing tension between radio and newspapers, many publishers were becoming wary of the way radio stations were using the free space they received in newspapers to promote programs. The central concern was that radio stations, which now had sponsored programs, were placing the sponsors' names right into the titles of the shows, which meant that whenever a newspaper listed or wrote about a particular show, the radio advertiser benefited from the free exposure. The publishers assumed that those crafty radio people were using this additional exposure as an inducement to secure more sponsors and take dollars away from the newspapers. So before the conference ended, another resolution the newspapermen passed banned any reporting on radio shows that included such direct advertising. However, since most major newspapers printed daily and weekly schedules of what was on the air, the sponsors whose names were part of the shows' name—e.g.,

The A&P Gypsies, or *The Eveready Hour*—still received the free mentions in the listings.

That fly in the ointment aside, the alliance between print and broadcasting seemed to be in fine shape when the publishers' radio committee report of 1925 concluded that "broadcasting, especially by newspapers, is still an experiment" that required further study, but that in general, "the broadcasting of news bulletins should help rather than retard the sale of newspapers." Then as if to symbolically strengthen this tenuous alliance, the speeches given at the luncheon of the publishers' meetings, including the keynote address by Vice President Charles Dawes, were aired over a group of five radio stations stretching from Detroit to Philadelphia.

For the next two years, America's newspapers and its radio stations continued their love/hate relationship. On the one hand, readers' fascination with everything radio made good copy and helped sell papers. On the other, as radio evolved from a public service to an effective and immediate way for advertisers to reach consumers, thus competing directly with newspapers, the publishers' view of the upstart industry dimmed. The relationship worsened when David Sarnoff launched the NBC network, followed by William Paley's creation of CBS. These networks suddenly provided advertisers with an incredibly efficient way to reach a national audience, giving radio networks a huge advantage over newspapers, which were only regional at best.

In terms of reporting the news itself, the print publishers still had little to fear; in 1927 the CBS network had but one teletype machine in its studios. Nonetheless, when the publishers met again in New York in April 1927, the interaction between radio and newspapers was one of the two lead items on the agenda. The highlight of the opening day was an address by President Coolidge, which was reported on in the following day's newspapers but was aired live by fourteen radio stations.

As in previous publishers' meetings, the radio committee issued its report based on research it had conducted during the previous year. Its conclusion was that "fortunately, direct advertising by radio is well-nigh an impossibility. The advertisers, therefore, are limited to the broadcasting of good-will programs on the air, thereby giving no serious competition to newspaper advertising." Had the committee's report been delivered just a little more than one month later, it might not have been so quick to dismiss, and therefore underestimate, radio's rapidly increasing market power.

MAY 20, 1927—A single engine airplane rolled down a runway and took off from Long Island carrying Charles Lindbergh on his flight to immortality. Thirty-three and a half hours later, the *Spirit of St. Louis* touched down in France, creating an instant American hero. Almost immediately, preparations were under way for an appropriate celebration to mark his triumphant return. When the announcer for Virginia's WSEA scooped the rest of the media by reporting a sighting of the flotilla carrying Lindbergh back to America, it was merely a pale indication of what radio and a newsworthy celebrity could accomplish together. Undoubtedly the printed stories about Lucky Lindy's triumph sold millions of extra newspapers, but the real winner was network radio. For an industry that had discovered the value of major events in building an audience, there was nothing bigger than Lindbergh's return, and the best part was that Lindbergh's return, which took more than two weeks from its initial announcements to its conclusion, made it an ongoing story. Every detail was fodder for the news, and when it was announced that the parade and presentation by President Coolidge would be in Washington, NBC dispatched their best announcers, headed by Graham McNamee, to cover the proceedings. RADIO MICROPHONES MAY BE INSTALLED ALONG FLIER ROUTE declared one newspaper headline. This would be the first broadcast ever attempted that originated from several sites, with announcers and microphones positioned at the Washington Navy Yard where the ship docked, at strategic spots along Pennsylvania Avenue, and at the Washington Monument, where President Coolidge would greet Lindbergh and bestow on him the Distinguished Flying Cross. The newspaper coverage was so detailed that the *Washington Post* even ran a biography of Graham McNamee, relating his amazing story, from the moment he walked into the studios of WEAF looking for a job, to the great sporting events he had announced, right through to his upcoming assignment: reporting on Lindbergh's return.

Meanwhile, as greeting committees planned the festivities, NBC was assembling a network of stations that could reach more than 50 million Americans. Seizing the marketing opportunity offered by this onetime event, NBC declared that Saturday, June 11, 1927, the day of the aviator's arrival and the parade, would be called Lindbergh Radio Day, even though the hero would actually be heard for only a few minutes, and the rest of the broadcast would consist of descriptions of the activities and President Coolidge's remarks.

In its own effort to drum up additional excitement, WRC in Washington announced they would carry President Coolidge's annual budget address on June 10, but that listeners would want to tune in early because sometime between 6:30 and 6:45 P.M., John Hays Hammond, the chairman of Washington, D.C.'s welcoming committee, would make a special announcement about Lindbergh's arrival.

SATURDAY, JUNE 11, 1927—a crystal-clear, warm, late spring morning—perfect weather for a parade. A large crowd—more than 100,000 people—gathered in Washington, D.C., and stood crammed into every inch of space between the Navy Yard and the Washington Monument, hoping for a glimpse of Charles Lindbergh. For the rest of the country, that Saturday was Lindbergh Radio Day, and at 11:30 A.M. tens of millions of listeners turned on their radios and heard

Ladies and gentlemen: This is the National Broadcasting Co. We will call the roll. This is Philips Carlin at the top of the Washington Monument. Are you ready? Ladies and gentlemen: this is Graham McNamee, announcing from the Navy Yard. We are broadcasting now from the Navy Yard at Washington, D.C.

After two more NBC announcers said hello from their particular locales, Graham McNamee picked up the narration:

Just a moment ago the last turn of the propellers of the Memphis *brought her close into the dock. This is the ship from Europe that carried a young man, who is up on the bridge now, a tall, slender stripling he seems from here, at least; an awfully nice looking boy, with wavy hair. He is taking it all in with extreme calm; he seems very interested in the proceedings. It is a tremendously romantic and interesting spectacle here.*

For the next two and a half hours, McNamee and his colleagues moved around Washington, following the parade route, describing every detail of the grand event for their radio audience. At a little after one o'clock, McNamee, now at the reviewing stand, turned his microphone over to President Coolidge, whose speech was repeatedly interrupted by wild cheering each time he mentioned Lindbergh by name. Then came the moment everyone had been waiting for: Charles Lindbergh would be heard. Speaking to the largest audience ever assembled, the aviator kept his remarks brief:

On the evening of May 21 I arrived at Le Bourget, France. I was in Paris for one week, in Belgium for a day and was in London and England for

several days. Everywhere I went, at every meeting I attended, I was re-
quested to bring a message home to you. Always the message was the
same. "You have seen," the message was, "the affection of the people of
France for the people of America demonstrated to you. When you return
to America take back that message to the people of the United States from
the people of France and of Europe." I thank you.

Though perhaps not the most imaginative, and certainly not the
longest speech ever given over the radio—the *New York Times* described it as "so brief that it was almost startling"—Lindbergh's words,
heard by those at the Washington Monument and by millions more
around the country, were thrilling simply because they were spoken by
America's newest hero. Summing up the day, Graham McNamee told
his loyal audience he was *just fearfully proud to have been just a tiny little*
spot in this great national and international affair.

The radio coverage of the event was itself big news, and writers,
though somewhat critical of the brevity of Lindbergh's speech, which
they deemed to be thirteen minutes shorter than the ideal time for a
radio talk, did note that the young aviator had a "fine radio voice and
delivery." Lindbergh's comments—actually just the sound of his
voice—set off a debate about how much money a full-length radio
speech by this newly minted hero would generate in terms of audience
and revenue. Speculation was that a station wishing to carry a Lindbergh talk would have to pay upward of $10,000 for the local rights,
and in their eagerness to secure Lindbergh, bidders might double or
triple that figure, which was at least four times what was believed to
have been the highest fee ever paid for a radio appearance.

But the mutually beneficial connection between Lindbergh and
radio had just begun to develop. When Lindy left Washington for celebrations in New York City, his comments, delivered at the unusual
hour of 7 A.M., were carried over Washington's WRC. Then in order

to relay every moment of the Lindbergh celebration to its listeners, WRC continued its coverage and detailed the enthusiastic reception given Lindbergh upon his arrival in New York. Even President and Mrs. Coolidge, though busy preparing for a trip, tuned the White House receiver to WRC and listened to coverage of the New York parade. The crowd shouted, "Lindy! Lindy! Lindy!" but Lindbergh didn't seem to be excited about anything, remaining cool and calm amid the amazing hoopla.

The coverage of the Lindbergh celebrations was the first triumph for national network radio. The following April, when the newspaper publishers met again in New York, their radio committee, realizing that radio had gradually encroached and was now threatening to upstage newspapers, "urged that publishers give serious consideration to the question of further publication of radio programs as news." Radio had finally become enough of an annoyance to newspapers that some action beyond limiting radio's access to the wire news services needed to be taken, and the most logical step would be eliminating the free publicity newspapers had been providing as a public service. One line in the radio committee's report told the story: "Interest in radio evidently may now be said to have moved distinctly away from its former status as a mechanical toy or a phenomenon of physics."

Despite some newspapers' efforts to starve the radio child by restricting its access to news content, some local stations around the country continued to find ways to insert news and informational programming into their broadcast day. In one arrangement, Westinghouse and its stations contracted with the Houston Publishing Company to create a weekly news feature called *The World through the Air.* Commenting on the experimental program, Herbert Houston of Houston Publishing said, "It is the first time, so far as I know, that the printed word and radio have been made to work together as allies to their mutual advantage in just this manner." Another such innovator was Fred Smith, who arranged to receive advance copies of *Time* magazine, from which he culled stories and created daily ten-minute news features that were heard over Cincinnati's WLW. Later in 1928 Smith moved to New York and joined the staff of WOR, where he continued to produce his show. Smith's show was listed every day on the radio pages of New York's many newspapers, but somehow when the listing was typeset, the words *News Casting* were put together, thus inventing the term as we know it today.

When the newspaper publishers met for the final time during the 1920s, they enjoyed listening to a special radio hookup with Commander Richard Byrd and his team from their base in Antarctica. Given the chance to speak over the wireless connection, many of the directors of the publishers association, including *Los Angeles Times* publisher Harry Chandler, gave short speeches that were transmitted via an experimental antenna through shortwave to the distant explorers at Little America. Another highlight of the publishers' meeting was the speech delivered by the newly inaugurated U.S. president and champion of radio, Herbert Hoover, whose successful run for the White House was greatly helped by the positive editorial power of the *Los Angeles Times* and the active support of its publisher. But after all the niceties were through and the publishers got down to their discussions about the state of their industry, radio remained high on the agenda, specifically the question of how to deal with the use of Associated Press dispatches over the airwaves, either by stations owned by newspapers or those that were simply supplied by the local paper. One publisher did suggest that if network radio news using Associated Press material for its content were to become a reality, any local newspaper that was an AP service client would have the right to block the local radio affiliate from broadcasting such news. However, since network news shows were few and far between, and since revenues from newspaper advertising had increased during the past twelve months, the publishers felt secure, and the proposal, along with the debate over the radio-newspaper relationship, was tabled until the following year.

By decade's end, while individual stations fit some local and regional news into their broadcast schedule—which was the kind of locally relevant programming Hoover always believed radio should deliver as part of its public-service function—the big radio networks themselves were staying out of the news business, although they were experimenting with less time-sensitive topical shows. Among the programs offered were David Lawrence's weekly series, *Our Government,* and Frederic William Wile's program, *The Political Situation in Washington Tonight.* Elliot Thurston gave his opinions in the series *Washington News,* while McKesson Drug was the proud sponsor of the *McKesson News Reel.* Finally, making its highly anticipated network debut at the outset of the 1929 autumn radio season was a brand-new show called *Current Events,* hosted by the "wandering voice of radio," H. V. Kaltenborn.

By the end of 1929, with the economy failing and newspaper advertising suddenly plunging, the relationship between the newspapers and radio would begin to change. Then early in the new decade, Charles Lindbergh would again be prominently featured on the radio, this time not playing the hero but a far more tragic role, and as a result the radio coverage for the real-life drama that gripped the nation would forever change how the print media and broadcasting would coexist, and would have a significant impact on the involvement of the electronic media with American jurisprudence.

Chapter 10

▲▲▲▲▲▲▲▲▲▲▲▲▲

The Rev. Dr. Elmer Gantry was the first clergyman in the state of Winnemac, almost the first in the country, to have his services broadcast by radio.

—*Elmer Gantry*

SINCLAIR LEWIS'S CONTROVERSIAL 1927 novel *Elmer Gantry* presented a cynical view of religious revivalists and their message of redemption at a price. His tale accurately depicted radio's ability to deliver religious messages to distant audiences, and there was no shortage of infamous and morally questionable religious radiocasters on which Lewis could have modeled the character of Elmer Gantry.

Before radio changed the religious landscape, the traveling tent revival was a staple of small-town American summers. These movable shows, many of which had their roots in the lyceum movement and the Chautauqua assemblies, provided towns with the chance for citizens to gather for a few days to enjoy the benefits of self-improvement, religious education, and even some entertainment. Dating back to the mid-1880s, these traveling revival and self-improvement meetings reached their greatest popularity in the years following World War I.

The tent shows were big business for the towns, the acts, the speakers, and the agents who organized the tours and booked the talent. The traveling revival meetings were similar to a vaudeville circuit, only with a stated higher moral purpose and less interesting entertainment, unless you found lengthy religious diatribes entertaining. William Jennings Bryan, himself a popular attraction on the circuit, called the Chautauqua movement "a potent human factor in molding the mind of the nation," while Theodore Roosevelt called it "the most American thing in America."

Whereas the Chautauqua circuit was geared toward self-improvement, intellectual pursuits, and a big dose of religion, there were other circuits traveled by troupes devoted exclusively to religion and salvation. These traveling assemblies, usually headlined by a magnetic preacher, visited towns across America presenting their fire-and-brimstone style of religion and revivalism. The message from the pulpit was often accompanied by music, usually provided by a brass band, which was a nice contrast to the drama of the fire-spitting preacher pulling forth revealing testimony from the sinful souls who came forward seeking salvation. One of the most famous revivalists of the era was a preacher with the fortuitous name of Billy Sunday. Sunday claimed to have led more than 300 revivals at which he preached to 10 million people. Of those millions of lost souls, he boasted that he had led more than one million of them down the road to salvation.

A revival does two things. First, it returns the Church from her backsliding and second, it causes the conversion of men and women; and it always includes the conviction of sin on the part of the Church. What a spell the Devil seems to cast over the Church today. When is a revival needed? When you feel the want of revival and the need of it.

Revivals were good entertainment and good business, and their message was well tuned to the same conservative forces in America that had endorsed Prohibition. Even without the subject of "devil liquor" to fire up the congregation, religious zealots found plenty of ready targets in the free spending and loose morals of the flapper era. During the summer of 1923, the primary Chautauqua circuit boasted appearances by politicians, government leaders, a host of religious notables, and other celebrities, and its image as "first aid to the ignorant" was supported by the belief that it had "become one of the most potent opinion-building forces in the United States." It was estimated that in 1922 alone more than 10 million people attended Chautauqua lectures. But a new message-delivery vehicle was making it possible to far exceed the audience reached through quaint tent shows.

THE UNHOLY MARRIAGE BETWEEN radio and religion began innocently enough on January 2, 1921, when Pittsburgh's KDKA installed three microphones in the Calvary Episcopal Church to air the Sunday morning services. The multimicrophone setup was designed to allow the radio audience to hear the organ, the choir, and the reverend equally well. The technical aspects of the broadcast were handled by two Westinghouse engineers, one Jewish and one Catholic, who held the equipment while cloaked in choir robes. Struck by radio's ability to reach out to unseen audiences, the Reverend Edwin Jan van Etten, pastor of the Calvary Church, thought the entire experiment represented the "universality of radio religion." The first Sunday morning church service that aired was so popular that it became a mainstay of KDKA's schedule. Two and a half years later, on June 8, 1923, Reverend Van Etten unveiled a bronze tablet in his church that had been paid for solely with contributions from his unseen congregation, the radio listeners. The dedication read: "January 2, 1921, from Calvary church, a church service was sent by radio telephone by the Westinghouse Electric and Manufacturing Company. This tablet was placed in 1923 by the Unseen Congregation." More than 4,700 listeners in forty states, plus some in Canada, Cuba, and Bermuda, contributed.

The Calvary Church's early use of radio to reach congregants far beyond its walls was not lost on other religious organizations. Congregations throughout the country reached out to local radio stations, which were pleased to provide the airtime because church services strengthened community ties while conveniently filling a few hours of programming. In December 1921 WJZ had the Reverend George P. Dougherty read a Christmas greeting that was so well received that early in January 1922 the station and the Christ Episcopal Church of Glen Ridge, New Jersey, agreed to air a weekly Sunday afternoon chapel service. Then in June of that year the station formed a relationship with the American Bible Society so that interest in the Bible would be "strengthened and abetted by daily Bible readings" carried over the airwaves.

By the middle of 1922, religious organizations had moved into station ownership: KJS was owned by the Bible Institute of Los Angeles; the First Presbyterian Church in Seattle owned KTW; and WDD in Washington, D.C., was owned by the Church of the Covenant. WDD's programming for Sunday, May 7, 1922, is representative of the station's offerings: An 11 A.M. service was broadcast in its entirety; the station then signed off until 3:30 P.M., when it returned to air the Sunday school anniversary exercises, followed by silence until 8 P.M., when it signed back on for the pastor's sermon and a program called "The Ministry of Music to the Soul: Mariam Gregory. Handel, Wagner."

A thoughtful sermon offset by some nice music had great audience appeal. An ever-increasing number of religious leaders, including many revivalists, turned to the radio pulpit as a way to reach more people, and since the entertaining speakers and the music provided the listeners with something worth hearing, acquiring airtime was not difficult. It was a simple calculation: Travel around on bouncy, dusty back roads setting up tents and benches in small towns where perhaps you could reach hundreds of folks at a time, or take to the airwaves and reach thousands, without ever leaving your pulpit.

SALFORD, ONTARIO; October 9, 1890—In the upstairs room of a small farmhouse, Aimee Elizabeth Kennedy was born to James Kennedy and his second wife, Minnie, who upon the birth of their daughter, dedicated the child's life to the service of God. However, despite learning the scriptures so completely that she could effectively debate virtually any point of religion, by the time Aimee was an adolescent she had begun to question the Bible and its teachings. She found that she could not reconcile the inconsistencies in the scriptures with the concepts espoused by people like Charles Darwin and Thomas Paine. Gradually, Aimee became an atheist and used her exceptional speaking and debating skills to defend the theories of evolution. Then in December 1907 an evangelist named Robert Semple came to Salford to preach and Aimee attended one of his meetings, intending to make fun of his talk. His sermon, or perhaps his good looks and commanding presence, changed the course of her life and set her on the path to becoming one of the great evangelists of the era. She married Semple and joined him in his work. At just nineteen years of age she reluctantly made her evangelical debut, thrilling a crowd of 15,000 in London's Albert Hall with her dynamic, gripping delivery. Robert Semple died suddenly the next year while doing missionary work in China. Pregnant with their daughter, who was born one month later, Aimee returned to her mother, who had moved to New York and was working for the Salvation Army. In New York, Aimee married Harold McPherson, with whom she had a son in 1913; but she also heard the voice of God calling her, telling her she had to preach. During the summer of 1915 Aimee began delivering sermons at meetings in Canada, and the popularity of her style and the overflow crowds she attracted forced her to purchase a large tent—her canvas cathedral in which to hold meetings.

Wanting to spread her message, she bought a used car and covered one side with a sign that read JESUS IS COMING SOON—GET READY and the other with a sign that read WHERE WILL YOU SPEND ETERNITY? In 1919, divorced from her second husband, Aimee, her mother, and her two children took to the road. They drove coast to coast in an era when women driving alone was rare, stopping for Aimee to preach wherever a crowd could be assembled. Aimee Semple McPherson's fame was spreading, aided by a story of how during one dramatic sermon a storm blew up and tore a hole in the tent just above her head. "Stop in the name of Jesus! I command you to stop right where you are, till this day's meetings are over!" she shouted, raising her hands toward the heavens. As luck, or providence, would have it, a rope pulling the seam together caught on a nail, pulling the tarp so it covered the hole until the service ended. It was just the kind of "miracle" that helped turn an ordinary evangelist into a legend.

McPherson made California her home base, traveling from city to city, preaching to huge crowds, saving souls and raising money to build a permanent home for her congregants in Los Angeles. Her brand of religion was different from the fire-and-brimstone shouting and histrionics used by the likes of Billy Sunday. Aimee's sermons were positive in nature: She avoided using fear as a motivator, instead emphasizing the more sunny aspects of religion. Her services were alive with music, storytelling, healing, speaking in tongues, visions, and theatrical presentations of biblical stories.

In Los Angeles, the mother-daughter team purchased a plot of land in the Echo Park section of town, where they planned to erect a magnificent temple. Aimee designed the building to be similar in shape to a megaphone, and it bore a slight resemblance to London's Albert Hall, where she'd given her first talk. The new building would be large enough to seat more than 5,000 congregants, a reflection of the grow-ing popularity of her brand of religion, and of her self-confidence.

With a final cost of more than $1.2 million, the Angelus Temple opened its doors at 2:30 on the afternoon of January 1, 1923. Facing a packed house of more than 5,300 people, Sister Aimee blessed the sanc-tuary, dedicating it to the cause of interdenominational and worldwide evangelism. The Church of the Foursquare Gospel, as it was called, was conceived as "a learning center for evangelism, whose chief object is the conversion experience." The outside of the temple's gold dome and the lighted cross could be seen for fifty miles around. On Easter Sunday 1923, the magnificent temple organ was dedicated; the organ, along with a fourteen-piece orchestra, a golden harp, and the temple's choir, were central to the entertainment, and the music they played was a mix of traditional a cappella singing, old hymns, and popular tunes arranged as jazz. In addition, with Hollywood's proximity Aimee found it easy to borrow costumes and props for the elaborately staged religious pageants she presented. These were brilliant shows, and the Angelus Temple and Sister Aimee's sermons became a must-see for Californians and visitors alike.

But Sister Aimee's messages took wing in a new way as well: She began recording sermonettes that local radio stations were more than happy to air. Station KHJ, the radio station of the *Los Angeles Times,* had offered airtime for local members of the clergy to deliver sermons, and Sister Aimee often took advantage of its offer. The voice and the dra-matic delivery she had so carefully developed made great radio listen-ing, which was a nice bonus for a station interested in building its listenership. Aimee Semple McPherson "spoke last night on 'Woman's Place in Religion.' An eloquent message from the heart and the soul," reviewed the *Times's* radio columnist. The success of her radio broad-casts convinced the temple's congregation that Aimee needed her own broadcast facility. Within months the necessary funds, about $25,000, were raised. To get her station designed and built, Aimee hired one of Los Angeles's most respected radio engineers.

Kenneth Gladstone Ormiston was the chief engineer of KHJ and had met Aimee when she visited the *Los Angeles Times*'s station to give her first radio talks. McPherson offered this handsome, impeccably dressed gentleman in his midthirties who walked with a slight limp an annual salary of $3,000, and asked him to design and construct a state-of-the-art broadcast and recording studio on the third floor of the Angelus Temple. In addition, she wanted the main auditorium equipped with microphones so that every element of her dynamic services would be heard clearly over the air. When her application for a radio license was granted by Hoover's Department of Commerce, the first one given to a woman, she was given the call letters KFNC, which were the next set of available sequential letters. McPherson sent a telegram to the Department of Commerce requesting her call letters be changed to KFSG, to stand for her teachings of the Four Square Gospel. On January 28, 1924, the Commerce Department wired back that her request had been granted. McPherson telegrammed her sincere thanks, and on the evening of February 6, 1924, KFSG made its debut.

> *ANGELUS TEMPLE*—*Powerful 500 Watt Radio Station*—
> *Now Broadcasting*— *Wave Length 278 Meters*—*K.F.S.G.*
> *Angelus Temple, Kall Four Square Gospel. Draw up your*
> *fireside chair, adjust your earphones and tune in, for the*
> *great Angelus Temple Revival is now on the air!*

So read the announcement in the February 1924 issue of McPherson's own magazine, *Bridal Call*.

The inaugural broadcast began at 8 P.M. with the hymn "Give the Winds a Mighty Voice." The service, delivered to an enthusiastic crowd, dedicated the new station to God and all of the people from

Mexico to Canada who could now join in McPherson's joyous brand of religion. In addition to Sister Aimee's words, radio listeners heard congratulatory statements by many of Los Angeles's civic and religious leaders, including the acting mayor; publisher Harry Chandler; Colonel J. F. Dillon, the regional supervisor of radio for the Department of Commerce; and Judge Carlos Hardy of the California Superior Court.

From the outset the station's schedule was demanding: Three times each day revival sermons, songs, and prayers were broadcast live from the sanctuary. There were special messages twice a week for shut-ins, and Aimee also recorded sermons to be aired when she was otherwise occupied. By April the station's schedule filled the air for part of every day except Mondays. KFSG usually signed on during the late morning hours and in the course of the next ten hours would sign on and off four or five times depending on what programming was available. But no matter what was aired, the centerpiece of the programming was always Sister Aimee's thrilling sermons and the ornate pageants that were really more like religiously themed vaudeville shows than religious gatherings.

KFSG's audience grew, and Aimee's voice became the most recognizable in the West. But her immense popularity had a price: She drew the wrath of some of her fellow Los Angeles ministers, most notably the Reverend Robert "Fighting Bob" Shuler, who in addition to being the minister of Los Angeles's Trinity Methodist Church, was the head of the Church Federation of Los Angeles. What Shuler realized was that McPherson's brand of religion, the happy redemption her revivalism offered, was outdrawing the more severe vision of damnation put forth by traditional church services. She offered a gospel that spoke of reconciliation and love, as opposed to the fear of hellfire and damnation preferred by her crosstown rivals. Famous for his sweeping tirades, Reverend Shuler vilified, in the most unbridled language, the sins of gambling, political corruption, and alcohol, and as her audience increased, he attacked Sister Aimee Semple McPherson and anyone associated with her. Late in 1924, Shuler published a vicious attack in his book *McPhersonism,* calling her manner in the pulpit "a disgrace to serious Christians everywhere." The growing feud between Shuler and McPherson would eventually be played out over the Los Angeles airwaves. But first, KFSG had to deal with a more important critic: the Department of Commerce and Secretary Hoover.

Soon after KFSG went on the air, radio stations near and far noticed that the signal emanating from the Angelus Temple studio had a habit of bouncing around and interfering with the signals being transmitted by other stations. KFSG's tendency to roam all over the wave band eventually became bothersome enough that stations complained directly to the Commerce Department. Hoover ordered the department's regional director, Colonel Dillon, who had been one of the guest speakers during KFSG's inaugural broadcast, to investigate. McPherson was warned that further violations of the station's licensed power restrictions would result in the department having to shut down the station. Angered by the threat and an eventual brief shuttering of her station, Sister Aimee fired off a telegram with an even more dire warning to Secretary Hoover:

PLEASE ORDER YOUR MINIONS OF SATAN TO LEAVE MY STATION ALONE. YOU CANNOT EXPECT THE ALMIGHTY TO ABIDE BY YOUR WAVELENGTH NONSENSE. WHEN I OFFER MY PRAYERS TO HIM I MUST FIT INTO HIS WAVE RECEPTION. OPEN THIS STATION AT ONCE. AIMEE SEMPLE MCPHERSON.

The station was reopened, and Chief Engineer Ormiston promised that KFSG would operate within the proper technical limits. With her station a weapon in her communications arsenal, McPherson's power, fame, and reach continued to grow, much to the annoyance of Bob Shuler and the other Los Angeles religious leaders. In essence, the two groups were in a pitched battle for congregants and their donations, and Sister Aimee was winning. Hundreds of thousands of listeners thought of McPherson's broadcasts as God's entrance into their homes and hearts. Another important show on KFSG was *The Sunshine Hour,* a six-days-a-week morning program hosted by McPherson and produced by Ormiston. Engineer and host quickly developed a close working relationship that raised some questions about propriety, especially since Ormiston was married. Bowing to the pressure of the nasty rumors and to avoid further scrutiny, Kenneth Ormiston quit his lucrative job at the Angelus Temple.

Aimee Semple McPherson would have probably gone down in history as another outspoken radio evangelist whose fame and power rose dramatically then quickly waned had it not been for the bizarre incident that followed her, and many others, for the balance of the decade and beyond.

JANUARY 11, 1926—Citing exhaustion, Aimee Semple McPherson embarked on a vacation to the Holy Land. Eleven days later, after reporting that her husband was missing, Mrs. Kenneth Ormiston left with the couple's child to live in Australia.

Meanwhile Aimee toured the Holy Land. Returning to the United States after stops in Ireland and London, she arrived in Los Angeles on April 24, 1926, and was greeted at the train station by the acting mayor and Judge Carlos Hardy, along with more than 12,000 of her faithful. Revived, she resumed her exhausting workload, leaving only time to go to the beach to take a daily swim in the Pacific Ocean. On May 18 she and her secretary, Emma Schaffer, went to Ocean Park. While the secretary left the beach to phone the temple, Aimee went into the ocean. More than an hour later, Emma Schaffer reported to the lifeguard that the evangelist was missing.

The horrible news that Aimee Semple McPherson may have drowned spread like wildfire. That evening, 5,400 of her faithful packed into the Angelus Temple; the usual joyous cries of *Hallelujah!* were replaced by quiet sobbing and silent prayer. Outside, newsboys hawked the latest extra edition of the newspapers containing the story of the possible drowning. For days, thousands of people with "A faith as strong and deep as the ocean" lined the Pacific shore "to watch hour after hour with aching eyes" for the evangelist's body, but it never surfaced. On the fourth day following the disappearance, her avid supporter on the bench, Superior Court Judge Carlos Hardy, went on KFSG to denounce rumors that Aimee Semple McPherson had staged her own disappearance.

Nine days after McPherson's disappearance, Kenneth Ormiston was brought in for questioning. Immediately upon his release, he made a highly public visit to McPherson's mother at the temple and declared, "I am glad to be with you and to do whatever I can to clear things up." He went on to discredit reports that he and the missing evangelist were romantically linked, and the word of his own disappearance, as reported to the police by his wife, was news to him.

That afternoon, McPherson's mother went on the temple's radio station to ask the church members and anyone else who was listening to come to the beach to search for her daughter's body. As days turned into weeks, the newspapers, despite the increase in circulation the dramatic story had given them, lost interest in the case and relegated the unsolved McPherson "drowning" to the back pages. To mark the one-month anniversary of Sister Aimee's disappearance, her mother organized a "day of rejoicing for Sister's victory," including special music and three services, all of which were broadcast. By the end of the day, thanks to donations from the crowds in the temple and radio listeners who phoned in their pledges, it was estimated that the Angelus Temple had raised $40,000. The glorious, and highly profitable, farewell was the final exclamation point on the Aimee Semple McPherson story—or so it seemed.

Woman Evangelist Escapes Abductors

JUNE 23, 1926—Looking exhausted and haggard, Sister Aimee mysteriously reappeared in the desert not far from the Mexican border.

Headlines across the country delighted the evangelist's followers, and the tale she told of being kidnapped at the beach and taken to Mexico, where she was held captive in a shack from which she had managed a Houdiniesque escape, was simply amazing—or as some of her critics were quick to say, entirely unbelievable. Offering to tell the whole story to the horde of reporters that had descended on the tiny town of Douglas, Arizona, McPherson gave a detailed account of what she had been through, including her escape from the cabin and her exhausting walk through the desert.

Elements of her tale simply didn't hold water, and after three useless searches through the Mexican desert by authorities to find the mysterious cabin, she offered a reward of $500 to anyone who could locate her prison. "Every word I have uttered about my kidnapping and escape is true," she protested. Two days after her miraculous escape, Aimee Semple McPherson and her entourage embarked on a journey back to Los Angeles. When the train stopped at Colton, California, 5,000 people crowded around her car while she gave a radio address that was carried by every radio station in Los Angeles and several others up and down the Pacific Coast.

In Los Angeles, plans were afoot for the celebration of Sister Aimee's glorious return. On the afternoon of June 27, more than 7,500 people crowded into the Angelus Temple while thousands more jammed the surrounding streets. When McPherson made her entrance, carrying an armful of red roses, the crowd jumped to its feet and screamed their *Hallelujah!*s When the congregation settled down, Sister Aimee ascended her pulpit and delivered a sermon titled "The Conquering Hosts," which retold the ordeal she had been through, including an explanation of how she had avoided getting sunburned while walking twenty miles through the desert. In the end, she attributed the whole plot to the work of the devil, who was miffed at being unable to stop the good work being done by her Angelus Temple.

It was a mesmerizing performance for the faithful in the temple and those listening on the radio. That evening, while delivering his own sermon from the pulpit of Trinity Church, Reverend Bob Shuler questioned the veracity of the McPherson miracle and challenged Los Angeles detectives to conduct a full investigation. His sermon included this astute observation: "Aimee Semple McPherson was born knowing all there is to know about mob psychology." McPherson counterattacked, suggesting Shuler himself might have been responsible for her kidnapping. The beneficiary of their on-air battle was radio; sales of receivers in the Los Angeles area boomed as listeners stayed current with every detail in the intriguing tale and the escalating war of words between the religious leaders.

By mid-July the district attorney was investigating the case. When reports surfaced that "Aimee Semple McPherson, Angelus temple evangelist, has been identified as the woman who accompanied Kenneth G. Ormiston, former radio operator at the temple, when he drove his automobile into a Salinas garage early on the morning of May 29, eleven days after the evangelist had disappeared," the story became even more sordid; it would remain the lead news item for the balance of the summer.

Kenneth Ormiston fled to the East Coast, where he traveled under an assumed name and, via letter, informed the Los Angeles DA that he refused to return to appear before the grand jury. In Los Angeles, the DA was actually investigating two parallel cases: McPherson's alleged kidnapping, and the possibility she had made the whole thing up as a way to sneak away alone with Kenneth Ormiston. As the legal wheels turned, McPherson used her pulpit, the one in the temple and its radiowave extension, to defend her tale and accuse her enemies. She even attacked the detectives investigating her story, whose names were Cline and Ryan; leaning toward her microphone for maximum effect, Sister Aimee pounced, "Both are Catholics, persecuting a Protestant minister."

Accusations flew from one side to the other in a battle between the McPherson faithful who believed her kidnapping story, and those, championed by Bob Shuler, who believed she had invented the tale to cover up her affair with Ormiston. When the grand jury was dismissed without proffering charges in the kidnapping case, it was evident to all except the blindly faithful that McPherson's story was fabricated. But the McPherson affair wasn't over. On August 3 the grand jury was reconvened to deliberate as to whether charges should be brought against McPherson and her mother. As the hearings dragged on and witnesses swore they had seen the evangelist with Mr. Ormiston during the period of her "abduction," Sister Aimee again used the pulpit to make her case: Each day following the hearings she returned to the temple and broadcast her version of what had transpired during the hearings. Her comments were so prejudicial that it eventually led the California State Senate to consider legislation making it a misdemeanor for anyone to broadcast comments on any case pending in the courts or to employ the far-reaching power of a radio station in any way that might influence prospective jurors.

Despite her attempts to spin the story, on November 3, 1926, Aimee Semple McPherson and her mother were bound over for trial in superior court to face the charge of "criminal conspiracy to commit acts injurious to public morals and to prevent and obstruct justice." If nothing else, the public repudiation allowed McPherson's enemies to call her a liar, and the Reverend Bob Shuler, now preaching over his own radio station, KFEG, which was given to him during that year by a devout spinster, led the charge. On December 9 Kenneth Ormiston was arrested in Harrisburg, Pennsylvania, prompting McPherson to state that his arrest had no significance to her. Eventually, Ormiston, who in every article was referred to as the "radio man," was brought to Los Angeles, where he testified he had been in Carmel with another woman during McPherson's disappearance.

McPherson seemed headed for a long trial and probable conviction, so on New Year's Day 1927 she announced that she would embark on a national "vindication tour." It was a bold and surprising move coming as it did on the same day that DA Asa Keyes pledged to continue pursuing the case against her. Then in an even greater surprise, just nine days later Keyes announced he would ask the court to dismiss all charges against McPherson, her mother, Ormiston, and all other participants in the case. McPherson, who was scheduled to leave the next day for her tour, "issued a statement after the charges were dismissed, declaring she was glad—'tremendously glad'—but added that she much preferred that the case would have gone to trial in order that she might have been vindicated in that manner."

Despite the shadows cast by the fiasco, Sister Aimee's vindication tour was met with some success. However, when the tour arrived in New York, she was informed that radio station WRNY, located at the Roosevelt Hotel, which had been scheduled to air her talks, had decided to cancel the engagement, believing it was bad policy to allow her to be heard over their station. As a favor to Reverend Robert Brown at whose tabernacle McPherson was scheduled to appear, WRNY's director Charles Isaacson spoke to three other stations, but all of them refused to carry Sister Aimee's talks on the grounds that they "might be 'too full of dynamite.'" As a last resort, station WODA in Paterson, New Jersey, was engaged to air McPherson's talks, but the damage to her image and standing was done.

The scandal followed Aimee McPherson and many of the story's key players for years. Battles with her mother, rifts within her congregation, accusations of financial misdeeds, and the ongoing radio attacks by Reverend Shuler gradually undercut Aimee McPherson's power and prestige. By August 1927 her position had deteriorated so much that the board of the temple took control of the organization's operations. Nonetheless, KFSG, with its entertaining blend of religion and amusements, remained one of Los Angeles's most popular radio stations.

Radio and religion were bound together, leading James Freeman, Episcopal bishop of Washington, D.C., to affirm, "Radio is the greatest agency that God Almighty has devised through human ingenuity to bring about the breaking down of barriers of different church beliefs."

During the autumn of 1926, just as the Los Angeles grand jury was weighing charges against Sister Aimee, across the country in a small suburb near Detroit, Michigan, another man of the cloth was discovering radio's amazing power, but his use of the medium would become far more insidious than any crime Aimee Semple McPherson may have committed.

ON OCTOBER 25, 1891, in Hamilton, Ontario, Charles Edward Coughlin was born. The son of devout Irish Catholics—his father was the sexton of the Hamilton cathedral—Charles fulfilled his mother's greatest dream when he entered the priesthood. Ordained at age twenty-three, he spent the first seven years of his career teaching in Canada before moving to Michigan to be a parish priest. Three years later he was assigned to a new parish in the Detroit suburb of Royal Oak, where he would live for the remainder of his career.

In 1926 the Archdiocese of Detroit was troubled by violent anti-Catholic attacks by the Ku Klux Klan, and the few parishioners Father Coughlin found in Royal Oak were hardly the grand congregation he had hoped to lead. Undeterred, he constructed a wooden church for $101,000, his "missionary oasis in the desert of bigotry," and named it the Shrine of the Little Flower in honor of the recent canonization of Sister Thérèse. Shortly after the church was completed, the Klan burned a large cross on the lawn and left a sign urging the priest to remove his congregation from Royal Oak. But Coughlin would not be intimidated, and instead of fleeing he resolved to defeat his enemies and build a more solid church with a cross so high that "neither man nor beast can burn it down."

To gain publicity for his shrine and to increase attendance at his sermons, Coughlin asked his friend Wish Egan, a scout for the Detroit Tigers baseball club, to bring some players to the church. Egan obliged with a few members of the Detroit team along with a couple of New York Yankees, including Babe Ruth. Word spread that the great Ruth was in Royal Oak, and that day the throng spilled out onto the church's lawn. So that everyone could hear his service, Coughlin installed loudspeakers to broadcast his sermon out to the street for the huge crowd there to enjoy. While Coughlin preached, Ruth and the other ballplayers moved among the congregation collecting contributions. More than $10,000 was collected that day, and Coughlin discovered that flamboyance, celebrity, and publicity were good for the religion business.

However, the big crowds did not return for his regular sermons; on August 15, 1926, only seventeen parishioners showed up to celebrate the Virgin's Assumption. Following the service, Coughlin talked with the congregants about his frustration. Then the young priest suddenly announced that he planned to broadcast services from the shrine via radio. His argument to the skeptical parishioners was simple: "Was it not explicitly expressed in the Scriptures that 'faith cometh through hearing?'" Coughlin, like Bishop Freeman, saw no conflict between faith and the science of technology; since God had created both science and faith, why not use "His latest gift to man, the radio, for the dissemination of faith?"

It was a convenient and timely rationalization, coming as it did during the height of the McPherson scandal, and Coughlin wasted no time putting his plan into action. WJR in Detroit was managed by Leo Fitzpatrick, another Irish Catholic, and in September 1926 he and Coughlin met. Whether he encouraged Coughlin to turn to radio, as

Coughlin's authorized biography claims, or if Coughlin convinced Fitz-patrick that Sunday afternoon sermons would be good radio, is debatable. Whichever way it happened, the end result was that on October 17, 1926, the Sunday afternoon time slot on WJR was filled by a program originating from the Shrine of the Little Flower. It would be a chance for the young priest to "explain Catholicism to the community."

Coughlin's voice was a rich, resonant baritone that had a spellbinding, intimate quality even when heard through the relatively poor sound of a radio receiver. With just a hint of an Irish inflection, Coughlin projected passionately over the airwaves. The first broadcast spurred five letters directly to Coughlin and more to the station. Encouraged by the response, WJR made the Coughlin sermons a weekly feature.

Initially the talks were simple and featured a clear exposition of the Sunday gospel delivered from the pulpit in Royal Oak. Gradually the contributions from radio listeners increased, as did the young priest's fame. Coughlin attributed his success to "remembering that he was an invited guest in the homes not only of Catholics but of Protestants and of irreligionists," and therefore found "it was easy to avoid the least taint of what even his bitterest critics would call bigotry." His claim that he "had none in his heart" would be severely challenged later in his career.

Perhaps influenced by the popularity of Aimee Semple McPherson's dynamic sermons and religious shows, Coughlin, too, brought drama to the radio listener. In April 1928 he produced a Good Friday broadcast, the "Biblical Scenes of the Trial and Crucifixion of Christ," featuring Jessie Bonstelle, a Broadway star and owner of the Bonstelle Theatre in Detroit. To heighten the drama, Coughlin timed the broadcast so the audio depiction was aired at the same hour at which the actual trial was supposed to have taken place. It was entertaining, innocent, and wholesome programming that engaged listeners.

Membership in the newly formed Radio League of the Little Flower cost just one dollar a year; the money flowed in, assuring Coughlin's success. In the fall of 1929 his sermons were picked up by Chicago's WMAQ and Cincinnati's WLW, dramatically increasing the size of his potential audience. He became known as the Radio Priest, and through the end of 1929 his talks remained focused on religious subjects. With the addition of these new stations he was now receiving more than 3,000 letters per week, many containing the one-dollar membership fee. As the decade ended, Coughlin's once-destitute parish was well on its way to accumulating enough money to construct a lavish new sanctuary.

NINETEEN TWENTY-NINE also saw the network radio debut of the Reverend Billy Sunday, whose fire-and-brimstone style had been a fixture of the evangelical tent shows early in the decade, although he, like literally hundreds of religious leaders, occasionally did question the "spiritual value of radio." Billy Sunday's *The Back Home Hour* was aired on the CBS network during the prime religion hour of 11 A.M. every Sunday. The show was instantly popular and equally controversial. Reverend Sunday attacked sin and sinners using questionable language and imagery: *I'll punch it, kick it, butt it, bite it, and when I'm old and fistless and toothless, I'll gum it.* Though criticized for being "one of the world's worst broadcasters," and for his virulently nasty anti-Catholic opinions, his dramatic sense, the theatrical savvy he developed in tent shows, served him well on the radio and kept him on the air. The Billy Sunday radio broadcasts included music sung by a "sweet-singing choir," dramatic testimony from converts who had turned to Jesus, and, of course, Billy's vivid preaching:

> *A man's body is only worth 85 cents and doesn't contain enough lime to whitewash a chicken coop, but his soul is worth $4,099. There may be another Homer, there may be another Milton, there may be another Shakespeare, there may be another Lincoln, there may be another Roosevelt, but there will never be another Jesus Christ!*

His show was so powerful that the only question was why had he waited so long to get on the air?

BACK IN LOS ANGELES, legal issues haunted the participants in the McPherson case, especially Judge Carlos Hardy and his vocal enemy, the Reverend Robert Shuler. However by February 1929 Shuler himself was the defendant in a libel case filed by the Knights of Columbus that was caused by attacks the reverend had made during the 1928 presidential campaign. Judge Hardy was also facing difficulties. It came to light that McPherson had acquired a hush fund of $800,000, some of which had been used to pay off participants in the 1926 hearings, including District Attorney Keyes. Then during the hearings into McPherson's disappearance it was revealed that Judge Hardy himself had accepted $2,500 from the evangelist. Sister Aimee called the payment nothing more than a "love offering" and insisted it had nothing to do with the judge's legal activities. Nonetheless, Hardy was charged, impeached, and ousted from the American Bar Association. The charges included counseling McPherson and her mother during their hearings, obstructing justice, accepting the $2,500 offering, and witness intimidation. But he was quickly acquitted of all charges and was back on the superior court bench on April 29, 1929. Later that year he would confront Aimee Semple McPherson's harshest critic, Reverend Robert Shuler, in a case that wove together the judicial, religious, and entertainment-industry strands of life in Los Angeles.

ALEXANDER PANTAGES was a social icon of the Roaring Twenties. Good-looking, married to a beautiful woman, and rich, Pantages owned and operated a chain of popular and profitable theaters that virtually controlled live entertainment in North America west of the Mississippi River. Perhaps anticipating a decline in vaudeville's popularity, he had hedged his bets and in 1925 formed a partnership with Famous

Players, a subsidiary of Paramount Pictures. In April 1929 Pantages announced he was selling fifteen theaters and his real-estate holdings to the Radio-Keith-Orpheum Corporation for $14 million, a handsome profit for a chain of theaters he had founded less than twenty years earlier. Headed by David Sarnoff, Radio-Keith-Orpheum, better known today as RKO Radio Pictures, blended the two main electronic media of the era: radio and moving pictures.

Within months of making the deal, Pantages's world crashed around him. His wife, Lois, was arrested and accused of causing the death of Juro Rokumoto in an automobile collision on June 16, 1929. She was released on $50,000 bond pending trial. Then on August 10, Alexander Pantages was arrested and charged with attacking and raping a seventeen-year-old female dancer who had gone to see him about her act. Released on $25,000 bond, he declared his innocence and claimed the girl's charges were a blackmail scheme spurred by the recent sale of his theater chain.

The two Pantages trials occurred within days of each other: His was filled with mysterious witnesses who suddenly couldn't be found, which led to accusations of witness tampering; Mrs. Pantages's was a case of vehicular manslaughter and included the eleventh-hour appearance of a surprise witness for the defense, who claimed another automobile had forced her off the road. But Mrs. Pantages's situation was worsened when the other witnesses at the scene testified that there was "a strong odor of liquor on her breath." The presiding judge, Carlos Hardy, became enraged when he found out that a supporter of Mrs. Pantages had been predicting there would be a hung jury even before the trial began. The vocal defender with a public platform was Reverend Robert Shuler, who used his pulpit and his radio station to decry the case and the judge. Hardy ordered the militant pastor to appear for questioning.

Justice was swift and both trials ended with convictions. Mr. Pantages sought a new trial while his wife asked for probation. As for

Reverend Shuler, his far-too-public involvement in the Pantages case opened him up to criticism and an investigation into whether his station belonged to the Trinity Church or to the reverend himself. His own vague statements about the station, including a preposterous claim that he owned the station but had made a verbal lease of the facility to his church, only encouraged the prosecutors. Unbowed, Shuler used his radio pulpit to defend his actions. His frequent use of radio to "slander public officials" as well as the more global concept of taxation of religious organizations came into question. His outrageous behavior and comments caused one *Los Angeles Times* reader to opine, "Surely the time has come for the citizens and taxpayers of this great city to protest this type of loudmouthed, irresponsible ministers."

Shuler's plight worsened when Judge Hardy ordered him brought to court during Mrs. Pantages's probation hearing. Under oath Shuler admitted that the information he used to issue his predictions about the trial had come to him from secondhand sources. Witnesses then testified that the information Shuler had was false. With Shuler twisting and turning in the witness chair, Judge Hardy declared, "This is just another illustration of what unfounded rumor and suspicion can cast upon a court and a jury." The reprimand was damaging to Shuler, but it only spurred him on in his battle against the government.

DURING THE 1920S, the bulk of religious broadcasting across America simply represented a new, effective way for pastors to extend the reach of their messages, to bring solace and kindness to those physically unable to attend services, and to literally bring the word of God into the home. The more notorious practitioners of electronic religion used their extended pulpits for personal gain or power, although even in those cases, at the core was the goal of extending the cleric's reach and influence. When in the autumn of 1929 Aimee Semple McPherson announced she was going to "send her sermons to the far corners of the earth through the medium of talking pictures," she was merely being an astute broadcaster keeping up with technological advancements to blend the sacred with the profane—religion and entertainment.

With the sanctimony of the pulpit supporting them, the pastors of the airwaves, some intentionally and others accidentally, demonstrated how easily their unseen congregations could be manipulated. At the end of 1929, as the fortunes of most Americans dropped precipitously and the Depression of the 1930s descended on the country, the ability to persuade from the pulpit and over the air would become an even more valuable, powerful, and dangerous talent.

As for Elmer Gantry, the fictional preacher who broadcast his sermons: When the novel was published in March 1927, clergy from coast to coast stood in their pulpits and spoke over radio stations to demand that the book be banned. One preacher predicted the novel would actually aid religion because the character was far too exaggerated to be believable, and that Lewis could never understand the soul of religion or of a minister. Perhaps Lewis knew this charming, hypnotic character only too well:

Thus Elmer increased the number of his hearers from two-thousand to ten thousand—and in another pair of years it would be a hundred thousand.

All of them listening to the Rev. Dr. Elmer Gantry as he shouted: "—and I want to tell you that the fellow who is eaten by ambition is putting the glories of this world before the glories of Heaven!"

Chapter 11

▲▲▲▲▲▲▲▲▲▲▲▲▲▲

IN ITS EARLIEST INCARNATION vaudeville was variety, organized hodgepodge, and at the beginning of the 1920s, variety was what Americans preferred. Unrelated acts—dancers, trained animals, comedians and comedy teams (some in blackface), jugglers, singers, ventriloquists, and even acrobats—tromped across the stage, one after the other, to do their bit. On Broadway and on tours across the country, the annual Ziegfeld Follies and George White's Scandals were the popular, big-name variety shows of the day. Routines, characters, and musical numbers were familiar mainstays of these gala productions. By the end of the decade, vaudeville's popularity was on the wane; though 1928 was a successful year, with nearly 1,000 theaters playing to an aggregate of nearly 2 million people a day, in 1929 the vaudeville audience started to disappear, drawn away by the mechanized entertainment powerhouses of talking pictures and coast-to-coast radio programming.

Ironically, neither talking pictures nor radio, both of which came to maturity during the 1920s, would ever have become so popular without the foundation built by vaudeville.

When radio began its journey from the hobbyists' garages into mainstream business and culture, vaudeville, in its many incarnations, had been entertaining Americans for more than half a century. Born in post–Civil War America, traveling shows provided varied and usually off-color entertainment for men. Then in 1881, impresario Tony Pastor opened his Fourteenth Street Theater in New York and presented less racy shows for "double audiences," audiences of men and women. By the end of the nineteenth century theater chains under the control of a single manager had become the norm. Performers were booked to tour the theaters in these circuits, the most prominent being the United Booking Office, also known as Keith-Albee, which controlled more than 400 theaters in the East and Midwest, and Martin Beck's Orpheum Circuit, which ran theaters from Chicago to California as well as the magnificent Palace Theatre in New York. The great number of acts needed to supply the hundreds of theaters in the circuits enabled the discovery and development of an amazingly varied pool of talented performers, many of whom would find second and third careers in radio, movies, and, eventually, television.

Early radiomen realized that once the thrill of listening to anonymous, invisible people chatting through static wore off, they were going to have to provide something more interesting if people were going to continue buying radio receivers. Frank Conrad, the engineer who masterminded KDKA's initial radio ventures, tested his home transmitting equipment by playing Victrola records in a microphone, creating "wireless concerts" for other enthusiasts. His program of September 20, 1920, included two orchestral numbers, a soprano solo, and a children's story. But anyone who could afford a Victrola and some shellac records could replicate the kind of programming Conrad was airing; clearly radio had to do something more, something that John Q. Public could not reproduce in his living room. Wireless entertainment had to feature talent, virtually any kind of talent, aired live.

As Westinghouse, General Electric, RCA, and hundreds of smaller companies became part of the new radio business, their expenditures went primarily toward the development and construction of transmitting equipment, and the first performance studios were usually outfitted with thick curtains and rugs that served not only as decoration but as natural sound deadeners. Performers and their managers saw radio as a new stage, and these studios, especially in the bigger cities, became destinations for artists of all kind. Though relatively barren of technical apparatus, at their center most studios had a grand piano surrounded by a few easy chairs and the microphone, often disguised as a floor lamp with a shade so as to decrease performers' mike fright. On an average summer day in 1922, a listener to Chicago's KYW could enjoy a children's bedtime story at 7:30 P.M. followed at 8 by a live musical program starring soprano Helen Collins accompanied on the piano by J. T. Ashford, a few numbers played by the Salvation Army Territorial Staff Band, and selections sung by the members of the Metropolitan Male Quartet. The program ended with the Salvation Army Band performing their rousing version of "Our Conquering Army."

Talent, if not great talent, was available everywhere. Instrumentalists, singers, whistlers, hummers, in fact anyone who could make an interesting sound found themselves performing before the local radio station's microphones. In Los Angeles, KHJ aired jazz sponsored by theater owner Alexander Pantages. In Fayetteville, Arkansas, KFMQ, "the voice of the Ozarks," aired the annual fiddlers' contest, where old-time fiddlers competed playing such classics as "Dry and Dusty" and "Leather Breeches." When Cedar Rapids, Iowa, got its first radio station in 1922, founder Douglas M. "Tex" Perham built his transmitter and studio in a converted garage on the southwest side of town. In the moments after WJAM's power switch was thrown for the inaugural broadcast, listeners all over the region were tapping their toes to the sounds of the Manhattan Dance Orchestra, which despite its name was made up entirely of local Des Moines musicians. After its initial broadcast, WJAM devoted its program schedule exclusively to educational lectures and performances by local musicians playing live for the radio audience.

Dr. John Brinkley's strategy of employing a stable of musicians and yodelers to entertain his patients and KFKB's audience in Milford, Kansas, demonstrated that stations could maintain a staff of entertainers in order to create their own varied content. Other stations found that committing to one kind of music was also an effective way to build an audience. Chicago's KYW debuted on November 11, 1921, with opera star Mary Garden performing. During the station's inaugural months, its program schedule consisted exclusively of opera, six days a week, including matinees and evening performances of the Chicago Civic Opera. Good content drove radio ownership; at the beginning of the 1921–22 opera season there were about 1,300 receivers in the Chicago area. By the end of that season, 20,000 sets were in operation. But when the opera season ended, KYW faced a new dilemma: what to broadcast? Hastily they built studios in the Commonwealth Edison building, which became a magnet for celebrities. Anyone of note who visited the Windy City was paraded before the KYW microphones: Rudolph Valentino, Al Jolson, Tito Schipa, and hundreds of other stars of varying degrees of fame discovered that appearing on the radio was good exposure.

WLS (owned by Sears, Roebuck and Company; the call letters stood for World's Largest Store) helped make Chicago the country music capital of the world at the time. On Saturday evening, April 19, 1924, the first Saturday following the station's debut, program manager George Hay introduced the *National Barn Dance,* a program of old tunes and traditionally called square dances. Station manager Edgar Bill said: "We had so much highbrow music the first week that we thought it would be a good idea to get on some of the old-time music. After we had been going about an hour, we received 25 telegrams of enthusiastic approval." Listeners were virtually transported to the hills, delighted by the quaint tunes and calls: *Big foot up—little feet down, / Like a jaybird walkin' on frozen ground.* The performers included Tommy Dandurand, Chubby Parker, and Pie Plant Pete. The program was so popular that stations all across the country copied its format. In 1925 George Hay moved to Nashville's WSM, where he re-created the show's format, naming it the *WSM Barn Dance.* One Saturday in December 1927, after the station had become an NBC network affiliate, the *Barn Dance* followed a network opera program. Hay is reported to have said, "For the past hour we have listened to music taken largely from Grand Opera, but from now on we will present 'The Grand Ole Opry.'" The name fit so well with the acts that trod across the *Barn Dance* stage, such as Dr. Humphrey Bate and the Possum Hunters, the Fruit Jar Drinkers, and the Clod Hoppers, that the name stuck and has been the calling card for country music ever since.

In their ongoing effort to find ready-to-air programming, radio station managers turned to vaudeville houses on Broadway, in New York, in search of varied offerings. In 1922 there was no more popular or respected vaudevillian than Ed Wynn. Born Isaiah Edwin Leopold in 1886, he ran away from home as a teenager to pursue a career in vaudeville; to spare his family the embarrassment of having a comedian in their ranks, he renamed himself by splitting his middle name—Ed-Win. Wynn worked as an assistant to W. C. Fields until the veteran performer caught him scene stealing and fired him. By 1912, Wynn had become a vaudeville star in his own right and in 1914 was a featured performer in the Ziegfeld Follies. Seven years later he was opening at Broadway's George M. Cohan's Theatre in a show of his own creation, a "Musical Riot" called *The Perfect Fool.*

The Perfect Fool was a revue made up of several scenes—like a vaude-ville show—that included mind reading, acrobatics, and song-and-dance numbers; "Ed Wynn can do almost anything," raved the *New York Times*. With barely a sensible line spoken by the comedian from the time the overture finished until his final appearance, audiences still laughed nearly every time Wynn opened his mouth. Yet despite *The Perfect Fool*'s being a highly visual romp, the program manager at WJZ thought Wynn's show would be good radio. On February 19, 1922, Wynn transported his troupe to the station's Newark, New Jersey, stu-dios for the broadcast. So anticipated was the event that all the other radio stations in the area agreed to go silent during the show so as not to interfere with WJZ's signal.

Though this show was being done for radio and he couldn't be seen by the audience, Wynn still wore his clown costume. As Wynn ap-proached the microphone, his severe anxiety seemed abnormal for a man so completely at ease on stage. As the show progressed, Wynn's nervousness decreased, but he was thrown off his rhythm by the lack of response, by the silence. Even the best bits in the show received no reaction, not even the slightest applause, but there was good reason: There was no live audience. Wynn told the station's staff announcer that he couldn't perform this way. The announcer gathered anyone standing around the studio—engineers, telephone operators, even artists who were scheduled to appear later—and invited them into the studio to enjoy the rest of the show. Their reactions—laughter, giggles, *oohs* and *aahs*, and applause—reenergized the show, and Wynn con-tinued more confidently. Although it wouldn't become common prac-tice for some time, *The Perfect Fool* broadcast introduced the idea of the studio audience. As for Wynn, while the broadcast ended up being a success, the mike fright he suffered would prevent him from returning to the airwaves on a regular basis for a decade.

Will Rogers, who early in 1922 had questioned whether anyone could actually hear him as he spoke into a WWJ microphone and then received hundreds of cards from listeners all over the Midwest, was starring in the Ziegfeld Follies of 1922 when excerpts of the show were aired live from the studios of KDKA. With a book by Ring Lardner, music by Victor Herbert, and a cast of music, dance, and vaudeville stars, the 1922 Follies must have been a fairly compelling show, but like Wynn, Rogers remained unsure about radio and its value as an entertainment medium and appeared on the air rather infrequently until the end of the decade.

The birth of legitimate drama as radio programming occurred far from the lights of Broadway. In Schenectady, New York, WGY signed on the air just two weeks before Ed Wynn's *The Perfect Fool* broadcast. Kolin Hager was the station's program manager and chief announcer, and despite the lack of success other regional stations had had presenting dramatic scenes, he decided that serious drama had a place on his station. During the summer of 1922, Edward H. Smith, a local actor in a troupe named The Masque that performed in nearby Troy, New York, suggested to Hager that his company perform radio adaptations of plays. Hager liked the idea and had Smith rework a three-act play by Eugene Walter titled *The Wolf,* turning it into a forty-minute radio drama. Written in 1908, *The Wolf* is a moralistic tale about an innocent young woman, raised by her strict father, who meets a man; the tale ends with her virtue intact. The adaptation was rehearsed and broadcast on August 3, 1922. The reaction was tremendous—the station received more than 2,000 letters—and Hager offered the troupe a regularly scheduled, weekly Friday-night time slot. By season's end, the group, now renamed the WGY Players, had presented forty-three specially made radio plays, and had begun to include sound effects to further enliven the dramas.

In Cincinnati, WLW, which was owned by Crosley Radio Corporation, was one of the most innovative radio stations in the country. On April 3, 1923, the station experimented with an entirely new source of content when they aired a drama written expressly for WLW by the station's manager, Fred Smith. The play was titled *When Love Wakens* (the first letters of the title's words represented the station's call letters, WLW), in which the narrator was called a "descriptionist."

Broadcasting plays, including some directly from Broadway theaters, was periodically attempted, but these live shows were not easy to air primarily because the radio audience could not see the relevant action or who was speaking, and that led to confusion. But there were other problems with serious drama unaltered for radio. First, the material had to be deemed suitable for the airwaves; second, the challenges of miking voices from all over a stage and even backstage created technical hurdles; and third, intervals between scenes and acts needed to be filled with new descriptive material or there would be silence. Then, still struggling to find its way, drama on the radio faced a new obstacle: Playwrights wanted to be paid if their works were going to be exploited on the air. After some miffed writers heard their words on the radio, the Society of American Dramatists and Composers proclaimed that airing a work without permission and compensation was a violation of copyright. The society's president declared: "Under such circumstances a station is liable for a fee both under the copyright law and common law. Now we propose to make it hot for any station that broadcasts our works without permission."

Further complicating the matter, live theater on the radio had to confront the same question sports broadcasting was facing: What impact would airing plays have on ticket sales? If you could hear a play for free on the radio, why would you pay for a ticket? The answer seemed to come from one WJZ listener who wrote thanking the station for airing the musical comedy *Mary Jane McKane*. Though he enjoyed the presentation, he was afraid he would have to stop listening to broadcasts of plays because "reception of the musical comedy cost him twenty dollars when his wife insisted that he take the entire family to see the show."

Even as plays and musicals became regular components of station programming, the debate as to whether they were good content continued. The key to success seemed to be in the choice of material; the drama had to be conveyed entirely through words, so the piece had to be suited to the medium. Despite an agreement between the famous Broadway producers the Shuberts and WJZ to place microphones between the footlights to air performances from the stage, those efforts during the autumn of 1925 were not rewarding, and the shows were discontinued. But plays airing from a radio studio were becoming accepted, and station WGBS in New York was one of the leaders in this arena. During the 1925 season they had success with presentations of *Salome, Emperor Jones,* and special adaptations of some Shakespeare classics, including *The Taming of the Shrew.* The station wanted to air the plays of George Bernard Shaw—though the call letters GBS looked as though they might refer to the playwright, they actually stood for the station's owner, Gimbel Brothers Department Store—and it entered into negotiations with the Irish author for the right to adapt his works for radio. Unfortunately, Shaw, like many other intellectuals, was not a radio fan, and the deal was never consummated. Shaw eventually warned that radio was threatening theater's viability: "All I can say is that if I could see and hear a play from my fireside I would never enter a theater again." Eight years later, after a visit to the United States, George Bernard Shaw sang a slightly changed tune. "There are only three things I'll never forget about America," he ventured: "the Rocky Mountains, Niagara Falls, and Amos and Andy on the radio."

Amos 'n' Andy, perhaps the most popular spoken entertainment show ever, did not begin its existence with that name. In 1924 Freeman Gosden and Charles Correll were bookers for the Joe Bren Producing Company. Based in Chicago, the two agents roomed together; to pass the time they harmonized, singing while accompanying themselves on the ukulele and piano, much like a vaudeville minstrel act. Urged by friends, they auditioned and were given a slot on WEBH, a small station with studios adjacent to the ballroom of the Edgewater Beach Hotel, from which the call letters were taken. Emboldened by the popularity of their "act," they quit their day jobs at the Joe Bren Producing Company, then moved their show to WGN, where they were paid $250 a week for their minstrel show. Gradually they added banter to their musical bits, and the team's popularity again grew, so much so that they were asked to develop a "strip show," a program patterned after a comic strip to be broadcast five days a week.

Instead of mimicking characters already appearing in strips in the newspapers, Gosden and Correll looked to the South to create their new radio show: It would be about two black southerners named Sam and Henry, who'd come to Chicago from Alabama seeking their fortunes. The show debuted on January 12, 1926, and its strip format enticed listeners to tune in every day for a fifteen-minute window into the characters' lives. Thanks in part to promotion provided by the *Chicago Tribune,* WGN's parent company, the show was tremendously popular in Chicago. But Gosden and Correll wanted more and asked to be allowed to record the shows and sell them, or syndicate them, to stations outside of Chicago. WGN refused, and when the team's two-year contract ended, they took their popular act across town to WMAQ, the station owned by the *Chicago Daily News.* Since WGN claimed to own the names Sam and Henry, the show's main characters needed to be renamed, and thus Amos and Andy were born.

Amos 'n' Andy debuted over WMAQ on March 19, 1928. In Chicago the shows were aired live, but the team recorded each episode for distribution to thirty other radio stations. The basic plot of the series was that after one year in Chicago, having come from Atlanta (they had to change Alabama to Atlanta to avoid problems with WGN), Amos and Andy owned one broken-down, topless automobile, one business—the Fresh Air Taxi Cab Company of America, Incorporated—

and one unpaid-for desk. The scenes were centered around the cab company and the rooming house where the boys lived. Every line of dialogue was written and delivered in the dialect Gosden and Correll created; phrases such as "I'se regusted," "Now ain't that sumpin?" and "Holy mackerel Andy," became catchphrases. Gosden and Correll believed in authenticity, and despite the fact that it was radio, they acted out every stage direction, even using props, as if the audience could see them. They were always pictured in blackface and never broke character or changed dialects; as far as the radio audience was concerned, they *were* Amos and Andy. In a 1929 poll conducted by WOL in Washington, D.C., *Amos 'n' Andy* was easily the most popular program, receiving 488 of a possible 557 votes. Even President Coolidge listening over WOL did not like to be disturbed while the show was on. Soon the show and the boys drew the interest of the NBC network executives.

During the summer of 1929, NBC announced that beginning with the August 19 broadcast of this comedy filled with "droll American-Afro witticisms," *Amos 'n' Andy* would join the NBC network. On the network the series was sponsored by Pepsodent toothpaste; their advertising commitment to the show marked the first time the network had sold a sponsorship for a fifteen-minute, six-days-a-week program. Until then sponsorships had been primarily for once-a-week, half-hour or hour-long programs. Initially *Amos 'n' Andy* aired at 11 P.M., but by mid-November its popularity forced the network to move it to prime time, at 7 P.M. But the shift meant the show was heard at 4 P.M. Pacific Time, which caused fans in the West to threaten a boycott against Pepsodent. Bowing to pressure, the network decided to air the show twice each evening, first from 7 to 7:15, then with a repeat airing at 10:30, mostly for listeners on the West Coast.

The network debut of the blackface comedians came nearly two years after the premiere of another entertainment milestone featuring a star in blackface, *The Jazz Singer,* with vaudevillian Al Jolson. While a relationship between the movies and radio had existed since 1923 with programs such as *The Movie Critic of the Air* and Quinn Martin's *Movie Notions,* the most meaningful union between the two technologies happened when silent movies added sound.

OCTOBER 7, 1927—Lined up outside the Warner Theatre in New York City, crowds of movie fans hoped to get a ticket to the world premiere of *The Jazz Singer.* Sensing the importance of the event, WRNY contracted to broadcast the premiere, including descriptions of the celebrities arriving for the show, in what was the equivalent of today's red-carpet ceremonies. At 8 P.M. listeners to WRNY heard Albert Howson describe the gala, from the arrival of the celebrities to the preliminary program, along with the music being heard in the theater and greetings from the notables in attendance, including Al Jolson himself.

The relationship between radio and movies developed further when the motion-picture industry, in an effort to ready the moviegoing public for the unstoppable arrival of talking pictures, turned to radio for promotional help. Hollywood arranged to have several leading stars speak over a nationwide hookup. Then, to build anticipation and audience interest, Hollywood leaked the names of the participants: Douglas Fairbanks, John Barrymore, Charlie Chaplin, Dolores del Rio, Norma Talmadge, and director D. W. Griffith would all be heard. Some movie palaces, all with newly installed sound equipment, would play the radio program in the theaters prior to that night's feature. Sponsored by Dodge Brothers, the automobile company, the broadcast originated from Mr. Fairbanks's bungalow in Hollywood and the WJZ studios, where Paul Whiteman and his band played interludes between the stars' talks.

It was a glittering event: The program opened with Whiteman and his band playing "Together," but before the galaxy of America's film stars were heard, the fifty-five-station NBC network was turned over to Detroit for special words from Edward G. Wilmer, president of Dodge Brothers, who announced the release of Dodge's new six-cylinder car, the Standard Six. After Wilmer's more than ten-minute pitch for the car, the broadcast returned to Hollywood and its stars. Fairbanks gave a talk titled "Keeping Fit"; Barrymore recited Hamlet's soliloquy; Miss Talmadge spoke about women's fashion; Miss del Rio sang "Ramona"; D. W. Griffith talked about love; and Charlie Chaplin told "characteristic" Jewish and cockney jokes. When he emerged from Fairbanks's bungalow, Chaplin told a *Variety* reporter that he had not enjoyed the experience because of mike fright.

But the broadcast was doomed by heavy rain in the Northeast and ice storms in the Midwest, which created interference in the form of loud echoing noises in the movie theaters, where the sound was being amplified. Audiences—at least those who stayed—stomped their feet and demanded that the offending sounds be turned off. Reporting on the initiation of sound in movie theaters, *Variety* called the effort "brutal."

While almost any kind of entertainment was potential radio content, ultimately music—live and on phonograph records—filled a great deal of the airtime during radio's first decade. Live music programs were easy to assemble and there was no shortage of available talent in every city, big or small. Paul Whiteman, for whose band George Gershwin composed *Rhapsody in Blue,* was one of New York's most powerful bandleaders; his band was often heard on the radio playing new songs of the day mixed in with classical favorites. While classical music—"serious" music, as it was usually called—received plenty of airtime, it was the new band music of the day that excited listeners most. President Hoover's belief was that radio had stimulated the appreciation of good music, despite the fact that it had given tenfold the "time to the worst music."

During the winter of 1923, WEAF in New York formed an in-house orchestra, and within the year, the ensemble of six musicians had developed a weekly show. Intrigued by the group's haunting melodies, an executive of a local food-store chain wanted to link his company to the group, and so on March 17, 1924, the ensemble was renamed the A&P Gypsies; they played exotic music with a nomadic motif. It was a novelty act that fit the marketing needs of the A&P food stores and, though they were never allowed to offer any merchandise during the show, A&P's sponsorship had a long run. Eventually the ensemble was enlarged to an orchestra of twenty-five, and on January 3, 1927, the A&P Gypsies became part of the NBC network; the show remained on the air until 1936, continuously sponsored by A&P.

While there were literally thousands of musicians and impresarios who contributed to music's prominence on the airwaves, two legends of entertainment deserve special attention because of the innovations they brought to radio: Samuel Lionel Rothafel and Rudy Vallée.

Born in Stillwater, Minnesota, on July 9, 1882 (and nicknamed Roxy by teammates in a Pennsylvania baseball league), Samuel Rothafel became one of the entertainment world's most imaginative presenters. Rothafel's first foray into entertainment was in Forest City, Pennsylvania, where he converted an empty storeroom into a movie theater. Not content to just show short, silent movies, Rothafel concocted elaborate presentations using lights, music, and changing colors harmonized with the silent pictures he presented. His ingenuity, imagination, and drive took him to New York, where beginning in 1913 he ran a series of important theaters, starting with the Strand on Broadway, then the Rialto, the Rivoli, and finally the grandest of them all, the Capitol, called the "World's Largest and Most Beautiful Theatre."

Rothafel, a superb self-promoter, made certain that whenever the Capitol Theatre announced the movies it had booked, it was always mentioned that the photoplays to be presented had been personally selected by S. L. Rothafel himself. In addition to choosing the movies, Rothafel was in charge of all the other aspects of the theater's programming, including vaudeville shows and recitals, some of which he presented either before or after the silent movies. Not surprisingly, as radio became a prominent part of entertainment, Roxy Rothafel wanted to be part of the new industry. On November 19, 1922, microphones installed at the Capitol Theatre at Broadway and Fifty-first Street captured what was advertised as "An Epochal Musical Event." With Erno Rapee conducting an enlarged Capitol Grand Orchestra, WEAF's listeners heard a special presentation of the American premiere of Richard Strauss's tone poem *A Hero's Life*.

That radio show and those that followed were high-class, well-produced presentations, and within the year, Sunday evening at 7:20 became *The Capitol Theatre Gang* broadcast time. The shows brought listeners a variety of entertainment, including opera highlights along with some lighter fare, usually movie music, all played by the Capitol's superb orchestra. These lavish shows were held together by breezy on-air introductions and commentary by Roxy himself; within months the show's name was changed to the catchier *Roxy and His Gang*. Roxy was the master of ceremonies who welcomed listeners everywhere into his theater and introduced them to incredible talents. The weekly show was so successful that it was expanded to two hours, including an additional segment for the radio audience only that was aired not from the stage, but from specially constructed studios above the theater. Roxy and his cast of regular performers became huge stars, and when they toured to Washington, D.C., in February 1924 for the First Annual Radio Show, they were invited to the White House to meet President and Mrs. Coolidge.

Catherine Kenney, a sixteen-year-old Washington "radio bug," wrote a column for the *Washington Post* that explained why *Roxy and His Gang* was the best thing on radio. "The atmosphere of fun and good fellowship which exists over there in the Capitol Theatre seems to float through the air to the listeners-in." She added: "But what makes the gang the most popular feature on the air? Their leader Roxy! Roxy, with the pleasing voice, now sending out a word of cheer to his disabled buddies, now joking with Frank or Gamby; now praising those about him—but always forgetting himself."

Roxy didn't have to talk about himself—undoubtedly he was the star of the show and Americans felt comfortable inviting him into their homes every Sunday evening. But his conversational, easygoing manner, so far removed from the formal, stilted announcing style that was the norm in that era, eventually led J. A. Holman, broadcasting manager of WEAF, to ask Roxy to curb his enthusiasm; he wanted "Roxy to be a little more dignified."

Roxy obliged and began speaking in a more straightlaced style: "He read no telegrams. He asked after the health of no maiden aunts. He made no personal allusions to real or fancied sheiks or flappers." The audience reacted with an overwhelming outpouring of negative fan mail. By the next broadcast WEAF had reconsidered, and the ebullient Roxy of old returned. "But folks," he said, "all is well. The differences are all gone. The American Telephone and Telegraph Company [owners of WEAF] and I have fixed everything up, and it's all glorious. They want to give you what you want and so do I. Don't be harsh or unmindful of what the company has done for radio."

Roxy's fame spread as other stations in markets from the East Coast to the Midwest began carrying the weekly extravaganza. In March 1925 Roxy became a syndicated newspaper columnist, and the announcements boasted that "ROXY, The King of the Air," who, with his famous "gang" entertained millions on the radio every Sunday, would now have a daily column about radio called *Hello, Everybody!,* the name of which was the written echo of his cheerful radio sign-on. Three months later a syndicate of private investors announced they were financing the construction of the world's largest motion picture theater for Samuel L. "Roxy" Rothafel, "the radio entertainer." The flamboyant impresario called the new 6,000-seat theater "the realization of my ambition to have a motion picture theatre of my own with entertainment features and radio broadcasting."

In July Roxy was released from his Capitol Theatre contract by his boss, Major Edward Bowes, vice president of Metro-Goldwyn-Mayer (MGM), which owned the Capitol. Instead of referring to his final broadcast as a good-bye, Roxy called it an "au revoir" since he would be back better than ever in the new theater, which would be named for him. Major Bowes took over all of Roxy's duties, including radio broadcasting, changing the Sunday evening show's name to *Major Bowes' Capitol Family*. Though still primarily a music show broadcast live from the stage, Bowes mixed in some talk and comedy bits to add variety. He went on to develop the *Major Bowes' Original Amateur Hour*, which became one of the most popular talent shows in broadcasting history, and within its fun format he developed the idea of having listeners call in to vote for their favorite amateur performers. "Murray Hill 8–9933 [the show's phone number] became the most famous telephone number in the world."

Construction of the Roxy Theatre took a little more than one year. By March 1927, days before the theater's actual opening, Roxy's familiar *Hello, Everybody!* was heard once again on the air. Using the theater's state-of-the-art radio studio, he, with members of his gang standing around for support and to provide background ambiance, renewed his relationship with the radio listeners by confessing he was nervous but vowing that everything would be ready for the grand opening.

FRIDAY, MARCH 11, 1927—Outside the Roxy Theatre crowds gathered hoping to catch a glimpse of the hundreds of celebrities attending the new theater's opening festivities. Gloria Swanson, Charlie Chaplin, Harold Lloyd, New York's dapper mayor Jimmy Walker, Ralph Pulitzer, Irving Berlin, and four United States senators were all there, but the star of the evening was the 6,200-seat theater itself. Just two weeks later, the theater, which was called the "Cathedral of the Motion Picture," was sold to the Fox Theatres Corporation. The agreement arranged for Roxy to manage the facility and to operate any theaters Fox might add to their chain. William Fox praised the arrangement, saying, "This entire chain of theatres will, therefore, benefit through management by a man who has directed many of the large and important theatres of New York, and who has become a world figure through his radio broadcasts."

Roxy was an American original, but without radio his fame would have been limited to the confines of his theater. As the head of his new entertainment venue and another one in Washington, D.C., he was the nation's impresario. The NBC network, always in the market for more talent, needed Roxy and his gang, which now included a studio orchestra of sixty players and a chorus of more than 100 voices. Roxy was a national sensation, so it wasn't unexpected that when Charles Lindbergh landed in Paris, Roxy was among the first to cable an offer to the triumphant flyer, but Roxy's was the largest: He guaranteed Lindbergh $25,000 a week to appear on the stage of the Roxy Theatre, appearances that would be broadcast. Lindbergh declined.

Radio fans loved Roxy, and Roxy was radio's biggest fan. "Radio has done more for me than anything else in the world. It has given me insight into the psychology of people's likes and dislikes far greater than that which I could have obtained by personal contact with audiences in the theatres. It has been an inspiration to me, and as long as I can I shall broadcast and carry on along these lines." By the autumn of 1928, more than 4 million letters from fans all over the country had been sent to Roxy, most of them expressing how his broadcasts had become part of their family's entertainment. The letters, which he called "the measuring gauge for our radio activities," and the gifts that often accompanied them, were the invisible audience's applause.

The growth in popularity of *Roxy and His Gang* paralleled the industry's expansion, and Roxy was the right showman at the right time: He knew how to manipulate the radio audience and involve them in the casual, friendly world he created. His programs showed that good music, well played, and presented with a healthy dose of bravado, attracted listeners. But beyond the movie palaces and theaters, there was another important source of music available to radio programmers: hotel ballrooms and the swanky clubs that were prohibited from serving liquor.

Dr. Isham Harris, the superintendent of the Brooklyn State Hospital for the Insane, placed the blame for the increase in insanity commitments during 1924 squarely at the feet of the pressures of the modern world. Among the complexities that were creating abnormal and exaggerated conditions, Dr. Harris cited radio, jazz, and bad liquor.

Fancy parties, jazz, and bad liquor were part and parcel of the Roaring Twenties, especially in the ballrooms of major hotels and the clubs that provided radio stations with an amazing amount of musical talent. Whether at swank midtown hotels or "slumming" at the clubs in Harlem, wealthy New Yorkers, socialites in flowing gowns and dashing men nattily attired in white tie and tails, enjoyed the freedoms of the era. America was having a party, and music was central to the celebration. Radio listeners benefited from a plethora of live music; on a typical night in 1924 listeners could hear Joska DeBabary's orchestra playing in the Louis XIV Room broadcast on KYW; the Symphonic Dance Orchestra playing in the radio ballroom of Philadelphia's Majestic Hotel over WFI; the Coconut Grove Orchestra on Los Angeles's KFI; George Freeman's Sooner Serenaders and the Texas Hotel Orchestra on Fort Worth's WBAP; the Coon-Sanders Nighthawks from Kansas City's Muehlebach Hotel on WDAF; or the Chubb-

Steinberg Orchestra de Luxe on Cincinnati's WLW. Then in Chicago there was WMBB—World's Most Beautiful Ballroom—whose sole mission was to air dance music nightly from the luxurious Trianon Ballroom, while WBBM, which broadcast from the Broadmoor Hotel, featured an all-jazz format. WBBM was the original radio home of Guy Lombardo and His Royal Canadians, who broadcast their first New Year's Eve bash in 1927, launching a tradition that would continue for decades.

Jazz, in its pure form, the kind being developed and promulgated by Duke Ellington, Fletcher Henderson, and Louis Armstrong, was heard on the radio, but not without criticism. Station managers were reluctant to broadcast hot jazz, and some stations would not allow saxophones to be heard because they were thought to have "an immoral influence." While jazz had some influence on the "dance orchestras," as they were called, what these society orchestras and bands played was, in reality, a cooled-down version of jazz that gave a taste of the real thing, but without its true, hot flavor.

Radio's seminal role in developing African American musical talent would not really occur until later in the decade, but in the meantime hundreds of dance orchestras brought the live atmosphere and ambiance of the ballroom right into the living rooms of radio listeners everywhere. Every evening, radio stations aired some form of this evocative opening: *And now, from the beautiful Starlight Room of the Smith Hotel in downtown* [name any city] *station* [fill in call letters] *brings you the dancing music of* . . . But nowhere was it more prevalent than in New York, where white-tie-clad men and evening-gowned women danced the nights away in the city's fabulous hotels, each of which featured at least one dance orchestra. At the Waldorf, twelve orchestras supplied dance music, while on any given night partiers at the Astor Hotel could enjoy music by eighteen ensembles. Hotels throughout the city needed music for their partying patrons, and some, like the Roosevelt Hotel

(WRNY) and the McAlpin Hotel (WMCA), had the radio station studios installed right in the hotel.

The Hotel Pennsylvania, across Seventh Avenue from Pennsylvania Station, was home to Vincent Lopez and His Orchestra. Many of their nightly shows were aired over WJZ during the station's earliest years. By 1924 the band was so identified with the hotel that the group became known as the Pennsylvania Orchestra. Lopez's sign-on was the simple, yet catchy *Lopez speaking*. Lopez and Paul Whiteman, whose weekly radio show was sponsored by Old Gold Cigarettes and who was cross-promoted in the cigarette's newspaper ads, which referred to Whiteman as the "King of Jazz," were the musical captains of New York. They lent their names to many orchestras and ensembles that played around town and in nearby cities, and took fees from each group, collecting a surcharge if the named bandleader himself showed up for the engagement. Getting a steady gig in one of their ensembles was a sought-after prize for any New York musician. Appearing one night a week in one of Lopez's ensembles was a tall, handsome saxophone player from New England—via Yale and London—named Rudy Vallée.

Hubert Prior Vallée was born in Vermont on July 28, 1901. When he was a child his parents moved to Maine, where his father worked as a pharmacist. Hubert was expected to follow in his father's footsteps, but the young man fell in love with the sound of the saxophone, developing the dreaded disease he called "saxophobia." He taught himself to play, and when he heard a recording by sax virtuoso Rudy Wiedoeft he found his idol. Attending the University of Maine, Vallée developed a fixation with Wiedoeft that earned him the nickname Rudy, which stuck and followed him when he transferred to Yale; there he joined an ensemble that played private engagements and some vaudeville gigs. It was the beginning of the 1920s and there was no shortage of work for young, talented bands like those described in *The*

Great Gatsby; "no thin five-piece affair, but a whole pitful of oboes and trombones and saxophones." Rudy Vallée became a raccoon-coat–wearing, megaphone-holding, tall, handsome, bronze-haired bandleader ideally suited to the party-happy era.

There was so much work for talented bands that groups were often booked to play multiple gigs on the same night. Engaged as the main dance band for a socialite's debutante party in Baltimore, Vallée and an ensemble played tune after tune while the crowd danced. Then during one of the band's breaks, another ensemble, this one called the Rhythm Boys, which had been put together by Paul Whiteman, came in to entertain. They set up, played a few tunes, and then one of the group's members sang "Montmartre Rose." A hush came over the crowd, and when the song was over they burst into wild cheering. Vallée watched as the young man, "oblivious to their shouts and applause, almost as if he were hard of hearing," threaded his way through the tables. "I was struck," Vallée remembered, "by the lack of expression on his face, which was a mask of complete indifference. Bing Crosby was a hit and didn't even know it!"

Shortly after that Baltimore date, Vallée got the break that would launch one of the great radio careers: On January 8, 1928, he was asked to lead a band at the Heigh Ho Club on New York's fashionable East Side. Owned by George Dickerman and George Putnam, Amelia Earhart's husband, the club had opened on New Year's to bad reviews, including a slam in the *New Yorker* complaining "that the floor was rough and the band looked very Jewish."

Vallée pulled together a group that included Jules de Vorzon, who would be the lead singer when vocals were needed. Vallée dressed his band in "tuxedo pants with satin Russian blouses buttoned at the neck, long sleeves, and a sash around the waist." As they played their opening set to a crowd of about fifteen people, Dickerman seemed annoyed, and when Vallée asked if he liked their music the owner complained that the lead singer was no good. So during the next set Vallée sang the numbers. Dickerman smiled, and Rudy Vallée remained the lead singer so the band could keep the job, which kept them busy every night from seven until three in the morning, all for the sum of ninety dollars a week. Their entrance into radio came in February when WABC, a fledgling radio station with studios in the Steinway Building on West Fifty-seventh Street (soon thereafter WABC changed its call letters to WCBS and became the flagship of the CBS Radio Network), decided the Heigh Ho house orchestra could be a source of high-quality musical programming. The station could not afford to send an announcer to the club, which meant that Rudy Vallée would have to do triple duty as leader, singer, and announcer. With the wonderful naiveté that comes from inexperience, Vallée stepped up to the microphone, and using the welcome with which the club's doorman greeted every guest, began his radio career with *Heigh-ho everybody, this is Rudy Vallée announcing and directing the Yale Collegians from the Heigh-Ho Club at Thirty-five East Fifty-third Street, New York City.*

Vallée's on-air style was casual, and his song introductions, which told the listener something about each composition, generated a dozen letters from listeners impressed by his different on-air sound. By the end of the first week, WABC increased the show from the agreed-on three times a week to every night; a few weeks later WOR asked Vallée if they could air a different segment of his nightly gig; then WMCA asked if another segment might be available for them to broadcast. Though he had to deal with the challenge of avoiding duplication of songs on the three stations, the radio exposure increased the size of the nightly crowd at the club, although Vallée believed that some of the increase was due to the fact that despite the club's restrictive, anti-Semitic policies, the German doorman had begun to let in some nongentile listeners.

While the Heigh Ho Club was closed during the summer of 1928, Vallée and his band played the Milton Point Casino in Rye, New York, from where their shows were broadcast by WMCA. One night the announcer told the radio audience they could write in for a signed picture of Rudy Vallée. More than 50,000 listeners responded. That autumn, Vallée and his band returned to the Heigh Ho Club, but Dickerman fired them, ostensibly because too many of the well-to-do male patrons complained that their dates were fawning over the good-looking bandleader and his musicians. But as often seemed to happen with Vallée's career, setback turned into advancement when he and his band—now renamed the Connecticut Yankees—were hired to play the Versailles, a struggling club on East Sixtieth Street, the site that years later would become the infamous Copacabana.

The Versailles needed an audience. "Put in a radio wire and watch what happens," Vallée told the management. Within three weeks the place was doing turn-away business and was being called the Villa Vallée. More proof of radio's amazing power came when Vallée convinced Bill McCaffrey, who booked the Keith vaudeville theaters, to give him a chance at a three-day run of two concerts a day at one of the Keith houses. McCaffrey agreed, and Vallée saturated the airwaves with announcements during the weeks before the gig: The result was that on the opening day hordes of radio fans pushed the manager out into the lobby; demand for tickets was so great that Vallée's engagement was extended, the only time such a thing had occurred in that theater. By year's end, Vallée was the toast of New York: He was doing nightly shows at the club, vaudeville house dates, and daily tea dances at the Lombardy Hotel, and was one of the most popular radio voices in the East.

During 1929 he and his band continued to play multiple gigs almost every day in sold-out theaters, fancy hotel rooms, and supper clubs. Intrigued by what was called Vallée's "almost mesmeristic power over women," Hollywood beckoned. With the advent and improvement of sound in movies, the strikingly handsome Vallée and his tender, impassioned crooning were ideally suited to the silver screen. While in

California he filmed one short feature, *Radio Rhythm,* in which he played a bandleader who steps out of a radio to lead the Connecticut Yankees through a few numbers; and the feature-length *The Vagabond Lover.* In the latter, Vallée played the part of a college senior and bandleader, Rudy Bronson, who gets embroiled in a convoluted plot of mistaken identity. Though the movie and his acting were panned, Vallée's "soft voice was roundly applauded by the audience and his songs caused many to leave the theatre humming." As he watched the New York premiere, Vallée realized he "had been a party to a resounding flop."

Nonetheless, Vallée had become the star of every available form of entertainment. He was America's first pop-singing radio idol, and, as it had done so many times before, the NBC Radio Network recognized a performer who had a vast and growing appeal, and had the ideal time slot picked out for him: Thursday evenings at eight. Vallée was sure to appeal to women: After all, the "enraptured women" who attended his shows referred to him as a cross between the Prince of Wales and Charles Lindbergh, and when he sang, these same women let out "a sigh as strong and as fervent as a tropical monsoon." NBC had a sponsor lined up for Vallée's show: Fleischmann's Yeast had been acquired in a merger during the summer of 1929, and along with Royal Baking Powder, Chase & Sanborn Coffee, and the E. W. Gillette Company, Ltd., had become part of a new consumer conglomerate called Standard Brands. Fleischmann's Yeast was the centerpiece of the company because of its amazing, reliable distribution system. Every Fleischmann's retailer knew that his scheduled quota of yeast would arrive as certainly as the morning paper, the morning milk, and the day's mail. A business of national import like that needed national exposure, and Rudy Vallée's show was the vehicle to carry their message.

THURSDAY NIGHT, OCTOBER 24, 1929, 8 P.M. EASTERN STANDARD TIME—As Rudy Vallée led his Connecticut Yankees through a rendition of "Down the Road to Sunshine," the NBC announcer stepped up to the microphone: *Good evening, ladies and gentlemen of the radio audience. This is Graham McNamee announcing the program sent to you by the makers of Fleischmann's Yeast.* McNamee, the best-known announcer in the country, then painted a vivid audio portrait of a *luxurious supper club, where soft, mellow blue lights cast their shadows over white linen and sparkling glass and silver . . . clear-eyed, clean-cut men dancing with beautiful girls in lovely gowns . . .* McNamee then introduced Vallée, who greeted the audience with his signature *Heigh-Ho everybody. We are playing "Vagabond Lover" and after this we'll have the "Pagan Love Song," then "Little By Little" and then back to "Vagabond Lover" again.*

For the next hour McNamee set up Vallée's brief introductions and read the commercials for Fleischmann's Yeast, which did not sell the product's ability to make better bread, but rather boasted of a discovery made by a Dr. Catalina that revealed yeast's astounding ability to help cure digestive disorders and give users extra energy: *Yeast may well be called the complement to the successful treatments of many ailments—to build up the energy, force and power of the patient, to maintain his vigor and help in convalescence. Now Rudy Vallée will sing his special arrangement of "Song of India."*

After McNamee read more testimonials from other "famous" doctors about yeast's curative powers, the show ended with the band reprising "Down the Road to Sunshine." McNamee wrapped up: *This concludes our Fleischmann's Yeast Hour. We hope you liked it and we'll be glad to hear from you. This is Graham McNamee speaking. Goodnight, all!*

"We flew the Fleischmann Hour by the seat of our pants," Vallée recalled. Nonetheless the result was a resounding success. The show was an aural fantasy of Gatsbyesque musical partying, an odd yet ideal environment in which a corporate conglomerate and its advertising agency, J. Walter Thompson, could convince a giddy America that health and vitality could be found in packets of yeast. It didn't hurt that female homemakers, Fleischmann's target audience, were captivated by the program's star.

Five days after the show's debut, on Tuesday, October 29, 1929, the economy's fantasy-bubble burst. But the Rudy Vallée show, always sponsored by Standard Brands' Fleischmann's Yeast—a "magnanimous and understanding" sponsor—maintained the top rating in its Thursday night time slot for the next 520 weeks. It was an amazing run during which Vallée redefined radio entertainment while amusing an economically and spiritually depressed nation.

Chapter 12

▲▲▲▲▲▲▲▲▲▲▲▲▲▲

ON THE VERY DAY THAT Rudy Vallée's NBC Network Radio show debuted, the *New York Times* front-page headline read:

Prices of Stocks Crash in Heavy Liquidation;
Total Drop of Billions

Black Thursday, as that day became known, was a shock to the millions of once-giddy investors who had enjoyed the unprecedented run-up in stock values during the previous decade, a rise that had fueled the free-spending, fun-filled partying of the 1920s. The losses of Black Thursday, an exacerbation of a steady decline that had begun weeks earlier, would be trumped the following Tuesday, October 29, when the stock market's prices tumbled even faster. Cornerstone stocks whose values had increased dramatically during the previous years were suddenly significantly lower. For example, on September 3, 1929, American Telephone had been $304 per share; General Electric had been $396.25; U.S. Steel had been $261; and General Motors had been $72.75. By November 13, two weeks after the precipitous decline and even after the markets had stabilized and had experienced a modest recovery, those same stocks were valued at $197.25, $168.50, $150, and $36 respectively, representing a nearly a 47 percent average decline in value.

As the country teetered toward financial crisis, President Hoover's administration took to the radio to reassure Americans. For the first time since the advent of radio, the president of the United States addressed the nation on three successive days, over the coast-to-coast NBC and CBS radio networks; the overarching theme of the talks was technology. The first talk, delivered at a dinner in Dearborn, Michigan, was part of the celebration marking the fiftieth anniversary of the invention of the electric light. In addition to the talk by Hoover, the radio audience heard speeches by Thomas Edison and Henry Ford. Following dinner, the assemblage moved to a nearby laboratory, where Edison, using the same kind of materials he'd employed in 1879, would build a copy of the original light. The entire scene from within the laboratory was described in great detail for the radio audience by Graham McNamee.

President Hoover next went to Cincinnati, where he participated in a ceremony marking the newly completed lock system on the Ohio River. Then it was on to Louisville, where he announced the inception of a project to build an inland waterway at the staggering cost of $20 million. The subtext of all three talks was clear: The American pioneering spirit and knack for invention, coupled with a massive government project, could help restore the country's economy and lift its sagging spirits. His talks were akin to sales pitches and had a sense of rallying the troops. "The American people, I believe, are convinced," he concluded. "What they desire is action, not argument."

Just three days later, as the financial markets slid further, President Hoover could no longer avoid making a public statement about the brewing economic crisis. Issuing a statement, he gave the American people a rosy assessment: The nation was "on a sound and prosperous basis." Hoover was using his national platform to calm a jittery nation, but his words must have seemed hollow and out of touch with reality as the crisis deepened.

On Tuesday, October 29, following the market's stunning drop, Assistant Secretary of Commerce Julius Klein, one of President Hoover's closest friends and advisors, confidently declared that America's economy was "hardly affected" by the collapse. Speaking over the CBS network, he recalled and echoed the conviction expressed by President Hoover that the fundamental business of the nation was on a firm basis. Klein ended his radio talk reassuringly: "Regardless of regrettable speculative uncertainties, the industrial and commercial structure of the Nation is sound. Good-night and thank you!"

If there was one person seemingly unaffected by the market collapse, it was Rudy Vallée, who was happily hosting his Thursday evening hour of delightfully upbeat music. Within weeks of the show's debut Vallée was being promoted as "Radio's GREATEST Personality." His timing may have been superb, because his show was an aural continuation of recent years' happy times and provided a backward-looking escape from the economic reality descending on the country. But Vallée's incredible overnight rise to national celebrity did have one small drawback: Agnes O'Laughlin, a Broadway showgirl, served him with a $200,000 breach-of-promise suit claiming he had jilted her. His official statement merely said he was "greatly surprised and deeply hurt." In many ways, the chorus girl's claim reinforced the free-swinging playboy image Vallée promoted and that kept his legions of female fans wishfully enthralled.

The indirect beneficiaries of Vallée's multimedia stardom were RCA, NBC's parent company, and its dynamic leader, David Sarnoff. Sarnoff, through shrewd business acumen and a prescient vision of how electronic entertainment would become central to the American lifestyle, had built RCA, or "Radio," as it was listed on the New York Stock Exchange, into one of America's giant corporations. The year 1929 had been one of consolidation and acquisition: Sarnoff completed deals with the Victor Talking Machine Company, creating RCA Victor, which he saw as "the alliance of two industries to the greater service of a single art"; with the Keith-Albee-Orpheum theater chain, creating Radio-Keith-Orpheum, or RKO, which marked "the entrance of Radio Corp. into the motion picture field on a large scale"; and with General Motors, creating General Motors Radio Corporation, which Sarnoff saw as a tremendous "opportunity for the development of the radio business as an adjunct to the automobile." The last of these deals did generate some negative reactions, not from businesspeople afraid of RCA's tentacle-like reach into every facet of American life, but from traffic authorities who warned that radios in cars would be a tremendous hazard. "Music in the car might make him [the driver] miss hearing the horn of an approaching automobile or fire or ambulance siren. Imagine 50 automobiles in a city street broadcasting a football game! Such a thing as this, I am sure, would not be tolerated by city traffic authorities."

Rudy Vallée personified Sarnoff's aggressive business strategy of merging RCA with allied industries, creating synergies across audiences: Vallée was a star on the NBC network, he recorded for Victor records, and *The Vagabond Lover* was made by RKO. But the core of RCA's business galaxy was radio, which Sarnoff had helped guide from its inception a decade earlier. Nineteen twenty-nine was seemingly just another year of spectacular results in radio sales that would benefit Sarnoff and his shareholders. The production of radio sets reached another annual record, exceeding the 1928 total by more than 1.2 million units to achieve a staggering 4,428,000 sets, for which Americans spent more than $750 million. More important, the number of U.S. house-holds that now had at least one radio exceeded 10,250,000. In the decade between 1919 and 1929, RCA's annual revenue had increased from $2 million to $182 million, with more than 90 percent of that coming from the sale of radio devices and licensing. National advertising, the kind that Fleischmann's Yeast was exploiting on Vallée's show, had reached a new peak in 1929 with total expenditures topping $3 billion, nearly $20 million of which went directly to radio—this despite Hoover's efforts, first as commerce secretary and then as president, to dissuade industry leaders from sullying the national treasure of radio by allowing hucksters to advertise their wares. The need for revenue to support more hours of programming, especially entertainment programs, increased the presence of advertising on radio, which was becoming ever more noticeable and annoying. Writing in his daily newspaper column, Will Rogers complained that "it's the height of something terrible when forty million people have been listening intently to Graham McNamee for two hours describe a thrilling world's series game and then hear: 'We will now switch you back to the studio for the Safety Can Opener Hour.'" But it was exactly that power, radio's ability to humanize products and put a recognizable, friendly voice like that of Graham McNamee behind consumer goods like yeast, that made radio an appealing vehicle for manufacturers with products to sell. A steadily increasing number of advertisers blended program content with their sales messages: *The Dutch Masters Minstrels, The Palmolive Hour,* and *The Planters Pickers* (sponsored by Planters Nuts) were just three of the more than 150 sponsored programs on the NBC and CBS networks.

However, even Sarnoff's visionary leadership could not prevent RCA from being just as susceptible as all the other corporate giants to market difficulties: The company's stock price on September 3, 1929, after a beneficial split, had been $101; by November 13 RCA was worth just $26 a share. The drop in RCA's stock hurt the portfolios of millions of Americans, including such leading lights as celebrities Scott and Zelda Fitzgerald, who had invested in the hot new technology of the era. Ironically, Sarnoff himself was unharmed by the stock's precipitous drop: That June, going on a hunch, Sarnoff had sold all his shares.

Despite the downturn in Wall Street's fortunes, the business of the nation needed to continue. On Monday, October 28, the Federal Radio Commission extended the licenses of every radio station in the country for a period of ninety days, at which time another review would be undertaken. But the question of licensing was merely one aspect of the control of the airwaves the government was debating. One issue that had begun to rear its head was censorship. The main function of the FRC had been, in essence, to act as the traffic cop of the ether, an independent agency determining the power, frequency, and hours of operation of the country's radio stations, always with an eye toward maximizing listeners' enjoyment by minimizing station interference. The FRC was supposed to concern itself with the technological aspects of radio, not its content. However, as radio became a more vital source of information and opinion, there were calls for the government to strictly control the content and the quality of the programming. Not surprisingly, the radio industry feared that kind of control, and some within the business preemptively proposed that radio-station owners and the networks, in cooperation with the government, should self-monitor. Another proposal hearkened back to the Fourth National Radio Conference in 1925, at which then-secretary Hoover had proposed that the federal government be responsible for traffic regulation, including the allocation of wavelengths and dealing with questions of signal interference, leaving local communities to dictate what was broadcast over the frequencies in their area. Under such a plan, citizens would communicate directly with the FRC to let the commissioners know what kind of programming they desired. Appearing before Congress, NBC president M. H. Aylesworth, showing where the network's priorities really lay, testified that his network had no problem with governmental regulation of broadcasting, but that governmental regulation of advertising rates would not be tolerated. Meanwhile, Democrats in Congress were charging that the Hoover administration was using the FRC as a "political football," that the naming of commissioners was nothing more than another example of partisanship. All of the conflicts Hoover had assiduously tried to avoid as he championed radio's earliest years were now appearing, just as the industry was beginning to reach maturity.

As 1929 drew to a close, President Hoover, trying to reclaim his position as the leader of radio, began urging Congress to make the FRC a permanent body, fully backed by the federal government, so that it would be less susceptible to local political interference, especially in light of the fact that FRC commissioners were often pressured by members of Congress into interceding on behalf of station owners in their district. With the arrival of real advertising revenues, radio-station values had risen, and with that owners were more concerned when the FRC, sometimes seemingly randomly, reduced their power or moved their station to a lesser-quality frequency. A negative change in power or position now equated with a reduction in money coming in.

Testifying before the Senate Interstate Commerce Committee, David Sarnoff urged the Senate to craft legislation that would do everything possible to encourage radio's growth and further development. He claimed that intense competition between wireless communication services would retard rather than advance the radio industry. "At a time when the nation calls for industrial initiative," he said, "when our government is properly using every effort to quicken and develop private enterprise, when large capital investments require encouragement and security, and when a new art is knocking at our door, an open road for radio development would help to maintain public confidence in the radio industry."

Maintaining confidence in American industry was on President Hoover's mind as well. On December 5, he addressed a nationwide radio audience, outlining the steps that a recently formed group of twenty business leaders—including Hoover's close friend and advisor Harry Chandler of the *Los Angeles Times* and KHJ—and the United States government planned to undertake to evaluate business conditions. Though the talk was given at 10:15 in the morning, its significance and relevance to a staggering country was not lost on radio's leaders: Both networks cancelled all other programming to air the speech.

The chairman of Hoover's blue-ribbon business-leaders committee, Julius Barnes, tried to spur Americans by telling them that "there is nothing to cause further timidity or hesitation," and that every sign pointed to "early stabilization of business activity." That optimistic view of business conditions was echoed by the radio industry, which had continued its triumphant march forward to establish itself as a central, if not the most unifying, component of American society; radio had become the thing Americans turned to when seeking information or entertainment. Asked to comment on the impact, if any, that the stock-market crash might have on radio, industry leaders provided a uniformly positive outlook. Inventor Lee De Forest predicted that a record number of radio sets would be sold; H. B. Richmond, president of the Radio Manufacturers Association, also foresaw nothing but increased sales; CBS president William Paley chose to put his faith in the spirit of Christmas to carry the industry forward. All were echoing the view of reality expressed by NBC president Aylesworth, who said, "Radio is not a luxury and should be accepted as a necessity in every American home." To a man, the leaders of the radio industry believed the formula for continued success required more varied and interesting programming—for which they expected to invest more than $12 million during 1930, which in turn would generate more radio set sales, increasing listenership and advertising revenues.

Despite the blip caused by the market's instability, the nation's holiday spirit seemed unbowed. At precisely 5:55 P.M. on Christmas Eve, President and Mrs. Hoover stepped onto the snow-covered grounds of Sherman Square, just outside the Treasury Building in Washington, D.C., to take part in the lighting of the National Community Christmas Tree. After some introductory speeches, a selection played by a cornetist, and a performance by pupils from a local high school accompanied by the U.S. Marine Band of "O Come All Ye Faithful," the president turned on the lights, a signal flare lit the sky, and Boy Scout buglers sounded a call, announcing to all the people of the land that Christmas was officially ushered in. President Hoover then spoke some words of greeting to "the assemblage and the nation," which he was able to reach because the entire ceremony was being carried by a radio hookup sending the festivities from coast to coast.

One week later, as the troublesome last few months of the decade came to a close, New Year's Eve revelers' exuberance was seemingly undiminished. In New York, the hotels were as crowded as ever. With Prohibition more than a decade old and still a topic of debate, with its proponents claiming that "young recruits to the army of drunkards have fallen off," those who wanted liquor had no trouble getting it. New Year's Eve was just another wild party that filled cabarets, clubs, hotels, and even spilled onto the streets of New York; in Times Square the crowds jammed every inch of space. The celebrations were dampened only by the raids conducted by Major Maurice Campbell, New York's federal Prohibition administrator, and his team of 150 agents, who that night visited twenty speakeasies and nightclubs, mostly in Harlem, where they arrested forty-two proprietors and employees.

For those who preferred to spend New Year's Eve at home, radio provided a celebratory atmosphere by transporting listeners to any number of appropriate venues and happy soirées. The excitement of the crowds in Times Square was picked up by microphones and sent out across the country over the CBS network, which led one reporter to describe the street noise as the "highlight of the night." If listening to music was the desired New Year's Eve entertainment, then listeners were well served, because between the hours of 9 P.M. and 1 A.M., New York's radio stations alone featured performances by more than thirty-five orchestras and ensembles. Among the highlights were shows by Paul Whiteman's Old Gold Orchestra over WABC; a special program of New Year's Eve celebration for radio by the Danceland Orchestra on WNYC; and the Palais Orchestra on WOR. But no station anywhere could trump the special New Year's Eve programming provided by the two RCA-owned facilities, WEAF and WJZ, whose programs were fed over NBC's Red and Blue networks.

At WEAF the focus was international. At 7 P.M. Eastern Standard Time, listeners could tune in to hear the chiming of Big Ben in London marking the beginning of 1930 in England. It would be the first element in a night of "Pursuing Time Around the World," a programming concept continued nearly five hours later when WJZ picked up the thread and began "Pursuing Time Across the Country." The lead act of this special tour de force was Rudy Vallée and his Connecticut Yankees, who began their show at 11:55 P.M. EST and carried listeners in the East right through the stroke of midnight and into the first moments of 1930. It was a great night for Vallée, who, in addition to leading the band and singing a few numbers, was moved to make a sentimental and humble speech thanking the radio audience for making him the star that he had become. Following Vallée's fifteen-minute gig, WJZ, as the lead station of the network, presented performances by the Lyman Orchestra, the Ballew Orchestra, the Spitalny Orchestra, the Fiorito Orchestra, the Bernie Orchestra, the Sanders Orchestra, and the Hamp Orchestra, all originating from different locations across the country. At 1:55 A.M. EST, the NBC network turned on its microphones in Denver to air shows by orchestras playing there. One hour later they switched their microphones to San Francisco, from where they presented "Street Noise and Dance Music," followed by the St. Francis Orchestra at the St. Francis Hotel, the Musical Muske-teers, the Stafford Orchestra, the Chinese Orchestra, and a reprise by the Musical Musketeers, ending the show at 4 A.M. EST. The one draw-back of the programming turned out to be the homogeneity of the music; because there was so much standardization of the jazz orchestras they all sounded very much alike. Despite this slight musical disadvan-tage, the night was a triumph for radio, a New Year's Eve coming-out party that solidified its place as a national entertainment force.

That night radio also revealed a poorly hidden truth about America: Despite Prohibition and the efforts of agents in cities everywhere, America's taste for liquor was evident, even over the airwaves, as giddy, some would say tipsy, announcers talked freely of drinking the night away. "Tuning in on radio throughout the country after midnight one would have thought 'Hail, Hail, the Gang's All Here' was the national anthem." What the revelers that night could not yet know was that the decadelong economic party that had fueled the Roaring Twenties was enjoying its last hurrah. America's addiction to wild fun, to flap-pers, and to white-tie-and-tails extravagance was about to end.

Chapter 13

▲▲▲▲▲▲▲▲▲▲▲▲▲

New Year's Day 1930—As far as radio fans were concerned, this was the beginning of another year filled with just the kind of programming they had come to expect. That New Year's Day, Graham McNamee hosted the radiocast of the Tournament of Roses parade and the Rose Bowl game, which pitted the University of Southern California Trojans against the undefeated University of Pittsburgh Panthers. Writing his column from Hollywood, Will Rogers noted that McNamee's job was to describe the day's intense heat, which was the reason "we bring him out every year." But there was a new twist in 1930: Seeking a different on-air style, NBC assigned Carl Haverlin and Lloyd Yoder to call the game's action, while McNamee provided a "descriptive picture of the scene of the game before and after the contest and between halves." By giving the listener more descriptive matter, the network could make the radio fan feel more a part of the game. Unfortunately the newly created announcing crew was saddled with a less than dramatic game: USC destroyed an "outfought, outpassed, and thoroughly outclassed" Pittsburgh squad 47 to 14.

Radio sports was a popular fixture, but nothing topped the regularly scheduled entertainment shows, especially *Amos 'n' Andy,* which continued to be the most listened-to show on radio, along with Rudy Vallée's *Fleischmann's Yeast Hour.* Their standing among listeners must have delighted their sponsors. Standard Brands, the parent company of Fleischmann's, was reaping the benefits of radio advertising, so much so that despite the country's unstable business environment, Standard Brands' president Joseph Wilshire announced that his company was starting the most extensive advertising expansion program ever. Vallée's affable manner and soothing crooning, and a steady stream of fine musical guests, all blended with brief comic routines, made the Thursday at 8 P.M. time slot on NBC a delightful listening experience. As the summer of 1930 neared, the question about what to do about the broadcasts while Vallée and his band toured the summer concert circuit arose. At first it was rumored that Vallée's show would simply take a hiatus from the airwaves, returning in the fall, but the fan demand for Rudy was so great that the network decided to broadcast the show from whatever city Vallée happened to be in on Thursday evening. For the last two weeks of July and throughout August, Rudy Vallée and the Connecticut Yankees originated their show from the tour locations: Hampton Beach, New Hampshire; Rye, New York; Pittsburgh, Pennsylvania; Green Bay, Wisconsin; and Canton, Ohio. According to reports, in addition to Vallée's fee for the broadcasts, his immense and still-growing popularity gave him income for the tour's opening week that amounted to $32,000, a huge sum for 1930.

Amos 'n' Andy had settled into its nightly, fifteen-minute, 7 P.M. EST slot, with a rebroadcast at 10:30 P.M. aired by stations in the Midwest, and then sent on to the stations in the West and Southwest that were "the presiding deities of the twilight time." The pair's popularity was tremendous, due to some degree to America's tendency to seek lighter forms of entertainment as a form of escape in times of stress. The illusion created by Gosden and Correll and their imaginary lives was so complete that fans thought "of them as two colored boys instead of two blackface characters which are played by a pair of young white men, who look more like high-grade bond salesmen than like a pair of troupers." Unlike most other radio stars whose national fame had come from some combination of vaudeville performances, movies, and records, Gosden and Correll's stardom resulted entirely from their radio exposure, for which they were handsomely rewarded, earning a guaranteed fee in 1930 of $100,000. But that was just the beginning; in April the pair signed an agreement with RKO to make a talking picture for an estimated fee of one million dollars. Then NBC, acting as the pair's agent, signed a long-term deal with Pepsodent, the show's national sponsor, which gave the comedy team a signing bonus and a sliding-scale salary, making them the highest-paid radio entertainers ever. Furthermore, the deal guaranteed their presence on the air for the next five years. Certainly for Gosden and Correll, 1930 was shaping up to be an excellent year.

In the nine years since KDKA had placed three microphones in a church to broadcast services, religion on the radio had assumed many guises, but overall had become an expected part of any station's schedule. But the programming had become even more controversial as some members of the clergy had taken to opining from their pulpits on political and social matters, especially Prohibition. However, no member of the clergy received as much attention as Aimee Semple McPherson, although not all of it was welcome, as journalists focused on the numerous scandals surrounding her, including accusations by her own temple pastors, who alleged misuse of church funds. Public disagreements with her mother about the operation of the temple, rumors of her frail health, several lawsuits about lesser matters, and repeated well-publicized preaching jaunts to distant lands made McPherson notorious and kept her name in the news. But with the great acclaim she once enjoyed now on the wane, the crowds attending her services were noticeably smaller and less generous.

On the other side of Los Angeles, McPherson's rival both on the air and in the pulpit, Reverend Robert Shuler, continued his rise to stardom and infamy. With a radio station, a monthly magazine, and home-printed pamphlets dealing with political topics, the controversial Shuler also kept himself in the public eye. Despite the repeated warnings from authorities about meddling in the legal system and making public comments during the 1929 Pantages trials, Shuler continued to use his radio platform to try to unduly influence court proceedings in Los Angeles. On May 5, 1930, Superior Court Judge Clair S. Tappaan gave Shuler a twenty-day jail sentence and a $100 fine for utterances he made over the radio concerning the procedures of the superior court in connection with a stock-fraud case. For the balance of the year, Shuler's apparent influence over Los Angeles's government and legal system were hotly debated in the press without providing any clear resolution either for or against him. His case, however, did lead to an important legal decision: The California Supreme Court ruled that "the constitutional guarantee of free speech does not protect a citizen when he comments on pending court cases in an attempt to interfere 'with the orderly administration of justice.'"

The constant on-air sniping and public battling gradually reduced McPherson and Shuler to almost laughable annoyances. Meanwhile in Detroit, Father Charles Coughlin was reaching new levels of popularity; with the power and reach radio gave him, he used the pulpit to air his beliefs, both religious and societal. On January 12, 1930, Coughlin strayed from his expected Sunday religious homily and in a sermon titled "Red Fog" attacked the dual enemies of America: Bolshevism and socialism. For the next nine Sundays, Coughlin continued his diatribes about the spread of Communism, drawing an aural picture of "this red serpent as it crawled from campus to campus" of America's universities, warning Americans of the threat posed to the country. Unimpeded and emboldened, he went on to accuse groups and individuals he deemed anti-American, including Bertrand Russell, "the atheist, the advocate of free love, the exponent of anarchy"; and Henry Ford, whom Coughlin charged with aiding the spread of Communism and with financially supporting the Soviet government, all the while abusing American workers. Being on the radio seemed to sanctify Coughlin as an authority on Communism, and he was called to testify before a congressional committee investigating Red activities. There the radio priest boldly called Henry Ford "the greatest force in the movement to internationalize labor throughout the world."

Radio was clearly working for Coughlin; at midyear his tiny parish, which was made up of only thirty-two families, had raised enough money to erect a "shrine to tolerance" to be built on the exact spot where just four years earlier the Ku Klux Klan had burned a cross protesting the establishment of his small Catholic church. The cost of the stone tower was estimated at $250,000, to be paid for primarily by money raised from his invisible radio parish of 7 million, from whom he received about 14,000 letters a week, most containing contributions. To acknowledge their generosity, the words *And other sheep I have that are not of this fold. Them also I must bring. They shall hear my voice and there shall be one fold and one shepherd* would be carved into the tower.

Even in the early days of broadcasting, audience appeal trumped most, if not all, other considerations. In 1930 CBS was still far behind the two RCA-owned networks in terms of recognition and popularity. Sensing Coughlin was a ratings winner, CBS offered him the chance to have his program heard on the stations of the CBS network.

At 7 P.M. on Sunday, October 5, 1930, Father Coughlin went on the air over the network with his *Golden Hour of the Little Flower.* His ability to crisply articulate political commentary, the way he targeted the rags-and-riches disparities that had resulted from the Coolidge-Hoover prosperity, all couched within Catholic theology, resonated with listeners from coast to coast. Soon the one-hour weekly commentaries by the bespectacled priest from Michigan made him an immensely influential national voice whose popularity neared that of *Amos 'n' Andy* and Rudy Vallée. Most astounding was the mail generated by Coughlin's talks: It was reported that one broadcast alone brought in more than one million letters—most containing one-dollar contributions—which entitled the donors to a one-year membership in the Shrine of the Little Flower. It was money that Coughlin declared would be spent to defend "the principles of Christianity and Patriotism against the modern heresy of Communism." Generously, in a big-tent sort of way, Coughlin did not limit membership in his Radio League of the Little Flower to Catholics, as he urged Protestants and Jews to join in his movement for "truth, charity, and patriotism."

Coughlin's ascendant popularity was not good news for President Hoover, whose administration was desperately trying to convince America that all was well with the economy. As a business, radio was clearly in better condition in 1930 than the rest of the country. It was the growth technology of the day, and the Commerce Department portrayed radio as the ideal place for a young man to turn if he wanted employment because it was an industry with limitless opportunity.

The Commerce Department's rosy picture of the radio industry was consistent with the way the administration's advisors—including Harry Chandler of KHJ and the *Los Angeles Times*—characterized the business situation of the entire country: They were advising President Hoover that economic conditions were normal. That blind optimism was repeated by members of the administration who publicly pronounced, usually over the radio, that all was well with the American economy and the business outlook. Reassuringly they told American audiences that the "evils of speculation" had been curbed, and that unemployment would decline. As if willing their way to recovery, stock prices did climb in part as a reaction to the administration's optimistic pronouncements, but the gains were minimal in comparison with the losses of the previous fall. Using radio as his bully pulpit, Hoover took to the air as if he were the nation's designated cheerleader. He had become a very competent radio speaker, and his address to the annual meeting of the Red Cross; his Memorial Day speech remembering the nation's war dead delivered at Gettysburg, Pennsylvania; and his appeal to the people of Washington, D.C., for contributions to the Community Chest, during which he said that "charity is the obligation of the strong to the weak," were all featured radio programs.

As the election season heated up, members of the administration, aware that the economic downturn was now being called a depression, again took to the airwaves in an effort to stem the tide of anti-Republican sentiment sweeping the country. Secretary of Labor James J. Davis, speaking over the CBS network, pointed out that "no president we have ever had has launched so many broad movements for the benefit of the people." But the political backlash was a huge problem for the incumbent Republicans. Secretary of the Interior Ray Lyman Wilbur, speaking over the NBC network, pointed to the need for a Republican Congress to aid the president's fight against the Depression, urging the nation to elect "men and women who will back the captain who inevitably must navigate our ship of state for the next two years through the troubled waters before us."

Thousands of hours of radio airtime, on the networks as well as on local stations, were devoted to speeches by America's political leaders, and not surprisingly President Hoover was the most frequently heard on-air politician. During his five years in the White House, President

Coolidge delivered thirty-seven radio addresses; Hoover broke that record in less than two years.

Radio's ability to instantly connect with large swaths of the population had blurred the line between public service and celebrity. More so than ever, politicians needed to be stars, just as performing stars were beginning to use their celebrity to influence politics. Will Rogers understood perhaps better than anyone the public power of media platforms. His daily newspaper column took the nation's leaders, Democrat and Republican alike, to task for mismanaging the country. But even America's homespun humorist-philosopher and sometime outspoken critic of radio, despite a severe case of mike fright, could not resist the temptations and rewards of radio. His initial network contract was for a thirteen-week series of half-hour talks over the CBS network. Rogers's show debuted on Sunday, April 6, 1930, at 10 P.M. EST, originating from the KHJ studios in Hollywood. Sponsored by Squibb Corporation, his fee for the six and a half hours of radio time was reported to be a hefty $72,000. Rogers's program dealt with current affairs and was spiced by his wry observations. "Tonight all I know is this—just what I read in the papers during the day," he would begin. On subsequent shows he talked about Charles Lindbergh, President Hoover, the Democrats (whom he called "the Lord's chosen people—he wanted to keep them exclusive, and that is why he made so few of them"), Henry Ford, and the crime wave in Chicago. It was a brief venture into series radio for Rogers, but it helped establish him as a tremendously influential voice in the country.

There was nothing new about Graham McNamee calling a title bout, and when Jack Sharkey and the challenger from Germany, Max Schmeling, stepped into the ring at Yankee Stadium on June 12, 1930, McNamee was ringside to call the action. In another first for sports radio, McNamee was joined by Carmen Ogden, whose task was to add color and some feminine appeal to the broadcast by describing the society and fashions seen at the fight. Using a multiple microphone set-up, NBC did a magnificent job of bringing the fight into the homes of millions of Americans. McNamee's graphic, blow-by-blow calls were polished and exciting. But perhaps more important, the technologically advanced setup allowed listeners to savor the sounds of the fight, the clanging bell tolling the rounds and the shouts of ringside spectators all clearly audible on any good home set, bringing the radio audience right into Yankee Stadium.

The bout itself was a dramatic, brutal affair with punches exchanged at a breathtaking clip. Sharkey seemed to be ahead as the fourth round progressed; then at the two-minute fifty-five-second mark he let fly a powerful left hook that sent Schmeling writhing to the canvas. It was a low blow. Pandemonium and confusion ensued as the referee hesitated before consulting with the judge, Harold Barnes. The bell signaling the end of round four sounded as Schmeling was helped to his corner. Then just after the bell for the fifth round clanged, the referee disqualified Sharkey for the low blow and awarded the victory to Schmeling. "Neither boxer could be brought to the microphone," McNamee told the audience; Schmeling was too dazed, while Sharkey walked off disconsolately. The result of the fight was that Max Schmeling, the "alien," took the throne, and for the first time in modern history would carry the title to Europe.

By 1930 radiocasts of the World Series, seemingly always hosted by Graham McNamee, had become a tradition, but as the St. Louis Cardinals prepared to face Connie Mack's Philadelphia Athletics, fans, perhaps tired of the same old thing, were questioning how baseball should be covered on radio. There were two schools of thought: one that believed there should be no advertising and that announcers should merely state the facts and keep their opinions to themselves; and the other, which viewed the radiocasts as entertainment that needed a colorful method of broadcasting in which the announcer painted "a picture to hold the listeners spellbound and give them a more interesting account rather than a cut-and-dried play-by-play description of the game's progress."

For the first game of the 1930 series both NBC and CBS were on the scene in Philadelphia's Shibe Park, airing coverage to millions of baseball fans from coast to coast. In St. Louis, thousands of St. Louisians forgot all about business duties, choosing instead to listen to radio reports of the opening game, which Philadelphia won. When the Athletics took a two-game-to-none lead, interest in the series waned. Play shifted to St. Louis, and despite the home team's winning game three, CBS decided to not broadcast game four, opting to stay with their previously scheduled programs. But since the networks hadn't paid anything for the rights to air the games, there was no real consequence other than that radio fans were limited to the coverage provided by Graham McNamee over the NBC network.

When St. Louis won game four, tying the series, interest in the games reignited, and CBS returned for game five in St. Louis. Unfortunately for the hometown fans, Philadelphia shut out the powerful St. Louis lineup, sending the series back to Philadelphia for what would be a series-ending game six. When the last out was made and the Athletics were again world champions, NBC listeners were treated to another radio first when within a minute of the game's conclusion the joyous shouts of Connie Mack's players were heard as they rushed into the clubhouse. Waiting for them, microphone in hand, was Graham McNamee, who called to each of the players to "say just a word." Many of the Philadelphia greats who obliged included Jimmy Foxx, Lefty Grove, and Connie Mack himself.

But there was one person who may not have been entirely thrilled by the fan interest in baseball. While the fifth game of the series was being played in St. Louis, President Hoover was speaking to the American Federation of Labor in Boston. Originally, officials wanted to postpone the baseball game so the president's important address could be aired around the country. But the game won out, which caused one *Washington Post* columnist to observe that "given a choice between a presidential address and a baseball game, it [the American citizenry] will tune in to the baseball game every time, although the address has a demonstrable relation to its fortunes and the baseball game has not." Despite Hoover's ever-improving delivery and on-air presence, presidential addresses had become old hat; there was no news there, and radio, thanks to its inherent immediacy, was being transformed into a place to find current events, not set pieces. More than speechifying, radio fans wanted entertainment, excitement, and action. They wanted two seemingly contradictory things: escape and reality.

IT WAS REALITY THAT GRIPPED radio fans in April 1930. On the night of April 21, shortly after the guards had marched the prisoners back to their cells in the old stone fortress known as the Ohio State Penitentiary at Columbus, a fire, perhaps set by inmates wanting to escape and sparked by some rags dipped in an oil preparation being used to repair the roof of the prison, erupted. The prison was an old rambling stone structure that had once held a prisoner named William S. Porter, who spent his time in the pen collecting materials for the stories he would write as O. Henry. Within the prison were cotton and wool mills, and as the flames spread they quickly engulfed the old structure, which was known to be in terrible condition and horribly overcrowded; built to incarcerate 1,500 inmates, at the time of the fire it was housing more than 4,300 convicts.

As the flames raced from area to area, the inmates, most locked in cells, struggled to get to safety and begged to be let out. But the guards, afraid to allow a breakout, refused to give up their keys and left many of the cells locked. The greatest devastation was in the oldest unit of the prison. Prisoners trapped in their cells yelled for release, rattled the bars, and screamed frightfully. "The bellowings of trapped men, grilled alive, ceased when the west block roof collapsed." Bodies were dragged from the burning buildings, while in the yard federal and state troops used bayonets to keep the unruly mob of scared convicts in order. More than 320 prisoners died that night, and more than two hundred others were injured and in need of treatment in the prison hospital.

In the days following the conflagration there were repeated threats of uprisings among the prisoners. The warden feared a massive prison break, especially since many of the cells no longer had functioning locks, but a tenuous calm prevailed as many of the convicts returned to their cells, leaving the doors ajar, entertaining themselves by playing cards and checkers and listening to radios. But one week after the disaster, the calm was again shattered as prisoners broke windows and threatened more violence. National Guard troops, who had been patrolling the scene since the night of the fire, set up machine guns on the lawn in front of the prison just outside the cell block housing the angry convicts. Eventually order was restored, and as the warden, the governor, and the legislature engaged in a fierce blame game, the Ohio Penitentiary convicts gradually returned to their normal schedules.

There was, however, an unexpected immediacy to the horrific fire and its aftermath that spread far beyond the prison's walls. Almost as soon as the curtain rose on that spectacle of fire and disorder, radio was there reporting, and it stayed there until the "show," from the news standpoint, had ended. In an effort to improve conditions in the overcrowded prison, the warden, just weeks before the fire erupted, had established a weekly concert for the inmates. Station WAIU in Columbus, in search of unusual local programming, had asked for and was granted permission to broadcast these events. When the fire broke out, WAIU's fully wired broadcast facility was already set up in the prison and ready to broadcast. Within an hour of the first alert, WAIU had an announcer in the warden's office, where he reported live. As the fire spread and the death toll and number of injured rose, the on-the-scene reporter used the broadcast facility to put out an emergency call for doctors, nurses, undertakers, ambulances, and anyone else who might be of help. Heightening the frenzied drama heard over the radio were the sounds of crackling fire, the crash of the collapsing roof, and the screams of the trapped convicts echoing pitifully within the prison's walls. The sounds were so horrific that some listeners refused to believe that what they were hearing was actually happening. Furthermore, since WAIU was part of the CBS network, the coverage was sent to the network's flagship station, WABC in New York, where Ted Husing, CBS's lead announcer, contacted other stations in the network and told them to pick up the WAIU coverage. For what may have been the first time in broadcast history, radio listeners heard the resounding, powerful phrase *Ladies and gentlemen, we interrupt this program to bring you an important news broadcast.*

At one point during the groundbreaking radio coverage, the warden asked WAIU to allow one of the inmates, a black preacher from the South, to tell the story himself. His words, accompanied by the horrific sounds of the conflagration, were powerful:

> *The fire came fast, touching us like a red-hot iron. Men were trapped in their cells. They didn't have a chance. They screamed. They moaned. Some prayed. Some who prayed never had prayed before. They learned how. They learned how fast.*

During the days of unrest following the fire, radio, this time unwittingly, aided the prisoners. When the state militia was called in to quell the unrest, all newspaper reporters were banned from the prison to ensure that the convicts would have no way to find out what was happening. However, since some of the convicts had barricaded themselves in one of the cell blocks with their radios, they had advance knowledge of everything that was occurring because WAIU continued to broadcast news of the prison troubles.

The live coverage of the tragedy was one of radio's defining moments, and its role in the aftermath of the fire was not yet complete. Somehow, days after order had been restored, two local broadcasters slipped another microphone into the prison, set it up in the prison yard, and connected it to station WLW in Cincinnati. The reporters then invited prisoners in the yard to share their stories with the radio audience. One by one, convicts told the story of the prison fire and the dreadful conditions in the prison. It was emotional, moving radio that continued until prison officials ended the show by snipping a wire connected to the transmitter.

The penitentiary fire was a tragedy of mammoth proportions and the entertainment industry was ready to exploit it. Within three days of the blaze, a country-music–styled song called "Ohio Prison Fire" was written and recorded by Bob Miller. His twangy tenor, blended with a weepy violin and the sobbing of a mother who has to identify her son's charred remains, was a powerful condemnation of what had happened. Within a month, three other renditions of the song were recorded, and all of them, in what may have been the first instance of national catharsis, were played on the radio.

More globally, the tragic fire opened the eyes of some broadcasters to the value of on-the-spot news reporting. Clearly one of radio's great strengths was its ability to bring the outside world into the home with dramatic immediacy, a capability that did not please newspaper editors, one of whom remarked, "Radio is making today's newspaper yesterday's newspaper."

THE EARLIEST KIND OF REPORTING on radio was election coverage, and as President Hoover listened on the White House radio on the night of November 4, 1930, he must have been hoping for better news.

Unfortunately for him, the results being reported were grim. Surrounded by a few close friends and advisors, President Hoover heard the initial election results, including news of the landslide reelection of New York's governor Franklin Roosevelt, before retiring to his private quarters. When he awoke the next morning, the news was even worse; Republican leaders were dazed, unable to understand the extent of their defeat. While immediately after the election the Republicans clung to a slim majority in the House of Representatives, in the months between the election and the end of the year they lost nineteen more seats in special elections to replace representatives who had died, which put the Democrats in control of the House.

There was more bad news for Hoover in the Senate, where Republicans hoped to maintain a slim majority, or at least a tie, so that Hoover's vice president could cast deciding votes. In Louisiana, the popular Democratic governor, Huey Long, was running virtually unopposed for the Senate seat. Long—who because he and his cronies enjoyed listening to *Amos 'n' Andy* had been nicknamed Kingfish, after one of the show's main characters—was a shrewd politician who had brilliantly used radio in his previous campaigns and during his tenure as governor. Long's method was to undertake incredibly long broadcasts, during which he alternated his remarks with music played by a live band: *This is Huey P. Long speaking to you. Ring up your friends and tell them to tune in on WDSU if you want to know what is going on around here.* He was often heard on KWKH in Shreveport, which was owned by a friend of his, and all of his lengthy speeches, campaign talks, as well as the long diatribes he delivered as governor, were carried free of charge.

Long was a compelling speaker: His voice was vibrant and had the quality and tone one might expect to hear from a circus sideshow barker. His rambling talks, more like sermons, were grand theater; he spoke for long periods seemingly without effort, delivering rapid-fire soliloquies that couched brutal attacks on political foes in vivid biblical imagery. He was part politician, part motivational speaker, and part fire-and-brimstone preacher. When asked why he did not submit his speeches to radio stations for them to vet before broadcasting, a common practice at that time, Long replied, "I don't write out my speeches. I make 'em up as I go along. I'll show you my notes though." He then handed the questioner his dog-eared copy of the Bible. Long's popularity in Louisiana was so great that it was said that when he spoke over the radio you could hear a pin drop anywhere in the state.

Huey Long was a developing national force for the Democratic Party. The only good news for President Hoover was Long's decision to retain the governorship of Louisiana until he could find an appropriate and loyal replacement, which meant he would not assume his Senate seat until January 1932. Radio's power to create political mischief was stunning to an establishment that had played by a set of unwritten rules designed when newspapers allowed time and space for proper investigation and rebuttal. In no uncertain terms, radio had changed the political discourse and the nation's political landscape. Though Long's use of radio to control the information his constituents received and to limit his opponents' opportunity to counter what he had to say was revolutionary, it was not the most bizarre use of radio during the 1930 elections. That claim belonged to a radio entrepreneur and medical innovator, the sexual rejuvenation king from the great state of Kansas: Dr. John Romulus Brinkley.

Chapter 14

▲▲▲▲▲▲▲▲▲▲▲▲▲▲

IN A NATION WHERE thousands of hours of local radio programming and countless more hours of network shows, originating primarily in New York, kept listeners turning their radio dials, there was one man who seemed to know how to use radio more effectively than anyone else: Dr. John R. Brinkley of Milford, Kansas. Known as a warm and concerned radio doctor, but becoming famous far and wide for his miracle sexual rejuvenation cure, Brinkley became the subject of one of the day's most popular jokes:

> Q: What's the fastest thing on four legs?
> A: A goat passing Doctor Brinkley's hospital.

With revenue pouring in from his surgeries and his national network of local pharmacies, which sold his numerically coded vials of made-up elixirs and kicked back part of each sale to the good doctor, Brinkley was far and away the wealthiest man in Milford, if not in all of Kansas. When his son rode his tricycle to school, a bodyguard walked alongside while Doc and Mrs. Brinkley rode behind in one of their specially built Lincolns with gold-plated hubcaps, or in one of the Cadillacs with *JRB* emblazoned in gold all over the vehicle. Brinkley flaunted his wealth by wearing an eleven-carat ring on his right hand, which was outshone only by the fourteen-carat stone he sported on his left hand. While it is impossible to assess precisely Brinkley's income during the bountiful years between 1926 and 1929, the combination of drug sales and the surgeries his clinic performed brought his gross annual income to somewhere around $2 million. It was no wonder he could readily follow Herbert Hoover's admonishment that radio was not a venue for product advertising: With that kind of money, Brinkley could afford to refuse the advertising dollars that were defraying the programming and management costs for most of America's stations.

But even immense popularity and excessive wealth can be problematic. By 1928 Brinkley's practices were drawing the attention of the American Medical Association (AMA) and the editor of the *Journal of the American Medical Association,* Dr. Morris Fishbein. It wasn't Brinkley's questionable surgery as much as the over-the-air diagnostic and prescription service that troubled the medical community, and after nearly two years of monitoring Dr. Brinkley, the AMA, assisted in no small part by negative editorial content in the *Kansas City Star,* began attacking Brinkley and his unchecked messages and claims.

But the AMA was not alone in its effort to rid the airwaves of medical quacks. In New York, the health commissioner, Dr. Shirley W. Wynne, announced he was launching an effort to eliminate medical advertising that made remedial claims, either directly or by inference. Wynne decided it was only appropriate to attack these charlatans by using their own methods, so he went on the radio. The freedom enjoyed by broadcasters during the pioneering years of commercial radio, when everything was still new, had allowed medical frauds and quacks to find their place on the air, and a gullible audience was awaiting them. By the end of the decade these medical men had become a widespread problem, and Brinkley, thanks to his brilliant use of the medium and his timely and appealing message of good sexual health, was the highest-profile target, the best-known practitioner among America's new medicine men of the airwaves. Morris Fishbein claimed that the AMA had in its files the names of more than 200,000 quacks, but that Brinkley was the most dangerous because of his daring and the fact that he could get attention via his own radio station.

Brinkley sued, charging that Fishbein, out of jealousy, was leading a conspiracy to ruin him. But Fishbein persisted, requesting an investigation by the AMA into Brinkley's training and his practice. In response, Brinkley resorted to what he knew best: He counterattacked on the air, claiming the AMA was nothing more than a "meat cutters' union" whose acronym actually stood for Amalgamated Meatcutters Association. All of this drama drew more unwanted attention to Milford's leading citizen, one result of which was an increase in the number of former patients who came forward claiming they had been injured by Dr. Brinkley's surgery or harmed in some way by one of his prescriptions. While men who had had the sexual rejuvenation surgery were reluctant to complain about the operation's lack of success, another group of patients who had suffered from prostate issues were far more willing to speak out against Brinkley, and they did.

In addition to the AMA's investigation, an exponentially increasing number of complaints about Brinkley's use of the public airwaves for personal gain and quackery made their way to the offices of the Federal Radio Commission in Washington, D.C. On May 21, 1930, Brinkley was called before the FRC to show why his license to operate KFKB should be renewed. Unfortunately for Brinkley, his old friend from Kansas State, Sam Pickard, had resigned his commissionership at the FRC and had moved to greener pastures as vice president of the CBS radio network. Before undertaking the journey to Washington, Brinkley threatened to invade the capital with an army of several thousand satisfied patients and radio listeners who would testify in his behalf, but in the end his "army" consisted of just thirty-five loyal supporters who had to pay their own way. Countering Brinkley at the FRC was his nemesis, Dr. Fishbein, along with other qualified doctors who after three days of hearings were able to convince the members of the FRC that Brinkley needed to be silenced. On Friday, June 13, 1930, the commission voted three to two to remove Brinkley's right to broadcast over KFKB on the grounds that the "station no longer met proper standards." Specifically, the commission determined that the practice of prescribing treatment for a patient the doctor had never seen was a threat to public health and safety. Furthermore, the commission found that KFKB was being operated for the personal interest of Dr. Brinkley and not "in the interest of the listening public." How ironic it must have seemed when, not long after the FRC's decision, KFKB won *Radio Digest*'s nationwide popularity contest.

Friday, June 13 was also the day the Kansas Supreme Court rejected Brinkley's attempt to halt an investigation into his medical practices by the Kansas Medical Board. Needing to save his businesses, Brinkley had his lawyers appeal the FRC's decision to the Court of Appeals of the District of Columbia, a strategy that enabled him to remain on the air at least until the court could review his case. In mid-July the state medical board hearings began. With nothing to lose, Brinkley dared the doctors on the board to come to his hospital and witness the gland implant operation for themselves. They accepted, and on September 15, before a large audience of reporters and doctors, Brinkley skillfully performed his famous sex-enhancement operation. Despite being impressed by his skills as a surgeon, the board returned to Topeka and promptly voted to revoke John Brinkley's medical license.

Desperate to stave off complete defeat, Brinkley hired a few properly trained surgeons for his clinic just to maintain some revenue that would support the infrastructure he had built. Then in an absolutely stunning move, he announced his intention to run for the governorship of Kansas. Too late to get his name on the ballot, Brinkley ran as a write-in candidate, and using his gift of gab and the strong KFKB signal, he went on the air to explain why he should be governor.

With a keen appreciation of the discontent that was weighing on the nation as a result of constantly rising unemployment and general economic distress, Brinkley developed a platform of platitudes and promises, a potent attack "against many of the evils that were paralyzing the social progress of the state." His promises included the granting of contracts to Kansas firms for Kansas work, help for poor workers against employers, "the purest and best medicines absolutely free to those who could not afford to pay," along with the best medical and surgical care, free school textbooks, lower taxes, artificial lakes for every county in the state, and guaranteed old-age pensions.

Barnstorming in his private airplane, his rallies, which were carefully choreographed and organized events, attracted huge crowds. Using a sound truck and cheerleaders to warm up his audiences, the veteran radio genius in Brinkley knew exactly how to work a crowd into a frenzy. His fiery talks about the ills of the current government led to the development of the clever and resonant slogan "Clean out, clean up, and keep Kansas clean."

Also seeking the Kansas governorship were two inexperienced, youngish men: Democrat Harry Woodring and Republican Frank Haucke. At first Brinkley's candidacy was viewed merely as an entertaining sidelight to the campaign; the *Kansas City Star* predicted he would be lucky to receive 10,000 votes. But as the final days of the campaign approached, the Brinkley candidacy gained traction and was drawing national attention to the race. Despite having been found guilty of gross immorality and unprofessional conduct in connection with his goat-gland transplantation operations and his practice of prescribing for human ailments by radio, as election day neared, Brinkley was more than a viable candidate: He had become a legitimate threat to the major parties.

Fearing that Brinkley might actually become governor, the two major parties sent letters to every election board in the state, instructing that "unless the ballot on which Brinkley's name was written in had the name correctly and flawlessly spelled," unless it was exactly "John R. Brinkley," the ballots were to be rejected. Brinkley countered, going on the air to deliver detailed instructions for his listeners and supporters that explained exactly how to write in his name. When the votes were tallied, Woodring had 215,340, Haucke had 215,208, and Brinkley 181,216, with thousands more Brinkley ballots tossed out for minor mistakes in spelling.

The election was so close that a recount was probably needed, but realizing that if a full recount were done more of Dr. Brinkley's discarded votes might be allowed, thus handing him the governorship, the Democrats and Republicans hastily agreed that Democrat Harry Woodring would be declared the winner and would assume the governorship for the next two years. Brinkley was locked out by the established party powers. Ironically, in addition to the estimated 239,000 votes he actually received in Kansas, because radio signals knew no borders, Brinkley was also credited with 20,000 write-in votes in the neighboring Oklahoma gubernatorial election. Though a disappointment to Brinkley and his supporters, his candidacy did provide an important media lesson for all politicians about how powerful radio could be in swaying and informing voters.

Despite his strong showing, the bad news for Brinkley continued. Stripped of his medical license and defeated in his political bid, he became a three-time loser when, on February 2, 1931, the Federal Court of Appeals upheld the FRC's ruling denying Brinkley's license renewal to operate KFKB. The court's decision affirmed the FRC's power and noted that Congress intended that "broadcasting should not be a mere adjunct of a particular business but should be of public character." Brinkley then tried to sell his station to a local insurance company, but the FRC ruled he could not do that since the state of Kansas already had more stations than they had been allocated by the commission. Vice President Charles Curtis, himself a Kansan, went to President Hoover and pleaded Brinkley's case, warning the president that preventing Brinkley from selling his station would make the doctor a martyr, which would mean that Hoover would lose the state of Kansas in the 1932 election. The FRC quickly changed its position and allowed the sale of the KFKB facility to the Farmers & Bankers Life Insurance Company of Milford, Kansas, for $95,000. On February 21, 1931, Brinkley said good-bye to his faithful radio followers; but if the FRC thought they were rid of John Romulus Brinkley, they were wrong.

Using his windfall from the sale of KFKB and some money put up by supporters and investors, Brinkley made a deal with the Mexican government that granted him permission to erect a massive 100,000-watt transmitter in Villa Acuna, about three miles from Del Rio, Texas. Then Brinkley purchased a phone line that ran from Milford all the way across the Texas–Mexico border to his new broadcast facility, which was given the call letters XER. With no broadcasting treaty between the United States and Mexico in place, Brinkley simply moved his radiocasts beyond the reach of the FRC. But since his new station was so powerful, his radio shows, now produced in Milford and transmitted from Mexico, could be heard on radios throughout most of the United States, far beyond the area originally reached by KFKB. With new listeners hearing about his medical cures, Brinkley's revenue once again soared.

THE FRC's POWER to reject radio license renewals, while not used frequently, did become a tool to control what station operators were doing. As an example, charging that station KVEP in Portland, Oregon, had repeatedly broadcast indecent and profane language and had drifted off their assigned frequency, the FRC ordered the station off the air. Another West Coast target of the commission was Fighting Bob Shuler, who despite repeated warnings continued to use KFEG in Los Angeles to attack local politicians and members of the government and judiciary. After an initial investigation, Ellis Yost of the FRC urged that the station's license be renewed. But when the full commission reviewed the case in November 1931, they determined that Shuler had been using his station as a personal outlet, rendering the station "undesirable and obnoxious to several religious organizations"; in short, he was accused of using the airwaves to promote religious strife and antagonism. In their decision, the commission focused on the "sensational" rather than "instructive" character of Shuler's broadcasts. Shuler's license was suspended, placing him in the "bad boys of the air" group along with Dr. Brinkley and another notorious on-air broadcaster-doctor, Norman Baker, the owner of KTNT in Muscatine, Iowa.

Despite his claims of having helped elect Herbert Hoover to the presidency, Norman Baker was vulnerable to FRC discipline because his radio station repeatedly promoted the miraculous and medically unproven cancer cures available at the Baker Institute in Muscatine. Using his magazine *The Naked Truth* in conjunction with his station, Baker, the onetime Calliaphone manufacturer, urged cancer sufferers to turn their backs on traditional medicine and try the wonderful, pain-free, even medicine-free cures he had developed. With a staff of chiropractors, osteopaths, and mail-order diploma doctors, who were encouraged to sell desperate patients the herbal concoctions available in the Baker pharmacy, his clinic was a booming business that drew local attention. Leading the attack was the *Muscatine Journal,* which repeatedly challenged Baker's credentials and cures. Angered by the assault, Baker went on the air on May 9, 1930, speaking continuously for seven hours in a tirade meant to discredit the *Muscatine Journal* and its publisher.

Soon thereafter, the Kansas Health Board filed charges with the FRC accusing Baker of broadcasting information "derogatory to the best interests of the public health." As could be expected, Baker's wild medical claims also drew the attention of the AMA and Dr. Fishbein. Like Brinkley, Baker took to the air attacking the AMA and maligning Fishbein, whom he called "the Jewish dominator of the medical trust of America." In subsequent radio attacks, Baker hammered away at his opponent's Jewish heritage; he wouldn't be the last radioman to turn to anti-Semitism, either in the United States or in Europe.

While fighting to keep his radio license, Baker repeatedly engaged in antigovernment battles, including a call to midwestern farmers to ignore the federal government's order mandating bovine tuberculosis testing; his calls helped incite a minirebellion among Iowa's farmers and helped foster his image as the farmers' champion. But his outrageous behavior eventually forced the FRC to revoke KTNT's license, and as the commission wrapped up its work in the summer of 1931, they ordered the station closed. Their decision found that Baker had used the station as his "private mouthpiece" to promote a number of his businesses and to attack the medical profession.

Baker challenged the ruling and the constitutionality of the 1927 Radio Act, claiming the law abrogated his right to free speech. His appeals were denied. Baker's downfall was swift: Without a station at his disposal to promote his businesses, his income dropped precipitously. In January 1932 his receipts totaled just $7,008, down from nearly $76,000 only eighteen months earlier. Undeterred, Baker sued the

AMA for libel, but a jury of Iowa farmers and merchants agreed that "it was no libel to call Norman Baker a quack." By June 1932, defeated and nearly broke, just like Dr. Brinkley, Baker headed across the Mexican border to a new, more powerful radio transmitter, this one in Nuevo Laredo.

Unlike Brinkley, Shuler, and Baker, Father Coughlin did not own a radio station and was therefore beyond the licensing control of the FRC. The Commerce Department's position was that the FRC did not have the power to regulate content; that was up to radio station owners to control, so long as they kept the public interest in mind. Far from being an angry station owner spewing for personal gain over the airwaves, Coughlin was a star, the Sunday talent on the CBS radio network whose religious messages were carried from coast to coast. For his first show of 1931 Coughlin planned to give a talk titled "Prosperity," an ironic title at a time when unemployment and business failures were reaching all-time highs. In the speech, scheduled for January 4, Coughlin was going to blame the high rate of unemployment on poor government decisions, but the "sermon" was aborted when CBS officials, having received advance warning of the incendiary tone of the speech, asked him to temper his remarks. Coughlin claimed that moment as the turning point in his career. He charged that CBS's censorship was spurred by the White House, which feared to have the truth, at least as Coughlin perceived it, told to the American people. But he acquiesced, substituting a vituperative talk that accused the CBS network and its executives of censorship, and the government of violating his right of free speech. He called on his loyal radio audience to rally around him and "express their pleasure whether or not these sermons would be continued."

More than 35,000 letters protesting the "censorship" of Father Coughlin inundated the CBS offices. One week later, Coughlin daringly returned to his originally planned "Prosperity" speech; pointedly he blamed the 1919 Treaty of Versailles, the international bankers, and the ideas of Karl Marx, "a Hebrew," for America's economic ills. It was a bold talk that played to the fear and discontent of a nation mired in the Depression. But when the contract for the 1930–31 season ended following the April 5 broadcast, CBS declined to renew Coughlin's show; the risk of government intervention against an entire network of stations airing inflammatory, antigovernment material was simply too great. Undaunted, Coughlin worked with Detroit's WJR to cobble together an independent network that grew to include twenty-seven stations. Some of these were part of the NBC network and some were affiliated with CBS, but all of them were willing to chance carrying the Radio Priest's weekly show despite, or perhaps because of, the compellingly nasty messages and antigovernment rhetoric.

As his outright attacks on President Hoover became increasingly incendiary, Coughlin's popularity rose; controversy attracted listeners. The mail flowing into Royal Oak forced Coughlin to employ a staff of ninety-six clerks and required the construction of a new post office. However, the publicity about his removal from CBS spurred other groups to challenge limitations placed on the right to express opinions over the air. By early 1932, religious organizations, citing the Shuler incident and CBS's cancellation of Coughlin's network show, claimed that the freedom of religious expression was being abrogated by radio and those who controlled the medium. Responding to the charges, CBS denied any intent to remove religion from the airwaves, explaining they had merely made a corporate decision to no longer sell airtime to preachers, choosing instead to create their own series of religious talks called *Church of the Air,* which premiered in September 1931.

Not insulated from having to defend himself, Father Coughlin faced a new accuser: Cardinal William Henry O'Connell of Boston, who questioned why a religious leader would use his radio time to speak about social issues when there were religious questions that should be discussed. Coughlin fired back, claiming that his talks about poor economic conditions and the social ills plaguing America were based on the teachings and writings of popes Leo XIII and Pius XI. Unfazed, and probably inspired by the debate he was sparking, Coughlin continued his controversial talks, and the prominence they gave him would make him a major participant in two of the stories that dominated the United States during 1932.

Much to Herbert Hoover's chagrin, radio was now beyond his control. It had become a vast arena for those who argued publicly about an America in which the gap between the haves and the have-nots had widened. At the 1931 annual dinner of the Bureau of Advertising of the American Newspaper Publishers Association, the keynote speaker was the chairman of Bethlehem Steel, Charles M. Schwab. During his talk he felt compelled to defend the $1.6 million salary and bonus he had given the company's president; by way of explaining the exorbitant compensation, Schwab told the gathering that during a period in which he spent an average of $1 million a week to improve and expand Bethlehem Steel, he himself had never taken one dollar out of the company. He then called for the media to cease claiming that President Hoover and his policies were responsible for the economic difficulties of the nation. The tone of the gathering shifted dramatically when one of radio's biggest stars, Will Rogers, got up to speak. Unable to restrain himself, Rogers immediately challenged Schwab's optimistic views, urging the audience to look at the facts of what was really going on in America, to see the economic devastation for what it was. Rogers then went for the jugular: Reacting to Schwab's boast that he'd spent $1 million a week to support Bethlehem Steel without ever taking a dollar for himself, Rogers said, "Well, Mr. Schwab, if you did that you're also the greatest sucker in the world."

DURING THE PREVIOUS YEAR, Schwab's friend and fellow "have" John D. Rockefeller had announced a plan to construct the largest office and cultural center ever built. Designed to occupy an area of three city blocks on Manhattan's West Side between Fifth and Sixth avenues, the site would include three skyscrapers and an entertainment complex complete with a new Metropolitan Opera House. Joining Rockefeller in the venture was RKO, NBC, and General Electric, all of which would have homes in the new complex. The projected cost of the buildings was more than $200 million, which not only represented the largest construction effort in New York's history, but also heralded "the installation of broadcasting as a national industry."

What spurred the notion to build a complex that, in addition to having lots of office space, would provide a national home for broadcasting was a meeting that had brought Rockefeller together with David Sarnoff of RCA, Merlin Aylesworth of NBC, Hiram Brown of RKO, and an effervescent radio icon and producer with the catchy name of Roxy Rothafel, who told Rockefeller that Americans wanted "diversified entertainment organized with all the best modern resources." Once Rockefeller heard Rothafel's presentation, he agreed to set aside his original plan to build a new opera house and instead construct a 7,500-seat variety theater. The good news in all of this for Charles Schwab and other industrialists was that the new center, which was initially called "A City of Radio," would require tons of steel and other construction materials at a time when factories were being closed and people put out of work.

Demolition of the buildings on the designated city blocks commenced during the autumn of 1930 as plans for the center were finalized. In March 1931 the largest steel order in history was placed: $10 million for 125,000 tons of steel, all destined for the new center, which, though still lacking an official name, was alternately referred to as Metropolitan Square, Rockefeller City, and Radio City. Estimates were that the generous order would result in the hiring of between 8,000 and 10,000 men. Orders for other materials—by October 1931 the value of the awarded contracts exceeded $50 million—sparked other industries back to life and generated some optimism in the Depression-plagued nation.

In a country filled with dying businesses, radio itself, which awaited the construction of its majestic new home, was thriving. In May 1931 the *Washington Post* marked the ninth anniversary of its radio column by looking back at the industry's remarkable climb to prominence. There were more than 12,800,000 radio sets in use around the country, and most of the nation's more than six hundred radio stations provided full program schedules of regular daily and weekly features. Gone were the days of on-and-off-again program hours; now stations signed on in the early morning and, for the most part, stayed on until the 1 A.M. sign-off time. Programming of every kind filled the airwaves: music of all sorts mostly performed live, comedy, drama, women's serial dramas—which later became known as soap operas—news, commentary and information, public affairs talks, religion, daytime children's features, helpful hints for the homemaker, and sports.

Despite the ailing economy and the ongoing debate over the advisability and desirability of advertising on the radio, the revenue from companies desperate to promote commodities to the army of American radio listeners continued to grow; more than $30 million in advertising revenue fueled radio during 1931. Though some critics complained about the ever-increasing amount of advertising, no one had yet come up with a better way to support America's radio addiction.

Radio's success also led to more criticism of the industry; it was no longer good enough to be able to listen to just anything. Fully matured, the audience demanded more of the medium. But while critics clamored for more serious programming, especially asking to hear less "jungle-noise," as jazz was often called, musicians who filled the airwaves with lighter fare, especially Rudy Vallée, were becoming big celebrities. While millions of Americans were out of work, radio's stars were reaping the benefits of popularity; for example, beyond their network fee of

$100,000, Gosden and Correll, Amos and Andy, earned more than $250,000 in royalties from toys that bore their likenesses and a candy bar named for them. But even this most popular of shows was not beyond reproach: Angered by the use of dialects, African American leaders circulated a petition to have the show removed from the air because "their mannerisms and the material of their skits are regarded as tending to hold the Negro race in ridicule." The attempt failed, but this was an era filled with grave inconsistencies in terms of race relations, many of which were reflected in radio. How odd was it for Duke Ellington and his band, whose shows from New York's Cotton Club were broadcast over WHN, to perform for a whites-only audience? But those were the accepted mores of the day, even in New York.

As the new buildings on Rockefeller's site rose from the rubble, during the fall of 1931 Americans tuned their radios to hear Graham Mc-Namee on NBC calling his ninth consecutive World Series. If they preferred something newer, they could listen to Ted Husing on the CBS stations, but either way the series featured a rematch between the St. Louis Cardinals and the Philadelphia Athletics. Apparently American radio sports fans had become jaded: It was no longer enough to have the series—won in seven games by the Cardinals—brought into their homes via radio. Now they wanted more: They wanted brilliant accuracy. Complaints about the descriptions, about the quality of the announcing and announcing errors, became commonplace and quite public. What was once exciting because it was new had now grown old, and listeners demanded constant improvement.

That fall, as college football took its place as the Saturday-afternoon fixture of network radio, one important icon was missing from the sidelines. Notre Dame's vibrant head coach, Knute Rockne, the man who had led the Fighting Irish to the 1930 national championship, who had coached the legendary Four Horsemen, who had inspired his players with the gripping "Win one for the Gipper" pep talk, and who had compiled an astounding .881 winning percentage, had been killed earlier that year in a plane crash. On November 4 the nation listened to tributes by President Hoover, the mayors of Chicago and New York, three of the Four Horsemen, and Will Rogers, who eulogized the great coach saying, "If they had built athletic institutions instead of monuments to Napoleon, France might have been an athletic nation and sent a second team to play Notre Dame."

But no radio show that aired during the autumn of 1931 was as bizarre and unfortunate for President Hoover as a special program meant to bring together the financially challenged nation. Perhaps hoping to convince Americans through repetition that all was well, Hoover had become a far-too-frequent radio speaker. Throughout 1931 he took to the airwaves to speak to the nation and had become so proficient at the art of radio addresses that one reporter called him "radio's ideal speaker." In one talk, Hoover appealed to "the heart of the nation" to contribute to the Red Cross so their work to aid those suffering from the calamity of the droughts could continue; in February his tribute to President Lincoln was aired by every station in both national networks; in the space of two days in April he delivered three more national addresses about how Americans could help one another get through the nation's problems; between May 21 and June 17, Hoover was heard over NBC seven more times, including an address to the nation's newspaper editors meeting in Indianapolis in which he "called upon the people to replace the fear and apprehension of the depression with an armor of confidence." In July he addressed the International Christian Endeavor societies. There was a talk on August 1 to the World Conference of the YMCA, and with less than thirty-six hours' notice, the two networks arranged to carry Hoover's address to the American Legion meeting in Detroit. That talk dealt with World War I veterans' demand for bonuses due to be paid by the government; it was another critical speech for the embattled president, who seemed to be trying to talk his way through the national crises.

Hoover saved his biggest radio gambit for the night of October 18. Billed as a plea to help the unemployed, this radio spectacular was designed to raise money for the nation's many relief funds. NBC and CBS worked cooperatively to carry the one-hour program on all of their affiliates, which meant that more than 150 stations would air the special. Speaking from Fort Monroe, Virginia, the president opened the country's appeal for contributions to help the unemployed. In his impassioned address, Hoover called on Americans to make the upcoming Thanksgiving memorable: *that we have each of us contributed our full part; that we, in each of our communities, have given full assurance against hunger and cold among our people; that upon this Thanksgiving Day we have removed the fear of the forthcoming Winter from the hearts of all who are suffering and in distress—that we are our brother's keeper.*

Following Hoover's appeal, the special broadcast continued with musical entertainment provided by legendary march composer John Philip Sousa conducting the U.S. Marine Band, Leopold Stokowski conducting the Philadelphia Orchestra, operatic numbers sung by Lily Pons and Sophie Breslau in New York, and bass Lawrence Tibbett in San Francisco. But the highlight, or lowlight from President Hoover's perspective, was the bitter and harsh talk delivered by Will Rogers. Rogers attacked Hoover and the bankers who controlled the nation's financial resources; he decried the country's inability to share and provide for the less fortunate; he ridiculed the stupidity of Prohibition, saying, *What does Prohibition amount to if your neighbors' children are not eating? It's food, not drink, is our problem now.* He noted that depression used to be a state of mind, but all that had changed since it moved from the head to the stomach. He bemoaned the incredible waste of the 1920s, then added that he had faith that 1932 would be a better year.

*Why? Why because it's an election year, and the Republicans always see
to it that things look good on election years. They give us three bad years
and one good one, but the good one is the voting year. Elections are always just a year too late for the Democrats.*

It was a staggering partisan rant, and Rogers concluded by calling on
those with the means to help those without; then he thanked the president for allowing him to appear on the program.

As a result of the appeal, Americans gave what they could to local
charities, but the emotional reaction to Rogers's speech, to the harsh
reality he spoke of, was astounding; he was inundated with telegrams
and letters, and many of America's Community Chest organizations
asked permission to use a reprint of his speech as ad copy to help raise
more money.

As the Depression deepened and unemployment continued its un-
abated rise during the last two months of the year, the men lucky
enough to be employed in Midtown Manhattan building the Rockefeller buildings and America's first broadcasting complex marked the
end of the year in a novel way: They erected a twenty-foot-high
Christmas tree in the mud that was the construction site. Then on
Christmas Eve they lined up in front of the tree to get their paychecks.
It was a somewhat hopeful symbol at a time when hope was in short
supply. What was more hopeful, and truly amazing, was that just one
year later the office and entertainment complex Rockefeller envisioned
would be open for business. But in the intervening months, a year that
would be the young medium's greatest, radio and the men who dominated the industry, both behind the microphone and in front of it,
would help chart a new course for the nation while redefining the ways
radio could be a factor in all elements of American life.

Chapter 15

FOR LEGIONS OF THE UNEMPLOYED, the dawn of 1932 was dark. The Depression was the harsh reality lived by millions of Americans throughout the country. Despite the repeated claims, many made in radio speeches by members of the Hoover administration, that economic improvements were on the horizon and would occur naturally as the business cycles turned, the economy continued to spiral downward, led by the failures of 2,294 banks with $1.7 billion on deposit during 1931. Finding work became work itself; word of a factory hiring drew crowds that needed to be controlled by police; when they didn't find work, the unemployed congregated anywhere they could, passing the time, hoping something might happen to change their lot. Even those who found jobs were barely surviving: By 1932, factory workers were averaging just thirty-five hours per week at a time when the average five-and-a-half-day workweek should have totaled forty-four hours. The plight of the American farmer was no better: By 1932 one-third of all American farmers had lost their land, while the overall unemployment rate in the country hovered above 20 percent.

Despite the increase in the number of makeshift communities known as Hoovervilles—housing built of scrap wood, cardboard, metal, and anything else that might provide shelter—the president continued to insist that the economy would correct itself and improve without the government doling out money. "The people will, of course, provide against distress, but the purpose of the national government must be to restore employment by economic recovery." Hoover believed in the need for Americans to help one another, in the idea that it was the role of private charities to aid the less fortunate. It was the "thousand points of light" of its era, but the reality was that even organized charities such as churches and soup kitchens were struggling and, at best, only provided some of the unemployed and homeless with limited assistance in the way of food. Soup kitchens and breadlines were painful, visual reminders of America's plight. On February 15, 1932, the American Legion and the American Federation of Labor launched a national drive to find one million new jobs for unemployed Americans; one month later only 127,574 jobs had been found and filled. With little government help—government relief averaged about $1.67 per citizen annually—the American suicide rate increased by more than 20 percent.

But through all the economic and social struggles, radio continued to grow and thrive. More than 15 million American homes had a radio, and many had two or three sets; hotels advertised a radio in every room, and with 614 broadcasting stations, there was no shortage of programming. The free entertainment radio provided must have been a welcome distraction for the millions of destitute American workers who had no jobs to go to. However, ironically, studies showed that instead of seeking diversion from their problems, radio listeners craved hearing news, though most of the news in 1932 was bad.

Whatever it was they listened to, the daily audience for radio programs was estimated to be more than 50 million people. With an audience of that size, America's growing legion of national advertisers, desperate to find the people who could still buy their products, filled broadcasters' coffers. The 1931 gross revenue for the two national networks, NBC and CBS, approached $36 million, with combined profits of over $3 million.

The news for the radio industry was good, just as it was for the workers and tradesmen who benefited from the construction of Radio City and the Rockefeller complex of buildings in Manhattan. One estimate held that the project's construction would use more than 10 million eight-hour days of labor and that the total number of people employed by the project would be well above 56,000. Every aspect of the construction made news: the way the holes were dug in the rock to accommodate the huge elevators that would raise and lower the stage; the twenty-five-foot chandelier; the 20,000 cast-iron radiators—the largest such order in history—that were needed; the awarding of contracts to the Wurlitzer Company for the pipe organs that would fill Radio City with grand sounds; the mammoth RCA sign that would be placed atop the skyscraper, readable from one mile away; an announcement that the board of directors of the site had voted to name the entire complex Rockefeller Center in honor of the project's main sponsor; and the hiring of a man whose fame was directly attributable to radio, who gave the center and its showpiece, Radio City, added credibility. By early 1932 it was common knowledge that Roxy Rothafel would be pulling the strings and organizing the programming for America's newest and showiest theater.

Roxy was bold. In an era when most of America's orchestras were struggling to survive and were laying off musicians, he increased the size of his radio orchestra and added concerts to keep more musicians employed. Early in 1931 Rothafel announced his intention to retire from the management of the Roxy Theatre, leaving his future plans obscure, saying only that he wanted to "enter a much wider field of activity." It didn't take much imagination to figure out that the planned scope and size of the Rockefeller development and Radio City Music Hall, "the most colossal playhouse in the world," held great appeal to an ego like Roxy's, and though his role in the project had not been officially announced, by November 1931 he had been given the unofficial title "the Mayor of Radio City."

However, not even Roxy was entirely safe from the Depression's realities: During 1931, the Roxy Theatre Company suffered financial losses of over $160,000, and shareholders were none too happy with their company's namesake and his decision to resign and pursue other options. Apart from that minor setback, nothing slowed Roxy's march toward power and greater renown. Often compared to the brilliant showmen P. T. Barnum and Oscar Hammerstein, Roxy was acknowledged as the greatest impresario of the day, and any hint of his plans for Radio City made news. He viewed Radio City as a beacon that would beam great musical programs out, thus sealing America's prominence throughout the world, and since the radio announcements would be made in English, he predicted that radio would eventually make English the world's language.

Bit by bit, Roxy teasingly unveiled his vision of the kind of entertainment that would fill Radio City and be broadcast to rapt listeners everywhere. He anticipated producing grand new shows every month and announced that he was determining what listeners really wanted based on a review of the more than 6 million letters he had received during his years on the air. He idealistically viewed the new enterprise as a chance to have practical artistic successes, but pragmatically understood that the institution's backers would want some financial return for the millions invested. In May 1932 radio listeners were treated to a taste of the kind of spectacular shows they could expect once Radio

City opened. It was a typical Roxy production, featuring a menu of everything from the Sisters of the Skillet to one of the day's leading contraltos, Madame Ernestine Schumann-Heink, to a special late-night appearance by Amos and Andy, comments from NBC president Aylesworth, and Roxy discussing plans for Radio City.

Meanwhile, as Rockefeller Center rose and Radio City was built and decorated, more stars of stage and screen were developing radio shows. Any sense that may have once existed that radio was not a place for America's stars to ply their trade had vanished. Among the leading and highest-paid luminaries who filled the radio galaxy were Fred Allen, Jack Benny, Burns and Allen, Morton Downey, Al Jolson, and Kate Smith; newscasters H. V. Kaltenborn and Lowell Thomas; and bands or orchestras led by Ben Bernie, Jack Denny, Guy Lombardo, Paul Whiteman, and countless others.

Even performers who had once tried radio but found their mike fright too great to overcome returned to the airwaves. Ed Wynn, whose 1921 foray into live radio was at once groundbreaking and disappointing, finally gave in to the calls for him to take his place among radio's pantheon of stars. At 9:30 on Tuesday evening, April 26, 1932, Wynn debuted his new show, which was broadcast from New York's WEAF and heard over the NBC network. Sponsored by Texaco, it was called *Ed Wynn and the Fire Chief Band* and was a mixture of Wynn's famous brand of slapstick humor, some vaudeville bits, and music. Serving as Wynn's straight man was the ubiquitous Graham McNamee. The show opened with the loud sirens of a fire truck, then the announcer introduced the orchestra and Graham McNamee, who, despite rumors of his demise as a radio artist, received excellent reviews for his performance. McNamee's introduction was followed by a burst of noise and Wynn's grand entrance, which included the clanging of bells, the tooting of horns, Wynn's hysterical laugh, and loud applause from the studio audience. During the shows, Wynn often said the word *so,* but he dragged it out to be as long as five syllables: *Soooooo-ooo-ooo.* Wynn's show became so popular that this silly one-word sound became a national catchphrase.

Another vaudeville veteran who made his way to radio was Eddie Cantor. His program, which debuted in September 1931, aired on Sunday evenings over the NBC network, and was sponsored by Chase and Sanborn. Despite a rocky opening, which Cantor blamed on a lack of rehearsal and the absence of the laughter of a live audience, the program developed into another hit, even though Cantor occasionally put the show on hiatus so he could fulfill other entertainment obligations, including making movies in Hollywood. But Cantor, whose clowning performances were high energy, also used his radio show as a soapbox from which he announced his candidacy for president of the United States. Though a joke, his satirical run drew more and more listeners, setting new audience records for an ongoing series. With his biting comedy, Cantor found a receptive audience for his merciless ridiculing of a government that had failed the people of the country. His fake run for the White House resulted in one of the recurrent cheers, and another catchphrase, of the era, which was reinforced through repetition on his show: *We want Cantor! We want Cantor!* Though his run was nothing more than a stunt, Cantor did end up getting some write-in votes in the November 1932 election.

For President Hoover, the constant criticism of his administration that echoed over the airwaves was troublesome. Hoover, perhaps better than anyone, understood the power of radio and the celebrity it created, and hoping to gain from being associated with America's popular entertainers, he was not shy about being pictured with radio stars. In May 1931 Freeman Gosden and Charles Correll, Amos and Andy, stayed with the president at his fishing camp in Maryland. However, Hoover's press secretary was quick to assure reporters that "politics had not been discussed" during the visit. Hoover was delighted to honor singing star Kate Smith for the way she had entertained America's veterans, then, as Hoover's popularity neared its nadir, he invited Rudy Vallée, whose popularity was rising, to the White House. Following their Oval Office meeting, Hoover's desperation about the nation's plight was all too evident. When asked by reporters what he and the president had talked about, Vallée replied that the president had told him that he would merit a medal if he could write and record a song to drive away the Depression. Later that year Vallée did record a song written by Yip Harburg and Jay Gorney that became a number-one hit; unfortunately for Hoover it was one of the most poignantly sad, Depression-inspired songs: "Brother, Can You Spare a Dime?"

Undoubtedly radio had the power to create national celebrities. But it was radio appearances by celebrities from other fields that had fueled radio's amazing growth. Opera singers, Broadway stars, vaudevillians, writers, politicians, international leaders, and homegrown heroes could always draw listeners. Since his 1927 transatlantic flight and triumphant return, Colonel Charles Lindbergh had become a national celebrity whose every activity was reported in the newspapers; and yet in the years following the broadcast of the celebrations and speeches marking his return in June 1927, Lindbergh had guarded his privacy and avoided radio exposure. In 1930, when his wife, Anne Morrow Lindbergh, let it be known she was pregnant, the country and the world waited eagerly for word of the birth. As the date neared, anticipation intensified; stores sold congratulatory greeting cards that had a drawing of a baby in a flower-covered airplane. The card came complete with a cloyingly sweet poem—"A wish for your dear little baby / That years may happily glide, / With mother to fondle and cherish / And father to counsel and guide"—and an envelope conveniently preaddressed to the Lindberghs in New Jersey.

On June 23 an eight-pound baby boy was born to the famous couple. The news was greeted joyfully in the United States and around the world, especially in France, where Lindbergh remained a larger-than-life hero. Visitors, gawkers, and reporters surrounded the Lindbergh home, hoping for details of the mother, the father, and the baby. While they only received a few unimportant updates, they did witness a steady stream of gifts, flower arrangements, and telegrams from around the globe being delivered to the New Jersey residence. The Western Union messenger, Johnny Sullivan, who carried the majority of the messages to the estate, admitted "he was tired and would welcome a little relief."

Lindbergh discouraged reporters from hanging around the neighborhood, and so once the birth announcement was finalized all news of the Lindbergh baby was kept secret. But the press would not stop annoying the family. One month later Lindbergh outlined what he considered to be acceptable journalistic practices, contrasting them with those acts he thought were an invasion of his privacy. Lindbergh drew the line "between the right of the press to report his activities as they relate to the scientific development of air travel," and personal curiosity, such as the "advance heralding" of the arrival of his baby.

Two weeks later, on August 8, Lindbergh stood before a battery of microphones to make his first in-studio radio speech. Both NBC networks, the Red and the Blue, and the CBS network cancelled all regular programming for the famed flier's talk about international aviation, which was aired live at 4:25 P.M. EDT and then rebroadcast at 11 that night. Not only would the entire United States be able to hear Lindbergh, but thanks to the use of shortwave, a live transmission of his talk was to be sent to Europe. However, weather conditions that day hindered the international transmission, so lacquer disc recordings of the colonel's speech were made and immediately shipped via the SS *Roosevelt* to London so the BBC could present a special, if somewhat delayed, broadcast of the talk.

During the summer of 1931, the Lindberghs again became newsworthy, this time for a daring trip they planned to make to the Orient. Their route would take them over some of the wildest and least-inhabited portions of the globe, including Point Barrow, Alaska, the northernmost territory in the United States. From there they planned to fly to Asia, ending their journey in Japan. One of the highlights of the trip would be the Lindberghs' use of radio to communicate during the flights. Bringing radio communication and aviation together—both were industries championed by Herbert Hoover when he was secretary of commerce and were two of the few growth businesses of the 1930s—would be an ideal way for Colonel Lindbergh to make his point about how radio transmission would improve air safety and open the world to air travel.

Departing from Maine, where they left their thirteen-month-old son in the care of his grandparents and a nurse, the Lindberghs headed to Canada on July 30, 1931, beginning what would be a dramatic journey that millions of people eagerly followed, including more than 2,000 radio amateurs who used their receivers to listen to Mrs. Lindbergh's direct transmissions from the plane. These radio amateurs were entrusted with the task of monitoring the plane's transmissions and providing information to the nearest points of contact along the route in the event of an emergency.

More than four weeks after their departure, having completed a journey of 7,132 miles, the Lindberghs arrived in Tokyo and were greeted with cheers of "Banzai." Immediately plans were set to transmit the official welcoming ceremonies back to the United States, with NBC and CBS airing the event. In addition to Colonel and Mrs. Lindbergh, Japan's ministers of communications and war were scheduled to speak. Despite some interference and static that occasionally drowned out the voices, the transmission exemplified Lindbergh's observation that radio and aviation were allied fields bridging vast distances to bring the world closer together. "With the advance of radio and aircraft, the mystery of distance can no longer exist. We are interested in many of the same things and confronted by similar problems. There are no longer distant countries," he concluded. The trip and the transmission were hallmarks for aviation and radio. Seven months later, Lindbergh would again be the center of radio's attention, this time much more reluctantly.

MARCH 1, 1932—That night, ignoring the unwritten rule about waiting for newspapers to issue an extra edition to announce breaking news, the CBS network interrupted a concert by a Chicago-based dance orchestra, shocking listeners across the nation with this bulletin:

> *Charles A. Lindbergh Jr., 1½ year-old son of Colonel and Mrs. Charles A. Lindbergh, was kidnapped just after dark tonight from his crib in the Lindbergh home at Hopewell, N.J. He was dressed in his sleeping clothes.*

During the days that followed, radio would establish and secure its place as a dominant source of breaking news and information; radio's immediacy had found its true calling. Stations issued a steady stream of bulletins and appeals for the baby's safe return. Network and station managers placed their transmitting equipment at the disposal of the authorities; phone lines and transmitting equipment were installed near the Lindbergh estate in an effort to assuage the flood of callers demanding more information. Regular programming was shunted, and instead of signing off during the overnight hours, stations remained on the air in case there was some news or information to be shared with anxious listeners. The networks, with their coast-to-coast reach, fed affiliated stations nonstop programming, remaining active, ready to provide bulletins twenty-four hours a day in case some piece of news broke. Not since the beginning of broadcasting had the radio facilities of the entire nation been turned over to one emergency, either public or private. Radio's undivided attention was focused on the return of America's hero's son.

In one of the more poignant moments of the Lindbergh case, one day after the kidnapping, NBC network announcer Ben Grauer took to the air to read a personal message from the baby's mother about the child's special dietary needs. The strict diet was to help the child recover from an illness, and it was Mrs. Lindbergh's wish that the kidnappers heard the detailed requirements, which included half a cup of prune juice after the baby's afternoon nap, and "fourteen drops of viosterol, a vitamin preparation, during the day." On the fourth day of the manhunt, America's religious leaders got involved, taking to the airwaves to appeal to the kidnappers for the child's safe return. Representatives of the Catholic, Protestant, and Jewish faiths spoke over a nationwide network arranged by CBS, all pledging immunity should the kidnappers return the child to one of their houses of worship. Speaking on behalf of the Catholic faith was Father Charles Coughlin, whose powerful oratory overshadowed all other radio speakers.

Do you realize that you have their first baby? Do you realize that you are holding away from the mother's arms flesh of her flesh and blood of her blood; that you are not injuring the baby half so much as you are crushing her heart in a great press, making her bleed the wine of sorrow?

He ended his talk by asking the kidnappers to find some sequestered church or orphanage and return the child, adding that he pledged his assurance that no questions would be asked. While the speech did not bring the baby back to his parents, its powerful message generated thousands of additional letters, and dollars, for Coughlin's church in Royal Oak.

For the next seventy-two days, radio announcers reported from the New Jersey scene, describing in detail every aspect of the hunt for the missing baby boy and telling anxious listeners about the hundreds of clues that had flooded in, none of which led to anything concrete.

Sensing that radio's news-delivery power might be greater than originally believed, the *New York Times* criticized the radio newspeople for
the way they issued bulletins without making certain the information
was anything more than rumor, arguing that radio's immediacy was
detrimental to the accuracy of the reporting. Delineating the difference between journalism and radio reporting, the *Times* went on to
point out that the cost of the extra reporting and airtime for the Lindbergh coverage was hurting radio. Nonetheless, the broadcasters vowed
to remain continuously on the air, ready to flash the news if the missing child should be found.

MAY 12, 1932—That evening, the news flashed that the infant's body
had been found in the woods near the Lindbergh home. Following the
national and international outpouring of sympathy for the Lindberghs,
cries of outrage and pain filled the airwaves. The White House and
members of the Senate and Congress publicly mourned; from Michigan, Father Coughlin sent his personal sympathy and extended his "fe-
licitations" to the family, for their child, in his mind, was not dead,
"merely waiting for them in the land of eternity." With the personal
thoughts out of the way, Coughlin seized the opportunity to call on his
listeners to view the kidnapping and murder of the Lindbergh baby as
a challenge to "eradicate the gangster and hoodlum from our country."
For Coughlin the tragedy was another chance to further his image as a
leader, both spiritual and societal. During the coming decade, the link between Coughlin and Lindbergh would develop and strengthen, as would
the importance of radio as a tool in the hunt for the baby's kidnapper,
and the eventual arrest, trial, and execution of Bruno Hauptmann.

Radio's coverage of the Lindbergh kidnapping was a significant
turning point. For those who had doubted the medium's ability as a
credible source for news, the coverage of the tragedy had to have been
eye-opening. Radio was no longer solely for entertainment; it could lay

aside "its jazz and comedy to play a greater role in mysterious dramas of life." What was significant was not that radio could report the news, but that it made it come alive in ways the print media could not. Radio had become the audio canvas of American life, providing escape and reality for millions of listeners.

IF ESCAPE IS WHAT RADIO FANS CRAVED, June 1932 was setting up to be a banner month for them. On the schedule was a heavyweight prizefight and two national political conventions, and that was great news for broadcasters because few events they aired stirred greater interest and enlarged the invisible audience more than a championship bout and the dramatic political oratory of a presidential race.

For months the boxing world had been taken by the idea that Jack Dempsey, America's boxing star of the 1920s, was going to return to the ring and challenge for the heavyweight crown. While Dempsey's large shadow loomed on the horizon, boxing fans anticipated the far more likely rematch between the current heavyweight champion, German Max Schmeling, and his American challenger, Jack Sharkey.

Eleven years after radio first broadcast a fight, NBC set up its microphones and transmitting equipment at a site in Long Island City, New York, called the Madison Square Garden Bowl to bring fans from coast to coast the blow-by-blow call. When Max Schmeling and Jack Sharkey entered the ring on June 21, 1932, seated at ringside was an announcer for German radio whose commentary would be shortwaved back to Schmeling's homeland. Just a few feet away, ready to call the fight for the NBC network, was the veteran of fight broadcasting, Graham McNamee, along with Charles Francis Coe, a well-regarded author of fight stories.

Unlike the bout two years earlier that ended after four rounds when Sharkey hit Schmeling with a low blow, the 1932 encounter was a fifteen-round affair that ended with Sharkey wobbling near his corner, one eye damaged and closed by a fierce Schmeling barrage. In the other corner, Schmeling waited for the decision, seemingly unmarked and confident he had retained the heavyweight championship of the world. Listeners to any one of sixty-nine radio stations, the largest network ever assembled for a fight, had heard McNamee and Coe alternate at the mike through the rounds, their different styles—McNamee deliberate and precise, while Coe nearly spat his words using a rapid-fire, staccato delivery—giving fans the clear sense that Schmeling had won by a safe margin. When the fight ended, McNamee sought comments from the fighters' managers, but their voices were drowned out by the thunderous roar of the crowd of more than 72,000 when ring announcer Joe Humphries read the decision: The judges had voted two to one for Sharkey, giving the American the heavyweight crown. It was a stunning upset that left McNamee and Coe breathless trying to explain this development to their listeners. Reviewing the bout and NBC's coverage, Alan Gould of the Associated Press called the fight "colorless," a quality not at all reflected by McNamee and Coe's dramatic call of the fight. Had the announcers injected excitement where none existed? Could radio alter reality? Could the media distort what was really happening? Could the absence of the visual allow radio announcers to relate exaggerated images of what they saw? Was radio objective? These challenging critical questions began to crop up just as the oratory of politics was providing radio audiences with a different kind of pugilism.

The 1932 heavyweight championship fight took place during the weeks between the two national nominating conventions, political battles that provided more real drama for America's radio audiences. The conventions were held in Chicago Stadium, which posed acoustic challenges for radio technicians. Weeks before the conventioneers descended on Chicago, plans were made to erect a platform at one end of the stadium. From there speakers would be heard by the 25,000 or

so people in the stadium and the millions more listening at home. Engineers installed banks of microphones around the stadium to allow for
maximum flexibility should a story develop somewhere other than on
the main platform. It was far more sophisticated than the setups used
in 1924 and 1928 when less receptive and sensitive microphones merely
captured the basic sounds of the conventions.

There was one more significant change: Between 1928 and 1932 the
price of doing business with radio had soared. While the networks
broadcast the conventions without charge—station managers hoped
for short conventions so they wouldn't lose too much advertising revenue—airing campaign speeches had become costly. The 1928 fee to
air a one-hour talk over the two major networks was around $15,500;
in 1932 the cost for a nighttime one-hour broadcast on the networks
had climbed to more than $35,000. Of course the audience was also
larger, up to a total of about 68 million Americans from a 1928 estimate
of 37 million.

The Republican convention was held during the second week of
June. Despite the disaster that was the American economy, Hoover's
renomination was a certainty, leaving little possibility for drama.
Nonetheless, radio was ready to cover any eventuality. Instead of using
one announcer as they had done in the past, the networks sent teams
of reporters and commentators to bring the spectacle of American politics to life. Representing CBS were commentators Frederic William
Wile and H. V. Kaltenborn, with anchoring provided by Ted Husing.
NBC sent political pundits William Hard and David Lawrence, newsman Floyd Gibbons, and their all-star utility anchor, Graham Mc-
Namee. Combined, CBS and NBC fed programming to nearly 200
radio stations, a new record for network transmission.

At noon on June 14, 1932, the Republican convention was called to
order. The thrilling sound of more than 20,000 shouting voices cas-
caded from one end of the country to the other. After the keynote ad-

dress, announcers and pundits filled the broadcast time between speeches by speculating on who might be nominated for vice president and by describing the celebrities they saw, the perspiring delegates desperately trying to get their planks into the party's platform, and the unbelievable impact of the sound of the crowd yelling, the force of which caused radio announcers to retreat behind the stadium's walls for protection. In his spitfire style, announcer Floyd Gibbons told of spotting "peerless leaders and beerless leaders" in the throng. Among those listening to the convention were members of the United States Senate, who, joined by Vice President Curtis, whose renomination was not secure, left the Senate chamber to go to a nearby room where a radio had been set up. President Hoover, whose renomination was never in doubt, listened to the proceedings from the White House.

Day two of the convention was more exciting as the debate intensified over whether to call for the repeal of Prohibition. National coverage over both networks usually began in the late morning and continued uninterrupted for more than four hours. The hoots and shouts from the crowd often caused the transmitted sound to crack and distort as engineers worked to control the modulating volume. As votes about the Prohibition plank were counted, the cheering grew even wilder, injecting some spirit into what was a basically lackluster convention. As one radio announcer put it: *This is an interesting and remarkable convention. At least it has developed into that. The "Grand Old Party" has shown that it is still full of fire and fight*—if not much fun; in the end, the "drys" won out.

The third and final day of the Republican convention drew a full house of more than 25,000 delegates and supporters to Chicago Stadium. At noon on June 16, President Hoover's name was placed into nomination by the chairman of the California delegation. Though his talk of keeping the nation on "an even keel" drew muted enthusiasm, the energy level increased when a military band accompanied by a loud organ played a stirring rendition of "Over There" while delegates marched around with their banners for Hoover. After the celebratory displays and the state-by-state roll call, Herbert Hoover was officially nominated for a second term at 2:23 P.M. EDT. Listeners throughout America heard the words from the podium: *Herbert Hoover, having received a majority of the votes, I hereby declare he is the Republican nominee for President of the United States.*

Though there were challengers, the Republicans did nominate Charles Curtis of Kansas to be their second-term candidate for vice president, and with all business done the Republican National Convention of 1932 was adjourned, and with that, the attacks began. On the following day, Jouett Shouse, chairman of the Democratic National Executive Committee, took to the airwaves, calling the Republican platform nothing more than a series of misleading hedges that "can be read by anybody into accord with anybody's idea." It was the first salvo in what would be a nasty campaign. But first the Democrats had to find their nominee, and that process began on June 28, when their delegates convened in Chicago.

As the Democrats arrived in the Windy City, engineers for the two radio networks were enhancing their technology. Using lessons learned during the Republican conclave, the engineers found ways to improve the sound pickup in the stadium to make the Democratic convention sound even more realistic and dramatic. Among the advancements being tried was a small microphone that could be inserted in a jacket's lapel. Around the convention floor, six pages, each wearing one of these special microphones, were strategically stationed so they could move quickly to be close to the delegation that was voting, making it possible for the radio audience to hear every detail of each state's roll call.

Excited by the possibility of unseating the unpopular Herbert Hoover, the Democrats anticipated a lively convention, with John Nance Garner of Texas and 1928 nominee Al Smith vying for the nomination. But it was the popular governor of New York, Franklin D. Roosevelt—positioning himself as the candidate capable of bridging the differences between the Southern prohibitionist wing and the more liberal Northern wing of the party—who truly excited the Democrats. Roosevelt, who had been the Democratic vice-presidential candidate when Harding beat Cox in 1920, had done well in his four years as New York's governor, including finding imaginative ways to have the government assist the needy. Not shy about using radio to get his message out to residents of New York State, Roosevelt often gave radio speeches, the frequency of which increased as the 1932 convention neared and the battle between FDR and Al Smith for primacy at the convention intensified.

The Democratic convention was at once great political theater and great radio. Aided by the new lapel microphones and a complex arrangement of additional microphones and loudspeakers, which made the convention sound as if it were being held in a specially built radio studio, every cheer, especially those reacting to calls for the repeal of Prohibition, echoed through millions of radio sets. Pleased with the quality of the "show," the radio networks stayed on the air with convention coverage for more consecutive hours than ever before: four hours the first day and more than six hours the second day. Another new element that made the proceedings more listenable was the Democrats' clever use of nonpolitical speakers to fill the once-silent gaps while backroom politicking was taking place. Thanks to radio, it was a far more produced convention than any previous one. During one afternoon session, radio stars stepped up to the platform and spoke to the conventioneers, their words carried by both networks, regardless of which network they were under contract to. The entertainment included radio crooner Eddie Dowling, former heavyweight champ Gene Tunney, Amos and Andy, and Will Rogers, who got tremendous laughs when he said, *As soon as enough members of the committee get sober,*

we probably will hear the prohibition plank. While these programming en-
hancements, combined with the improved audio quality, certainly
made the Democratic convention a better radio show than the one the
Republicans mounted, it is unlikely that these improvements markedly
helped the Democrats' political outlook in 1932; after all, with Hoover
in the White House and millions of Americans unemployed, their
chances were already good.

Three other notable speakers were heard during the Democratic
convention: famed Scopes trial lawyer Clarence Darrow; Huey Long
of Louisiana; and the man who had become known as the Shepherd of
the Air, Father Charles Coughlin. The relationship between Coughlin
and Roosevelt had its roots in one of Coughlin's 1930 radio sermons,
in which he predicted *Another Roosevelt shall have the courage to unlock the
hypocritical human factors who have debased our system . . . Another Roosevelt
shall labor for the development of our own country!* During his 1931 battle
with the CBS network over censorship, Coughlin had written to Governor Roosevelt asking him to intervene, but Roosevelt wrote only a
noncommittal reply offering his sympathy for the priest's difficulty.
Then in the spring of 1932, as Roosevelt's campaign for the Democratic nomination was heating up, he and Coughlin met at a New York
hotel and exchanged ideas about unemployment relief and ways to help
the common man. Coughlin was impressed by Roosevelt's plans and
claimed Roosevelt had been impressed by his understanding of economics. While there is some question as to how impressed Roosevelt
really was, there is no doubt that he appreciated the size of Coughlin's
radio audience and understood the value of the priest's support at the
ballot box.

Stepping up to the Chicago Stadium microphones, Coughlin made
his appearance sound as if it were spur of the moment, when in fact it
had been carefully staged. His opening remark was greeted by laughter: *Of course I am not a Republican and most people know that.* He quickly

added that religion should not be identified with any political party, and then unequivocally threw his full and rather consequential support behind Roosevelt, electrifying the crowd by coining the catchy phrase "Roosevelt or ruin."

In the governor's mansion in Albany, New York, Roosevelt listened to the convention's proceedings late into the night over the radio, interrupting the broadcast only to take calls from his lieutenants in Chicago. And while the entertainment and protracted hours of broadcast time made for good radio, the political theater was dynamite. When John E. Mack rose to place FDR's name into nomination, Al Smith scowled and left the stadium declaring, "Hell, I can listen to that at the hotel over the rad-dio." As Mack began his nominating speech, the booing of the Smith supporters, led by Chicago mayor Anton Cermak, drowned him out. It was all vividly captured for the American radio audience by the plethora of microphones.

When the balloting began at four in the morning on July 1, the first person to cast his state's votes by talking into one of the new lapel microphones was Alabama governor William Brandon, the politician who had become famous during the 1924 convention for his repeated cry of *"twenty-four votes for Oscarrrrrr W. Un-der-woooooooood."* The balloting was protracted and the backroom arm twisting and negotiating intense. At 8 P.M., as the fourth ballot began, the convention seemed to be deadlocked. When California's turn came, William Gibbs McAdoo asked to speak from the platform. There, struggling to be heard over the booing Smith supporters, he undeadlocked the convention: *California casts forty-four votes for Franklin Delano Roosevelt.* At 10:32 P.M. the Democrats' nominee was Governor Roosevelt, who was listening to the proceedings on the radio in Albany. President Hoover, vacationing at his camp in the Virginia mountains, where he planned to work on his own acceptance speech during the Fourth of July holiday, listened over the radio to the fourth ballot. Another interested listener was Governor

Roosevelt's seventy-year-old mother, who, when reached at her Hyde Park, New York, home, said, "My son called me up to tell me he had been nominated, but I had already heard it over the radio in my own home."

All that remained was for the convention to nominate John Nance Garner to be FDR's running mate, an event that Speaker of the House Garner heard while listening on a radio in the Washington, D.C., office of another congressman. The next morning Roosevelt left Albany via airplane and flew to Chicago, where, breaking with the custom of giving the acceptance speech sometime after the convention's conclusion, he delivered his acceptance speech live at the convention. Greeted by cheering fans, including hundreds of unemployed workers, Roosevelt addressed the crowd, rousing the delegates and presumably the radio audience as well with this ringing promise: *I pledge you, I pledge myself, to a new deal for the American people.* President Hoover did not hear Roosevelt's powerful acceptance speech; if he had, he may have realized early on how captivating and dynamic his opponent's oratory could be, not to mention how positive FDR's message was, especially when his talk was followed by the rousing rendition of the Roosevelt campaign song, "Happy Days Are Here Again."

The 1932 Democratic convention set all kinds of broadcasting records: A total of almost fifty hours of airtime were dedicated to the convention, including nearly twelve consecutive hours on the air, throughout the night; and at a cost to the radio networks of nearly $1 million. "Listeners heard the nomination of a potential Vice President by acclamation, the cheering of throngs that jammed the Stadium as Governor Roosevelt was being awaited, and the bedlam of cheers that greeted his arrival on the speakers' platform."

Radio had brought democracy into American homes in ways never before imagined; but the medium's incredible power—positive and negative—had become all too evident. Radio's role in nominating and electing America's leaders needed to be scrutinized; commentators warned that the equal-time provision, which was part of the 1927 Radio Act, must be strictly adhered to. Nasty on-air political tactics, such as those Huey Long used in Louisiana to defeat his opponents, were frowned on. No longer able to hide behind the "no censorship" provision of the Radio Act to avoid libel charges, broadcasters needed to guard themselves against the utterances of political candidates.

Between the end of the summer conventions and the fall political season, America's networks struggled to figure out what airtime they would give to the candidates as part of their public service, and what airtime the campaigns would have to pay for. For example, the networks had always given away time for presidential addresses, but based on that precedent, any time President Hoover spoke over the air would be free, while time used by candidate Roosevelt would have to be paid for, which created an immediate inequity. Clearly a distinction between President Hoover and candidate Hoover needed to be drawn so Roosevelt would not be at too great a disadvantage. The microphone had become a modern weapon of politics.

Looking ahead at the upcoming campaign, radio's leading political pundit, H. V. Kaltenborn, predicted: "Radio will certainly play a dominating part in the campaign this year. In a very real sense this will be a radio campaign." But the presidential campaign was only one piece of a far larger mosaic that would make the autumn of 1932 the moment that marked radio's final ascent to the peak of American life and culture.

Chapter 16

▲▲▲▲▲▲▲▲▲▲▲▲▲▲▲▲

Radio's entry into the mainstream of American life had begun just twelve years earlier with KDKA's coverage of the 1920 presidential election—an election that kept a young New Yorker named Roosevelt from becoming vice president and swept the Republicans, along with an energetic secretary of commerce named Hoover, into office. Despite radio's having become the print media's chief competitor for advertising dollars, marveling at and assessing the industry's development made great newspaper copy. One columnist, reviewing radio's incredible progress and the stars it had created, noted that before radio came along Graham McNamee had been a part-time church singer and salesman. Now, in 1932, his name and voice were instantly recognizable from coast to coast. Fine music programs had become the standard for radio, and America's greatest artistic institutions were prominently featured week after week, with broadcasts by the Metropolitan Opera, the New York Philharmonic, the Philadelphia Orchestra, the Cleveland Orchestra, and other prominent musical organizations. More and more regularly scheduled programming was broadcast; the widely varied offerings were targeted at every kind of listener, from children, to housewives, to businessmen, to sports fans, to music aficionados. And this huge increase in programming, all of which was expensive to produce, occurred despite a dip in the sale of radio sets during the first part of 1932, which, despite the ever-increasing advertising revenue, was still an accepted barometer for how the radio industry was doing.

Given the content-filled hours, station managers had to become adept at jettisoning regular programming to carry something of a special nature, whether it was breaking news such as the Lindbergh baby kidnapping or a sporting event like the Sharkey-Schmeling championship bout. Furthermore, radio's tremendous political and social clout had become even more evident during the in-depth coverage of both conventions. As Labor Day approached, radio was absolutely central to three important campaigns: the final days of the baseball season and the World Series, the vicious battle between FDR and President Hoover for the White House, and the efforts to complete Radio City Music Hall.

During the summer of 1932 baseball took its place in the forefront of American sports. In the National League, the Chicago Cubs were leading the pack, but it was a tight race as the Pittsburgh Pirates kept the pressure on the Cubs. The two teams traded the top position in the standings, leaving fans speculating as to which team would earn the dubious honor of confronting the awesome Yankees in the World Series. In New York, the Yanks were having one of the best seasons in team history, running away with the American League title while winning more than 70 percent of their games. At the beginning of the 1932 season, due in part to the country's economic difficulties, superstar slugger Babe Ruth had agreed to a $5,000 salary cut. When asked about the

Depression, Ruth quipped, "I didn't see much of a depression with the Yankees." It was an accurate assessment; the Yankees rolled over the American League and headed for the World Series. But shortly after Labor Day, Ruth, suffering from shooting pains in his side, left the team while on a road trip and returned to New York to consult with his doctor. He missed the next ten days of play and was in questionable health when the regular season ended.

While the baseball teams were positioning themselves for the fall classic, the run for the White House was captivating the country. The Republicans and President Hoover had assumed the president would be able to campaign from the White House by merely giving a few well-timed radio speeches. Their strategy was to show Hoover hard at work doing the people's business while his lieutenants went out on the stump, but by the end of September both campaigns realized that while radio was effective in reaching thousands of voters efficiently, it could not replace the power and intimacy of personal appearances. Hoover and Roosevelt were both excellent radio orators, but they were far more dynamic when the audience could see them, especially during the delivery of speeches that ran as long as forty-five minutes. In the case of the Roosevelt campaign, there was another important aspect of the "radio only" issue: Needing to show that the effects of polio had not made him too frail to lead, Roosevelt could not afford to stay home and hide behind a microphone.

For the voting public, the novelty of hearing famous people speak via radio in the comfort of their homes, which in 1928 had seemed so marvelous, had worn off. Nonetheless, radio's role in the reinforcement and repetition of key messages remained central, and both campaigns organized networks of stations to carry the talks the candidates and their surrogates delivered, in this way combining the excitement of live stump speeches with the reach of national radio. Attacks and rapid responses via radio became part of the campaigns' arsenals, and it was not unusual

for both candidates to broadcast speeches on the same day. The campaigns were honing the use of radio as a way to quickly counter charges
made by the other side before lasting damage could be done.

Still trying to campaign from the White House, Hoover found himself in for a far more arduous battle than he had anticipated. He or his
surrogates had to respond to attacks by FDR that were aired in carefully scripted speeches. Furthermore, the Republican Party was low
on funds for airtime and advertising, and so Hoover had to add fund-
raising to his already overtaxed schedule. In his speeches, Hoover portrayed himself as a victim, a busy, diligent man forced to waste time
fending off accusations that he didn't care about the plight of the American workers. It was a rough beginning to a grueling battle that would
include whistle-stop tours rivaling the kind of campaigns run in 1920.

With the presidential campaign as a constant backdrop, Americans
found some diversion in the back-and-forth battle to win the National
League. When the dust settled on the 1932 baseball season, the Chicago
Cubs claimed the right to face the New York Yankees and a still-
debilitated Babe Ruth in the World Series. As expected, both networks
covered the series; NBC's broadcasts were anchored by Graham Mc-
Namee, while at CBS Ted Husing was the main voice. In an effort to
drum up interest in their coverage, CBS announcer Hal Totten interviewed both managers on the eve of the first game during CBS's national broadcast of Ben Bernie's entertainment and music show. It
might have seemed odd to insert conversations with baseball managers
into the middle of a lighthearted music program like Bernie's, but it was
an effective way for CBS to promote their coverage of the series, just
as television networks today train their cameras on the stars of their fall
shows during baseball games in October.

The 1932 series opened in New York with 12–6 and 5–2 Yankee
victories before moving to Chicago. President Hoover, who had attended games during previous World Series, declined invitations to

attend any of the 1932 games, claiming he had work to do for his country. On the other hand, Roosevelt just happened to be campaigning in Chicago as the series arrived there; seeing an opportunity for free media attention, he accepted an invitation to game three. Played on Saturday, October 1, the game Roosevelt witnessed turned out to be one of the most memorable in World Series history.

There was bad blood between Babe Ruth and the Chicago Cubs; the Windy City team did not like the public comments the Babe had made about the way the Cubs were treating one of their players, who just happened to be a former Yankee. With 49,986 people jammed into Wrigley Field, the Yankees opened game three by putting two men on base. When Ruth stepped to the plate he was serenaded by loud booing from the Cubs' faithful. He responded by launching the third pitch he saw into the center-field stands, giving the Yankees a quick 3–0 lead. In the third inning Lou Gehrig homered, giving the Yankees a 4–1 advantage; but the Cubs scratched their way back, and by the time the fifth inning began the score was tied at four. Babe Ruth batted second in the inning; as he strode to the plate, the catcalling and name-calling coming from the Cubs' dugout was ferocious, loud enough for the radio commentators to explain the ruckus to their listeners. Ruth shouted back and then stared at the mound, never lifting the bat from his shoulder, as Cubs' pitcher Charlie Root threw his first four pitches. The count was two balls and two strikes when the pivotal moment arrived: The Babe held his right arm out and pointed two fingers toward center field, then yelled to the Cubs' dugout that the next pitch was going out. Angry, Root fired his next pitch. Ruth swung, launching a majestic shot into the stands right where he had pointed. Announcing over the CBS network, Tom Manning captured the event for radio listeners across the country, and his description of every detail of the incident, from the moment Ruth walked to the plate, to the instant the blast landed in the stands, was magical: *Babe Ruth connects and there it goes! The ball is going, going, going, high into the centerfield stands, into the scoreboard, and it's a home run.*

Manning's nearly hysterical call and the crowd noises made listeners feel as if they were right there in Wrigley Field. It was a dramatic moment that radio let the entire country hear. Later in that inning, Lou Gehrig homered again, and the Yankees went on to win the game 7–5. After observing the home-run display by Ruth and Gehrig, Roosevelt admitted that the game had taught him "more about the power situation in America than he had ever learned from books and commission reports."

The Yankees went on to sweep the series, smashing the Cubs 13–6 in game four. Commenting on the games, Will Rogers wrote:

> The old radio pays for itself every Fall during the world series. We listen to ads, crooners and politicians all year just to hear: "The count is three and two on Babe Ruth and the pitcher is winding up." That's America's greatest suspense. Babe is the only man in the world that was never "tuned out on."

Another personality radio listeners rarely tuned out was Rudy Vallée, who, sponsored by Fleischmann, had owned the Thursday at 8 P.M. slot on the NBC network since October 1929. Though he had become the unquestioned dean of radio hosts, Vallée was not content to rest on his laurels. Perhaps sensing increasing pressure from the growing crowd of competitive new programs, he decided his show's format needed to be freshened. In a letter to John Reber of J. Walter Thompson, the ad agency responsible for the show and for sales of Fleischmann's Yeast, Vallée wrote:

> I appreciate as well as you that competition is unusually keen on the air today. I have always felt that our program should not be

judged by sales, whether the sales are high or low, as I honestly feel that God himself could not sell Fleischmann's Yeast for health. Popularity data, however, is another matter, and if it shows that the hour is not up to scratch, you know well enough that I will move heaven and earth and spare no expense as far as it is humanly possible for me to do so, to make it greater than ever!

Later in that letter, almost as an aside, Vallée asked how the sponsor would feel if he included the tune "Okay Beer!" in a show, even though it might "antagonize the drys." That request was denied, but his efforts to improve his show were welcomed.

THURSDAY, OCTOBER 6, 1932, 8 P.M.—Three years after its network debut, the *Fleischmann's Yeast Hour* went on the air, but instead of the usual Graham McNamee introductions at the top of the show, the radio audience heard the orchestra playing the opening theme accompanying *Heigh ho everybody . . . this is Rudy Vallée announcing and directing the Fleischmann's Yeast Hour.* Vallée told his listeners that effective with this show he was assuming new duties: *It will be my task to find and bring to this microphone a great variety of entertaining people . . .* His idea was to have many different guests each week drawn from the stars of the stage and screen, the day's spectacular and interesting personalities, and people in the news. He hailed the show's newfound flexibility, which allowed him to react quickly to current events: *The keynote of our new program series then, is . . .* Vallée paused for effect, and then defined this new entertainment genre: *variety.*

Vallée organized these shows meticulously, setting new industry standards for radio production. In so doing, he gave birth to the American variety show, which, as Vallée himself said, was the "Palace Theater of the Air"—a direct descendant of vaudeville, now reshaped to please an audience that couldn't see the acts. Week after week, Vallée brought the superstars of entertainment, politics, theater, and sports to his show; he introduced talented newcomers, many of whom went on to have their own successful radio, and later television, shows; he presented scenes from plays, including *Coquette, Street Scene, Emperor Jones,* and *Romeo and Juliet,* with leading actors like Claude Rains, Helen O'Connell, Bela Lugosi, and Jimmy Cagney. Vallée also proudly brought forward many of the day's leading comedians and, albeit hesitantly, introduced America to its first successful radio ventriloquist, Edgar Bergen, about whom John Reber of J. Walter Thompson warned, "The guy better be funny if he hopes to overcome the limitations of the medium."

While the autumn of 1932 included a presidential campaign to determine the path the country would follow in its effort to escape the economic crisis, Rudy Vallée's bold move to bring true variety to radio, to present many different kinds of entertainment all within one hour, changed the course of American media entertainment, spawning the style of radio and television entertainment the country would enjoy for the next half century and launching the careers of artists who would grace the television screens in American homes for decades.

Just two days before Vallée changed the style of radio entertainment, President Hoover gave his initial address of the campaign. In a talk carried by both networks that originated in Des Moines, Iowa, Hoover recounted that the country's natural and economic disasters had been beyond his control. He talked about how he had fought valiantly in behalf of the American people, and promised, if reelected, to improve the country and help it emerge from its plight. Angered by the tone of the political discourse, he called the Democratic attacks on his administration "deliberate, intolerable falsehoods" that needed to be set right. It was a powerful if somewhat lengthy defense, and yet it backfired. Because his presentation ran forty-five minutes beyond the allotted time, NBC was forced to preempt the weekly broadcast of Ed Wynn's program. Wynn, his troupe, his musicians, and a studio audience of eight hundred waited for the cue to begin that never came. The cancellation generated more than 6,000 complaints to NBC and an additional 800 to the network's New York flagship station, WEAF. The good news for Ed Wynn and his troupe was that their contract required they be paid because the show was rehearsed and ready to be aired and preemption was not a reason for nonpayment. Presidential politics were important, but Americans wanted their entertainment, and they wanted it at its scheduled time. A presidential campaign speech could wait; Ed Wynn could not.

The race for the White House became a battle for radio airtime supremacy: a brutal struggle between the president, who just four years earlier had been successfully sold over the radio, against the "new product"—an articulate governor from New York who offered Americans a new deal. Trying to win at any cost, even though he did not trust Coughlin, Roosevelt co-opted some of the rhetorical devices and religious themes used by the Radio Priest in his broadcast sermons. In an important speech on October 2, Roosevelt suggested that the country needed to be steered on a course between laissez-faire capitalism and socialism; his text quoted from Pope Pius XI's 1931 encyclical, cloaking politics in a mantle of religion.

Father Coughlin, with his radio contract renewed, continued to be a major and vocal Roosevelt supporter and at the end of October began a series of radio "sermons" in which he accused Wall Street, and by inference Hoover and his cronies, of manipulating the gold standard and bringing on the Depression. His attacks on Hoover equaled his strong support for Roosevelt, and Coughlin fully expected that his loyalty to the Democrats would gain him some say in the policies of a Roosevelt administration. His value to the campaign was the sway he held over his loyal listeners, each of whom represented a potential vote.

During the final weeks of the campaign, listeners were literally bombarded by constant attacks and counterattacks launched over the airwaves by both sides, and as the weeks dwindled to days, the skirmishes grew more intense. The most reverberant salvo was fired on October 25; in a speech delivered to a cheering throng at Baltimore's Fifth Regiment Armory and broadcast to a national audience, Roosevelt accused the Hoover administration of failing to help Americans, especially during the years when the Republicans had control of all branches of government. Roosevelt's original speech—the text reprinted by newspapers the next morning—specifically cited the White House and both houses of Congress. But in the speech heard over the radio, the candidate extemporized, adding the phrase *and I may add, for full measure, to make it complete, the United States Supreme Court as well.*

It was a stunning accusation that riled loyal Republicans who begged former President Coolidge to get into the fray and rebut the upstart governor, to use his prominence as a past president and warn America about Roosevelt. Beyond the offhanded comment about the Supreme Court, what made that speech so memorable was Roosevelt's brilliant use of imagery and alliteration, which resonated powerfully on the air: *I am waging a war in this campaign—a frontal attack, an onset—against the "four horsemen" of present Republican leadership—the horsemen of Destruction. Delay. Deceit. Despair.*

Staggered by Roosevelt's speech, the Republicans took to the airwaves that day to retaliate. The thrust of their attack was that any man who would question the independence of the U.S. Supreme Court had to be a dangerous demagogue who needed to be stopped. The Republicans rallied their forces, turning Roosevelt's impromptu comment against him; repeatedly they insinuated that his suspicions about the Supreme Court and its lack of objectivity were not a criticism of the Republicans, but rather an indictment of the Democratic candidate's character. The Republicans declared that any man who believed the Supreme Court was a partisan body did not have the judgment to be president. These coordinated attacks by key Republicans who had been given the talking points by the campaign were orchestrated so that listeners across the nation would hear the same message and be made aware of the threat Roosevelt posed to the American way of life. Enraged, Roosevelt swore he would not allow Hoover to question his Americanism and was ready to take to the air to counter Hoover's counter. But cooler heads prevailed, and the candidate decided to move on and let the hollow Republican attacks fade away rather than keep the debate resonating over the airwaves.

During the final week of the campaign, hearing both candidates speak often one right after the other was a daily radio experience. Radio coverage gave voters sitting at home the ability to assess not only what the candidates said, which they could have done by reading the newspaper transcripts of the speeches, but how they sounded. Scheduled programming was pushed aside, replaced by the nation's great political orators. What listeners heard were increasingly bitter attacks; Hoover charged that Roosevelt's economic proposals would bankrupt the nation: *Grass will grow in the streets of 100 cities and weeds will overrun the fields of millions of farms.* Roosevelt responded, charging that the *most un-American episode in the campaign was President Hoover's alleged attempt, to arrogate himself and his handful of assistants in Washington the right to claim an exclusive interpretation of and ownership in the American system of government.*

Desperate to close the gap in the polls, President Hoover combined old and new campaign techniques: On November 3 he boarded a train in Washington and began a grueling whistle-stop campaign across the country. Everywhere he spoke, radio microphones picked up his talks, which even Democrats had to admit were becoming increasingly effective. Given that between 1929 and 1932 he had made ninety-five radio addresses, he should have been an effective radio communicator. Hoover's last nationwide appeal as a candidate came on election eve in Elko, Nevada, where "miners, sheep-herders, cattle ranchers and part of the 3,000 population of this little town clustered about his car." That night listeners also heard a rare talk by former president Coolidge; speaking from Northampton, Massachusetts, he told the nation that *all the teachings of common sense require us to re-elect President Hoover.* While Coolidge's endorsement was not the most effervescent, Hoover did receive support from Mrs. Benjamin Harrison, widow of the twenty-third president, who closed her radio address with a simple, direct message: *I feel that this is the best way out of our difficulties—vote for Hoover.*

While the Republicans had purchased the bulk of the election-eve airtime on both NBC and CBS—a move for which they were being hailed as brilliant strategists—the Democrats bought the later hours of airtime, comforted by the adage that "he who laughs last, laughs best." After a final day of campaigning, Roosevelt, speaking from his home in Poughkeepsie,* New York, asked the nationwide radio audience to rally to his cause, appealing for them to elect him as the "humble emblem of the new deal." He closed with: *On this very eve of the exercise of the greatest right of the American electorate, I bid you good night. And I add to that, God bless you all.*

As Americans went to the polls, pundits were handicapping the election based on the way key spokespeople sounded on the air. Since the millions of at-home listeners were unaffected by the campaigns' visual presentations—the fireworks, the bunting, the gestures, the banners—a candidate's speaking style was critical in altering perceptions and opinions. John Carlile, CBS's production manager, observed that Calvin Coolidge had a voice that is "hard—hard like that of most of those who live in climates like that of northern New England." Carlile critiqued the vice-presidential candidates: Republican Curtis's voice "depicts the rough and ready type of man," while Democrat Garner's voice "reveals determination." As for the presidential candidates, Carlile felt that President Hoover's voice "is a little heavy and reveals strain. The voice of a man who does not like to talk." As for Roosevelt: "His voice is a well-trained instrument capable of reflecting his moods and the

✶ HYDE PARK, MAYBE?

color of his thoughts. But to have heard him (never to have seen him) would be enough to convince the listener that he was sincere in utterance and good natured even in attack."

Though the total advertising expenditures for the two campaigns were less than they had been in 1928, the single largest budget item for each was their radio airtime; the two parties spent a total of $472,000 on NBC alone. Of the somewhat less than $2 million the Republicans spent on Hoover's reelection campaign, $400,000 went to radio. However, despite the money flowing to them, broadcasters were not pleased with having to air campaign speeches because of the disruption they caused to the regularly programmed shows. Nonetheless, both radio networks and local radio stations across the nation were willing to jettison regular programming for one more major event: election-night coverage of the voting results.

Though the radio networks began running election bulletins as early as election day afternoon, the official returns coverage was scheduled to begin at 6 P.M. Eastern Time. On CBS, F. W. Wile and Edwin C. Hill anchored the coverage of the national returns, but CBS added a wrinkle to their reporting: They had hired Dr. Salo Finkelstein, a "mathematical wizard," to add the numbers and keep the count accurate. At NBC, anchors David Lawrence and William Hard provided the commentary. Stations all across the country that regularly signed off during the late-night and overnight hours planned to stay on the air, right until morning if necessary, so Americans could get the election results with the immediacy only radio could provide. This far-reaching coverage seemed an appropriate way to mark the twelfth anniversary of KDKA's election-night broadcast of the 1920 Harding-Cox election, only now, instead of somewhere between 500 and 1,000 listeners, the audience for the election returns was over 60 million. Modern election coverage was born, and the audience loved it.

The candidates themselves were in that invisible audience: Roosevelt and his team at New York's Biltmore Hotel, where the early re-

Hello, Everybody!

turns indicating a Democratic sweep pleased them; and President Hoover, surrounded by family and friends at his home in Palo Alto, California, listening to the disappointing results on the local radio station. Shortly after midnight Eastern Standard Time, Hoover wired his concession to Roosevelt. Within minutes radio listeners from coast to coast knew that Roosevelt would be the next president of the United States. The following afternoon, President-elect Roosevelt delivered a national radio address in which he spoke of uniting the country. He ended his thankful, optimistic statement with *I invite your help, the help of all of you, in the task of restoration.* It was Roosevelt's first use of radio as a means of healing the nation, and it set the tone for the brilliant manipulation of the medium that marked his presidency.

With 16.5 million sets in operation, radio was also given credit for generating the largest voter registration and turnout in the country's history. The 7 million increase in the number of registered voters that had occurred in the United States between 1928 and 1932 was linked to the increase of 7 million radio sets that had been purchased during the same four-year period.

The 1932 election was devastating for the Republicans; they lost seats in the Senate and the House of Representatives, along with important governorships, all of which were reported on as part of radio's election-night coverage. Built into the network broadcasts were regularly scheduled opportunities for stations to break away to report on local races. This timed opening allowed local stations to report on elections in the communities to which they were licensed. While there were literally hundreds of local elections to cover, the candidates in three of those races drew special attention from radio fans and radio regulators alike.

In California, angered by the FRC's ruling that forced his station, KFEG, from the air at the end of 1931, Fighting Bob Shuler had appealed to the Court of Appeals of the District of Columbia to have the FRC ruling overturned. *Trinity Methodist Church v. FRC* was based on

Reverend Shuler's claim that the commission did not have the right to censor his broadcasts. Shuler, perhaps emboldened by a statement of support from *The Christian Century,* a liberal Episcopalian weekly that encouraged ministers to feel free to say anything they liked over the radio as long as it was not slanderous, vowed to take his case to the highest court in the land, convinced that the court would not "close the lips of a man battling for righteousness."

Waiting for the case to be heard, and with no radio station over which to denounce local politicians, Shuler bided his time, limiting his attacks to those he made in his church and during public appearances. Then on June 24, 1932, Shuler filed a declaration of candidacy for the United States Senate, choosing to run against the Republican incumbent, Senator Samuel Shortridge, and the Democratic challenger, William Gibbs McAdoo. As the campaign progressed, Shortridge withdrew and was replaced by the far more moderate and anti-Prohibition Tallant Tubbs. Determined to have an impact on the election, Shuler campaigned on the "keep America dry" plank. It was a divide-and-conquer strategy: If the "wets" split their votes between Tubbs and McAdoo, then perhaps the "drys" would concentrate their votes on Shuler and elect the reverend. Shuler's campaign was fueled by his supporters' indignation that such a wonderful man should be chased from his radio pulpit; to his vocal supporters, he was a martyr. Ironically, during the campaign Shuler was afforded protection under the same 1927 Radio Act he was challenging because as an announced candidate for the Senate, radio stations were required to give him the same amount of airtime they gave to the major party candidates. So even though he no longer had his own radio mouthpiece, thanks to the equal-time rule he still had access to the airwaves.

When election day rolled around, Tubbs and Shuler were swept away in the Roosevelt tidal wave that transformed California from a Republican to a Democratic stronghold. One columnist wryly noted that Shuler's defeat deprived the nation's capital "of the presence of one who would have added hitherto unwitnessed gyrations and music to the political carousel." But the news for Shuler got worse; three weeks after the election, the Court of Appeals vigorously sustained the FRC action, ordering KFEG off the air. The ruling supported the FRC completely and went on to deplore the possibility that radio, reaching from one corner of the country to the other as it did, might be turned into a vehicle that could "obstruct the administration of justice, offend the religious sensibilities of thousands, inspire political distrust and civic discord, or offend youth and innocence by the free use of words suggestive of sexual immorality." If that were to happen, the ruling concluded, then "this great science, instead of a boon, will become a scourge and the nation a theatre for the display of individual passions and the collisions of personal interests."

It was a huge blow to Shuler and a rousing endorsement of the FRC's power and its role as the protector of the airwaves. The most significant aspect of the court's decision was that what the FRC had done was neither censorship nor previous restraint, nor was it a whittling away of the rights guaranteed by the First Amendment. What the ruling really meant was that Fighting Bob Shuler's fifteen minutes of fame were over.

Meanwhile, Norman Baker, the owner of KTNT and also the first person to challenge the constitutionality of the FRC, was desperately trying to survive. Having fled to Nuevo Laredo, Mexico, in 1931 after losing his appeal to keep his station open, Baker was hastily constructing a superpowerful 150,000-watt transmitter, which would be able to reach most of the United States. His plan was to construct the most powerful station in North or South America, and since there was no agreement between the United States and Mexico concerning broadcasting, Baker felt confident he would evade the FRC's control.

But building a massive transmitter takes time, and despite the shortcuts he attempted, all of which led to further construction delays, Baker was unable to reach his audience. Following the precedent set by that broadcasting genius from Kansas, John R. Brinkley, Baker wanted to use his new superstation as the main vehicle to spread the word of his candidacy for the governorship of Iowa. Baker announced his intentions during the summer of 1932; his strategy was simple: become governor of Iowa and change the laws so he could again broadcast and run his medical clinic and other assorted businesses.

Running on an independent Farm–Labor ticket, Baker faced a unique problem: Since there was an outstanding warrant connected to a conviction for practicing medicine without a license, the Iowa attorney general's office announced that if Baker set foot in Iowa he would be arrested. But the brilliant promoter in Baker could not be stymied, and despite being exiled, he developed unique ways to campaign. As election day neared, sound trucks bearing colorful banners toured Iowa blaring Baker's promises to clean grafters out of state government. Recorded speeches delivered from loudspeakers mounted on the trucks informed voters that Baker would eliminate the unnecessary inspectors and regulators who drew salaries and cluttered government, and he promised he would continue his fight against the medical establishment. But his candidacy was doomed, damaged by the loss he had suffered to the AMA in an Iowa courtroom the previous spring, and by the fact that his name did not appear on the ballot. On election day, Baker received a mere 5,000 votes, with slightly over 10 percent of them coming from his hometown of Muscatine. Defeated, but pleased that his enemy, Governor Dan Turner, had also lost, Baker contented himself knowing that someday soon he would be able to broadcast over the most powerful radio transmitter on the continent.

As for Dr. John R. Brinkley, his near win in the 1930 Kansas governor's race inspired him to reprise the campaign in 1932, but this time he started with enough lead time. On February 15, 1931, promoters staged a massive rally for 20,000 supporters in Milford, at which Brinkley claimed he had no real political aspirations, but that he had a "duty to fight for the people," and with that he threw his hat into the ring. One year later, as the major parties prepared to choose their candidates, Brinkley was far more than a quack running for office; he was a legitimate threat who could use his oratorical skills and his Mexican transmitter to sway thousands of votes. United in their desire to defeat Brinkley, the parties, represented by incumbent Democrat Harry Woodring and Republican Alf Landon, charged Brinkley with failing to pay taxes. It became a nasty campaign in which the major party candidates spent more time discrediting and attacking Brinkley than debating each other.

Far better organized than he was during his 1930 run, Brinkley got his name on the ballot, eliminating the need for a write-in candidacy. With his powerful transmitter in Mexico—reportedly the most powerful in all of North America—sending out his messages, the campaign was catching fire. Still not content, the clever doctor added a new weapon: a Chevrolet truck mounted with massive loudspeakers that followed him around the state blaring his prerecorded campaign talks and slogans. Brinkley named the vehicle Ammunition Train No. 1— there was no No. 2—and it became his favorite campaign tool. He even figured out that those recorded speeches could be used in a variety of ways, including talks for boys and girls appropriate for Sunday-school use, which helped spread his message in new ways and to new audiences.

As the campaign sped into summer, it was clear that this three-way race could toss the state to the Republican side, or even to Brinkley. There was no doubt that he was a power, and as one writer put it, "Anything can happen in Kansas." Perhaps what made Brinkley such a fine candidate was that the man knew how to put on a show; his campaign rallies were an outgrowth of the kind of variety show he had pioneered on his radio station during its earliest years. It was an odd blend of down-home religion, folksy talks, and good old-fashioned entertainment and music. What made his campaign even more amazing was that the more the establishment, including his nemesis, the *Kansas City Star,* attacked him, the more popular Brinkley became. He countered attacks on him by claiming to have uncovered a conspiracy to kill his son in order to undermine his morale and thus force him to give up the fight. He even accused Governor Woodring of offering clemency to anyone who killed the good doctor before election day. Eventually both major party candidates shifted their strategies, and instead of attacking Brinkley they wooed those among his supporters who were not entirely committed to his rather bizarre campaign.

With two weeks remaining before election day, the race grew more intense, but much to the chagrin of the Democrats and Republicans, the increased interest in politics was spurring deeper support for the independent candidate. Brinkley was attracting huge audiences to his rallies: In Dodge City he brought in more people than the combined crowds at the Republican and Democratic rallies. With only a few days remaining, no one could predict the outcome; more astounding was that two days after the election, the results were still in doubt as the counting continued. Despite a Roosevelt victory in the state, the race for governor was too close to call; Landon had a slim lead over Governor Woodring, with Brinkley languishing in third place, though still hopeful that the rural vote—theoretically his strength—would carry him to victory.

When all the votes were tallied, Brinkley had carried more counties than either of his opponents but had failed to win a majority of the total, which he charged was because votes in the more populated areas had been stolen from him. Like Shuler and Baker, Brinkley came in third, but unlike the other independent radio upstarts, his was an impressive showing: He received 244,607 votes to Woodring's 272,944 and Landon's winning total of 278,581. However, the Brinkley candidacy had siphoned off enough votes from the Democrats to allow the Republicans to win, which was one of only five Republican governorships that wasn't lost in the Roosevelt sweep. Ironically, Brinkley's candidacy may have been hurt by a dirty radio trick he had not thought of. On election day, workers for both major parties, still fearing a Brinkley victory, broadcast fake election results designed to demoralize Brinkley's supporters and discourage them from voting. Whether that ruse cost him the election is hard to say, but either way, John Brinkley was a two-time loser.

In a note to his wife penned a few weeks later, a disconsolate Brinkley wrote, "Personally, I would like to discontinue every business project that I am in and shake loose of the whole mess and start life all over again on a different path." Despite the huge impact he had on broadcasting and on Kansas politics, Brinkley was a defeated man. Though beaten down and depressed, John Romulus Brinkley, radio maverick, would be heard from again. But if there were one lesson the defeats of Shuler, Baker, and Brinkley taught, it was that while America enjoyed its amusement, the order established by the government, whether in medicine or in broadcasting, was necessary if chaos were to be avoided.

Once the nation settled down after the 1932 election, radio returned to what had become its regular programming. Music of every kind, sports (especially college football), information features, children's programming, cooking shows, entertainment, and variety filled the broadcasting days and nights. The competition for audience was fierce, and sponsors looked for every way to use the medium to reach consumers. Radio was big business, and in no place was it bigger than in New York City, which was home to the major radio networks, the ever-growing advertising agencies on Madison Avenue, and radio's first true cathedral, Radio City Music Hall.

One year earlier, during the autumn of 1931, Roxy Rothafel, accompanied by a team of NBC technicians and studio designers, set off for Russia and Europe. Their grand tour had two purposes: to study great theaters and radio studios, and to scout for talent. The technicians were interested in finding ways to make a large theater seem light, sunny, and airy, while Roxy was interested in finding performers to import for the theater's grand opening. In London they visited the spanking-new studios of the BBC; in Berlin they studied the construction of the Grosses Schauspielhaus, which had been designed for Max Reinhardt, and saw the vast new studios of the German national radio stations that a few years hence would be used to broadcast Nazi propaganda; in Russia, Roxy met with the great Konstantin Stanislavsky. It was an idea- and fact-finding mission that, the team declared upon returning to New York, merely confirmed that American ingenuity was still the best in the world.

Despite some delays, including a work stoppage to negotiate a new wage scale for laborers during June 1932, the construction of Roxy's grand theater and the office buildings of the Rockefeller complex continued apace. As summer turned to fall, one legendary part of New York's entertainment scene faded away: the Palace Theatre, the best-known Broadway vaudeville house, was going to be turned into a film theater, officially ending its live shows.

While the nation was distracted by the presidential election, Roxy had been able to secretly plan a spectacular opening for his new theater without leaking the news prematurely. But as soon as the election was over, Roxy, a brilliant promoter, began strategically releasing tidbits to the press about his plans.

As the finishing touches were placed on the splendid sunburst interior of Radio City Music Hall, Roxy announced that the world's largest theater would open on December 27, with a "brilliant program." In another promotional maneuver, *Roxy and His Gang* returned to the air in mid-November with their old-fashioned show of musical favorites and classics, but because Radio City was not yet complete and the acoustics not yet perfected, they chose to broadcast from an NBC radio studio instead of from the grand hall. Being back on the air gave Roxy a platform from which to build anticipation for the theater's opening. Declaring that Radio City Music Hall would be a "pageant of the entire theatre" that would present a wide range of entertainment—from jazz to grand opera, and from circus numbers to dramatic sketches—Roxy told listeners that the opening show would include Martha Graham, contralto Vera Schwartz, the Tuskegee Choir, the comedy team of Weber and Fields, Ray Bolger, the Flying Wallendas, the Kikuta Japs, opera stars Tito Ruffo and Jan Peerce, and possibly the great Amos and Andy.

Understanding the power and draw of celebrity, Roxy let it be known that he had invited President Hoover to attend the gala, signaling that the music hall's opening night was sure to be a spectacular event attended by the famous. His instincts proved correct; when it was announced that tickets for the opening gala would be distributed, more than 60,000 people put in their requests.

On Christmas Day the new auditorium was ready and about 500 invited guests were spread out among the hall's 6,200 seats. To test the theater and its acoustics, Leopold Stokowski led a large orchestra and a chorus of more than 300 voices in a performance of a new work commissioned for the occasion called *Voices of Millions*. The concert was not only a test of the theater, but of the sound that would be broadcast from the hall. The performance was aired over NBC, and when the broadcast ended a special message from Roxy was read over the air: He wanted listeners and performers alike to know that he had listened to the mammoth musical performance on the air and was thrilled.

For the next two days the hall was taken over by rehearsals for the opening-night spectacular. Roxy looked exhausted and haggard. Then on the night of December 27, 1932, an elegant, formally attired crowd descended on the corner of Sixth Avenue and Fiftieth Street; more than

250 New York City policemen were assigned to the area to keep traffic moving. Radio City was the place to be, and radio was there with full coverage of the opening-night crowd, as the red-carpet presentation, including celebrity interviews, was aired live over NBC. Advertisements for the spectacle described Radio City as a "Christmas Gift to the World" and announced that the "World's largest playhouse . . . Presenting spectacular stage shows twice daily" under the "Personal Direction of Roxy" would open at precisely 8 P.M. But with rain falling and a crush of limousines and taxis jamming the streets, the traffic soon became unmanageable, delaying the curtain for more than thirty minutes.

Roxy, the showman of showmen, accomplished exactly what he had intended: The opening was hailed as a major event, with more than 500 performers entertaining a celebrity-studded crowd. Evidently recovered from the stress of the past few months, "Roxy was . . . beaming, fresh and happy." While President Hoover did not show up, the opening did attract the likes of Al Smith, Amelia Earhart, retail giant Bernard Gimbel, New York's Mayor-elect John O'Brien, former heavyweight champ Gene Tunney, and radio's greatest visionary, David Sarnoff. But the performance, which did not end until 12:55 A.M., was overshadowed by the venue itself and the technical marvels it contained. While the theater was hailed as an absolute triumph of design, Roxy's endless opening night gala was far less successful. Brooks Atkinson, reviewing for the *New York Times,* criticized the heavy-handed presentation, the gaudy pomp, and the endless string of performers: "And the truth seems to be that Maestro Roxy, the celebrated entrepreneur of Radio City, has opened his caravansary with an entertainment which, on the whole, does not provoke much enthusiasm. It is more the product of a radio and motion-picture mind than of a genius for the short turns and encores of the music hall stage." Perhaps the only good news for Roxy was that the sound of the broadcast, heard across America, was excellent, even if the performances were disappointing.

The construction of Radio City and of Rockefeller Center seemed to defy the economics of the Depression. These were gleaming new structures that sent a message of optimism to a nation and a world desperate for good news. These marvelous edifices seemed to be totally in harmony with the vision and hope embodied by President-elect Roosevelt; it was all so wonderfully new. While Radio City's opening night may have been a fiasco for Roxy, the pomp and splendor of the occasion announced to the world that radio was celebrating its coming-of-age. Once the province of men and boys tinkering in attics and garages with wires, dials, and antennas, radio had evolved into a dominant, transforming business and form of culture; it had reached a new level of maturity and was here to stay as a vital component of American life. As if to prove the point, both the NBC and CBS radio networks ended 1932 in the black: NBC's profit for the year was $1,050,113 and CBS's was $1,263,451.

On New Year's Eve, white-tie-and-tails-bedecked and ball-gown-attired partygoers in the major cities marked the end of another year, dancing the night away at swanky hotels. Meanwhile, hundreds of radio stations beamed their signals into the night air, carrying the magical, upbeat sounds of dance bands and the sweet voices of crooners to listeners in their homes in large towns, small villages, and isolated farms from coast to coast. Many Americans may have been home alone that New Year's Eve, but they were celebrating in the company of millions of others, all of whom were connected by radio.

Chapter 17

▲▲▲▲▲▲▲▲▲▲▲▲▲▲

THE PERIOD BETWEEN THE NOVEMBER 1932 election and Roosevelt's March 4, 1933, inauguration was a bitter time for Hoover, who believed the Democrats had won by using vicious personal attacks on him and on American life itself. His frustration must have been heightened by the fact that he had been outmaneuvered and outcampaigned via radio, the medium he had so carefully guided from infancy to maturity as secretary of commerce. The reality was that Hoover had become an incredibly unpopular man and president; he was the most prominent fall guy for a nation that wondered how the Republicans in the White House and in Congress could have squandered the great prosperity they had been handed in 1920. Hoover and his party paid the price in the 1932 elections.

During the five-month interregnum, the Depression reached its nadir. Homelessness and hunger were rampant; in New York, police had to remove an army of derelicts who were living in shacks in Central Park. At the center of their ragtag community was one "building" constructed of fruit boxes and egg crates. A torn American flag fluttered above this ersatz community center; inside, the homeless congregated around one battery-operated radio. A handmade sign over the shack's entrance told the story of the time: RADIO CITY.

It was cold and dank in Washington, D.C., on Saturday, March 4, 1933. Before the steps of the Capitol, 100,000 people watched as Franklin Delano Roosevelt was sworn in as president. Radio was there to air the great event not only to the United States, but to a worldwide audience estimated to be over 100 million people. As it had done nearly six years earlier for the triumphant Lindbergh return parade, NBC, now joined by CBS, covered the inauguration by reporting from locales all around Washington. Some of radio's great announcers anchored the coverage: Among the voices heard were those of Graham McNamee, H. V. Kaltenborn, Ted Husing, Charles Francis Coe, Floyd Gibbons, and a relative newcomer to the field named Arthur Godfrey. But the one voice everyone wanted to hear was that of the new president. Roosevelt stepped up to the microphones on the Capitol steps and spoke frankly and candidly to an anxious audience. His baritone voice resonated with confidence and warmth: *This is preeminently the time to speak the truth, the whole truth, frankly and boldly,* he began. Then, after a brief pause, he told America and the world: *So, first of all, let me assert my firm belief that the only thing we have to fear is fear itself.* It was that single line that would help carry the nation forward and would continue to resonate down through the decades. The balance of the speech, laid out in biblical and religious imagery, presented an overview of Roosevelt's plans for pulling the nation out of its morass. He spoke clearly, confidently, using the power of radio to communicate directly to his worried listeners. Some commentators likened the inauguration to a revival meeting. The actress Lillian Gish would later write to the new president to assure him that over the airwaves he had a distinct incandescence, as if he had been "dipped in phosphorus."

FDR's style provided a marked change from Hoover, who always sounded aloof and distant, as if he were delivering a formal address. Despite the formality of the occasion, FDR's inaugural speech provided another chance for him to talk directly with the American people, making them feel as if he were sitting right in their living rooms with them; he spoke to Americans as individuals, not as blocks of voters. On the Sunday night following the inauguration, the new president spoke to the nation about the banking crisis. Carefully explaining the run on the banks that had occurred and the bank holiday that had been called, Roosevelt, using a calm, intimate, reassuring tone, told his audience that putting money back into the banks was good for the country: *In other words, the bank puts your money to work to keep the wheels of industry and of agriculture turning around.*

Sixty million Americans listened to the president's address, and the next morning, when the banks reopened, money flowed into them rather than out of them. This talk was the first of what CBS's Harry Butcher called the president's "fireside chats." Throughout his presidency, Roosevelt used radio to bring the nation together, to inspire and to cajole. So effective and affecting were his talks that the number of letters written directly to the president reached unprecedented levels. Among the tens of thousands of letters received following the banking talk was one from Frank Cregg of New York, who had listened to the speech with some friends from both sides of the political aisle. Cregg wrote: "When your radio talk began everyone seemed to become hypnotized, because there wasn't a word spoken by anyone until you had finished and then as if one voice were speaking all spoke in unison 'We are saved.'" A widow from Alabama was inspired to write, "We all felt the magnetism, of the tone of your Voice—that you were sent for our delivery."

Thrilled with Roosevelt's triumph and probably aware that the new president was to some degree mimicking the way he couched speeches about social issues in religious imagery, Father Coughlin expected to be thanked for his support by being asked to become part of the new administration's inner circle—to become an advisor to the president. But Roosevelt was wary of the Radio Priest, and within months of taking office Roosevelt began to distance himself from Coughlin. Then in December 1934, Coughlin formed the National Union for Social Justice (NUSJ), which he described as a political party that would "organize for social united action which will be founded on God-given social truths."

The incident that obviated any possible working relationship between the president and Coughlin occurred in 1935 when the Radio Priest, skillfully aided in the Senate by another dangerous individual, Senator Huey Long, called the United States' membership in the World Court a stupid betrayal of the nation's independence. It was the start of a weekly airing of antiwar, isolationist positions articulated by Coughlin over his network of radio stations. As he had worked against Hoover in 1932, Coughlin and the NUSJ sought to unseat Roosevelt in 1936, but he discovered that true political power was harder to attain than radio popularity. Nonetheless, money continued to flow into the Royal Oak parish coffers even as Coughlin's radio addresses became more and more belligerent and nasty. He was no longer preaching the gospel; rather, his talks were blatant social commentaries with an increasingly dangerous antiwar, pro-German bent. He was a pioneer in hate radio, and his comments and followers became increasingly anti-Semitic. He blamed the Depression on the Jews, claiming that an international conspiracy of Zionism had brought about the world's troubles.

The combination of Roosevelt's immense popularity and Coughlin's extreme positions gradually caused the Radio Priest's popularity to wane, and by 1939 Coughlin and the radio stations that carried his program were confronted by protests from angry groups alarmed by the priest's rants. But in addition to radio, Coughlin had at his disposal a journal called *Social Justice* that he had created and published, and on its pages he repeatedly urged support of the Nazis in their war against Great Britain. The war in Europe hastened Coughlin's alienation from his radio audience, and only a few small radio stations were willing to go against public sentiment to carry his talks. In the September 23, 1940, issue of *Social Justice,* Coughlin announced that he was "temporarily retiring from the air." Though there were periodic reports of his imminent return, Father Coughlin's radio time was over. With America's entry into the war, his radical positions pushed him so far out of the mainstream that his superiors in the Catholic Church were forced to insist he remain silent on national issues. Then Attorney General Francis Biddle charged *Social Justice* with giving aid and comfort to the enemy and the U.S. Post Office barred it from the mail, permanently and completely ending Coughlin's days as a political force and commentator.

Coughlin retired from the priesthood in 1966 and lived out his life in Birmingham, Michigan, where he died in 1979. Though he initially saw radio as a mighty vehicle for good, he quickly realized its invisible power could be used just as easily to shape public opinion—his forum for demagoguery—especially at a time when uncertainty and discontent were foremost in the public psyche. His example taught an important lesson that has been passed down from one generation of opinionated, social-engineering evangelists to the next.

Ironically, one of the people who aided Coughlin's late-1930s push to keep the United States out of the European conflict was America's hero, Colonel Charles Lindbergh. In 1939 *Social Justice* editorially agreed with Lindbergh's stated opinion that the Nazis were too strong to be defeated and therefore the United States should remain out of the conflict. The magazine went so far as to propose that Lindbergh would be a superb Republican candidate for president in 1940, the hero America needed to get rid of Roosevelt, but the plan never took flight. While Lindbergh's importance as a subject of radio and news dates back to the parade that welcomed him upon his return from Europe in 1927, and to the kidnapping of his child in 1932, it was the coverage of the arrest, trial, and conviction of Bruno Hauptmann for that crime that altered broadcast news forever.

FOR MORE THAN TWO YEARS following the discovery of the Lindbergh baby's body, police around the world tracked down every lead in search of the baby's killer. Then on September 20, 1934, Bruno Richard Hauptmann, an immigrant German carpenter with a criminal past, was arrested and charged with the kidnapping and murder. Walter Winchell, a former vaudevillian who'd made it big as a New York newspaper columnist, and who had found a home on radio beginning in December 1932 as the well-paid host of the popular Sunday evening *Jergens Journal* carried on the NBC Blue Network, had been informed that the police were closing in on a suspect. Using restricted information probably leaked to him by the FBI, Winchell went on the air and hinted at an imminent arrest. Then one week later he told his audience that he was in part responsible for the apprehension of Hauptmann. Winchell's on-air style was fast paced and what he said was delivered in a manner that made it sound like hard news, while in reality his content moved between the facts and the story he wanted to tell. Winchell was the caricature of the hard-bitten newsman, brusque and almost angry, and it was a role he played to perfection during Hauptmann's trial, even though he was not a journalist either by training or skill.

Justice for Hauptmann was swift. The trial at the Hunterdon, New Jersey, courthouse began on January 3, 1935. During jury selection, with Winchell sitting front and center in the courtroom, Hauptmann's attorneys tried to establish that Winchell's comments in the newspaper had had a prejudicial effect. They asked one potential juror if he had read Winchell's column. "I wouldn't let a man like that influence me," the man replied before continuing with "I don't read his column, but I listen to him on the radio." Despite repeated recommendations by NBC's legal department that Winchell act responsibly, the newsman-*cum*-performer used his radio platform to reveal the state's evidence against Hauptmann; in essence, via radio, Winchell tried and convicted the German carpenter, serving as prosecutor and jury for his captivated national audience.

The trial was a true celebrity media circus, not unlike the ones we have come to expect today. Reporting on the proceedings for the *New York Times,* Edna Ferber acerbically commented that the courthouse and surrounding areas had become the chic place to be seen, and that celebrity sightings had become a sport. "Is that Winchell?" some gawkers were heard to say.

Winchell made himself a central character, and his direct involvement in the trial was great for his radio show's ratings. When Hauptmann was convicted on February 13, 1935, Winchell reportedly jumped to his feet and claimed credit for predicting the trial's outcome, yelling, "Oh, that's another big one for me!" Fourteen months later, Bruno Richard Hauptmann was executed in New Jersey's electric chair.

Winchell's *Jergens Journal* was a long-running hit and his staccato opening, which he crisply annunciated each week above the percussive hammering sound of a teletype machine, became a catchphrase of American pop culture: *Good evening, Mr. and Mrs. North America and all the ships at sea, let's go to press!* Winchell's power as a gossip columnist, insidious though it often became, was remarkable, but his greatest long-term impact on the media was the way he forever blurred the once well-defined lines between reporter and celebrity, and between news and entertainment.

Blurring lines was also the métier of Aimee Semple McPherson, whose mixture of entertainment and religion had cast a spell over American radio listeners. In one particularly amusing incident, a Mrs. Clara Ellis filed for divorce, claiming her husband, Paul, had stopped working because he had become a fan of McPherson's temple broadcasts. In addition, Mrs. Ellis charged that her husband listened to the services at such a high volume that it prevented her from sleeping. Without doubt, during radio's early days no one was more hypnotic than Aimee Semple McPherson; but once the veneer had been removed from her act and she was forced to defend herself against a steady onslaught of attacks and lawsuits, her power and fame ebbed at an amazing clip. Following a nervous breakdown, she attempted a comeback in 1931, but never again reached the height of popularity she had once attained. By September 1933 she was nothing more than the opening act at New York's Capitol Theatre, where she gave sermons before the showing of the MGM movie *The Solitaire Man*. In reviewing her performance, one critic wrote, "Yet so strongly does the performer suggest someone who is acting like somebody else that her auditors may fancy they are seeing an imitation." Though she remained the head of the Angelus Temple, the final years of her life were filled with challenges, including forty-five civil lawsuits brought against her. She died in 1944 at age fifty-three of a heart attack after taking sleeping pills for her nervous condition. Just one month before her death, Sister Aimee proudly declared that during her career she had preached to more people than any other evangelist of her time.

McPHERSON'S BRAND OF EVANGELISM was at least as much entertainment as it was religion, while for Roxy Rothafel, entertainment *was* his religion; like McPherson, controversy kept his name in the news. While he'd enjoyed more than a decade of tremendous successes, the gross failure of the grand opening night of Radio City was a blow from which the great impresario would never recover. By linking his name with every detail of the venture and letting it be perceived that, as *Radioland* magazine described it, he was "enthroned there," Roxy took an enormous personal gamble that backfired. Then during the months that followed the ill-conceived opening, the shows Roxy presented failed to attract audiences large enough to fill the thousands of seats in Radio City's main theater and the smaller house known as the RKO Roxy Theatre. Tired and sick, Roxy took a leave of absence from his post to convalesce from surgery. Returning in May 1933, he announced that the smaller theater would change its programming policy and become a vaudeville house with four shows a day, each containing fifteen acts. It was a throwback to an earlier time, but the economic realities of this era did not bode well for any entertainment that needed large audiences with the ability to pay, and as the failures mounted, Roxy's battles with Radio City's management became more severe. In September he lost a legal fight to keep his name on the marquee of the smaller theater; it was immediately renamed the RKO Center Theatre. Defeated by the constant struggle to re-create the kind of popular success he had achieved so easily during the 1920s, Rothafel, tired of the fights, the costs, and the constant criticism from his bosses, resigned his post at Radio City. Two years later, he tried to get his job back, but before any action could be taken, Samuel L. Roxy Rothafel, just fifty-three years old, died of heart disease. Though in the end he failed, his overall legacy was impressive. Chief among the lessons he left behind was one guiding principle: "There is some simple truth in broadcasting, and it is the key to success, and that is be natural, or the broadcast will 'B-flat,' and that is just too bad."

Roxy showed a generation of performers how to make the transition from the stage to the radio studio. Those he influenced included Al Jolson, Ed Wynn, Eddie Cantor, Burns and Allen, George Jessel, Fred Allen, Will Rogers, Jack Pearl, Jack Benny, Bob Hope, Kate

Smith, Jimmy Durante, and Bing Crosby. They all followed the Roxy model to varying degrees as they starred in radio's golden age, the era that began in 1933, which would have been far less shiny if it hadn't had the Roxy touch. Those former vaudevillians made radio *the* place for entertainment, and since money was hard to come by, the fact that all of that talent came into your living room for free only made it more appealing.

One constant that spanned radio's formative years through its golden age and even beyond was the comedy of *Amos 'n' Andy*. Year after year, Freeman Gosden and Charles Correll spun their tales of the lives lived by radio's beloved fictional characters. Into the 1930s the ratings held up well, but by the middle of the decade the show's popularity began to wane. In May 1939 the team kept listeners on the edge of their seats with an episode known as "Andy's Wedding." It was a cliff-hanger at its best: Just as Andy was about to answer the question, "Will you take this woman?" a shot rang out and Andy fell to the ground wounded, leaving the marriage question unanswered. A national debate—not unlike the "Who shot JR?" controversy nearly half a century later—ensued, including opinions from lawyers and clergymen about whether Andy was actually married. But despite this one intrigue, the show was a shadow of its former self. In 1943 changes in the format were made and the series continued on CBS for another dozen years, but it never again captivated the nation as it had during the 1920s. The root of the problem was that the characters were part of another era, throwbacks, caricatures who had once been welcome visitors in every home in America, but who may have simply overstayed their welcome.

While Gosden and Correll's impact is undeniable, it was the smooth-voiced bandleader from Maine who truly changed American radio and culture. Rudy Vallée's Thursday-night NBC show was the petri dish of entertainment. Week after week, Vallée brought stars—established and yet to be discovered—to the radio audience. Anyone who was anyone—sports heroes, Broadway stars, singing sensations, great classical music artists, comedians, and even ventriloquists—appeared on Vallée's show. For ten years—an amazing 518 consecutive weeks—Fleischmann's Yeast and its parent company, Standard Brands, sponsored the show. Vallée introduced a generation of performers to their audiences, and it was those performers who would become the standard-bearers of broadcast radio and television entertainment for most of the next half century.

Rudy Vallée was also a progressive in an era in which jazz, with its African American roots, had as its self-proclaimed king a Caucasian ironically named Whiteman. Vallée never hesitated to include great jazz performers on his program and was a friend to African American artists. He wrote the foreword to Louis Armstrong's autobiography and helped arrange for Fleischmann's Yeast to sponsor a series of half-hour shows hosted by Louis Armstrong during the summer of 1938. The short-lived series, called *The Harlem Revue,* marked the first time an African American was given the opportunity to host his own program.

On September 28, 1939, radio's longest association of sponsor and performer, Fleischmann's and Vallée, came to an end. Rudy Vallée had maintained his high standards and the high ratings in his Thursday-night slot for an entire decade, and his impact on the industry was astounding. His meticulous work ethic and belief in carefully produced shows and fine showmanship raised the quality of the radio variety show. He was radio's first truly important producer, and though he would for the next few decades reappear periodically on the radio, he never again attained the renown he achieved as the host of that first national variety show. Unfortunately, later generations only knew of his rather silly movies and viewed him as a megaphone-toting, raccoon-coat-wearing mascot of a long-gone flapper era. But his impact on American culture cannot be overestimated. Vallée died in California in 1986. If anyone doubted his popularity, especially with women, one need only note the story of a midwestern husband who interrupted the Vallée show by asking his wife, "Why don't you get something worth listening to?" Angered by the interruption, the woman shot her husband dead.

THE UBIQUITOUS GRAHAM MCNAMEE, America's first true announcer, was at Vallée's side for the entire run of the series. But his contribution to early radio is far greater than that one long-term engagement; McNamee pioneered so many kinds of announcing that he defined the job of announcer for generations to come. But during the 1935 World Series, which pitted the Detroit Tigers against the Chicago Cubs, NBC unceremoniously yanked McNamee from the assignment, replacing him with the young, hot announcing team of Red Barber and Bob Elson. For the balance of the decade, McNamee was far less important than he had been; though he served as Vallée's announcer and played the stooge for Ed Wynn's *Fire Chief* program, he never again received the plum announcing assignments. McNamee died in 1942 at age fifty-three. Remembering him and the trailblazing he had done, Red Barber said, "He'd lived a thousand years."

McNamee was the victim of evolving audience tastes; his removal from the World Series was a brutal acknowledgment that radio had become big business, and that stars, even onetime radio audience favorites, were subject to the need to continuously attract more and more listeners. After all, without an audience, advertisers couldn't convince America to buy their products, and without revenue from advertisers, radio stations and networks could not survive. National brands and national advertisers linked the country together; radio had thus homogenized America. But what happened to those innovative souls, the quacks and troublemakers who had defined radio's first important years?

By the autumn of 1933, Norman Baker had built and launched his Mexican radio station, which bore the call letters XENT. Its super-powerful transmitter blasted across the border from Nuevo Laredo and floated his programming well into the United States. His broadcasts were the usual eclectic mix he had developed in Muscatine: the recognizable calliope sign-on, a wide variety of music and musicians, an on-air psychologist, a radio astrologer, and several regularly scheduled daily talks by Norman Baker himself, some delivered live from his studio and others prerecorded. Revenue averaging more than $150,000 a year flowed into XENT. Despite treaties negotiated between Mexico and the United States to coordinate control of radio signals, Baker was able to keep XENT running because he strictly adhered to the Mexican broadcasting rules. Furthermore, he cultivated personal relationships with Mexican authorities who looked the other way when his talks bordered on the questionable, including frequent rants against the Jewish doctors who had spoken out against him back in Iowa.

Baker was living the good life, but he couldn't resist the temptation to go back to Iowa. Despite the outstanding warrant, he returned to Muscatine in 1936 to face the charges and run for the Republican Senate nomination. His antics, though crowd-pleasing, were for naught, and he ended up in fifth place in the election. As to the charges of medical conspiracy, Baker was convicted and received a sentence of one day in jail, which he served, claiming he did so for his followers.

Tired of losing to the Iowa authorities, Baker moved to Arkansas, a state more friendly to questionable medical practices. He bought the luxurious Crescent Hotel in Eureka Springs and converted it into a resort where patients could come to receive his unique medical treatments. Decorated in his flamboyant style with lavender walls, Baker's palace—the "World's Most Beautiful Health Resort"—with its wonder water, attracted patients seeking the doctor's cancer cures. Many heard about the great doctor and his resort by listening to the broadcasts over XENT, which, despite Baker's absence, continued to send its powerful signal well into the United States. Baker's luck ran out in 1940 when the United States government pressed charges of mail fraud. After a two-week trial, Baker was convicted and sentenced to four years in the federal penitentiary in Leavenworth, Kansas. Released after three years, Baker retired to Florida, where he lived on a yacht once owned by financier Jay Gould. In 1958, one week after telling a friend he was in such good condition that he felt like he would live to be 125, Norman Baker died of cirrhosis of the liver. Baker supposedly left behind a fortune in cash earned from his exploits; there was even a rumor that the money was buried somewhere in Mexico, but it was never found. As for XENT, Baker's real fortune maker, without the master to run the station it struggled to survive and was either sold or given away by Baker employees in 1944.

And then there was John R. Brinkley. It was a gloomy time for the residents of Milford, Kansas; more than half of them faced unemployment or a drastic reduction in their income when the colorful practitioner-politician who had rocked the medical establishment and Kansas politics packed up and left. On October 7, 1933, Dr. Brinkley, blaming the Depression for his financial difficulties, closed the Milford clinic, packed up all the equipment, and moved the entire operation to Del Rio, Texas. As he departed, a contractor he had hired razed all of his important buildings, leaving a pile of rubble in its place and Milford in dire straits.

The caravan of cars and trucks loaded with equipment rolled south to Del Rio, just across the Rio Grande from his powerful Mexican transmitter and station, XER. Earlier that year, the FRC had sent a delegation to Mexico to begin the delicate task of negotiating a radio broadcasting agreement with the Mexican government. Their unstated goal, among others, was to keep Dr. Brinkley in check. Undeterred, Brinkley bought the luxurious Roswell Hotel in Del Rio and set it up as his new sanitarium; as he had done in Milford, he curried favor with the local community by buying needed supplies for their use. Over his powerful radio station, in a folksy baritone, he spoke to susceptible listeners, telling them of the amazing cures they could find in Del Rio. By then he had switched his focus from testicles to the prostate: *You men, why are you holding back? You know your prostate's infected and diseased.* During his weekday radio talks he attacked the medical establishment, while on Sundays he would become more religious and preach to his listeners about the importance of compassion. Whatever he was doing, it worked: During a period of slightly more than four years between 1933 and 1938, Brinkley and his "surgeons" operated on more than 16,000 men, earning the clinic approximately $12 million.

Brinkley's station, XER, was a cornucopia of programming: There was music, including many of the acts that had starred on KFKB; a mentalist; an East Indian yogi who was in charge of spiritual phenomena; a parson who explained why the Jews could not be trusted; and the multitalented Rose Dawn, who read horoscopes, sold perfume, and, for a $1 contribution, would pray for a listener. Of course, listeners were encouraged to send in for a vial of any number of Dr. Brinkley's miracle elixirs, which would cure you of almost anything, if you could pay the price.

Money flowed in, and the Brinkley family was living lavishly, but the Mexican government grew concerned that Brinkley may not have been a real doctor, and after some police activity, Brinkley was forced to shut down his transmitter. A few months later, in 1935, Brinkley returned, this time with station XERA, and his broadcasting career continued; as the 1930s progressed, his radio talks increasingly assumed a more philosophical, even theological bent.

But even Dr. Brinkley was subject to the economic realities of price competition, and when another doctor began advertising on other radio stations offering the Brinkley procedures at a reduced price, Dr. Brinkley's revenues decreased. Angered by the competition, he again moved his operations, this time to Little Rock, Arkansas, though he continued to live in Del Rio. For the next few years, Brinkley ran an ever-shrinking empire. Embroiled in multiple lawsuits, including his own failed libel suit against Morris Fishbein and the AMA, as well as a number of malpractice suits, a charge for back taxes from the IRS, and increasing problems with transmitting from Mexico, not the least of which was a 1937 agreement between Mexico and the United States that sought to control and organize the cross-the-border stations, Brinkley was much diminished.

When in 1941, the 1937 agreement between Mexico and the United States, known as the Havana Treaty, was finally put into effect, Dr. Brinkley's XERA was no longer on the list of authorized Mexican broadcast stations. Mexican officials ordered the station off the air, and within hours of the edict the Mexican army dismantled the powerful transmitter. It was March 29, 1941, when the radio voice of Dr. Brinkley was finally silenced. With no way to charm an audience, Brinkley's once-great fortune dwindled and his health deteriorated. He filed for bankruptcy, and on May 26, 1942, while reading his Bible, "shorn of his once-vast fortune and pursued to the last by litigation," John R. Brinkley died.

What Dr. Brinkley and the other innovative broadcasters of those wonderful early years understood was that radio enabled them to bond with the masses by speaking to the individual. Their natural, folksy, let-me-pull-up-a-chair-and-chat-with-you on-air style made radio listeners all across the country warm to them, to hear them as a new friend, as someone who'd just come into their house to tell a story, to introduce them to an idea, to inform them, and yes, to even entertain them. Those wild men and women of radio's earliest years grasped the potential, the good and evil, of mass communication. What the Brinkleys, the Bakers, the McPhersons, the Coughlins, the Winchells, and the Vallées, the famous, the infamous, and the forgotten broadcasters of those formative years, demonstrated was that the radio audience, whether in Milford or Manhattan, was willing and eager to hear any story if it were well told, and told by someone they believed to be

credible; of course, some of that credibility came to them simply because they *were* on the radio.

The lessons those innovators taught were learned well by President
Roosevelt. When the Japanese attacked Pearl Harbor, Roosevelt took
to the air, proclaiming December 7, 1941, *a date which will live in infamy.*
His resonant voice, a sonic beacon on a somber day, was beamed from
coast to coast, giving Americans the confidence to fight the enemies of
freedom. Slightly more than three years later, when President Roosevelt, the man who cemented radio broadcasting's role as the most
important arrow in the political communications quiver, died suddenly,
the tragic bulletin spread from one end of the nation to the other.
Radio stations interrupted regularly scheduled programming to bring
the news to a saddened, mournful country. Stations immediately canceled all commercials and replaced regular programming with news,
appropriate music, memorial services, eulogies, and other special tributes to the late president.

Perhaps in some surreal way symbolic of the mysterious ether that
carries invisible radio signals across the sky, Roosevelt was not quite
ready to give up his national microphone. The night before he died he
had written the text for a speech scheduled to be delivered via radio the
next day. In this talk that America never heard, Roosevelt looked back
at the last years and the horrors the world had witnessed. *We seek
peace—enduring peace. More than an end to war, we want an end to the beginnings of all war.* Had he lived, the audience would have heard his familiar, comforting voice instruct that the conquest of our enemies was
not sufficient: *We must go on to do all in our power to conquer the doubts,
the ignorance and the greed, which made this horror possible.* And this chat
with his radio "family" would have ended with this hopeful thought:
*The only limit to our realization of tomorrow will be our doubts of today. Let
us move forward with strong and active faith.*

Author's Note

▲▲▲▲▲▲▲▲▲▲▲▲▲▲▲▲▲▲

LIVING IN THIS WORLD of 24/7 communication, where it is virtually impossible to avoid being in touch, where information and entertainment continuously stream at us, it's hard to fathom that less than a century ago the very idea of sound traveling through walls into people's homes must have seemed like some wild science fiction. I often imagine the lonely farmer in the middle of Nowhere, USA, trying to explain to his incredulous wife that this boxy contraption of wires, tubes, and dials would make it possible for them to listen to music played by an orchestra in some swanky New York hotel. But that's how it all began; radio provided the formidable foundation for all of the electronic mass media that followed. As with the Internet, radio's growth was incredibly swift, and the reaction to these two communication industries was quite similar: intrigue, dismissal, and acceptance, until finally each medium came to dominate its respective time. The comparisons, not only in technological growth and impact on society, but in the eras themselves, are remarkable.

In researching this book I realized that while there are many fine histories of the era and of the industry, radio's real story was best told in the daily newspaper articles that reported on every technological advance and every programming development. Radio seemed to infiltrate the newspapers, becoming central to every kind of story, from international business to celebrity gossip. Though newspaper publishers were slow to recognize that radio was eroding their papers' relevance, audience, and revenue, their radio columnists, the journalists, understood that the development and steady advance of radio was *the* story of the era. While most major newspapers had radio columns, the picture painted by two important reporters was invaluable, and I am indebted to their diligence and commitment to what was then a new medium. Orrin E. Dunlap Jr. of the *New York Times* and Robert D. Heinl of the *Washington Post,* both avid radio enthusiasts, were the columnists whose consistent reporting told the story of the developing industry. Their literally hundreds of articles, when read sequentially, tell the story of the birth of mass communication and the development of an entirely new segment of the entertainment industry.

Ultimately what they saw and revealed, especially as the Great Depression descended over the country, was that radio embodied much of the American spirit, and the way the industry developed here, without total government control, was typically American; here it was affirmed that the airwaves belonged to the people and not to the politicians. Those reporters inherently understood that radio was not only important news, but that it provided the platform from which to tell the real story of the American spirit—its comedy, its tragedy, its political dramas, its music, its entertainment, its athletic competition, its news, and its faith—and radio sent all of it from coast to coast, to unify the nation when it needed it most.

Acknowledgments

▲▲▲▲▲▲▲▲▲▲▲▲▲▲▲▲▲▲▲▲▲▲▲▲▲

IN A STRANGE WAY, writing and broadcasting are similar endeavors; in both instances words are sent out to an invisible audience that, for the most part, is unknown to the writer or announcer. Yet despite the lack of immediate response, we labor on, hoping what we do will be appreciated, will be moving, and might have an impact. The good news is that along the way there are people whose guidance, criticism, and, yes, belief help us make it from show to show, or chapter to chapter. There are many people who have been invaluable on this journey and my thanks to each of them is poor compensation for what they have given me.

To my family, Kristy, Rebecca, and Susannah: You bore the brunt of this effort; you have my love and thanks. To my father, Julius Rudel: Your eye for editorial detail is remarkable, and your guidance superb.

Acknowledgments

Few people have such perseverance and sense of what is good—and what is not—as my friend and agent, Eric Simonoff, and I thank him for pushing me in this direction.

At Harcourt, Rebecca Saletan's excitement for this project was motivating, and Thomas Bouman is the dream editor: focused, quick, responsive, and always right! Special thanks to David Hough and his eye for detail, and to Sara Branch. To the entire team at Harcourt, my sincere gratitude and appreciation is yours.

Maureen Kindilien was an invaluable resource who provided countless hours of assistance; without her I would have often found myself lost at some remote Web site. At the Paley Center (the Museum of Television and Radio), Rebecca Paller and Jane Klain were tremendously helpful as I journeyed back in time looking for the unusual.

As I discovered more and more about Rudy Vallée, Jeanette Berard and Klaudia Englund at the Vallée Collection were all incredibly generous with providing documents and time, and I thank them and Eleanor Vallée for all of their help.

Then there are special friends who listened to me retell these stories; their encouragement and interest provided much-needed audience reaction. To all of you, broadcasters and nonbroadcasters alike, my undying thanks: Phil Redo, Warren Bodow, Arthur Yorinks, Jimmy Nicholson, Terry Wrong, David Sand, Robert Heilbrun, Yung Chin, Alan Pollock, Bettyann Kevles, Dan Kevles, Richard Berman, Jeff Bens, and David Lugowski.

I thank my students for keeping me on my toes; and finally, I would like to send a special thank-you to all the broadcasters I have had the pleasure to work with, and the ones I have yet to meet. What we do on the air is the real American mosaic, crafted from that magical, invisible ether.

Endnotes

▲▲▲▲▲▲▲▲▲▲▲

Chapter 1

1 "'as I should urgently advise them to do'": Carson, Gerald. *The Roguish World of Doctor Brinkley.* New York: Rinehart, 1960, 30.

2 "October 1917": Wood, Clement. *The Life of a Man: A Biography of John R. Brinkley.* Kansas City, KS: Goshorn Publishing, 1934, 324.

2 "'Well, why don't you put 'em in me?'": Ibid., 97.

3 "goats as the donor": Lee, R. Alton. *The Bizarre Careers of John R. Brinkley.* Lexington: University Press of Kentucky, 2002, 31.

3 "'Compound Operation'": Ibid., 56.

3 "'physical and mental vigor'": Carson, *The Roguish World of Doctor Brinkley,* 35.

3 "in the anatomy": Lee, *The Bizarre Careers of John R. Brinkley,* 57.

5 "surgeon general of the army": Wood, *The Life of a Man,* 324.

6 "burst into tears": Lee, *The Bizarre Careers of John R. Brinkley,* 29.

6 "'American Medical Association'": Wood, *The Life of a Man,* 112.

6 "'super-powered salesman'": Ibid., 107.

6 "of the medical community": Ibid., 325.

7 "and needed money": Ibid., 113.

7 "'even realize it.'": Ibid., 115.

7 "and was intrigued": Ibid., 122.

7   "Doctor of Science degree": Ibid., 325.

8   "the *Los Angeles Times*": Ibid., 133.

9   "'$500,000 to $1,000,000'": *The Los Angeles Times,* June 19, 1922.

9   "'in modern journalism'": *The Los Angeles Times,* April 13, 1922.

10   "'and musical program'": *The Washington Post,* November 25, 1922.

10   "out over the air": *The Los Angeles Times,* August 6, 1922.

10   "September 1923": Fowler, Gene, and Bill Crawford. *Border Radio: Quacks, Yodelers, Pitchmen, Psychics, and Other Amazing Broadcasters of the American Airwaves.* Rev. ed. Austin: University of Texas Press, 2002, 24.

11   "*Goat Gland Baby*": Juhnke, Eric S. *Quacks and Crusaders: The Fabulous Careers of John Brinkley, Norman Baker, and Harry Hoxsey.* Lawrence: University Press of Kansas, 2002, 7.

11   "'to your heart'": Fowler and Crawford, *Border Radio,* 24.

11   "*1050 kilocycles*": Carson, *The Roguish World of Doctor Brinkley,* 87.

Chapter 2

14   "cacophony in the air": Larson, Erik. *Thunderstruck.* New York: Three Rivers Press, 2006, 94.

14   "*Cavalleria Rusticana*": Archer, Gleason Leonard. *History of Radio to 1926.* New York: The American Historical Society, Inc., 1938, 99.

14   "to that specific frequency": Barnouw, Erik. *A Tower in Babel: A History of Broadcasting in the United States, to 1933.* New York: Oxford University Press, 1966, 27.

14   "naming the transmissions Marconigrams": *The New York Times,* November 20, 1911.

14   "the reach of Marconigrams": *The Wall Street Journal,* April 4, 1912.

15   "onboard ship installations": Barnouw, *A Tower in Babel,* 42.

15   "wireless messages from sea": Archer, *History of Radio to 1926,* 111.

15   "United States since before 1910": Douglas, George H. *The Early Days of Radio Broadcasting.* Jefferson, NC: McFarland, 1987, 38.

16   "just idle gossip": Landry, Robert John. *This Fascinating Radio Business.* Indianapolis, New York: Bobbs-Merrill Co., 1946, 23.

16   "who were 'listening in'": *The Washington Post,* November 28, 1915.

16   "due to all the interference": *The Washington Post,* May 8, 1912.

16   "Department of Commerce": Godfrey, Donald G., and Frederic A. Leigh. *Historical Dictionary of American Radio.* Westport, CT: Greenwood Press, 1998.

18   "battlefields of Europe": *The Washington Post,* May 11, 1919.

18   "135 transmitting stations": *The Wall Street Journal,* September 28, 1914.

19   "their enemy's military moves": Archer, *History of Radio to 1926,* 126.

19   "'to or from another radio station'": *The Wall Street Journal,* September 25, 1914.

20   "was not on site": *The Washington Post,* September 11, 1914.

20 "action was indeed legal": *The Washington Post,* September 19, 1914.

20 "'to protect such relations'": *The Washington Post,* September 26, 1914.

20 "by April 1916": *The New York Times,* November 21, 1915.

20 "under constant surveillance": *The Washington Post,* April 23, 1916.

20 "homing pigeons": *The New York Times,* July 16, 1916.

20 "and radio groups alike": *The New York Times,* December 17, 1916.

21 "for the United States in wartime": *The New York Times,* November 21, 1915.

21 "for the duration of the ban": Landry, *This Fascinating Radio Business,* 26.

21 "'method of communication'": *The New York Times,* November 3, 1917.

21 "'its hour of need'": *The New York Times,* May 6, 1917.

21 "more wireless telegraphers": Archer, *History of Radio to 1926,* 143.

21 "outlined in that message": Ibid., 149.

22 "'by direct parley with the German people'": *The Washington Post,* May 5, 1919, and Archer, *History of Radio to 1926,* 145.

22 "within the United States": *The Wall Street Journal,* December 6, 1918.

22 "invisible-wave traffic problems": *The Wall Street Journal,* August 7, 1919.

22 "government control into law": *The Wall Street Journal,* October 9, 1919.

22 "government monopoly of radio": *The Washington Post,* December 19, 1918.

23 "and its domestic assets": *The Wall Street Journal,* September 4, 1919.

23 "the Radio Corporation of America": *The Wall Street Journal,* November 21, 1919.

23 "and communications companies": Landry, *This Fascinating Radio Business,* 31.

24 "the leaders of that industry": *The Wall Street Journal,* January 6, 1919.

Chapter 3

26 "communicate in English": Bilby, Kenneth W., *The General: David Sarnoff and the Rise of the Communications Industry.* New York: Harper & Row, 1986, 17.

27 "at the *New York Herald*": Ibid., 19.

27 "there on September 30, 1906": Ibid., 23.

27 "New York telegrapher's assignment": Ibid., 29.

27 "of the *Titanic* disaster news": Ibid., 31.

28 "'transmitted music received'": Barnouw, *A Tower in Babel,* 78.

28 "'of thousands of families'": Bilby, *The General,* 39.

28 "their receiving radius": Barnouw, *A Tower in Babel,* 78.

28 "far too visionary and fanciful": Bilby, *The General,* 40.

29 "further develop his idea": Ibid., 54.

30 "pieces at specific times": Spar, Debora L. *Ruling the Waves: Cycles of Discovery, Chaos, and Wealth from the Compass to the Internet.* New York: Harcourt, 2001, 161.

30 "the first bartered advertising": Archer, *History of Radio to 1926,* 199.

31 "'who have wireless sets'": *The Pittsburgh Sun,* September 29, 1920.

31   "'collective communication ever devised'": Archer, *History of Radio to 1926*, 201.

33   "'already fifteen minutes late'": *The New York Times*, August 15, 1920.

33   "the candidates speak": "American Leaders Speak: The Presidential Election of 1920." American Memory, Library of Congress. http://memory.loc.gov/ammem/nfhtml/nfexpe.html (Accessed June 15, 2006).

34   "should the KDKA experiment fail": Archer, *History of Radio to 1926*, 203.

34   "those historic election returns": Ibid., 204.

35   "truly social event": *The Washington Post*, January 9, 1921.

35   "and a successful test": *The Washington Post*, February 23, 1921.

36   "'recorded on phonograph records'": *The Christian Science Monitor*, February 26, 1921.

36   "'normal occupations for boys'": Hoover, Herbert. *The Memoirs of Herbert Hoover—Vol. 1, Years of Adventure*. New York: MacMillan, 1952, 5.

36   "An average student": DeGregorio, William A. *The Complete Book of U.S. Presidents*. 6th ed. Fort Lee, NJ: Barricade Books, 2005, 465.

37   "earned about two dollars a day": Pietrusza, David. *1920: The Year of the Six Presidents*. New York: Carroll & Graf Publishers, 2007, 106.

37   "and concentrated on organization": DeGregorio, *The Complete Book of U.S. Presidents*, 463.

37   "'human despair are paved with'": Hoover, *The Memoirs of Herbert Hoover—Vol. 1*, 26.

37   "inspecting possible mine sites": Ibid., 27.

37   "had reached $4 million": DeGregorio, *The Complete Book of U.S. Presidents*, 467.

37   "Garfield campaign in 1880": Hoover, *The Memoirs of Herbert Hoover—Vol. 1*, 9.

38   "to *hooverize*": DeGregorio, *The Complete Book of U.S. Presidents*, 467.

38   "'a great international figure'": Pietrusza, *1920: The Year of the Six Presidents*, 109.

38   "'also Merciful Providence'": Lyons, Eugene. *Herbert Hoover: A Biography*. Garden City, NY: Doubleday, 1964, 105.

38   "'worthy of the greatest glory'": Ibid., 149.

38   "both Republicans and Democrats": Pietrusza, *1920: The Year of the Six Presidents*, 113.

38   "'they were "too objective"'": Hoover, Herbert. *The Memoirs of Herbert Hoover—Vol. 2, The Cabinet and the Presidency*. New York: MacMillan, 1952, 35.

39   "'important than the Interior'": Ibid., 36.

39   "for the job of commerce secretary": *The New York Times*, March 11, 1921.

39   "'related to these problems'": Hoover, *The Memoirs of Herbert Hoover—Vol. 2*, 36.

39   "'of commercial radio facilities'": *The New York Times*, March 10, 1921.

39   "'build up, not tear down'": *The Washington Post*, February 27, 1921.

39   "'two hours of work a day'": Hoover, *The Memoirs of Herbert Hoover—Vol. 2*, 42.

40   "trade and commercial associations": *The Wall Street Journal*, March 12, 1921.

41   "'every year in the United States'": *The Washington Post*, August 10, 1921.

41   "system still in use today": *The Washington Post*, March 2, 1924.

Chapter 4

42 "'heretofore forbidden delights'": Zeitz, Joshua. *Flapper: The Notorious Life and Scandalous Times of the First Thoroughly Modern Woman.* New York: Crown Publishers, 2006, 23.

42 "of at-home enthusiasts": *The Christian Science Monitor,* April 14, 1922.

43 "with other enthusiasts": Landry, *This Fascinating Radio Business,* 40.

43 "'who takes up radio seriously'": *The Washington Post,* April 2, 1922.

43 "equipment had been set up": *The Washington Post,* June 26, 1921.

43 "'pioneer college broadcaster'": *The Washington Post,* April 16, 1922.

44 "and extracurricular scene": *The Christian Science Monitor,* March 24, 1922.

44 "'pursuits of the radio wave'": *The Washington Post,* March 26, 1922.

44 "speeches were about radio": *The Washington Post,* July 5, 1922.

44 "training for Boy Scouts": *The Washington Post,* April 7, 1922.

44 "a popular party game": Ibid.

44 "between fire calls": *The Washington Post,* June 1, 1922.

44 "an afternoon radio concert": *The Washington Post,* March 22, 1923.

44 "hobby to a staple luxury": *The Christian Science Monitor,* March 18, 1922.

45 "'its kind in the radio world'": *The Washington Post,* August 19, 1922.

45 "that morning on the radio": Smulyan, Susan. *Selling Radio: The Commercialization of American Broadcasting, 1920–1934.* Washington, D.C.: Smithsonian Institution Press, 1994, 21.

45 "the bird, he reasoned": Barnouw, *A Tower in Babel,* 103.

45 "a local school building": *The Washington Post,* June 6, 1922.

45 "'every aspect of human life'": Hoover, *The Memoirs of Herbert Hoover—Vol. 2,* 139.

46 "'Hoover wrote years later'": Ibid.

46 "'such control in a new art'": Ibid.

46 "hearing radio signals increasingly difficult": *The Christian Science Monitor,* March 6, 1922.

47 "of their leisure time": Landry, *This Fascinating Radio Business,* 46.

47 "celebrate the nation's birthday": *The Washington Post,* July 12, 1922.

48 "used in the baking of bread": *The Washington Post,* May 22, 1922.

48 "Ninety-nine new stations": Archer, *History of Radio to 1926,* 241.

48 "home receiving sets": Landry, *This Fascinating Radio Business,* 40.

49 "more densely populated areas": *The Washington Post,* July 17, 1922.

49 "manufacturer and the merchant": *The Washington Post,* December 23, 1923.

49 "'from $10 up'": *The Washington Post,* June 7, 1922.

49 "already on the air": *The Washington Post,* August 29, 1922.

50 "of other people listening in": *The Washington Post,* March 26, 1922.

50 "radio amateurs": "Maxim, Hiram Percy." *Encyclopedia Britannica Online.* http://search.eb.com (Accessed November 11, 2007); and Barnouw, *A Tower in Babel,* 54.

51 "'community at the same time'": Hoover, *Memoirs—Vol. 2,* 141.

52 "Hoover as probusiness": Barnouw, *A Tower in Babel,* 95.

52 "the politician's remarks": Ibid., 93.

52 "'home on election night'": *The Christian Science Monitor,* March 24, 1923.

53 "of Ridgewood, New Jersey": *The Christian Science Monitor,* March 21, 1923.

53 "'on the same wave lengths'": *The New York Times,* January 3, 1923.

53 "'to the public good'": *The New York Times,* March 25, 1923.

54 "was a public service": Bensman, Marvin R. *The Beginning of Broadcast Regulation in the Twentieth Century.* Jefferson, NC: McFarland & Co., 2000, 52.

54 "with the larger stations": Barnouw, *A Tower in Babel,* 121–22.

54 "*Radio Broadcast's* editor": Archer, *History of Radio to 1926,* 318.

55 "abrogated his rules": Ibid., 319.

55 "'squeals and eternal misery'": Barnouw, *A Tower in Babel,* 122.

55 "'are practically unclimbable'": *The Washington Post,* May 5, 1924.

56 "'notable visitors these days'": *The New York Times,* August 19, 1923.

56 "'drowned in advertising chatter'": Hoover, *Memoirs—Vol. 2,* 140.

57 "'You can't miss it'": Landry, *This Fascinating Radio Business,* 44.

57 "libraries had been funded": Archer, *History of Radio to 1926,* 253.

57 "or sponsor public lectures": Ibid., 254.

57 "for the public good": Bensman, *The Beginning of Broadcast Regulation in the Twentieth Century,* 52.

57 "*plan can be secured*": Barnouw, *A Tower in Babel,* 111.

58 "which topped $385 million": Landry, *This Fascinating Radio Business,* 42.

58 "animal they were hearing": *The New York Times,* March 19, 1923.

58 "(all times Eastern Standard)": *The Hartford Courant,* October 12, 1924.

59 "primarily to hear music": *The Hartford Courant,* October 5, 1924.

59 "'voluntary regulation of radio'": *The Christian Science Monitor,* August 27, 1924.

59 "Oakland, California (KGO)": *The New York Times,* October 5, 1924.

59 "'finally decide in any event'": Landry, *This Fascinating Radio Business,* 49.

59 "a direct tax on listening": *The New York Times,* December 22, 1924.

60 "'slander through these channels'": *The Hartford Courant,* October 9, 1924.

60 "that reception would be clearer": *The Hartford Courant,* October 11, 1924.

60 "'those administering radio today'": *Radio Broadcast,* March 1925.

61 "and good church music": *The Washington Post,* November 2, 1924.

61 "'pursuit of their hobbies'": *The Washington Post,* September 1, 1924.

61 "'ornaments to the home'": *The Hartford Courant,* October 5, 1924.

61 "better-informed voters": *The New York Times,* July 13, 1923.

61 "the 1924 presidential candidates": *The Washington Post,* July 23, 1924.

62 "'next to nothing'": *The Washington Post,* September 21, 1924.

62 "'I cannot at present accept'": Herbert Hoover letter to Congressman Wallace White; *The Christian Science Monitor,* December 5, 1924.

62 "to give or receive": Barnouw, *A Tower in Babel,* 162.

62 "'worth-while things that are going on'": *The Washington Post,* November 30, 1924.

62 "'what is put on the air'": *The New York Times,* December 22, 1924.

Chapter 5

63 "on the air in June 1922": "June 30, 1922 Broadcast Station List." http://earlyradiohistory.us/220630ci.htm (Accessed November 25, 2007).

64 "(the Church of the Covenant)": Ibid.

65 "Wonders of Chiropractic": "Col. BJ Palmer." http://www.cmshowcase.com/halloffame/col_bj_palmer.htm (Accessed November 30, 2007).

65 "the freedom to travel": Lee, *The Bizarre Careers of John R. Brinkley,* 47.

65 "might be misinterpreted": Carson, *The Roguish World of Doctor Brinkley,* 48.

65 "the farmer's mouthpiece": Juhnke, *Quacks and Crusaders,* 9.

66 "Kansas First, Kansas Best": Ibid., 10.

66 "'Home of the Gland Transplantation'": Carson, *The Roguish World of Doctor Brinkley,* 48.

66 "patients at the clinic": Chase, Francis Seabury. *Sound and Fury: An Informal History of Broadcasting.* New York, London: Harper & Bros., 1942, 61.

66 "in Milford, Kansas": Carson, *The Roguish World of Doctor Brinkley,* 89.

67 *"for an examination"*: Chase, *Sound and Fury,* 64.

68 *"Possum Point, Missouri"*: Carson, *The Roguish World of Doctor Brinkley,* 91.

68 "by KFKB's transmitter": Lee, *The Bizarre Careers of John R. Brinkley,* 70.

68 "and uplifting his audiences": Wood, *The Life of a Man,* 213.

68 "from thirty-nine states and Canada": Barnouw, *A Tower in Babel,* 171.

68 "on December 1, 1924": Lee, *The Bizarre Careers of John R. Brinkley,* 71.

69 "to the Brinkley Hospital": Chase, *Sound and Fury,* 65.

69 "Dr. Brinkley's medical help": Juhnke, *Quacks and Crusaders,* 10.

70 "'The terms used were nauseating'": Bensman, *The Beginning of Broadcast Regulation in the Twentieth Century,* 124.

70 "to more than 5,000": "People & events: The site of the trial: Dayton, Tennessee." *The Monkey Trial.* http://www.pbs.org/wgbh/amex/monkeytrial/peopleevents/e_dayton.html (Accessed August 27, 2006).

71 "about three hundred people": *The New York Times,* July 14, 1925.

71 "'We're the radio guys from outer space'": "People & events: The site of the trial: Dayton, Tennessee." *The Monkey Trial.* http://www.pbs.org/wgbh/amex/monkeytrial/peopleevents/e_dayton.html.

71 "'the Drake Hotel, Chicago'": *The New York Times,* July 5, 1925.

72 "and vocal music": *The New York Times,* February 18, 1925.

72 "'that would sweep the country'": *The New York Times,* July 10, 1925.

72 "'official act of mine'": Ibid.

72 "by a member of the clergy": *The Washington Post,* July 15, 1925.

73   *"sunrise over Key West"*: "People & events: The site of the trial: Dayton, Tennessee." *The Monkey Trial.* http://www.pbs.org/wgbh/amex/monkeytrial/ peopleevents/e_dayton.html.

73   "listened on a radio": "WGN Radio Timeline, 1920s–30s." http://wgngold .com/timeline/1920s1930s.htm (Accessed September 5, 2006).

73   "he announced midtrial": *The Wall Street Journal,* July 13, 1925.

74   "atheist in the United States": "People & events: The site of the trial: Dayton, Tennessee." *The Monkey Trial.* http://www.pbs.org/wgbh/amex/monkeytrial/ peopleevents/e_dayton.html.

74   "for schoolteacher Scopes": *The Christian Science Monitor,* July 21, 1925.

74   "after the trial ended": "WGN Radio Timeline, 1920s–30s." http://wgngold .com/timeline/1920s1930s.htm.

74   "AND HOOVER IS THE MAN": *The Washington Post,* July 19, 1925.

74   "'and I simply have to have a license'": *The New York Times,* September 13, 1925.

75   "'solution of the problem'": *The New York Times,* February 28, 1925.

75   "'radio sets in every household'": *The New York Times,* September 13, 1925 (R–3).

76   "'the distant station programs'": *The New York Times,* Ibid., (R–1).

76   "as an emerging problem": *The New York Times,* Ibid., (R–5).

76   "service to listeners": *The New York Times,* Ibid., (R–1).

76   "many New York stations": *The New York Times,* September 6, 1925.

77   "'and the Government'": *The New York Times,* September 15, 1925.

77   "to broadcast the festivities": *The New York Times,* September 16, 1925.

77   "star Rudy Wiedoeft": Archer, *History of Radio to 1926,* 366.

77   "'Echoes of New York'": *The New York Times,* September 17, 1925.

77   "his resonant baritone voice": McNamee, Graham, and Robert Gordon Anderson. *You're on the Air.* New York, London: Harper & Brothers, 1926, 19.

77   "hired on the spot": Barnouw, *A Tower in Babel,* 149.

77   "seven to ten weekday evenings": McNamee, *You're on the Air,* 20.

78   "had entered the radio business": *The New York Times,* September 21, 1925.

78   "'and the radio industry end'": *The New York Times,* September 17, 1925.

79   "around $5,000 per month": Chase, *Sound and Fury,* 67.

79   "which they won": Wood, *The Life of a Man,* 212.

80   *"be welcomed in every home"*: Ibid., 225.

81   "'eye at his radio station'": Ibid., 215.

81   "'in the Heart of the Nation'": Carson, *The Roguish World of Doctor Brinkley,* 98.

81   "'warfare against germs'": Wood, *The Life of a Man,* 217.

81   "a thousand letters a day": Ibid., 218.

82   "at his clinic in Milford": Juhnke, *Quacks and Crusaders,* 11.

82   *"after three months' persistent use"*: Carson, *The Roguish World of Doctor Brinkley,* 101.

82   "from the druggists themselves": Wood, *The Life of a Man,* 222.

82   "Dr. Brinkley Pharmaceutical Association": Carson, *The Roguish World of Doctor Brinkley*, 100.

83   "Dr. Brinkley": Ibid., 90.

84   "three-quarters of an inch wide": Lee, *The Bizarre Careers of John R. Brinkley*, 80.

84   "one doctor declared": Carson, *The Roguish World of Doctor Brinkley*, 104.

84   "was drastically reduced": Wood, *The Life of a Man*, 226.

85   "make it national champion": Ibid.

85   "as one of the nation's leading stations": Lee, *The Bizarre Careers of John R. Brinkley*, 84.

85   "'nefarious Milford Messiah'": Chase, *Sound and Fury*, 68.

85   "'I get fat on fights'": Lee, *The Bizarre Careers of John R. Brinkley*, 85.

Chapter 6

86   "pearl button factory": Juhnke, *Quacks and Crusaders*, 38.

87   "'two-by-four town'": Winston, Alvin. *Doctors, Dynamiters, and Gunmen: The Life Story of Norman Baker; a Fact Story of Injustices—Confiscation and Suppression.* Muscatine, IA: TNT Press, 1936, 34.

87   "the Mental Marvel": Juhnke, *Quacks and Crusaders*, 39.

87   "denounce her as a fraud": Winston, *Doctors, Dynamiters, and Gunmen*, 47.

87   "year exceeded $200,000": Ibid., 62.

88   "from food products to clothing": Juhnke, *Quacks and Crusaders*, 39.

88   "'the whole world knows about'": Spence, Stephen. "Pure Hoax: The Norman Baker Story." http://www.crescent-hotel.com/bakerstory.htm (Accessed January 16, 2008).

89   "freedom of the airwaves": Winston, *Doctors, Dynamiters, and Gunmen*, 83.

90   "hotel lobby to conventioneers": Hoffer, Thomas William. *Norman Baker and American Broadcasting.* Master's Thesis. Madison: University of Wisconsin, 1969, 48, 570.

90   "United Fruit Company": Ibid., 83.

90   "for independent broadcasters": Ibid., 50.

90   "fight the 'gang'": Ibid., 83.

91   "'Time will tell the truth of my statements'": Norman Baker speech given on December 12, 1925.

91   "beyond the area of its license": Juhnke, *Quacks and Crusaders*, 40.

91   "crowded part of the dial": *The Washington Post*, January 17, 1926.

92   "'his discretion in administration'": *The New York Times*, February 28, 1926.

92   "administered radio affairs": *The New York Times*, March 2, 1926.

92   "more independent stations": *The New York Times*, June 6, 1926.

92   "circuit of vaudeville theaters": *The New York Times*, June 20, 1926.

93   "with restraint of trade": Barnouw, *A Tower in Babel*, 184.

93   "'central broadcasting organization'": Ibid.

93   "National Broadcasting Company, Inc., or NBC": Ibid., 185.

93   "for broadcasting in the United States": *The New York Times,* September 14, 1926.

94   " 'whether it be cooperative or competitive' ": Ibid.

94   " 'no service to render' ": Harvard University and Graduate School of Business Administration. *The Radio Industry: The Story of its Development, as Told by Leaders of the Industry to the Students of the Graduate School of Business Administration, George F. Baker Foundation, Harvard University.* Chicago: A. W. Shaw and Co., 1928, 109.

94   "acceptance of the electrical industry": Bilby, *The General,* 86.

94   " 'have exceeded the income' ": *The New York Times,* September 13, 1926.

95   "by humorist Will Rogers": Chase, *Sound and Fury,* 39.

95   "Roughly six weeks": Barnouw, *A Tower in Babel,* 191.

95   "signed on the air": Chase, *Sound and Fury,* 22.

96   " 'for direct advertising' ": Smulyan, *Selling Radio,* 41.

97   "underwritten by General Mills": Summers, Harrison Boyd. *A Thirty-Year History of Programs Carried on National Radio Networks in the United States, 1926–1956.* New York: Arno Press, 1971, 7.

97   "Smith Brothers Cough Drops": Chase, *Sound and Fury,* 105.

97   "with political candidates": Hoffer, *Norman Baker and American Broadcasting,* 79.

97   "by the end of 1926": Douglas, *The Early Days of Radio Broadcasting,* 95.

98   "independent commission to control radio": Barnouw, *A Tower in Babel,* 199.

98   " 'to destroy its great value' ": Douglas, *The Early Days of Radio Broadcasting,* 95.

98   "as a tool of partisan politics": Goodman, Mark, and Mark Gring. "The Ideological Fight over Creation of the Federal Radio Commission in 1927." *Journalism History* 26.3 (Autumn 2000): 117.

98   "in an efficient, effective manner": Ibid.

99   "both houses of Congress": Barnouw, *A Tower in Babel,* 199.

99   "acting in the public's interest": Douglas, *The Early Days of Radio Broadcasting,* 96.

99   "to serve the public interest": Goodman and Gring, "The Ideological Fight over Creation of the Federal Radio Commission in 1927," 117.

99   "partisan control of the airwaves": "The Radio Act of 1927." *Columbia Law Review* 27.6 (June 1927): 726–33. www.jstor.org.

100   "existing radio stations operating in the country": *The New York Times,* February 25, 1927.

100   "for the others to thrive": Barnouw, *A Tower in Babel,* 214.

101   "to a less desirable frequency": *The New York Times,* May 29, 1927.

101   "its power to 1,000 watts": *The Christian Science Monitor,* October 11, 1927.

101   "power to 2,000 watts": Hoffer, *Norman Baker and American Broadcasting,* 149.

101   "testified Senator Smith W. Brookhart of Iowa": *The New York Times,* November 2, 1927.

102   "to either 10,000 or 14,000 watts": *The New York Times,* January 22, 1928.

102   "he provided to rural citizens": Hoffer, *Norman Baker and American Broadcasting,* 161.

102 "reach more of America's farmers": Ibid., 171.

102 "to a merely advisory role": *The New York Times,* March 15, 1928.

102 "reorganizing the radio spectrum": *The New York Times,* March 16, 1928.

102 "appeared before the commission": *The New York Times,* July 10, 1928.

103 "argued candidate Thomas": Ibid.

103 "in the Midwest to discontinue broadcasting": *The New York Times,* September 2, 1928.

103 " 'because of the crowded radio conditions in New York' ": *The New York Times,* October 10, 1928.

103 "was being sacrificed": *The New York Times,* November 8, 1928.

104 " 'in their own neighborhoods and States' ": *The New York Times,* November 11, 1928.

104 " 'a high class service to your listeners' ": Hoffer, *Norman Baker and American Broadcasting,* 188.

104 "President Hoover seeking his intercession": Ibid., 202.

105 " 'The Naked Truth' ": *The Washington Post,* September 29, 1929.

105 "and the AMA": Hoffer, *Norman Baker and American Broadcasting,* 203.

105 "of the entire United States population": Harvard University and Graduate School of Business Administration, *The Radio Industry,* 253.

105 "to below $20 a share": Bilby, *The General,* 102.

106 " 'debate, drama, and information' ": Harvard University and Graduate School of Business Administration, *The Radio Industry,* 244.

Chapter 7

108 " 'It is bright with hope' ": Graff, Henry F., and United States Presidents. *Inaugural Addresses of the Presidents of the United States from W. H. Taft to G. W. Bush.* The Lakeside Classics; no. 103. Chicago: Lakeside Press, R. R. Donnelley, 2005, 124.

109 "he never fired a single employee": DeGregorio, *The Complete Book of U.S. Presidents,* 431.

109 "played poker": Ibid., 433.

109 "near the president's office": Ibid., 435.

109 "unsavory group of men": Ibid., 440.

109 "with jobs and preferential treatment": Maier, Pauline. *Inventing America: A History of the United States.* 2nd ed. New York: W. W. Norton, 2006, 732.

109 " 'business in government administration' ": Graff, *Inaugural Addresses,* 71.

109 "angered Democrats and thrilled Republicans": Pietrusza, *1920: The Year of the Six Presidents,* 420.

110 "president was delivering his rendition of it": "Chronomedia: 1921." www.terramedia.co.uk/Chronomedia/years/1921.htm (Accessed December 4, 2007).

110 "properly tuned radio receiving set": *The Washington Post,* October 22, 1921.

110 "'picking up the receiver and listening'": *The Washington Post*, February 8, 1922.

111 "south side of the executive grounds": *The Washington Post*, April 22, 1922.

111 "'and gossip flying through the air'": *The Washington Post*, February 9, 1922.

111 "'Mr. Harding laughingly told friends'": *The Washington Post*, January 27, 1923.

112 "ever addressed by a president": *The Washington Post*, April 22, 1923.

112 "'in all parts of the country'": *The New York Times*, June 21, 1923.

112 "'but cripples his oratory near by'": *The New York Times*, June 27, 1923.

112 "'landscape in search of an idea'": DeGregorio, *The Complete Book of U.S. Presidents*, 443.

113 "'to both orator and audience'": *The New York Times*, June 25, 1923.

113 "to Round Hill, Massachusetts": *The New York Times*, July 26, 1923.

113 "some panic in major cities": *The Washington Post*, August 1, 1923.

114 "probably of a massive stroke": DeGregorio, *The Complete Book of U.S. Presidents*, 442.

114 "the balance of the week": *The Washington Post*, August 6, 1923.

114 "'newspapers and press associations'": *The New York Times*, August 4, 1923.

115 "his third radio appearance": *The New York Times*, February 17, 1924.

115 "ten of the country's largest stations": *The New York Times*, April 18, 1924.

115 "for as little as twenty-five dollars": *The Washington Post*, June 8, 1924.

115 "rank and file": *The Washington Post*, June 1, 1924.

115 "for personal gain": Maier, *Inventing America*, 732.

116 "'It could have been done by postcard'": Barnouw, *A Tower in Babel*, 148.

117 "'of the Democratic national convention'": *The New York Times*, July 8, 1924.

117 "any particularly nasty speeches": Barnouw, *A Tower in Babel*, 148.

117 "the report on a local radio station": *The Washington Post*, July 10, 1924.

117 "house to listen to the convention coverage": *The Washington Post*, July 12, 1924.

118 "who actually were there": *The New York Times*, July 6, 1924.

118 "to an already burgeoning audience": Ibid.

118 "'to carry out their promise'": *The Washington Post*, July 5, 1924.

118 "'check up on your tubes, batteries, etc.'": *The Washington Post*, August 10, 1924.

119 "each case on its merits": Craig, Douglas B. *Fireside Politics: Radio and Political Culture in the United States, 1920–1940*. Baltimore, MD; London: Johns Hopkins University Press, 2006, 117.

119 "'utterances of his opponents'": *The Washington Post*, August 14, 1924.

120 "'housecleaning of the Government'": *The New York Times*, November 4, 1924.

120 "scattered reports began to come in": *The New York Times*, November 5, 1924.

120 "and the humor of Joseph Spree": *The New York Times*, November 2, 1924.

120 "*campaign songs of all time*": *The New York Times*, November 4, 1924.

121 "not food and booze": *The New York Times*, November 2, 1924.

121 "in which they were interested": *The New York Times*, November 5, 1924.

121 "power to pardon prisoners": Ibid.

Endnotes

121 "Democrats spent about $40,000": Ward, Geoffrey C. "1932: A New Deal Is Struck." *Smithsonian* 35, no. 7 (October 2004): 61.

121 "'the audience was nobody knows'": *The New York Times,* November 6, 1924.

121 "'do not care for long speeches'": *The Washington Post,* November 30, 1924.

122 "in the entire country": *The Wall Street Journal,* January 22, 1925.

122 "over 22,800,000": *The New York Times,* March 5, 1925.

122 "calling those assembled to order": *The Washington Post,* March 2, 1925.

122 "though uninspired speech": Graff, *Inaugural Addresses,* 80.

122 "United States Marine Band": *The Washington Post,* June 21, 1925.

122 "the senator announced": *The Washington Post,* May 11, 1925.

123 "COOLIDGE ALSO WILL BE BROADCAST": *The Washington Post,* April 18, 1926.

123 "'of the reception of his message'": *The Washington Post,* February 23, 1927.

123 "to hear an event simultaneously": *The Washington Post,* February 1, 1927.

123 "'best radio speaker in the nation'": *The New York Times,* April 17, 1927.

123 "'any other man in public life'": Ibid.

123 "'makes no mistakes in his delivery'": Ibid.

124 "'I do not choose to run for President in 1928'": *The Washington Post,* August 3, 1927.

124 "'manufacturer of the Calliphone [*sic*]'": *The New York Times,* November 3, 1927.

124 "message to be 'cryptic'": Hoover, *The Memoirs—Vol. 2,* 190.

124 "'you better keep them'": Ibid., 193.

124 "together in September 1927": Barnouw, *A Tower in Babel,* 222.

125 "Mervin H. Aylesworth, president of NBC": *The New York Times,* May 17, 1928.

125 "which secured the nomination": Hoover, *Memoirs—Vol. 2,* 195.

125 "convention was on the air": *The Washington Post,* June 20, 1928.

125 "'National and Columbia broadcasting companies'": *The New York Times,* June 28, 1928.

125 "'all of it bad'": DeGregorio, *The Complete Book of U.S. Presidents,* 476.

125 "hadn't heard a word of it": *The New York Times,* August 14, 1928.

126 "virtually every corner of the country": *The New York Times,* August 22, 1928.

126 "'with twenty minutes of entertainment'": *The New York Times,* September 1, 1928.

126 "every speech had to be original and new": Hoover, *Memoirs—Vol. 2,* 199.

127 "installed at the White House": *The Washington Post,* September 30, 1928.

127 "preferred the Republican to Governor Smith": Hoffer, *Norman Baker and American Broadcasting,* 185.

127 "with the Republican nominee": Ibid., 184.

127 "'which you will note is a strong one'": Ibid., 185.

127 "'REMAINING FARM NETWORK SCHEDULES'": Ibid., 186.

127 "one million dollars for radio time": Ibid., 184.

128 "'the spellbinders out'": *The Washington Post,* October 21, 1928.

128 "'I say "Good Night"'": *The New York Times,* November 4, 1928.

128 "entirely from the candidates' homes": *The Wall Street Journal*, January 9, 1929.
129 "recognizable voice on the American scene": *The Washington Post*, February 3, 1929.
129 "through which he had spoken to the nation": *The Washington Post*, March 2, 1929.
129 "of the FRC and of radio in his hands": *The Washington Post*, November 18, 1928.
129 "McNamee, Carlin, and Brokenshire": *The Washington Post*, March 2, 1929.
129 " 'to which you have called me' ": Graff, *Inaugural Addresses*, 124.

Chapter 8

130 "whose real name was Giuseppe Carrora": Halberstam, David J. *Sports on New York Radio: A Play-By-Play History*. Chicago: Masters Press, 1999, 3; and Boxing Hall of Fame Web site.
131 "eager to find out what had happened": *The New York Times*, July 5, 1919.
132 " 'rivaled that of a world war' ": Halberstam, *Sports on New York Radio*, 2.
132 "set up listening equipment for the bout": Bilby, *The General*, 56.
132 "to Jersey City to cover the bout": *The New York Times*, June 29, 1921.
133 " 'supplying bulletins in the usual places' ": *The New York Times*, July 1, 1921.
133 " 'will be posted blow by blow' ": Ibid.
133 "knockout of his French opponent": Bilby, *The General*, 57.
134 "he preferred large outdoor venues": "Tex Rickard." *Enshrinees*. http://www.ibhof.com/rickard.htm (Accessed January 16, 2008).
134 "gross revenues would exceed $1.3 million": *The New York Times*, September 11, 1923.
134 "thus widening the audience": *The New York Times*, September 12, 1923.
135 " 'Every Home Should Have a Radio!' ": *The New York Times*, September 15, 1923.
135 "sprang up everywhere": *The Washington Post*, September 16, 1923.
135 "in as many movies as championship bouts": Zeitz, *Flapper*, 61.
135 "speak into a radio microphone": *The Washington Post*, March 16, 1924.
135 "and, more important, to the promoter": *The Washington Post*, November 26, 1924.
136 " 'was just as good as seeing the fight' ": *The New York Times*, January 16, 1926.
136 " 'who were unable to attend these events' ": *The New York Times*, March 21, 1926.
136 "to broadcasting sporting events": *The New York Times*, April 6, 1926.
137 "greatest sports promoter of his time": *The New York Times*, April 2, 1926.
137 "interested in buying the radio rights": *The New York Times*, September 12, 1926.
137 "The motion was never seconded": *The New York Times*, September 16, 1926.
138 "using copy furnished by newswire services": *The New York Times*, September 19, 1926.

138   "reporter from covering the event": *The New York Times*, September 18, 1926.

138   "would be revoked": *The Washington Post*, September 19, 1926.

138   "the call of the fight over loudspeakers": *The New York Times*, September 21, 1926.

138   "by announcer Graham McNamee": *The New York Times*, September 22, 1926.

138   "and Flo Ziegfeld": "Eighty Years Ago this Month—Philadelphia Hosts 'Greatest Fight in Boxing History'—But Was It Fixed?" November 14, 2006. http://www.philly.future/Org/node/4448 (Accessed January 17, 2008).

138   *"with no steam behind it"*: *The New York Times*, September 24, 1926.

139   *"It is a dressing gown with a red back"*: Ibid.

139   *"to try to defend it as becomes a marine"*: Ibid.

139   "was 'quite satisfactory'": *The New York Times*, September 25, 1926.

139   "'in all heavyweight history'": *The Washington Post*, July 19, 1927.

140   "'It is a boon to boxing'": *The New York Times*, July 21, 1927.

140   "the chance to fight Dempsey": "The Time Tunnel: When Dempsey Kayoed Sharkey and Whipped Father Time." *East Side Boxing*. http://www.eastsideboxing.com/news.php?p=3970&more=1 (Accessed January 16, 2008).

140   "the rights to handle the radio coverage": *The New York Times*, September 9, 1927.

140   "enthused the *New York Times*": *The New York Times*, September 16, 1927.

140   "privilege of hearing the bout": *The New York Times*, September 23, 1927.

140   "so that the celebrants could listen to the fight": Ibid.

141   "neither boxer would be injured": *The Washington Post*, September 22, 1927.

141   "read and transmitted": *The New York Times*, September 22, 1927.

141   "to more than 50 million people": Ibid.

141   "just stormed by and left without a word": *The New York Times*, September 23, 1927.

141   "'and remained there until the decision was announced'": Associated Press wire report, September 23, 1927.

142   "'of the announcer's voice from ringside'": *The New York Times*, September 28, 1927.

142   "claiming radio had ruined the show": *The New York Times*, July 28, 1928.

142   "Rickard returned the money": *The New York Times*, July 29, 1928.

142   "that day's radio column": *The Washington Post*, May 4, 1929.

143   "'who arrived on the same train'": *The New York Times*, June 29, 1929.

143   "Jackie Fields and Vince Dundee": *The New York Times*, September 29, 1929.

143   "boxing matches back on the air": *The New York Times*, October 6, 1929.

144   "was actually hearing his voice": Halberstam, *Sports on New York Radio*, 139.

144   "had dubbed Murderers' Row": Montville, Leigh. *The Big Bam: The Life and Times of Babe Ruth*. New York: Doubleday, 2006, 139.

144   "every play made in the World Series": *The New York Times*, October 2, 1921.

144   "pieces moving around a board": *The New York Times*, October 6, 1921.

144 "'sent out as the game progresses'": Ibid.

145 "could know what was going on": *The New York Times*, October 22, 1921.

145 "gave his play-by-play": "The History of WMT." *The 80th Anniversary Cookbook.* http://www.n-connect.net/lynxy/book6.html (Accessed January 19, 2007).

146 "'comment on all interesting occurrences'": *The New York Times*, October 3, 1922.

146 "'and before Babe crosses the home plate'": Ibid.

146 "'*Play that is Made—At Home!*'": *The New York Times*, October 4, 1922.

146 "first two games of the series were aired": Sullivan, George, and John Powers. *The Yankees: An Illustrated History.* Philadelphia: Temple University Press, 1997, 27.

147 "would also carry reports of the contests": *The New York Times*, October 9, 1923.

147 "wanted the plum assignment": Halberstam, *Sports on New York Radio*, 141.

147 "*The Broadcast Shop*": *The Washington Post*, October 11, 1923.

147 "for as little as ten dollars": *The Washington Post*, October 10, 1923.

147 "eager to be part of the event": McNamee and Anderson, *You're on the Air*, 51.

147 "'was the buying or selling of stocks'": *The Wall Street Journal*, October 11, 1923.

148 "leaving Graham McNamee to step in": Halberstam, *Sports on New York Radio*, 141.

148 "'apparently motionless but giving signals all the time'": McNamee and Anderson, *You're on the Air*, 52–53.

148 "by a whopping 50 percent": *The Washington Post*, October 5, 1924.

149 "between those price points": Ibid.

149 "Senators' manager, Bucky Harris": *The Washington Post*, October 6, 1924.

149 "'one of the miracles of the age'": *The Washington Post*, October 26, 1924.

149 "Pittsburgh Pirates was airing on radio": *The Washington Post*, October 8, 1925.

149 "could be adjusted downward": *The Washington Post*, October 10, 1925.

149 "as a 'veteran announcer'": *The Washington Post*, October 11, 1925.

149 "*ladies and gentlemen of the radio audience*": Ibid.

149 "led more than 50,000 listeners to write in": Kyvig, David E. *Daily Life in the United States, 1920–1940: How Americans Lived through the "Roaring Twenties" and the Great Depression.* Chicago: Ivan R. Dee, 2004, 78.

150 "'carried an informing eloquence'": McNamee and Anderson, *You're on the Air*, v.

150 "more than 1.5 million people": Montville, *The Big Bam*, 232.

150 "'for these are the days of radio'": *The New York Times*, October 6, 1926.

150 "the news of Ruth's three home runs": *The New York Times*, October 8, 1926.

150 "his hero would again homer": *The New York Times*, October 9, 1926.

151 "*the ardor of a real baseball fan*": *The New York Times*, October 11, 1926.

151 "*takes off his hat to the crowd*": Ibid.

151 "*down to the sovereign State of Missouri*": Ibid.

151 "he died in 1990 at age seventy-four": *The New York Times*, January 11, 1990.

152 "'they are written in air'": *The New York Times*, October 8, 1927.

152 "WNYC, WABC, and WOR—carried the series": *The New York Times*, October 4, 1928.

152 *"It's over the fence'"*: *The New York Times*, October 10, 1928.

153 *"A score of disgusted listeners'"*: *The Washington Post*, June 2, 1929.

153 "Ted Husing anchoring for CBS": *The Washington Post*, October 9, 1929.

153 *"It's a great set"*: *The Washington Post*, October 6, 1929.

153 *"in regard to winning the series'"*: *The New York Times*, October 15, 1929.

153 "to the winning Philadelphia rally": Ibid.

154 *"play by play, on the radio'"*: *The New York Times*, November 9, 1923.

154 "college-football-mad son cheering in his room": *The New York Times*, September 21, 1925.

155 "by Pittsburgh, 21–14": "Great Moments from 100 Games of the Backyard Brawl." KDKA. December 1, 2007. http://kdka.com/unassigned/Pitt.West .Virginia.2.599082.html (Accessed January 16, 2007).

155 "it was simply too demanding": McNamee and Anderson, *You're on the Air*, 61.

155 "game every Saturday afternoon": *The Washington Post*, November 13, 1922.

156 "college songs as well": *The New York Times*, October 12, 1922.

156 "sorted out what had just happened": Halberstam, *Sports on New York Radio*, 36.

156 "au courant with the action": Ibid., 35.

156 "and radio's biggest stars": "Red 'The Galloping Ghost' Grange." Hall of Famers. *College Football Hall of Fame.* http://www.collegefootball.org/famersearch .php?id=20071 (Accessed January 16, 2008).

157 *"they spell Grange'"*: Schwartz, Larry. "Galloping Ghost Scared Opponents." *ESPN.com.* http://espn.go.com/sportscentury/features/00014213.html (Accessed January 16, 2008).

157 *"technique of cooperative announcing'"*: *The Washington Post*, October 11, 1925.

157 "Twin Announcers": *The Washington Post*, November 8, 1925.

157 "the Army-Navy game": *The New York Times*, November 28, 1926.

157 "and the radiocasts resumed": *The New York Times*, October 7, 1927.

158 "hookup was Graham McNamee": Halberstam, *Sports on New York Radio*, 37.

158 "and all the rest of the splendid pageantry": *The Washington Post*, January 2, 1928.

158 "Estelle Taylor, and Colleen Moore": *The New York Times*, January 2, 1928.

158 *"a college football romance'"*: *The Washington Post*, November 25, 1929.

Chapter 9

160 *"a large amount of mail'"*: *The Washington Post*, June 19, 1927.

161 "planning and operations": *The Washington Post*, April 7, 1921.

162 "fetching the highest prices": *The Christian Science Monitor*, May 29, 1922.

162 *"insects devouring his crops'"*: *The New York Times*, February 4, 1923.

162 *"accepted without discussion'"*: Ibid.

162 *"It's the farmer's friend'"*: *Successful Farming*, September 1924.

162 "'and action of our farm population'": From a speech about radio delivered by David Sarnoff at the University of Missouri, 1924. Craig, Steve. "'The Farmer's Friend': Radio Comes to Rural America, 1920–1927." (no date) http://www .rtvf.unt.edu/html/craig/pdfs/rural.PDF (Accessed May 4, 2007).

162 "farms around the country": *The Washington Post,* September 14, 1924.

163 "'have requested the privilege of handling'": *The Washington Post,* March 28, 1926.

163 "*Newark Sunday Call*": Douglas, *The Early Days of Radio Broadcasting,* 99.

163 "a spot on the air": Ibid., 101.

163 "'heard by a radio audience'": Kaltenborn, H. V. *Fifty Fabulous Years, 1900–1950: A Personal Review.* New York: Putnam, 1950, 109.

164 "that Kaltenborn disapproved of": Ibid., 112.

164 "'cease all editorial comment'": Ibid.

164 "'the wandering voice of radio'": Ibid., 113.

164 "'used regularly on the air'": Ibid., 115.

165 "articles about the new medium": Barnouw, *A Tower in Babel,* 98.

165 "new acts for future broadcasts": Barnouw, *A Tower in Babel,* 132.

166 "as that used strictly in newspapers": *The New York Times,* April 26, 1923.

166 "'received many appreciative letters'": Ibid.

166 "radio was discussed at greater length": *The New York Times,* April 25, 1924.

166 "'and the demand for them'": *The New York Times,* April 24, 1924.

167 "'rules of the Associated Press were adopted'": *The New York Times,* April 21, 1925.

167 "'by its very nature be exclusive'": Ibid.

168 "free mentions in the listings": *The New York Times,* April 25, 1925.

168 "'retard the sale of newspapers'": *The New York Times,* April 23, 1925.

168 "but one teletype machine in its studios": Dunning, John. *On the Air: The Encyclopedia of Old-Time Radio.* New York: Oxford University Press, 1998, 485.

168 "lead items on the agenda": *The New York Times,* April 25, 1927.

168 "aired live by fourteen radio stations": Ibid.

169 "'competition to newspaper advertising'": *The New York Times,* April 28, 1927.

169 "one newspaper headline": *The Washington Post,* June 4, 1927.

170 "reporting on Lindbergh's return": *The Washington Post,* June 12, 1927.

170 "and President Coolidge's remarks": *The Washington Post,* June 8, 1927.

170 "about Lindbergh's arrival": *The Washington Post,* June 10, 1927.

171 "*interesting spectacle here*": *The Washington Post,* June 12, 1927.

172 "'I thank you'": *The New York Times,* June 12, 1927.

172 "'it was almost startling'": Ibid.

172 "*and international affair*": *The Washington Post,* June 12, 1927.

172 "'radio voice and delivery'": Ibid.

172 "for a radio appearance": *The Washington Post,* June 5, 1927.

172 "carried over Washington's WRC": *The Washington Post,* June 13, 1927.

173 "the amazing hoopla": *The Washington Post,* June 14, 1927.

173 "'of radio programs as news'": *The New York Times,* April 26, 1928.

173 "'or a phenomenon of physics'": Ibid.

173 "'in just this manner'": *The New York Times*, January 10, 1925.

174 "thus inventing the term as we know it today": Douglas, *The Early Days of Radio Broadcasting*, 107.

174 "distant explorers at Little America": *The New York Times*, April 20, 1929.

174 "the active support of its publisher": *The New York Times*, April 22, 1929.

174 "from broadcasting such news": *The New York Times*, April 23, 1929.

175 "H. V. Kaltenborn": Summers, *A Thirty-Year History of Programs Carried on National Radio Networks in the United States, 1926–1956*, 12.

Chapter 10

176 *"to have his services broadcast by radio"*: Lewis, Sinclair. *Elmer Gantry*. Signet Classic. New York: New American Library, 1980, 384.

176 "following World War I": "Organization History," Redpath Agency. Redpath Chautauqua Collection, Special Collections Department, University of Iowa Libraries (Iowa City). http://sdrc.lib.uiowa.edu/traveling-culture/inventory/MSC150.html (Accessed February 23, 2007).

177 "'the most American thing in America'": Ibid.

177 "down the road to salvation": "Sunday, Billy." *Encyclopedia Britannica Online*. http://search.eb.com (Accessed November 11, 2007).

177 "'and the need of it'": "What a Revival Does." From *Billy Sunday: The Need for Revivals*. http://www.biblebelievers.com/billy_sunday/sun2.html (Accessed March 3, 2007).

178 "'forces in the United States'": *The Christian Science Monitor*, June 4, 1923.

178 "attended Chautauqua lectures": Ibid.

178 "and the reverend equally well": Archer, *History of Radio to 1926*, 212.

178 "'universality of radio religion'": Barnouw, *A Tower in Babel*, 71.

179 "Cuba, and Bermuda, contributed": *The Washington Post*, June 9, 1923.

179 "Sunday afternoon chapel service": Archer, *History of Radio to 1926*, 243.

179 "'daily Bible readings' carried over the airwaves": *The Washington Post*, June 15, 1922.

179 "Church of the Covenant": "June 30, 1922 Broadcast Station List." http://earlyradiohistory.us/220630ci.htm (Accessed November 25, 2007).

179 "Mariam Gregory. Handel, Wagner": *The Washington Post*, May 7, 1922.

180 "like Charles Darwin and Thomas Paine": Epstein, Daniel Mark. *Sister Aimee: The Life of Aimee Semple McPherson*. New York: Harcourt Brace Jovanovich, 1993, 35.

180 "for the Salvation Army": "Aimee Semple McPherson." *Notable Biographies*. http://notablebiographies.com/Ma-Mo/McPherson-Aimee-Semple.html (Accessed December 10, 2007).

180 "sermons at meetings in Canada": "Aimee: A Short Biography." http://www.libertyharbor.org/aimee.htm (Accessed February 21, 2007).

181   "her canvas cathedral": Ibid.

181   "until the service ended": Epstein, *Sister Aimee*, 86.

181   "presentations of biblical stories": "Aimee Semple McPherson." *America National Biography Online*. http://www.anb.org (Accessed February 21, 2007).

182   "'chief object is the conversion experience'": Epstein, *Sister Aimee*, 247.

182   "and popular tunes arranged as jazz": Ibid., 253.

182   "Californians and visitors alike": Ibid., 259.

182   "were more than happy to air": Ibid., 263.

182   "reviewed the *Times*' radio columnist": *Los Angeles Times*, March 27, 1923.

183   "*Bridal Call*": Hilliker, Jim. *History of KFSG*. 2002. http://radioheritage.net/kfsg.html (Accessed November 22, 2007).

183   "the hymn 'Give the Winds a Mighty Voice'": Epstein, *Sister Aimee*, 264.

184   "of the California Superior Court": *Los Angeles Times*, February 5, 1924.

184   "was the head of the Church Federation of Los Angeles": Epstein, *Sister Aimee*, 283.

184   "her crosstown rivals": Ibid.

185   "'a disgrace to serious Christians everywhere'": Epstein, *Sister Aimee*, 284.

185   "roam all over the wave band": Hoover, *The Memoirs of Herbert Hoover—Vol. 2*, 142.

185   "'Aimee Semple McPherson'": Ibid.

185   "the proper technical limits": Ibid., 143.

185   "into their homes and hearts": Epstein, *Sister Aimee*, 285.

186   "at the Angelus Temple": Ibid., 289.

186   "to live in Australia": Ibid.

186   "quiet sobbing and silent prayer": Thomas, Lately. *The Vanishing Evangelist: The Aimee Semple McPherson Kidnapping Affair*. New York: Viking Press, 1959, 8.

187   "'hour after hour with aching eyes'": *Los Angeles Times*, May 20, 1926.

187   "had staged her own disappearance": Thomas, *The Vanishing Evangelist*, 19.

187   "was brought in for questioning": *The Washington Post*, May 28, 1926.

187   "was news to him": Thomas, *The Vanishing Evangelist*, 31.

187   "for her daughter's body": Ibid.

187   "'day of rejoicing for Sister's victory'": Ibid., 48.

187   "'WOMAN EVANGELIST ESCAPES ABDUCTORS'": *The New York Times*, June 24, 1926.

188   "tiny town of Douglas, Arizona": Thomas, *The Vanishing Evangelist*, 60.

188   "walk through the desert": Ibid., 64–65.

188   "'escape is true,' she protested": *The Washington Post*, June 26, 1926.

188   "up and down the Pacific Coast": Thomas, *The Vanishing Evangelist*, 88.

188   "the ordeal she had been through": *The Washington Post*, June 28, 1926.

188   "being done by her Angelus Temple": Thomas, *The Vanishing Evangelist*, 97.

189   "'know about mob psychology'": *Los Angeles Times*, June 28, 1926.

189   "responsible for her kidnapping": Thomas, *The Vanishing Evangelist*, 100.

189   "between the religious leaders": Ibid., 116.

189 " 'after the evangelist had disappeared' ": *The Washington Post*, July 16, 1926.

189 "appear before the grand jury": *The Washington Post*, July 21, 1926.

189 " 'persecuting a Protestant minister' ": Thomas, *The Vanishing Evangelist*, 174.

190 "her affair with Ormiston": *Los Angeles Times*, July 23, 1926.

190 "during the hearings": Thomas, *The Vanishing Evangelist*, 245.

190 "might influence prospective jurors": *Los Angeles Times*, January 19, 1927.

190 " 'prevent and obstruct justice' ": Epstein, *Sister Aimee*, 312.

190 "that year by a devout spinster": *Time*, February 8, 1932.

190 "had no significance to her": *The Washington Post*, December 10, 1926.

190 "during McPherson's disappearance": *The Washington Post*, January 2, 1927.

191 "a national 'vindication tour' ": Epstein, *Sister Aimee*, 315.

191 "participants in the case": *The New York Times*, January 11, 1927.

191 " 'have been vindicated in that manner' ": Ibid.

191 "heard over their station": *The New York Times*, February 26, 1927.

191 "her image and standing was done": *The New York Times*, February 17, 1927.

191 "the organization's operations": *Los Angeles Times*, August 4, 1927.

192 " 'barriers of different church beliefs' ": *The Chicago Tribune*, August 30, 1925.

193 " 'neither man nor beast can burn it down' ": Fishwick, Marshall W. "Father Coughlin Time: The Radio and Redemption." *Journal of Popular Culture* 22.2 (Fall 1988): 33.

193 "services from the shrine via radio": Ward, Louis B. *Father Charles E. Coughlin: An Authorized Biography*. Detroit: Tower Publications, 1933, 24.

193 " 'for the dissemination of faith' ": Ibid.

194 " 'explain Catholicism to the community' ": *The New York Times*, October 28, 1979.

194 "spellbinding, intimate quality": Brown, Robert J. *Manipulating the Ether: The Power of Broadcast Radio in Thirties America*. Jefferson, NC: McFarland & Co., 1998, 85.

194 "passionately over the airwaves": Phillips, Cabell B. H. *From the Crash to the Blitz, 1929–1939*. New York: Fordham University Press, 2000, 305.

194 "more to the station": *The New York Times*, October 28, 1979.

194 "he 'had none in his heart' ": Ward, *Father Charles E. Coughlin*, 28.

194 "that engaged listeners": *The Wall Street Journal*, April 5, 1928.

195 "focused on religious subjects": *The New York Times*, October 28, 1979.

195 " 'spiritual value of radio' ": *The Washington Post*, January 25, 1925.

195 "*and toothless, I'll gum it*": Dunning, *On the Air*, 571.

195 " 'one of the world's worst broadcasters' ": *The Washington Post*, March 18, 1929.

195 "nasty anti-Catholic opinions": *The Washington Post*, November 28, 1929.

195 " 'sweet-singing choir' ": *The Washington Post*, January 12, 1930.

196 "so long to get on the air": Ibid.

196 "another Jesus Christ": *The Washington Post*, January 12, 1930.

196 "1928 presidential campaign": *Los Angeles Times*, February 25, 1929.

196 "including District Attorney Keyes": *The New York Times*, November 13, 1928.

196 "with the judge's legal activities": *The Washington Post,* January 29, 1929.
196 "from the American Bar Association": *The New York Times,* January 18, 1929.
196 "and witness intimidation": *Los Angeles Times,* February 27, 1929.
196 "on April 29, 1929": *Los Angeles Times,* April 28, 1929.
197 "less than twenty years earlier": *The New York Times,* April 18, 1929.
197 "sale of his theater chain": *The New York Times,* August 11, 1929.
197 "'liquor on her breath'": *The Washington Post,* September 11, 1929.
197 "appear for questioning": *The Washington Post,* September 17, 1929.
197 "wife asked for probation": *The Washington Post,* October 7, 1929.
198 "radio pulpit to defend his actions": *Los Angeles Times,* December 19 and December 27, 1929.
198 "'irresponsible ministers'": *Los Angeles Times,* September 26, 1929.
198 "'cast upon a court and a jury'": *Los Angeles Times,* November 8, 1929.
199 "'the medium of talking pictures'": *Los Angeles Times,* October 3, 1929.
199 "soul of religion or of a minister": *The New York Times,* March 14, 1927.
199 "'the glories of Heaven!'": Lewis, *Elmer Gantry,* 384.

Chapter 11

200 "vaudeville was variety": Knapp, Raymond. *The American Musical and the Formation of National Identity.* Princeton, NJ: Princeton University Press, 2005, 62.
200 "and coast-to-coast radio programming": Gilbert, Douglas. *American Vaudeville: Its Life and Times.* New York: Dover Publications, 1968, 6.
201 "audiences of men and women": Ibid., 10.
201 "Palace Theatre in New York": Ibid.
201 "and a children's story": Barnouw, *A Tower in Babel,* 68.
202 "barren of technical apparatus": *The New York Times,* March 26, 1922.
202 "'Our Conquering Army'": *The New York Times* and *The Washington Post,* July 1, 1922.
202 "theater-owner Alexander Pantages": *Los Angeles Times,* November 11, 1923.
202 "and 'Leather Breeches'": *The New York Times,* February 14, 1925.
203 "for the radio audience": "The History of WMT." *The 80th Anniversary Cookbook.* http://www.n-connect.net/lynxy/book6.html (Accessed January 19, 2007).
203 "20,000 sets were in operation": Barnouw, *A Tower in Babel,* 88.
203 "on the radio was good exposure": Ibid., 90.
204 "'telegrams of enthusiastic approval'": "The WLS National Barn Dance." http://www.wlshistory.com/NBD (Accessed April 15, 2007).
204 *"Like a jay-bird walkin' on frozen ground"*: "National Barn Dance: WLS National Barn Dance." http://www.hillbilly-music.com/programs/story/index.php?prog=190 (Accessed August 4, 2004).
204 "country music ever since": "Grand Ole Opry." Country Music Planet's History of Country Music. http://countrymusicplanet.com/history/grandoleopry.htm (Accessed May 27, 2004).

204 *"The Perfect Fool"*: *The New York Times*, February 21, 1922.

205 "song-and-dance numbers": *The New York Times*, November 8, 1921.

205 "raved the *New York Times*": Ibid.

205 "Wynn opened his mouth": *The Christian Science Monitor*, May 9, 1922.

205 "with WJZ's signal": *The New York Times*, February 4, 1922.

205 "the idea of the studio audience": Archer, *History of Radio to 1926*, 244.

206 "Ziegfeld Follies of 1922": Hilliard, Robert L., and Michael C. Keith. *The Broadcast Century and Beyond: A Biography of American Broadcasting*. 3rd ed. Boston: Focal Press, 2001, 32.

206 "from the studios of KDKA": Settel, Irving. *A Pictorial History of Radio*. New York: Grosset & Dunlap, 1967, 47.

206 "specially made radio plays": *Radio Broadcast*, November 1923.

207 "was called a 'descriptionist'": Barnouw, *A Tower in Babel*, 137.

207 "'our works without permission'": *The New York Times*, February 8, 1924.

207 "'family to see the show'": *The New York Times*, March 2, 1924.

208 "and the shows were discontinued": Chase, *Sound and Fury*, 199.

208 "was not a radio fan": *The New York Times*, April 19, 1925.

208 "'enter a theater again'": *The New York Times*, April 4, 1925.

208 "'Amos and Andy on the radio'": Lackmann, Ronald W. *The Encyclopedia of American Radio: An A–Z Guide to Radio from Jack Benny to Howard Stern*. New York: Facts On File, 2000, 16.

209 "named Sam and Henry": Nachman, Gerald. *Raised on Radio: In Quest of the Lone Ranger*. Berkeley: University of California Press, 2000, 279.

209 "to thirty other radio stations": Barnouw, *A Tower in Babel*, 226.

210 "and one unpaid-for desk": Ibid., 227.

210 "of a possible 557 votes": *The Washington Post*, June 2, 1929.

210 "while the show was on": Barnouw, *A Tower in Babel*, 226.

210 "join the NBC network": *The New York Times*, July 28, 1929.

210 "six-days-a-week program": "Pepsodent's Success Story." http://www.old-time .com/commercials/1920's/Pepsodent's%20Success%20Story.htm (Accessed January 11, 2008).

210 "prime time, at 7 P.M.": *The Washington Post*, November 13, 1929.

210 "for listeners on the West Coast": *The New York Times*, November 14, 1929.

211 "Quinn Martin's *Movie Notions*": *The New York Times*, July 20, 1924.

211 "Al Jolson himself": *The Washington Post*, October 6, 1927.

211 "between the stars' talks": *The New York Times*, March 28, 1929.

212 "Jewish and cockney jokes": *The New York Times*, March 30, 1928.

212 "called the effort 'brutal'": Farr, Rob. "Screened But Not Heard: The Big Broadcasts of 1928." (2000) http://www.otr.com/1928.html (Accessed May 4, 2007).

212 "'time to the worst music'": Hoover, *The Memoirs—Vol. 2*, 146.

213 "'and Most Beautiful Theatre'": *The New York Times*, February 20, 1921.

214 *"A Hero's Life"*: *The New York Times*, November 19, 1922.

214   "studios above the theater": Hilmes, Michele. *Radio Voices: American Broadcasting, 1922–1952*. Minneapolis: University of Minnesota Press, 1997, 61.

214   "President and Mrs. Coolidge": *The Washington Post*, February 24, 1924.

215   "'but always forgetting himself'": *The Washington Post*, January 25, 1925.

215   "'to be a little more dignified'": *The Washington Post*, February 4, 1925.

215   "'sheiks or flappers'": Ibid.

215   "'has done for radio'": *The New York Times*, February 9, 1925.

215   "his cheerful radio sign-on": *The Washington Post*, March 14, 1925.

216   "'and radio broadcasting'": *The New York Times*, June 3, 1925.

216   "which owned the Capitol": *The New York Times*, July 23, 1925.

216   "would be named for him": *The New York Times*, July 27, 1925.

216   "in broadcasting history": Lackmann, *The Encyclopedia of American Radio*, 47.

216   "'telephone number in the world'": Chase, *Sound and Fury*, 227.

216   "for the grand opening": *The New York Times*, March 8, 1927.

217   "6,200-seat theater itself": *The New York Times*, March 12, 1927.

217   "'through his radio broadcasts'": *The New York Times*, March 26, 1927.

217   "more than 100 voices": *The Washington Post*, February 27, 1927.

217   "that would be broadcast": *The Washington Post*, May 22, 1927.

217   "'on along these lines'": *The New York Times*, March 31, 1926.

217   "of their family's entertainment": *The New York Times*, October 14, 1928.

218   "'for our radio activities'": *The New York Times*, September 29, 1929.

218   "radio, jazz, and bad liquor": *The New York Times*, March 6, 1925.

218   "at the clubs in Harlem": Douglas, Ann. *Terrible Honesty: Mongrel Manhattan in the 1920s*. New York: Farrar, Straus, and Giroux, 1995, 373.

219   "on Cincinnati's WLW": Taken from the *Washington Post* radio listings for February 27 and April 29, 1924; and Dunning, *On the Air*, 61.

219   "luxurious Trianon Ballroom": Chase, *Sound and Fury*, 255.

219   "an all-jazz format": Barnouw, *A Tower in Babel*, 130.

219   "would continue for decades": Dunning, *On the Air*, 62.

219   "'an immoral influence'": Barnouw, *A Tower in Babel*, 131.

219   "by eighteen ensembles": *The New York Times*, January 1, 1926.

220   "*Lopez speaking*": Dunning, *On the Air*, 61.

220   "'King of Jazz'": *The New York Times*, November 26, 1929.

220   "showed up for the engagement": Vallée, Rudy, and Gil McKean. *My Time is Your Time: The Story of Rudy Vallée*. New York: Obolensky, 1962, 3.

220   "'saxophobia'": Ibid., 22.

220   "and some vaudeville gigs": Dunning, *On the Air*, 593.

221   "'trombones and saxophones'": Fitzgerald, F. Scott. *The Great Gatsby*. New York: Scribner, 2004, 40.

221   "'and didn't even know it!'": Vallée, Rudy. *Rudy Vallée Kisses and Tells*. Rev. ed. Canoga Park, CA: Major Books, 1976, 57.

221   "'looked very Jewish'": Ibid., 61.

221   "'and a sash around the waist'": Ibid., 62.

222   "of the CBS Radio Network": Douglas, *The Early Days of Radio Broadcasting*, 181.

222   "*New York City*": Vallée and McKean, *My Time is Your Time*, 63.

222   "nongentile listeners": Ibid., 73.

223   "50,000 listeners responded": Ibid., 74.

223   "and his musicians": Ibid., 75.

223   "out into the lobby": Ibid., 76.

223   "in that theater": *Screenland*, September 1929.

223   "at the Lombardy Hotel": *The New York Times*, December 27, 1928.

223   "'almost mesmeristic power over women'": *Screenland*, September 1929.

224   "'to leave the theatre humming'": *The New York Times*, November 27, 1929.

224   "'to a resounding flop'": Vallée and McKean, *My Time is Your Time*, 84.

224   "'as a tropical monsoon'": *Screenland*, September 1929.

224   "called Standard Brands": *The New York Times*, July 6, 1929.

224   "and the day's mail": *Time*, July 1, 1929.

225   "'*Vagabond Lover*' again": Excerpt taken from Rudy Vallée's script for the show.

225   "'*Song of India*'": Ibid.

225   "*This is Graham McNamee speaking. Goodnight, all!*": Ibid.

225   "'by the seat of our pants'": Vallée and McKean, *My Time is Your Time*, 86.

226   "a 'magnanimous and understanding' sponsor": Ibid.

Chapter 12

227   "TOTAL DROP OF BILLIONS": *The New York Times*, October 24, 1929.

228   "NBC and CBS radio networks": *The Washington Post*, October 17, 1929.

228   "by Graham McNamee": *The Washington Post*, October 21, 1929.

228   "'What they desire is action, not argument'": *The Washington Post*, October 24, 1929.

229   "'and prosperous basis'": *The Washington Post*, October 26, 1929.

229   "'Good-night and thank you!'": *The New York Times*, October 30, 1929.

229   "'Radio's GREATEST Personality'": *The Washington Post*, December 25, 1929.

229   "'greatly surprised and deeply hurt'": *The Washington Post*, December 20, 1929.

230   "'greater service of a single art'": *The Wall Street Journal*, January 5, 1929.

230   "'on a large scale'": *The Wall Street Journal*, June 25, 1929.

230   "'as an adjunct to the automobile'": *The Wall Street Journal*, October 15, 1929.

230   "'by city traffic authorities'": *The Washington Post*, December 15, 1929.

231   "spent more than $750 million": *The New York Times*, December 28, 1929.

231   "of radio devices and licensing": Bilby, *The General*, 102.

231   "$20 million of which went directly to radio": *Broadcasting Magazine* (Washington, D.C.). *The First 50 Years of Broadcasting: The Running Story of the Fifth Estate.* Washington, D.C.: Broadcasting Publications, 1982, 2.

231   "''for the Safety Can Opener Hour''": *The New York Times*, October 14, 1929.

231 "on the NBC and CBS networks": Summers, *A Thirty-Year History of Programs*, 15.

232 "Sarnoff had sold all his shares": Bilby, *The General*, 102.

232 "another review would be undertaken": *The New York Times*, October 29, 1929.

232 "should self-monitor": *The Washington Post*, November 3, 1929.

233 "programming they desired": *The Washington Post*, October 26, 1929.

233 "rates would not be tolerated": *The Washington Post*, January 16, 1930.

233 "as a 'political football'": Ibid.

233 "a permanent body": *The Washington Post*, December 16, 1929.

234 "'confidence in the radio industry'": *The Wall Street Journal*, December 13, 1929.

234 "'early stabilization of business activity'": *The Washington Post*, December 13, 1929.

234 "its triumphant march forward": *The New York Times*, December 29, 1929.

234 "to carry the industry forward": *The Washington Post*, December 30, 1929.

234 "'as a necessity in every American home'": *The New York Times*, November 17, 1929.

235 "listenership and advertising revenues": *The New York Times*, December 29, 1929.

235 "was officially ushered in": *The Washington Post*, December 25, 1929.

235 "'young recruits to the army of drunkards have fallen off'": *The New York Times*, January 27, 1929.

235 "forty-two proprietors and employees": *The New York Times*, January 1, 1930.

236 "'highlight of the night'": *The Washington Post*, January 2, 1930.

236 "thirty-five orchestras and ensembles": *The New York Times*, December 31, 1929.

236 "'pursuing time around the world'": Ibid.

236 "the star that he had become": *The Washington Post*, January 2, 1930.

237 "at 4 A.M. EST": *The New York Times*, December 31, 1929.

237 "they all sounded very much alike": *The Washington Post*, January 2, 1930.

237 "'"Hail, Hail, the Gang's All Here" was the national anthem'": Ibid.

Chapter 13

238 "'we bring him out every year'": *The New York Times*, January 2, 1930.

238 "'and between halves'": *The New York Times*, January 1, 1930.

239 "'outfought, outpassed, and thoroughly outclassed'": *The Washington Post*, January 2, 1930.

239 "advertising expansion program ever": *The New York Times*, December 31, 1929.

239 "happened to be in on Thursday evening": *The Washington Post*, July 17, 1930.

239 "amounted to $32,000": *The Washington Post*, August 7, 1930.

240 "'the presiding deities of the twilight time'": Archer, Gleason Leonard. *Big Business and Radio*. New York: The American Historical Company, Inc., 1939, 354.

240 "as a form of escape in times of stress": Chase, *Sound and Fury*, 215.

240 "'than like a pair of troupers'": *The New York Times*, February 2, 1930.

240 "in 1930 of $100,000": Ibid.

240 "an estimated fee of one million dollars": *The New York Times*, April 13, 1930.

240 "highest-paid radio entertainers ever": *The New York Times,* August 17, 1930.

240 "especially Prohibition": *The New York Times,* September 14, 1930.

240 "misuse of church funds": *The Washington Post,* October 12, 1929.

241 "and kept her name in the news": Stories about McPherson's legal problems appeared in the country's major newspapers throughout 1930.

241 "in the public eye": *The New York Times,* July 27, 1930.

241 "with a stock-fraud case": *The Washington Post,* May 9, 1930.

241 " ' "with the orderly administration of justice" ' ": *The New York Times,* October 3, 1930.

242 " 'from campus to campus' of America's universities": Ward, *Father Charles E. Coughlin,* 70.

242 " 'the exponent of anarchy' ": Ibid.

242 " 'labor throughout the world' ": *The New York Times,* July 26, 1930.

242 "would be carved into the tower": *The New York Times,* July 6, 1930.

243 "the Coolidge-Hoover prosperity": Phillips, *From the Crash to the Blitz, 1929–1939,* 305.

243 " 'truth, charity, and patriotism' ": Ibid., 307.

243 "with limitless opportunity": *The New York Times,* January 26, 1930.

243 "economic conditions were normal": *The Washington Post,* January 24, 1930.

244 " 'evils of speculation' had been curbed": *The Washington Post,* January 1, 1930.

244 "that unemployment would decline": *The New York Times,* January 2, 1930.

244 "optimistic pronouncements": *The Washington Post,* January 21, 1930.

244 "annual meeting of the Red Cross": *The Washington Post,* May 4, 1930.

244 "delivered at Gettysburg, Pennsylvania": *The New York Times,* May 11, 1930.

244 " 'charity is the obligation of the strong to the weak' ": *The Washington Post,* February 6, 1930.

244 " 'for the benefit of the people' ": *The Washington Post,* August 8, 1930.

244 " 'the troubled waters before us' ": *The Washington Post,* October 28, 1930.

244 "by America's political leaders": *The Washington Post,* August 17, 1930.

245 "in less than two years": *The Washington Post,* December 30, 1930.

245 "half-hour talks over the CBS network": *The New York Times,* March 20, 1930.

245 "a hefty $72,000": *The Washington Post,* April 3, 1930.

245 "he would begin": Dunning, *On the Air,* 723.

246 "fashions seen at the fight": *The New York Times,* June 11, 1930.

246 "right into Yankee Stadium": *The New York Times,* June 13, 1930.

246 "carry the title to Europe": Ibid.

247 " 'description of the game's progress' ": *The New York Times,* September 14, 1930.

247 "millions of baseball fans from coast to coast": *The New York Times,* October 1, 1930.

247 "Graham McNamee over the NBC network": *The New York Times,* October 5, 1930.

247 "CBS returned for game five in St. Louis": *The New York Times,* October 6, 1930.

248   "'and the baseball game has not'": *The Washington Post,* October 3, 1930.

248   "ever-improving delivery and on-air presence": *The Washington Post,* March 18, 1929.

248   "in terrible condition and horribly overcrowded": *Current History,* June 1930, 561.

249   "'west block roof collapsed'": *Time,* April 28, 1930.

249   "treatment in the prison hospital": *The New York Times,* April 23, 1930.

249   "and listening to radios": *The Washington Post,* April 25, 1930.

249   "housing the angry convicts": *The New York Times,* April 28, 1930.

249   "from the news standpoint, had ended": *The Washington Post,* May 18, 1930.

249   "and ready to broadcast": Husing, Edward B. *My Eyes Are in My Heart.* New York: B. Geis Associates, 1959, 110.

250   "who might be of help": *The Washington Post,* May 18, 1930.

250   "were hearing was actually happening": Ibid.

250   *"to bring you an important news broadcast"*: Husing, *My Eyes Are in My Heart,* 111.

250   *"They learned how fast"*: Ibid., 113.

251   "WAIU continued to broadcast news of the prison troubles": Ibid.

251   "the wire that connected to the transmitter": Ibid.

251   "written and recorded by Bob Miller": *The Washington Post,* December 6, 2007.

251   "her son's charred remains": Ibid.

251   "'Radio is making today's newspaper yesterday's newspaper'": Husing, *My Eyes Are in My Heart,* 113.

252   "retiring to his private quarters": *The Washington Post,* November 5, 1930.

252   "the extent of their defeat": *The New York Times,* November 6, 1930.

252   "in control of the House": *The New York Times,* November 8, 1930.

252   "Kingfish, after one of the show's main characters": Williams, T. Harry. *Huey Long.* New York: Knopf, 1969, 313.

252   *"what is going on around here"*: Ibid., 629.

252   "were carried free of charge": Sterling, Christopher H., Michael C. Keith, and Museum of Broadcast Communications. *The Museum of Broadcast Communications Encyclopedia of Radio.* New York: Fitzroy Dearborn, 2004, 881.

252   "a circus sideshow barker": *Current History,* November 1934, 172.

253   "his dog-eared copy of the Bible": *Harper's Monthly,* June/November 1935, 697.

253   "hear a pin drop anywhere in the state": Sitkoff, Harvard. "Huey Long: Film Review." *Film and History* 17.2 (May 1987): 46–47. http://pao.chadwyck.co.uk (Accessed December 14, 2007).

Chapter 14

255   "all over the vehicle": Lee, *The Bizarre Careers of John R. Brinkley,* 73.

255   "somewhere around $2 million": Ibid., 80.

255   "his unchecked messages and claims": Juhnke, *Quacks and Crusaders,* 13.

255   "directly or by inference": *The New York Times,* December 31, 1929.

256 "via his own radio station": Lee, *The Bizarre Careers of John R. Brinkley*, 92.

256 "leading a conspiracy to ruin him": Juhnke, *Quacks and Crusaders*, 14.

256 "'meat cutters' union'": Chase, *Sound and Fury*, 70.

256 "Amalgamated Meatcutters Association": Juhnke, *Quacks and Crusaders*, 14.

256 "speak out against Brinkley, and they did": Lee, *The Bizarre Careers of John R. Brinkley*, 96.

257 "KFKB should be renewed": Chase, *Sound and Fury*, 72.

257 "of the CBS radio network": *The New York Times*, January 30, 1929.

257 "had to pay their own way": Juhnke, *Quacks and Crusaders*, 14.

257 "'station no longer met proper standards'": Ibid., 15.

257 "'in the interest of the listening public'": Jones, William K. *Cases and Materials on Electronic Mass Media: Radio, Television, and Cable.* Mineola, NY: Foundation Press, 1976, 173.

257 "nationwide popularity contest": Carson, *The Roguish World of Doctor Brinkley*, 143.

257 "by the Kansas Medical Board": Carson, *The Roguish World of Doctor Brinkley*, 146.

257 "review his case": Chase, *Sound and Fury*, 73.

258 "John Brinkley's medical license": Ibid., 72.

258 "and guaranteed old-age pensions": Wood, *The Life of a Man*, 270.

258 "'and keep Kansas clean'": Carson, *The Roguish World of Doctor Brinkley*, 157.

259 "to receive 10,000 votes": Wood, *The Life of a Man*, 271.

259 "human ailments by radio": *Hartford Courant*, November 2, 1930.

259 "the ballots were to be rejected": Chase, *Sound and Fury*, 77.

259 "and Brinkley 181,216": *The Washington Post*, November 8, 1930.

259 "actually received in Kansas": Wood, *The Life of a Man*, 273.

259 "Oklahoma gubernatorial election": Carson, *The Roguish World of Doctor Brinkley*, 166.

260 "'of public character'": Jones, *Cases and Materials on Electronic Mass Media*, 173.

260 "in the 1932 election": Wood, *The Life of a Man*, 277.

260 "Kansas, for $95,000": *The Washington Post*, February 23, 1931.

260 "originally reached by KFKB": Barnouw, *A Tower in Babel*, 259.

261 "ordered the station off the air": *The Washington Post*, May 30, 1930.

261 "religious strife and antagonism": *The Washington Post*, November 14, 1931.

261 "Herbert Hoover to the presidency": Hoffer, *Norman Baker and American Broadcasting*, 184.

262 "in the Baker pharmacy": Juhnke, *Quacks and Crusaders*, 46–47.

262 "*Muscatine Journal* and its publisher": Hoffer, *Norman Baker and American Broadcasting*, 271.

262 "'interests of the public health'": *The New York Times*, August 10, 1930.

262 "opponent's Jewish heritage": Juhnke, *Quacks and Crusaders*, 52.

262 "among Iowa's farmers": Ibid., 53.

262 "ordered the station closed": *The Washington Post*, June 28, 1931.

262   "to attack the medical profession": *The Chicago Tribune,* June 6, 1931.

262   "his right to free speech": *The Washington Post,* June 24, 1931.

263   "'to call Norman Baker a quack'": *Time,* March 28, 1932.

263   "this one in Nuevo Laredo": Juhnke, *Quacks and Crusaders,* 58.

263   "the public interest in mind": Bensman, *The Beginning of Broadcast Regulation in the Twentieth Century,* 215.

263   "a talk titled 'Prosperity'": Warren, Donald I. *Radio Priest: Charles Coughlin, the Father of Hate Radio.* New York: Free Press, 1996, 34.

263   "spurred by the White House": Ibid., 36.

263   "violating his right of free speech": Ward, *Father Charles E. Coughlin,* 85.

263   "'these sermons would be continued'": Warren, *Radio Priest,* 34.

264   "'a Hebrew'": Ibid., 35.

264   "for America's economic ills": *The New York Times,* January 12, 1931.

264   "to include twenty-seven stations": Warren, *Radio Priest,* 38.

264   "Radio Priest's weekly show": Ward, *Father Charles E. Coughlin,* 29.

264   "of a new post office": Warren, *Radio Priest,* 34.

264   "controlled the medium": *The New York Times,* January 25, 1932.

264   "*Church of the Air*": *Time,* February 8, 1932.

265   "popes Leo XIII and Pius XI": *The New York Times,* May 10, 1932.

265   "'greatest sucker in the world'": *The New York Times,* April 24, 1931.

266   "and General Electric": *The New York Times,* June 14, 1930.

266   "'the installation of broadcasting as a national industry'": *The New York Times,* June 16, 1930.

266   "'with all the best modern resources'": Ibid.

266   "'A City of Radio'": *The New York Times,* June 22, 1930.

266   "between 8,000 and 10,000 men": *The New York Times,* March 19, 1931.

267   "in the Depression-plagued nation": *The Wall Street Journal,* October 17, 1931.

267   "more than 12,800,000 radio sets": *The Washington Post,* June 1, 1930.

267   "daily and weekly features": *The Washington Post,* May 24, 1931.

267   "for the homemaker, and sports": Summers, *A Thirty-Year History of Programs Carried on National Radio Networks in the United States, 1926–1956,* 25–30.

267   "fueled radio during 1931": *The Wall Street Journal,* March 22, 1932.

267   "jazz was often called": *The Washington Post,* October 11, 1931.

268   "a candy bar named for them": *The New York Times,* May 3, 1931.

268   "'Negro race in ridicule'": *The Washington Post,* June 28, 1931.

268   "were broadcast over WHN": Douglas, *Terrible Honesty,* 420.

268   "ninth consecutive World Series": *The Washington Post,* September 24, 1931.

268   "Husing on the CBS stations": *The Washington Post,* October 1, 1931.

268   "become commonplace and quite public": *The Washington Post,* October 8, 1931.

269   "in a plane crash": *The Washington Post,* April 1, 1931.

269   "'a second team to play Notre Dame'": *The New York Times,* November 5, 1931.

269   "'radio's ideal speaker'": *The New York Times,* January 18, 1931.

269   "of the droughts could continue": *The New York Times*, January 23, 1931.

269   "both national networks": *The Washington Post*, February 12, 1931.

269   "the nation's problems": *The Washington Post*, April 12, 1931.

269   "over NBC seven more times": *The Washington Post*, May 11, 1931.

269   "'with an armor of confidence'": *The Washington Post*, June 16, 1931.

269   "Christian Endeavor societies": *The Washington Post*, July 17, 1931.

269   "of the YMCA": *The Washington Post*, July 21, 1931.

270   "for the embattled president": *The Washington Post*, September 21, 1931.

270   "many relief funds": *The Washington Post*, October 15, 1931.

270   "'that we are our brother's keeper'": *The New York Times*, October 19, 1931.

270   "in San Francisco": *The Washington Post*, October 16, 1931.

271   "allowing him to appear on the program": *The New York Times*, October 19, 1931.

271   "help raise more money": *The New York Times*, October 22, 1931.

271   "of the tree to get their paychecks": "Rockefeller Center Christmas Tree." http://Rockefeller_Center_Christmas_tree (Accessed January 21, 2008).

Chapter 15

272   "$1.7 billion on deposit during 1931": Kyvig, *Daily Life in the United States, 1920–1940*, 218.

273   "have totaled forty-four hours": Ibid., 222.

273   "one-third of all American farmers had lost their land": Brinkley, Alan. *American History: A Survey*. 12th ed. Boston: McGraw-Hill, 2007, 682.

273   "hovered above 20 percent": Maier, *Inventing America*, 755.

273   "might provide shelter": Kyvig, *Daily Life in the United States, 1920–1940*, 228.

273   "'by economic recovery'": Phillips, *From the Crash to the Blitz, 1929–1939*, 45.

273   "assistance in the way of food": Kyvig, *Daily Life in the United States, 1920–1940*, 224.

273   "one million new jobs for unemployed Americans": *The Washington Post*, February 8, 1932.

273   "jobs had been found and filled": *The Washington Post*, March 2, 1932.

273   "by more than 20 percent": "The Great Depression." National Parks Service. http://www.nps.gov/archive/elro/glossary/great-depression.htm (Accessed July 27, 2007).

273   "no shortage of programming": *The New York Times*, March 27, 1932.

273   "news in 1932 was bad": *The New York Times*, April 3, 1932.

274   "more than 50 million people": Ibid.

274   "approached $36 million": *The New York Times*, January 31, 1932.

274   "with combined profits of over $3 million": Craig, *Fireside Politics*, 32.

274   "well above 56,000": *The Wall Street Journal*, September 9, 1931.

274   "would raise and lower the stage": *The New York Times*, January 3, 1932.

274   "twenty-five-foot chandelier": *The Washington Post*, July 31, 1932.

274   "that were needed": *The Wall Street Journal*, August 26, 1931.

274   "fill Radio City with grand sounds": *The Wall Street Journal*, May 17, 1932.

274   "from one mile away": *The Washington Post*, February 21, 1932.

274   "the project's main sponsor": *The Wall Street Journal*, February 25, 1932.

275   "leaving his future plans obscure": *The Washington Post*, January 28, 1931.

275   "'enter a much wider field of activity'": *Time*, February 9, 1931.

275   "'the Mayor of Radio City'": *The New York Times*, November 8, 1931.

275   "resign and pursue other options": *The New York Times*, February 2, 1932.

275   "make English the world's language": *The New York Times*, January 3, 1932.

275   "for the millions invested": *The New York Times*, February 20, 1932.

276   "Roxy discussing plans for Radio City": *The Washington Post*, April 30, 1932.

276   "*Ed Wynn and the Fire Chief Band*": *The Washington Post*, April 25, 1932.

276   "excellent reviews for his performance": *The Washington Post*, April 28, 1932.

277   "became a national catchphrase": Dunning, *On the Air*, 219.

277   "laughter of a live audience": *The Washington Post*, October 5, 1931.

277   "new audience records for an ongoing series": Dunning, *On the Air*, 223.

277   "in the November 1932 election": Ibid.

277   "during the visit": *The Washington Post*, May 26, 1931.

278   "entertained America's veterans": *The Washington Post*, February 11, 1932.

278   "a song to drive away the Depression": *The New York Times*, May 24, 1932.

278   "to the Lindberghs in New Jersey": *The Washington Post*, June 12, 1930.

279   "'he was tired and would welcome a little relief'": *The New York Times*, June 26, 1930.

279   "the arrival of his baby": *The New York Times*, July 26, 1930.

279   "was to be sent to Europe": *The New York Times*, August 8, 1930.

279   "broadcast of the talk": *The Washington Post*, August 11, 1930.

280   "ending their journey in Japan": *The Washington Post*, July 25, 1931.

280   "open the world to air travel": *The New York Times*, May 26, 1931.

280   "his grandparents and a nurse": *The New York Times*, July 29, 1931.

280   "in the event of an emergency": *The Washington Post*, August 17, 1931.

280   "cheers of 'Banzai'": *The New York Times*, August 26, 1931.

280   "communications and war were scheduled to speak": *The New York Times*, August 27, 1931.

281   "'There are no longer distant countries,' he concluded": *The New York Times*, August 29, 1931.

281   "*He was dressed in his sleeping clothes*": *The New York Times*, March 3, 1932.

281   "shared with anxious listeners": Ibid.

281   "America's hero's son": *The New York Times*, March 6, 1932.

282   "special dietary needs": McLeod, Elizabeth. "The Lindbergh Baby Tragedy, 1932–1936." http://www.old-time.com/mcleod/top100html (Accessed June 27, 2004).

282 "'during the day'": *The New York Times,* March 3, 1932.

282 *"bleed the wine of sorrow?":* Fishwick, "Father Coughlin Time," 42.

282 "that no questions would be asked": *The New York Times,* March 6, 1932.

283 "child should be found": *The New York Times,* March 13, 1932.

283 "sympathy for the Lindberghs": *The New York Times,* May 13, 1932.

283 "'hoodlum from our country'": Ibid.

284 "'dramas of life'": *The New York Times,* March 13, 1932.

284 "oratory of a presidential race": *The New York Times,* June 19, 1932.

284 "for the heavyweight crown": *The Washington Post,* February 13, 1932.

284 "Coe, a well-regarded author of fight stories": *The Washington Post,* June 19, 1932.

285 "retained the heavyweight championship of the world": *The New York Times,* June 22, 1932.

285 "that Schmeling had won by a safe margin": Ibid.

285 "excitement where none existed": *The Washington Post,* June 24, 1932.

286 "on the main platform": *The Washington Post,* May 29, 1932.

286 "to more than $35,000": *The New York Times,* June 12, 1932.

286 "record for network transmission": Ibid., and *The Washington Post,* June 13, 1932.

287 "'peerless leaders and beerless leaders'": *The New York Times,* June 15, 1932.

287 "where a radio had been set up": *The Washington Post,* June 15, 1932.

287 "from the White House": *The New York Times,* June 16, 1932.

287 *"is still full of fire and fight":* Ibid.

288 "'for President of the United States'": *The New York Times,* June 17, 1932.

288 "'accord with anybody's idea'": *The Washington Post,* June 19, 1932.

288 "every detail of each state's roll call": *The New York Times,* June 24, 1932.

289 "who truly excited the Democrats": Maier, *Inventing America,* 761.

289 "to have the government assist the needy": Brinkley, *American History,* 699.

289 "primacy at the convention intensified": *The New York Times,* May 1, 1932.

289 "millions of radio sets": *The New York Times,* June 28, 1932.

289 "more than six hours the second day": *The New York Times,* June 29, 1932.

290 "'we probably will hear the prohibition plank'": *The New York Times,* June 30, 1932.

290 "Shepherd of the Air": Ibid.

290 *"for the development of our own country":* Warren, *Radio Priest,* 40.

290 "and ways to help the common man": Marcus, Sheldon. *Father Coughlin: The Tumultuous Life of the Priest of the Little Flower.* Boston: Little, Brown, 1973, 45.

291 "not be identified with any political party": Warren, *Radio Priest,* 43.

291 "'Roosevelt or ruin'": Marcus, *Father Coughlin,* 46.

291 "from his lieutenants in Chicago": *The New York Times,* July 1, 1932.

291 "'at the hotel over the rad-dio'": Morgan, Ted. *FDR: A Biography.* New York: Simon and Schuster, 1985, 350.

291 "was listening to the proceedings on the radio in Albany": Ibid., 353.

291 "over the radio to the fourth ballot": *The New York Times,* July 3, 1932.

292 "'over the radio in my own home'": Ibid.
292 "hundreds of unemployed workers": Ibid.
292 "*to a new deal for the American people*": Brinkley, *American History*, 699.
292 "powerful acceptance speech": *The New York Times*, July 4, 1932.
292 "radio networks of nearly $1 million": *The New York Times*, July 1 and 3, 1932.
292 "'on the speakers' platform'": *The New York Times*, July 3, 1932.
293 "the utterances of political candidates": *The New York Times*, June 27, 1932.
293 "a modern weapon of politics": *The New York Times*, July 10, 1932.
293 "'will be a radio campaign'": *The New York Times*, June 12, 1932.

Chapter 16

294 "part-time church singer and salesman": *The New York Times*, June 19, 1932.
295 "other prominent musical organizations": *The New York Times*, July 3, 1932.
295 "during the first part of 1932": *The New York Times*, October 2, 1932.
296 "'I didn't see much of a depression with the Yankees'": Montville, *The Big Bam*, 307.
296 "to consult with his doctor": Ibid., 308.
296 "his lieutenants went out on the stump": *The New York Times*, October 31, 1932.
297 "to add fund-raising to his already overtaxed schedule": Lyons, *Herbert Hoover*, 292.
297 "plight of the American workers": Morgan, *FDR*, 362.
297 "rivaling the kind of campaigns run in 1920": Craig, *Fireside Politics*, 179.
297 "Ben Bernie's entertainment and music show": *The Washington Post*, September 27, 1932.
298 "had work to do for his country": *The New York Times*, September 23, 1932.
298 "accepted an invitation to game three": *The New York Times*, September 29, 1932.
298 "toward center field": Garner, Joe, and Bob Costas. *And the Crowd Goes Wild: Relive the Most Celebrated Sporting Events Ever Broadcast*. Naperville, IL: Sourcebooks, 1999, 4.
299 "*and it's a home run*": Ibid.
299 "'had ever learned from books and commission reports'": *The Washington Post*, October 2, 1932.
299 "'tuned out on'": *The New York Times*, September 29, 1932.
300 "'to make it greater than ever!'": Excerpted from Rudy Vallée letter to John Reber, June 11, 1932.
300 "*variety*": Vallée's radio script for the program of October 6, 1932.
300 "new industry standards for radio production": Chase, *Sound and Fury*, 217.
300 "'Palace Theater of the Air'": Vallée and McKean, *My Time is Your Time*, 87.
301 "Bela Lugosi, and Jimmy Cagney": The guests for all of Vallée's shows are listed in the log of his shows.
301 "'overcome the limitations of the medium'": Dunning, *On the Air*, 226.
301 "emerge from its plight": *The Washington Post*, October 5, 1932.
301 "that needed to be set right": *The New York Times*, October 6, 1932.

302 "flagship station, WEAF": *The New York Times*, October 23, 1932.

302 "not a reason for nonpayment": *The New York Times*, October 9, 1932.

302 "Pope Pius XI's 1931 encyclical": Warren, *Radio Priest*, 43.

302 "and bringing on the Depression": Marcus, *Father Coughlin*, 47.

303 *"the United States Supreme Court as well"*: *The New York Times*, October 27, 1932.

303 *"Delay, Deceit, Despair"*: *The New York Times*, October 26, 1932.

303 "did not have the judgment to be president": *The New York Times*, October 27, 1932.

304 "debate resonating over the airwaves": Morgan, *FDR*, 363.

304 *"in the American system of government"*: *The New York Times*, November 6, 1932.

304 "ninety-five radio addresses": Chase, *Sound and Fury*, 113.

304 "'clustered about his car'": *The New York Times*, November 8, 1932.

305 *"re-elect President Hoover"*: Ibid.

305 *"vote for Hoover"*: *The New York Times*, November 6, 1932.

305 "'he who laughs last, laughs best'": *The Washington Post*, October 25, 1932.

305 *"And I add to that, God bless you all"*: *The New York Times*, November 8, 1932.

306 "'good natured even in attack'": *The New York Times*, November 6, 1932.

306 "for each was their radio airtime": *The New York Times*, October 9, 1932.

306 "spent a total of $472,000 on NBC alone": Craig, *Fireside Politics*, 134.

306 "$400,000 went to radio": *The Wall Street Journal*, November 18, 1932.

306 "as early as election day afternoon": *The Chicago Tribune*, October 30, 1932.

306 "and keep the count accurate": *The New York Times*, November 6, 1932.

306 "was over 60 million": *The New York Times*, November 8, 1932.

307 "a Democratic sweep pleased them": Morgan, *FDR*, 363.

307 "to the disappointing results on the local radio station": Lyons, *Herbert Hoover*, 308.

307 *"in the task of restoration"*: *The Wall Street Journal*, November 10, 1932.

307 "during the same four-year period": *The Wall Street Journal*, November 7, 1932.

307 "with important governorships": *The Washington Post*, November 9, 1932.

307 "to report on local races": *The New York Times*, November 6, 1932.

308 "as long as it was not slanderous": *Time*, February 8, 1932.

308 "'close the lips of a man battling for righteousness'": *The Washington Post*, November 14, 1931.

308 "William Gibbs McAdoo": *The Washington Post*, June 25, 1932.

309 "'and music to the political carousel'": *The Washington Post*, November 14, 1932.

309 "'of sexual immorality'": Jones, *Cases and Materials on Electronic Mass Media*, 174.

309 "'collisions of personal interests'": *The New York Times*, November 29, 1932.

309 "by the First Amendment": Craig, *Fireside Politics*, 76.

309 "150,000-watt transmitter": Hoffer, *Norman Baker and American Broadcasting*, 427.

309 "further construction delays": Ibid., 428.

310 "he would be arrested": *The Washington Post*, July 8, 1932.

310 "coming from his hometown of Muscatine": Juhnke, *Quacks and Crusaders*, 58–59.

311 "'duty to fight for the people'": Lee, *The Bizarre Careers of John R. Brinkley*, 133.

311 "failing to pay taxes": Ibid., 135.

311 "the most powerful in all of North America": *The Washington Post*, January 3, 1932.

311 "new ways and to new audiences": Carson, *The Roguish World of Doctor Brinkley*, 170.

311 "'Anything can happen in Kansas'": *The New York Times*, July 17, 1932.

312 "the more popular Brinkley became": *The New York Times*, August 31, 1932.

312 "killed the good doctor before election day": Juhnke, *Quacks and Crusaders*, 22.

312 "the Republican and Democratic rallies": *The New York Times*, October 23, 1932.

312 "as the counting continued": *The Washington Post*, November 10, 1932.

312 "would carry him to victory": *The Washington Post*, November 9, 1932.

312 "had been stolen from him": Chase, *Sound and Fury*, 78.

312 "and Landon's winning total of 278,581": Carson, *The Roguish World of Doctor Brinkley*, 173.

313 "discourage them from voting": Lee, *The Bizarre Careers of John R. Brinkley*, 149.

313 "'on a different path'": Juhnke, *Quacks and Crusaders*, 24.

314 "for the theater's grand opening": Krinsky, Carol Herselle. *Rockefeller Center*. New York: Oxford University Press, 1978, 65.

314 "American ingenuity was still the best in the world": Ibid., 66.

314 "scale for laborers during June 1932": *The Wall Street Journal*, June 25, 1932.

314 "officially ending live shows": *The New York Times*, October 10, 1932.

314 "'brilliant program'": *The New York Times*, November 18, 1932.

314 "musical favorites and classics": *The Washington Post*, November 20, 1932.

315 "instead of from the grand hall": *The New York Times*, November 27, 1932.

315 "circus numbers to dramatic sketches": *The New York Times*, November 22, 1932.

315 "Amos and Andy": *The New York Times*, December 14, 1932.

315 "more than 60,000 people put in their requests": Krinsky, *Rockefeller Center*, 78.

315 "and was thrilled": *The New York Times*, December 26, 1932.

315 "Roxy looked exhausted and haggard": *The New York Times*, December 28, 1932.

316 "to keep traffic moving": *The New York Times*, December 27, 1932.

316 "was aired live over NBC": Ibid.

316 "'beaming, fresh and happy'": *The New York Times*, December 28, 1932.

316 "David Sarnoff": Ibid.

316 "'of the music hall stage'": Ibid.

317 "defy the economics of the Depression": Barnouw, *A Tower in Babel*, 267.

317 "a vital component of American life": Landry, *This Fascinating Radio Business*, 57.

317 "and CBS's was $1,263,451": Barnouw, *A Tower in Babel*, 272.

Chapter 17

318 "on American life itself": Lyons, *Herbert Hoover*, 297.

319 "RADIO CITY": Barnouw, *A Tower in Babel*, 269.

319   "over 100 million people": *The Washington Post,* March 4, 1933.

319   "named Arthur Godfrey": *The Washington Post,* March 5, 1933.

319   *"to fear is fear itself"*: Graff, *Inaugural Addresses of the Presidents of the United States,* 129.

319   "to a revival meeting": Morgan, *FDR,* 375.

320   "'dipped in phosphorous'": Ibid., 376.

320   "was good for the country": *The New York Times,* March 13, 1933.

320   "rather than out of them": Maier, *Inventing America,* 763.

320   "'fireside chats'": Dunning, *On the Air,* 495.

320   "reached unprecedented levels": Maier, *Inventing America,* 763.

320   "'"We are saved"'": Levine, Lawrence W., and Cornelia R. Levine. *The People and the President: America's Conversation with FDR.* Boston: Beacon Press, 2002, 37.

320   "'you were sent for our delivery'": Ibid., 45.

321   "'God-given social truths'": Marcus, *Father Coughlin,* 71.

321   "of the nation's independence": Ibid., 83.

321   "had brought about the world's troubles": Sayer, James Edward. "Father Charles Coughlin: Ideologue and Demagogue of the Depression." *Journal of the Northwest Communication Association* 15.1 (Spring 1987): 22.

322   "alarmed by the priest's rants": *The New York Times,* January 2, 1939.

322   "war against Great Britain": Marcus, *Father Coughlin,* 198.

322   "'temporarily retiring from the air'": Ibid., 177.

322   "remain silent on national issues": *The New York Times,* October 28, 1979.

322   "discontent were foremost in the public psyche": Brown, *Manipulating the Ether,* 88.

323   "but the plan never took flight": Marcus, *Father Coughlin,* 202.

323   *"Jergens Journal* carried on the NBC Blue Network": Dunning, *On the Air,* 708.

323   "leaked to him by the FBI": Gabler, Neal. *Winchell: Gossip, Power, and the Culture of Celebrity.* New York: Knopf, 1994, 201.

324   "'but I listen to him on the radio'": Ibid., 209.

324   "evidence against Hauptmann": Ibid., 210.

324   "'Is that Winchell?' some gawkers were heard to say": *The New York Times,* January 28, 1935.

324   "'Oh, that's another big one for me!'": Gabler, *Winchell,* 212.

325   "prevented her from sleeping": *Los Angeles Times,* July 14, 1926.

325   "she attempted a comeback in 1931": Epstein, *Sister Aimee,* 306.

325   "'they are seeing an imitation'": *The Wall Street Journal,* September 25, 1933.

325   "any other evangelist of her time": *The Washington Post,* September 28, 1944.

326   "'enthroned there'": Dunning, *On the Air,* 590.

326   "containing fifteen acts": *The New York Times,* May 3, 1933.

326   "the RKO Center Theatre": *The New York Times,* September 6, 1933.

326   "resigned his post at Radio City": *The New York Times,* January 9, 1934.

326   "he tried to get his job back": Krinsky, *Rockefeller Center,* 80.

326 "died of heart disease": *The New York Times*, January 14, 1936.

326 "'and that is just too bad'": *The New York Times*, November 26, 1933.

327 "the show was a shadow of its former self": Dunning, *On the Air*, 34.

328 "Fleischmann's and Vallée, came to an end": *The New York Times*, July 30, 1939.

329 "shot her husband dead": *The New York Times*, July 4, 1986.

329 "'He'd lived a thousand years'": Dunning, *On the Air*, 360.

330 "and others prerecorded": Hoffer, *Norman Baker and American Broadcasting*, 466, 469–70.

330 "more than $150,000 a year": Ibid., 484.

330 "against him back in Iowa": Ibid., 511–12.

330 "a sentence of one day in jail": Fowler and Crawford, *Border Radio*, 98.

330 "with lavender walls": Juhnke, *Quacks and Crusaders*, 61.

331 "charges of mail fraud": Ibid.

331 "cirrhosis of the liver": Ibid., 62.

331 "was buried somewhere in Mexico": Fowler and Crawford, *Border Radio*, 102.

331 "a drastic reduction in their income": *The Washington Post*, October 8, 1933.

331 "and Milford in dire straits": Carson, *The Roguish World of Doctor Brinkley*, 190.

331 "buying needed supplies for his use": Lee, *The Bizarre Careers of John R. Brinkley*, 184.

332 *"infected and diseased"*: Ibid., 185.

332 "the importance of compassion": Juhnke, *Quacks and Crusaders*, 29.

332 "approximately $12 million": Lee, *The Bizarre Careers of John R. Brinkley*, 187.

332 "even theological bent": Carson, *The Roguish World of Doctor Brinkley*, 218.

333 "'pursued to the last by litigation'": *The Washington Post*, May 27, 1942.

334 "canceled all commercials": *The New York Times*, April 14, 1945.

334 *"and active faith"*: *The Washington Post*, April 14, 1945.

Bibliography

"Aimee: A Short Biography." http://www.libertyharbor.org/aimee.htm (Accessed February 21, 2007).

"Aimee Semple McPherson." *America National Biography Online.* http://www .anb.org (Accessed February 21, 2007).

"Aimee Semple McPherson." *Notable Biographies.* http://notablebiographies .com/Ma-Mo/McPherson-Aimee-Semple.html (Accessed December 10, 2007).

"American Leaders Speak: The Presidential Election of 1920." American Memory, Library of Congress. http://memory.loc.gov/ammem/nfhtml/ nfexpe.html (Accessed June 15, 2006).

"The Beginnings of Radio and Sports Programming." http://www.americansportscasteronline.com/radiohistory.html

"Chronomedia: 1921." www.terramedia.co.uk/Chronomedia/years/1921.htm (Accessed December 4, 2007).

"Col. BJ Palmer." http://www.cmshowcase.com/halloffame/col_bj_palmer .htm (Accessed November 30, 2007).

"Eighty Years Ago this Month—Philadelphia Hosts 'Greatest Fight in Boxing History'—But Was It Fixed?" November 14, 2006. http://www.philly .future/Org/node/4448 (Accessed January 17, 2008).

377

"Emergence of Radio in the 1920s and its Cultural Significance." http://xroads
.virginia.edu/~UG00/30n1/radioshow/1920radio.htm (Accessed October
30, 2005).

"The Golden Age of Radio." Broadcasting, Radio and Television.
http://autocww.colorado.edu/~blackmon/E64ContentFiles/
CinemaAndBroadcasting (Accessed July 9, 2004).

"Grand Ole Opry." Country Music Planet's History of Country Music.
http://countrymusicplanet.com/history/grandoleopry.htm (Accessed
May 27, 2004).

"The Great Depression." National Parks Service. http://www.nps.gov/
archive/elro/glossary/great-depression.htm (Accessed July 27, 2007).

"Great Moments from 100 Games of the Backyard Brawl." KDKA. December
1, 2007. http://kdka.com/unassigned/Pitt.West.Virginia.2.599082.html
(Accessed January 16, 2007).

"The History of WMT." *The 80th Anniversary Cookbook.* http://www
.n-connect.net/lynxy/book6.html (Accessed January 19, 2007).

"June 30, 1922 Broadcast Station List." http://earlyradiohistory.us/220630ci
.htm (Accessed November 25, 2007).

"Leisure in the Interwar Era, 1920–1945." http://www.encyclopedia
.chicagohistory.org/pages/735.html (Accessed June 10, 2007).

"Life Goes to a Hate Rally." *Columbia Journalism Review* 35.3 (September/
October 1996).

"National Barn Dance: WLS National Barn Dance." http://www
.hillbilly-music.com/programs/story/index.php?prog=190 (Accessed August
4, 2004).

"Ohio Penitentiary Fire." http://www.ohiohistorycentral.org/entry
.php?rec=558 (Accessed May 13, 2007).

"Organization History" Redpath Agency. Redpath Chautauqua Collection,
Special Collections Department, University of Iowa Libraries (Iowa City).
http://sdrc.lib.uiowa.edu/traveling-culture/inventory/MSC150.html
(Accessed February 23, 2007).

"People & events: The site of the trial: Dayton, Tennessee." *The Monkey Trial.*
http://www.pbs.org/wgbh/amex/monkeytrial/peopleevents/e_dayton.html
(Accessed August 27, 2006).

"Pepsodent's Success Story." http://www.old-time.com/commercials/1920's/
Pepsodent's%20Success%20Story.htm

"Pioneering Amateurs (1900–1917)." http://earlyradiohistory.us/sec012.htm
(Accessed August 28, 2005).

"The Radio Act of 1927." *Columbia Law Review* 27.6 (June 1927): 726–733.
www.jstor.org.

"Red 'The Galloping Ghost' Grange." Hall of Famers. *College Football Hall of Fame.* http://www.collegefootball.org/famersearch.php?id=20071 (Accessed January 16, 2008).

"Rockefeller Center Christmas Tree." http://enc./Rockefeller_Center_Christmas_tree (Accessed January 21, 2007).

"Sunday, Billy." *Encyclopedia Britannica Online.* http://search.eb.com (Accessed November 11, 2007).

"Tex Rickard." *Enshrinees.* http://www.ibhof.com/rickard.htm (Accessed January 16, 2008).

"The Time Tunnel: When Dempsey Kayoed Sharkey and Whipped Father Time." *East Side Boxing.* http://www.eastsideboxing.com/news.php?p=3970&more=1 (Accessed January 16, 2008).

"Voice-Broadcasting the Stirring Progress of the 'Battle of the Century.'" *The Wireless Age,* August 1921: 11–21. http://earlyradiohistory.us/century2.htm (Accessed January 7, 2007).

"WGN Radio Timeline, 1920s–30s." http://wgngold.com/timeline/1920s1930s.htm (Accessed September 5, 2006).

"The WLS National Barn Dance." http://www.wlshistory.com/NBD (Accessed April 15, 2007).

"Westinghouse Company Enters Wireless Field." *Electrical Review,* October 16, 1920: 615. http://earlyradiohistory.us/1920west.htm (Accessed October 28, 2005).

"What a Revival Does." From *Billy Sunday: The Need for Revivals.* http://www.biblebelievers.com/billy_sunday/sun2.html (Accessed March 3, 2007).

Allen, Frederick Lewis. *Only Yesterday: An Informal History of the 1920s.* 1st Perennial classics ed. New York: Perennial Classics, 2000.

Arbuckle, Mark. *Herbert Hoover's National Radio Conferences and the Origin of Public Interest Content Regulation of U.S. Broadcasting: 1922–1925.* 2001.

Archer, Gleason Leonard. *Big Business and Radio.* New York: The American Historical Company, Inc., 1939.

———. *History of Radio to 1926.* New York: The American Historical Society, Inc., 1938.

Bahr, Robert. *Least of All Saints: The Story of Aimee Semple McPherson.* Englewood Cliffs, NJ: Prentice-Hall, 1979.

Bailey, Thomas Andrew. *The American Pageant: A History of the Republic.* Lexington, MA: Heath, 1971.

Barnouw, Erik. *A Tower in Babel: A History of Broadcasting in the United States, to 1933.* New York: Oxford University Press, 1966.

Basie, Count, and Albert Murray. *Good Morning Blues: The Autobiography of Count Basie.* New York: Random House, 1985.

Benjamin, Stuart Minor, Douglas Littman, and Howard A. Shelanski. *Telecommunications Law and Policy.* Carolina Academic Press Law Casebook Series, 2nd ed. Durham, NC: Carolina Academic Press, 2006.

Bensman, Marvin R. *The Beginning of Broadcast Regulation in the Twentieth Century.* Jefferson, NC: McFarland & Co., 2000.

Bilby, Kenneth W. *The General: David Sarnoff and the Rise of the Communications Industry.* New York: Harper & Row, 1986.

Bormann, Ernest G. "A Rhetorical Analysis of the National Radio Broadcast of Senator Huey Pierce Long." *Speech Monographs* 24.4 (1957): 244.

———. "Huey Long: Analysis of a Demagogue." *Today's Speech* 2.3 (September 1954): 16–19.

Brindze, Ruth. *Not to be Broadcast: The Truth about the Radio.* New York: Vanguard Press, 1937.

Brinkley, Alan. "Comparative Biography as Political History: Huey Long and Father Coughlin." *The History Teacher* 18.1 (November 1984): 9.

———. *American History: A Survey.* 12th ed. Boston: McGraw-Hill, 2007.

———. *Voices of Protest: Huey Long, Father Coughlin, and the Great Depression.* New York: Knopf, 1982.

Broadcasting Magazine (Washington, D.C.). *The First 50 Years of Broadcasting: The Running Story of the Fifth Estate.* Washington, D.C.: Broadcasting Publications, 1982.

Brown, Robert J. *Manipulating the Ether: The Power of Broadcast Radio in Thirties America.* Jefferson, NC: McFarland & Co., 1998.

Bunis, Marty, and Sue Bunis. *The Collector's Guide to Antique Radios: Identification & Values.* 3rd ed. Paducah, KY: Collector Books, 1995.

Burns, Ken. *Empire of the Air: The Men Who Made Radio.* Directed by Ken Burns. PBS Home Video, 1996.

Buxton, Frank, and Bill Owen. *The Big Broadcast, 1920–1950.* New York: Avon, 1973.

Carroll, Carroll. *None of Your Business: Or My Life with J. Walter Thompson (Confessions of a Renegade Radio Writer).* New York: Cowles Book Co., 1970.

Carson, Gerald. *The Roguish World of Doctor Brinkley.* New York: Rinehart, 1960.

Casey, Michael, and Aimee Rowe. "'Driving Out the Money Changers': Radio Priest Charles E. Coughlin's Rhetorical Vision." *Journal of Communication & Religion* 19.1 (1996): 37–47.

Chase, Francis Seabury. *Sound and Fury: An Informal History of Broadcasting.* New York, London: Harper & Bros., 1942.

Chester, Giraud, and Garnet R. Garrison. *Television and Radio: An Introduction.* 2nd ed. New York: Appleton-Century-Crofts, Inc., 1956.

Columbia Broadcasting System. *The Sound of Your Life: A Record of Radio's First Generation.* New York: 1950.

Craig, Douglas B. *Fireside Politics: Radio and Political Culture in the United States, 1920–1940.* Reconfiguring American Political History. Baltimore, MD; London: Johns Hopkins University Press, 2006.

Craig, Steve. "'The Farmer's Friend': Radio Comes to Rural America, 1920–1927." (no date) http://www.rtvf.unt.edu/html/craig/pdfs/rural.PDF (Accessed May 4, 2007).

DeGregorio, William A. *The Complete Book of U.S. Presidents.* 6th ed. Fort Lee, NJ: Barricade Books, 2005.

Douglas, Ann. *Terrible Honesty: Mongrel Manhattan in the 1920s.* New York: Farrar, Straus, and Giroux, 1995.

Douglas, George H. *The Early Days of Radio Broadcasting.* Jefferson, NC: McFarland, 1987.

Dunning, John. *On the Air: The Encyclopedia of Old-Time Radio.* New York: Oxford University Press, 1998.

Epstein, Daniel Mark. *Sister Aimee: The Life of Aimee Semple McPherson.* New York: Harcourt Brace Jovanovich, 1993.

Farr, Rob. "Screened But Not Heard: The Big Broadcasts of 1928." (2000) http://www.otr.com/1928.html (Accessed May 4, 2007).

Fishbein, Morris. *The Medical Follies: An Analysis of the Foibles of some Healing Cults, Including Osteopathy, Homeopathy, Chiropractic, and the Electronic Reactions of Abrams, with Essays on the Antivivisectionists, Health Legislation, Physical Culture, Birth Control, and Rejuvenation.* New York: Boni & Liveright, 1925.

Fishwick, Marshall W. "Father Coughlin Time: The Radio and Redemption." *Journal of Popular Culture* 22.2 (Fall 1988): 33. http://proquest.umi.com/pqdweb?did=1691890&Fmt=7&clientId=65345&RQT=309&VName=PQD.

Fitzgerald, F. Scott. *The Great Gatsby.* New York: Scribner, 2004.

Fowler, Gene, and Bill Crawford. *Border Radio: Quacks, Yodelers, Pitchmen, Psychics, and Other Amazing Broadcasters of the American Airwaves.* Rev. ed. Austin: University of Texas Press, 2002.

Gabler, Neal. *Winchell: Gossip, Power, and the Culture of Celebrity.* 1st ed. New York: Knopf, 1994.

Garner, Joe, and Bob Costas. *And the Crowd Goes Wild: Relive the Most Celebrated Sporting Events Ever Broadcast.* Naperville, IL: Sourcebooks, 1999.

Gilbert, Douglas. *American Vaudeville: Its Life and Times.* New York: Dover Publications, 1968.

Godfrey, Donald G., and Frederic A. Leigh. *Historical Dictionary of American Radio*. Westport, CT: Greenwood Press, 1998.

Goodman, Mark, and Mark Gring. "The Ideological Fight over Creation of the Federal Radio Commission in 1927." *Journalism History* 26.3 (Autumn 2000): 117.

Goslich, Siegfried, Rita H. Mead, and Timothy Roberts. "Radio: Impact on Musical Life." *Grove Music Online*. http://www.grovemusic.com/shared/views/article.html?section=music.42011.5 (Accessed October 30, 2005).

Graff, Henry F., and United States Presidents. *Inaugural Addresses of the Presidents of the United States from W. H. Taft to G. W. Bush*. The Lakeside Classics; no. 103. Chicago: Lakeside Press, R. R. Donnelley, 2005.

Halberstam, David J. *Sports on New York Radio—A Play-By-Play History*. Chicago: Masters Press, 1999.

Harvard University and Graduate School of Business Administration. *The Radio Industry: The Story of its Development, as Told by Leaders of the Industry to the Students of the Graduate School of Business Administration, George F. Baker Foundation, Harvard University*. Chicago: A. W. Shaw and Co., 1928.

Hilliard, Robert L., and Michael C. Keith. *The Broadcast Century and Beyond: A Biography of American Broadcasting*. 3rd ed. Boston: Focal Press, 2001.

Hilliker, Jim. *History of KFSG*. 2003. http://radioheritage.net/kfsg.html (Accessed January 21, 2008).

Hilmes, Michele. *Radio Voices: American Broadcasting, 1922–1952*. Minneapolis: University of Minnesota Press, 1997.

Hoffer, Thomas William. *Norman Baker and American Broadcasting*. Master's Thesis. Madison: University of Wisconsin, 1969.

Hogan, J. Michael, and Glen Williams. "The Rusticity and Religiosity of Huey P. Long." *Rhetoric & Public Affairs* 7.2 (Summer 2004): 149.

Hoover, Herbert. *The Memoirs of Herbert Hoover—Vol. 1, Years of Adventure*. New York: MacMillan, 1952.

———. *The Memoirs of Herbert Hoover—Vol. 2, The Cabinet and the Presidency*. New York: MacMillan, 1952.

Husing, Edward B. *My Eyes Are in My Heart*. New York: B. Geis Associates, 1959.

Johnson, David, and Betty Johnson. *Guide to Old Radios: Pointers, Pictures, and Prices*. Radnor, PA: Wallace-Homestead Book Co., 1989.

Jones, William K. *Cases and Materials on Electronic Mass Media: Radio, Television, and Cable*. University Casebook Series. Mineola, NY: Foundation Press, 1976.

Jonnes, Jill. *Empires of Light: Edison, Tesla, Westinghouse, and the Race to Electrify the World*. New York: Random House, 2003.

Juhnke, Eric S. *Quacks and Crusaders: The Fabulous Careers of John Brinkley, Norman Baker, and Harry Hoxsey.* Lawrence: University Press of Kansas, 2002.

Kaltenborn, H. V. *Fifty Fabulous Years, 1900–1950: A Personal Review.* New York: Putnam, 1950.

Kazin, Michael. "The First Radio Populist: A Lesson from the 1930s." *Tikkun* 10.1 (1995): 37ff.

Knapp, Raymond. *The American Musical and the Formation of National Identity.* Princeton, NJ: Princeton University Press, 2005.

Krinsky, Carol Herselle. *Rockefeller Center.* New York: Oxford University Press, 1978.

Kyvig, David E. *Daily Life in the United States, 1920–1940: How Americans Lived through the "Roaring Twenties" and the Great Depression.* Chicago: Ivan R. Dee, 2004.

Lackmann, Ronald W. *The Encyclopedia of American Radio: An A–Z Guide to Radio from Jack Benny to Howard Stern.* New York: Facts On File, 2000.

Landry, Robert John. *This Fascinating Radio Business.* Indianapolis, New York: Bobbs-Merrill Co., 1946.

Larson, Erik. *Thunderstruck.* New York: Three Rivers Press, 2006.

Lee, R. Alton. *The Bizarre Careers of John R. Brinkley.* Lexington: University Press of Kentucky, 2002.

Leuchtenburg, William Edward. *The Perils of Prosperity, 1914–32.* Chicago: University of Chicago Press, 1958.

Levine, Lawrence W., and Cornelia R. Levine. *The People and the President: America's Conversation with FDR.* Boston: Beacon Press, 2002.

Lewis, Sinclair. *Elmer Gantry.* New York: New American Library, 1980.

Lynd, Robert Staughton, and Helen Merrell Lynd. *Middletown: A Study in American Culture.* Harvest book/HBJ Book. San Diego: Harcourt Brace, 1957.

Lyons, Eugene. *Herbert Hoover: A Biography.* Garden City, NY: Doubleday, 1964.

Maier, Pauline. *Inventing America: A History of the United States.* 2nd ed. New York: W. W. Norton, 2006.

Marcus, Sheldon. *Father Coughlin: The Tumultuous Life of the Priest of the Little Flower.* Boston: Little, Brown, 1973.

Marinacci, Michael. "Dr. John Brinkley (1885–1941): Getting America's Goat." http://pw2.netcom.com/~mikalm/brinkley.htm (Accessed July 15, 2004).

"Maxim, Hiram Percy." *Encyclopedia Britannica Online.* http://search.eb.com (Accessed November 11, 2007).

McLeod, Elizabeth. "Eddie Cantor Runs for President, Winter 1931–Fall 1932." http://www.old-time.com/mcleod/top100html (Accessed June 27, 2004).

————. "The Lindbergh Baby Tragedy, 1932–1936." http://www.old-time .com/mcleod/top100html (Accessed June 27, 2004).

McNamee, Graham, and Robert Gordon Anderson. *You're on the Air.* New York; London: Harper & Brothers, 1926.

Montville, Leigh. *The Big Bam: The Life and Times of Babe Ruth.* New York: Doubleday, 2006.

Morgan, Ted. *FDR: A Biography.* New York: Simon and Schuster, 1985.

Nachman, Gerald. *Raised on Radio: In Quest of the Lone Ranger.* Berkeley: University of California Press, 2000.

Nevins, Allan, and Henry Steele Commager. *The Pocket History of the United States.* The Pocket Library. New York: Pocket Books, 1969.

Phillips, Cabell B. H. *From the Crash to the Blitz, 1929–1939.* New York: Fordham University Press, 2000.

Pietrusza, David. *1920: The Year of the Six Presidents.* New York: Carroll & Graf Publishers, 2007.

Sanger, Elliott M. *Rebel in Radio: The Story of WQXR.* 50th anniversary edition. Millwood, NY: Kraus Reprint, 1986.

Sayer, James Edward. "Father Charles Coughlin: Ideologue and Demagogue of the Depression." *Journal of the Northwest Communication Association* 15.1 (Spring 1987): 17–30.

Schwartz, Larry. "Galloping Ghost Scared Opponents." ESPN.com. http://espn .go.com/sportscentury/features/00014213.html (Accessed January 16, 2008).

Settel, Irving. *A Pictorial History of Radio.* New York: Grosset & Dunlap, 1967.

Sitkoff, Harvard. "Huey Long: Film Review." *Film and History* 17.2 (May 1987): 46–47. http://pao.chadwyck.co.uk (Accessed December 14, 2007).

Smulyan, Susan. *Selling Radio: The Commercialization of American Broadcasting, 1920–1934.* Washington, D.C.: Smithsonian Institution Press, 1994.

Spar, Debora L. *Ruling the Waves: Cycles of Discovery, Chaos, and Wealth from the Compass to the Internet.* New York: Harcourt, 2001.

Spence, Stephen. "Pure Hoax: The Norman Baker Story." http://www .crescent-hotel.com/bakerstory.htm (Accessed January 16, 2008).

Sterling, Christopher H., Michael C. Keith, and Museum of Broadcast Communications. *The Museum of Broadcast Communications Encyclopedia of Radio.* New York: Fitzroy Dearborn, 2004.

Sullivan, George, and John Powers. *The Yankees: An Illustrated History.* Philadelphia: Temple University Press, 1997.

Summers, Harrison Boyd. *A Thirty-Year History of Programs Carried on National Radio Networks in the United States, 1926–1956.* New York: Arno Press, 1971.

Terrace, Vincent. *Radio Programs, 1924–1984: A Catalog of Over 1800 Shows.* Jefferson, NC: McFarland, 1999.

Thomas, Lately. *The Vanishing Evangelist: The Aimee Semple McPherson Kidnapping Affair.* New York: Viking Press, 1959.

Vallée, Eleanor, and J. Amadio. *My Vagabond Lover: An Intimate Biography of Rudy Vallée.* Dallas: Taylor Publishing, 1996.

Vallée, Rudy. *Rudy Vallée Kisses and Tells.* Rev. ed. Canoga Park, CA: Major Books, 1976.

Vallée, Rudy, and Gil McKean. *My Time is Your Time: The Story of Rudy Vallée.* New York: Obolensky, 1962.

Ward, Geoffrey C. "1932: A New Deal Is Struck." *Smithsonian* 35, no. 7 (October 2004): 60. http://proquest.umi.com/pqdweb?did =707697751&Fmt=7&clientId=65345&RQT=309&VName=PQD

Ward, Geoffrey C., and Ken Burns. *Jazz: A History of America's Music.* New York: Alfred A. Knopf, 2000.

————. *Baseball: An Illustrated History.* 1st ed. New York: Alfred A. Knopf, 1994.

Ward, Louis B. *Father Charles E. Coughlin: An Authorized Biography.* Detroit, MI: Tower Publications, 1933.

Warren, Donald I. *Radio Priest: Charles Coughlin, the Father of Hate Radio.* New York: Free Press, 1996.

Watterson, John Sayle. *College Football: History, Spectacle, Controversy.* Baltimore: Johns Hopkins University Press, 2000.

White, Llewellyn, and Commission on Freedom of the Press. *The American Radio: A Report on the Broadcasting Industry in the United States from the Commission on Freedom of the Press.* Chicago: University of Chicago Press, 1947.

Whittingham, Richard. *Saturday Afternoon: College Football and the Men Who Made the Day.* New York: Workman Publishing, 1985.

Williams, T. Harry. *Huey Long.* New York: Knopf, 1969.

Winston, Alvin. *Doctors, Dynamiters, and Gunmen: The Life Story of Norman Baker; a Fact Story of Injustices—Confiscation and Suppression.* Muscatine, IA: TNT Press, 1936.

Wood, Clement. *The Life of a Man: A Biography of John R. Brinkley.* Kansas City, KS: Goshorn Publishing, 1934.

Zeitz, Joshua. *Flapper: The Notorious Life and Scandalous Times of the First Thoroughly Modern Woman.* New York: Crown Publishers, 2006.

Index